MATERIAL CULTURE AND JEWISH THOUGHT
IN AMERICA

Material Culture
and Jewish Thought
in America

KEN KOLTUN-FROMM

Indiana University Press

Bloomington & Indianapolis

This book is a publication of

Indiana University Press
601 North Morton Street
Bloomington, IN 47404-3797 USA

www.iupress.indiana.edu

Telephone orders   800-842-6796
Fax orders   812-855-7931
Orders by e-mail   iuporder@indiana.edu

♾ The paper used in this publication
meets the minimum requirements of
the American National Standard for
Information Sciences—Permanence
of Paper for Printed Library Materials,
ANSI Z39.48-1992.

Manufactured in the United States of
America

Library of Congress Cataloging-in-
Publication Data

Koltun-Fromm, Ken.
  Material culture and Jewish thought
in America / Ken Koltun-Fromm.
    p. cm.
  Includes bibliographical references
and index.
  ISBN 978-0-253-35454-9 (cloth : alk.
paper) — ISBN 978-0-253-22183-4
(pbk. : alk. paper) 1. Judaism—United
States. 2. Jews—United States—
Identity. 3. Jews—United States—
Intellectual life. 4. United States—
Civilization—Jewish influences. 5.
Jews—Cultural assimilation—United
States. I. Title.
  BM205.K65 2010
  306.6'960973—dc22

2009052337

1 2 3 4 5 15 14 13 12 11 10

For ARNOLD EISEN

CONTENTS

· ACKNOWLEDGMENTS · ix

Introduction: Material Culture and
Jewish Identity in America · 1

1 The Material Self: Mordecai Kaplan
and the Art of Writing · 13

2 The Material Past: Edward Bernays,
Joshua Liebman, and Erich Fromm · 53

3 Material Place: Joseph Soloveitchik
and the Urban Holy · 108

4 Material Presence: Abraham Joshua Heschel
and *The Sabbath* · 141

5 The Material Narrative: Yezierska, Roth,
Ozick, Malamud · 180

6 The Material Gaze: American Jewish Identity
and Heritage Production · 225

Conclusion: American or Jewish
Material Identity? · 270

· NOTES · 279
· BIBLIOGRAPHY · 315
· INDEX · 329

ACKNOWLEDGMENTS

I enjoy telling my friends that finally, after a rather long and circuitous search, I have found my authorial voice in this book. But that voice has been deeply inflected by the far more melodious tones of friends, family, colleagues, and students. My voice, as I have come to understand it, resonates with those whom I admire and trust. It echoes, but also travels beyond those who have influenced me as a writer and person. I want to acknowledge some of those voices here, and dedicate this book to one very eloquent voice in particular.

In temperament I am still a student at Haverford College, and so I find many of my most valuable colleagues among the student body here. Josh Mikutis and Carolyn Warner read this book in its entirety, offered trenchant critique when I needed it most, tracked down footnotes and missing citations, and provided support and courage to carry forward. They represent the very best that Haverford has to offer. Jessie Post helped to polish this manuscript into a readable form, and I am very grateful for her generosity. Karen Terry and I have worked closely together over the past two years. She knows how much this book resounds with her influence, and for that I am deeply grateful. Students in my Jewish Images, Material Religion, and American Judaism courses never fail to remind me of the richness of a college that still prizes creativity, demands intellectual energy, and cultivates honorable lives.

Like the students, my colleagues are hard working, generous with their time, and dedicated to their profession. The members of the Haverford Religion Department—David Dawson, Naomi Koltun-Fromm,

Tracey Hucks, Terrence Johnson, Anne McGuire, and Travis Zadeh—are, to my mind, family in the most meaningful way. Comfort at home allows me to venture out in new and sometimes uncertain paths. Colleagues beyond my institutional home have been supportive, encouraging, and committed. A special and heartfelt appreciation to Lila Corwin Berman, Zak Braiterman, Nathaniel Deutsch, Andrew Heinze, Leah Hochman, Barbara Kirshenblatt-Gimblett, Laura Levitt, John Modern, David Morgan, Robert Orsi, Riv-Ellen Prell, Nora Rubel, Jonathan Sarna, Jenna Weissman-Joselit, and Michael Zank. My collaborators in the Works in Progress Group in Modern Jewish Studies have also guided and challenged my work from its inception, and it is that much better for their effort. My friends at Indiana University Press, especially Janet Rabinowitch and Joyce Rappaport, have moved this project along with speed, humor, and dedicated work. I thank all of you for your generosity and passion.

I have been undeservedly supported by the Mellon New Directions grant, Haverford Research grants, and the Hurford Humanities Center at Haverford College. The folks at the Hurford Center have tirelessly supported my projects from the beginning, and to Emily, James, Kim, and Richard I owe far more than I have received. A portion of chapter 1 appeared in "Performing the Material Self: Mordecai Kaplan and the Art of Writing," *AJS Review* 31, no. 1 (2007): 109–31, and I am grateful for the permission to reproduce much of that article here.

Support comes in many forms, of course, and I feel that sense of gratitude for those closest to me. My daughter Talia will tell you I spend too much time at the computer, and she is undoubtedly right. But playing whatever sport that includes a ball with her, and running after Isaiah while imagining new railroad scenes and birds along the horizon with Ariel—all this brings me back to what is really important and central in my life. Without them and Naomi, all of whom live more fully than I, working at the computer would be lonely indeed.

Some fifteen years ago I first read many of the texts discussed in this book with my teacher and friend, Arnold Eisen. Though both Arnie and I have traveled far from those first days at Stanford University, in many ways this book returns me to that time of initial fascination and concern. Arnie did not teach me to read these texts as I do (I cannot blame him for that), but he did guide me in listening well, in cherishing learned texts, in cultivating disciplined habits, and in writing with care and integrity. But more, far more than all that, Arnie modeled then, and continues to demonstrate now the life of commitment, of Jewish engagement, of honest living, and of responsible faith. I dedicate this book to Arnold Eisen because it could be for no other.

Ken Koltun-Fromm
Haverford College

MATERIAL CULTURE AND JEWISH THOUGHT
IN AMERICA

Material Culture and Jewish Identity in America

On a train bound for Schenectady in December 1928, Mordecai Kaplan continued his obsessive journal writing, this time in the third-person. He chides himself for turning to "his latest fad," once again postponing a harder look at "the metaphysical problem which he set before himself." As Kaplan reflects on his "weakness for formulas" and the "universe of words," he regrets that he never had "the fortune of experiencing the thrill of firsthand contact with things." The journal became that sensual thing for Kaplan, and it promised exposure to a material world. Writing in the third person, Kaplan venerates the empowering technology of things:

> But he never lost sight of the greater reality of the universe of things which was denied to him. He never heard the phonograph, radio or telephone without wishing it were appropriate to kneel down and worship. If he had his way would have created a ritual and recommended specific benedictions to be recited before making use of these great products of human ingenuity.[1]

Things fail to solve metaphysical problems, but they do attract reverence and religious homage. Kaplan draws a "universe of things" into the orbit of ritual activity: hearing things compels appropriate devotion. Is this false idol worship, offering to dead objects what should be God's own? Or has Kaplan tapped into the ways in which things move us, the modes in which we see, touch, and hear things, and the magnetic appeal in and through which physical objects inflect and shape personal identity? Perhaps Kaplan even senses the effervescent quality of things that speak—the radio, phonograph, and telephone. These things come alive, as it were, and so deserve his ritual worship and attention. In this material universe, Kaplan can experience the thrill, firsthand, of sensual touch and religious reverence.

For Jewish immigrants like Kaplan, America offered many such enticing goods. Material temptations surrounded the immigrant world, and seduced Jews, as they did Kaplan, into the "greater reality" of enlivened things. Through such physical exposure, Jews fashioned a material Jewish identity in America. It is an identity steeped in the magnetic and alluring quality of things. Even more, American Jews produced second-order reflections on the nature of things and their material charms. Jews were profoundly embedded in the very culture that provoked their own musings on identity and materiality. The dynamic interplay between American Jewish thought and culture is the subject of this study.

This book explores how American Jews work with things, and how they think about them in ways that produce distinctive identities. By linking the material dimensions in culture to Jewish identity in order to create what I call *material Jewish identity,* I seek to inscribe the very thing I want to uncover: the material features of Jewish thought and practice. American Jews like Kaplan constructed their selves in and through material objects. Kaplan is mesmerized by things, but he is not the only Jew in America to be drawn to the vivifying effect of the material landscape. Yet he does capture the central preoccupations of this book: the modes by which Jews confront objects; how devotion to the past (living only in a "universe of words") limits material abundance and success; the ways in which place—the "universe of things" or a local train to Schenectady—inspires Jewish thought and practice; the presence of physical objects in Jewish ritual life; the formation of character tethered to material things; the visual paradigms in and by which Jews see things; and the manner in which those objects, in turn, speak to Jews. This book explores how American Jewish thinkers as diverse as Joseph Soloveitchik, Abraham Joshua Heschel, Joshua Loth Liebman, Eric Fromm, and Mordecai Kaplan fantasize about objects, and the impact of those things on American Jewish thought. But it is also a book about visual and literary culture, and the methods by which narrative, film, and photography trace the material formations of Jewish heritage and character. Jewish thought is a cultural practice, and that practice generates compelling accounts of an identity steeped in material culture. This is what I mean by material Jewish identity in America.

For too long, scholars have stuffed Jewish thought into intellectual, social, or political straitjackets. Reflections on Jewish thought have become critical—and still important—exercises in epistemology, social critique, aesthetics, as well as philosophical and social ethics.[2] Some, as reflected in Jonathan Freedman's impressive work *Klezmer America,* have turned to cultural studies to reinvigorate a multifaceted and creative Jewish ethnicity. But Freedman has little to say about Jewish religious thought, and often neglects it for the staple cultural issues of ethnicity and race.[3] This book, in contrast, weaves religious discourse into the fabric of cultural studies, fastening the physical, bodily, and sensual pleasures of material life to religious thought. It broadens the rubric of cultural studies to include the theoretical but deeply material musings of Soloveitchik, Kaplan, Heschel, Liebman, and other Jewish thinkers. But it also recaptures the stuff of Jewish culture—literary works, as well as *The Jazz Singer* films and *Lilith* magazine glossies—to better understand the material dimensions of Jewish identity in America. Kaplan evokes this sense of cultural depth as a "greater reality of the universe of things": a world, so he claims, worthy of veneration. This book is but one form of tribute to the charms of the material world.

Those charms reveal the material roots of American Jewish thought. In stating it this way, I want to expose the cultural patterns that inform Jewish thinking about things, and the visual and literary paradigms that ground Jewish identity in objects. In short, I seek to wed cultural studies to Jewish thought. A marriage like this does not come easily, especially for those trained in modern Jewish philosophy. In my graduate school days, students of religion would study the great European, American, and Israeli thinkers, while historians stuck to cultural trends. Religion types like myself rarely cared about social worlds; we had great thoughts to think, problems to solve, intellectual patterns to trace, and a philosophical heritage to recount. When I first read Soloveitchik, I turned to Kant and Kierkegaard, together with Jewish law and biblical texts, to understand his world of *halakhah.* But you will not find that philosophical heritage in my discussion of Soloveitchik's *Halakhic Man* and *Lonely Man of Faith* in chapter 3. Instead, I turn to cultural theories of urban religion, and how city images and landscapes inform Soloveitchik's theory of Jewish law. I situate his work within notions of the urban holy and the transformative potential of the streets. In other words, I want to turn Soloveitchik into a cultural theorist, one who thinks deeply about his material landscape and its impact on Jewish observance. It is a thinking about identity within the physical spaces and material objects of experience. Cultural studies drags Jewish thought into the messiness and allure of city life, into the "universe of things" that seduce, enliven, and transfigure Jewish identity. One can certainly study Kaplan's theory of civilization, or his appropriation of Durkheim's social theory, or even Soloveitchik's philosophical dance with Kant and Kierkegaard. These are all worthy pursuits. But this book does not walk along those theoretical paths. Instead, it reveals the material culture within Kaplan's Jewish thought, and the urban roots of Soloveitchik's legal world. I uncover artistic performances that deliver the material stuff of civilizations, show how Kaplan personifies his journal as a material friend in lieu of community, and explore Boston's urban streets that inflect Soloveitchik's view of Jewish law. If Kaplan turns to material products, like his journal, to bear witness to a life well-lived, then Soloveitchik transforms urban chaos into a holy grid of religious byways. Journals and holy grids bind Jewish thought to culture.

In more than one way, Kaplan is the hero of this book. He introduces all the thematic concerns that situate my portrayal of American Jews—the cultivation of material identity in America; the weight of the past on material success; the chaotic allure of cityscapes; the presence, seductive appeal, and inescapable texture of things; and the ways in which Jews visualize heritage through artistic mediums. Each of the following chapters takes up these issues in some detail, working through Jewish texts that foster material identity. The chapters are ordered in roughly chronological order, critically addressing a central theme in the construction of Jewish identity in America.

Chapter 1 focuses on Kaplan's description of his journal as a material friend—as a physical exposure of self that cultivates and situates his presence in America. Kaplan becomes American in and through his journal as he reflects on the meaning of journal writing and its relation to personal identity. A study of his journal from 1913 to 1934 reveals what Barbara Kirshenblatt-Gimblett calls "the constitutive power of display." Objects become particular, recognizable things in and through contextual performances. Kaplan's journal is one such performance and display. It is an arranged and classified item that explores identity through an "exhibitionary logic." Kirshenblatt-Gimblett rightly emphasizes the staging of identity that also captures Kaplan's imagination: "The agency of display . . . is not to be folded into 'the image of the Jew' or even representation, whether discursive or demographic. Display not only shows and speaks, it also *does*—with greater or lesser success."[4] Kaplan's journal witnesses to this power of display, for it materializes his Jewish identity in a cultural, artistic medium. This is but one of the material artifacts that make up a civilization—Kaplan's embracing term for the cultural, artistic, and religious products and folkways of ethnic groups. Kaplan's Jewish self is on display in a journal that exposes his modernist anxieties of self-fashioning. The journal also physically embodies Kaplan's desire as an immigrant to create something of permanence in his new homeland. He fashions his Jewish American identity by inscribing it in his journal—that "agency of display" in which Kaplan labors "to be seen and heard."[5] The journal does not represent Kaplan, nor does it signify deeper or more transcendent meanings. Instead, the journal embodies what Kaplan calls his "self-aspect" because it enacts his material self in America. For Kaplan, writing is a kind of material act of exposure, in which he embodies his Jewish identity within an American social world.

Immigrants like Kaplan struggled with their past inheritance to cultivate a home in America. Jewish ancestors and their claims upon religious and cultural observance often inhibited a full exposure to the American scene. It was a heavy weight to sustain and nurture, and a good many American Jews sought a lighter freight with fewer obligations. Matthew Frye Jacobson observes how Americans deny a difficult and conflicted past to make room for another, more congenial heritage. He describes the contrivance of a "roots trip" that dislodges a cumbersome, often tragic history, in order to nurture a more exultant, glorious narrative. Immigrants often absorb or even create this kind of story as they establish "roots" in a new country. They displace past burdens with more liberating blessings. It is a willful forgetting that forges new beginnings.[6] This is precisely what Edward Bernays, Joshua Loth Liebman, and Eric Fromm sought to do for America—the subjects of chapter 2. Bernays, the nephew of Sigmund Freud, appropriated his uncle's psychology to liberate Americans from repressive desires inherited from the past.

He freed consumers to heed only their deepest, individual desires, even as he enslaved them to appetites created by his public relations counsel. In the exodus to freedom, Bernays returned the American consumer to slavery of a different sort: material cravings that promote the capitalist interests of Bernays's business clients. The new beginnings he sought only created additional burdens. His narrative, however progressive and modern, established roots all the same. He emancipated one "herd" mentality only to reinforce another.

Bernays reappropriates many of the psychological and cultural burdens he finds so confining in the herd mentality. I call this kind of inescapable heritage the material past: a form of cultural inheritance that shapes the possibilities of material human flourishing in the present. Such a past both informs, and for Bernays, Liebman, and Fromm, deforms material self-flourishing. The "herd" mentality, as Bernays describes that term, frustrates material success in the future. Enslavement to inherited desires of consumption merely restrains the progressive capacities of individual desires. Bernays turned to Freud to help liberate the self from irrational burdens, and to see clear to brighter futures.

So, too, did Joshua Loth Liebman, perhaps the most famous liberal American Jewish preacher after the Second World War. Liebman, like many of his progressive contemporaries, translated the stern, tragic, "European" Freud into a more compassionate, hopeful, "American" psychologist. An American populous yearning for a "peace of mind" after the horrors of war required a kinder Freud. Liebman explored how modern Americans could turn past curses into healthy blessings. This would be a narrative of American maturity that overcomes the sins of the fathers. It is a "roots trip" that unties tragic moorings to encourage a more promising future. Erich Fromm traveled even further, severing the past, and the false idol worship that defined it, so that a free and unrestrained personality could emerge in love and mutual responsibility. The material past weighed down human flourishing, for Bernays, Liebman, and Fromm, because it tethered Americans, and especially American Jews, to a heritage that inhibited material success: one would not purchase, love, or relate to the appropriate things. Jews could not become progressive, free, and productive American citizens if they harbored strong ties to their religious, cultural, and familial pasts. They had to give up inherited desires (Bernays), childhood inhibitions and fears (Liebman), and restrictive social networks (Fromm) to flourish as American Jews. Yet the material past continued to haunt Bernays, Liebman, and Fromm. Though each Jewish thinker labored mightily to weaken the inherited past, they could not but recognize the power of that past to inform American Jewish identity. A "roots trip" is far more twisted and contentious than their more linear narratives would suggest.

American Jews think a good deal about wrong turns, and the maps they draw seek tighter navigational direction and clarity. Bernays, Liebman, and Fromm offered such guides for Americans and American Jews. But so did other Jewish thinkers who lived in and among observant Jewish communities in the city. When Jews came to America in the latter part of the nineteenth and early twentieth centuries, they overwhelmingly arrived in cities, and the urban religion fashioned there textured their practice of material identity. This is especially true for the Orthodox Jewish thinker Joseph Soloveitchik, whose account of Jewish law is the focus of chapter 3. Images of the city infuse and inflect his masterful accounts of *Halakhic Man* (1944) and *The Lonely Man of Faith* (1965). Soloveitchik creates byways of holiness and maps of the city that enable Orthodox Jews to travel with certainty, clarity, and purpose amid urban chaos. We can better appreciate Soloveitchik's unique blend of Jewish law and the American urban imaginary through the prism of Robert Orsi's work on urban religion, especially his account of the urban holy— that imagined space of renewal in which one sinks lower into the chaos only to rise up more holy and cleansed. Orsi's interpretive task, I believe, should be applied to a reading of Soloveitchik's religious work:

> This is the challenge of studying urban religion generally: we must read through and across the fantasy of the city as it has emerged over the last two centuries, attending to both the forces that have shaped this fantasy and their impress on the ways in which we construe urban popular experience, religious and secular.[7]

Soloveitchik appropriated fantasies of the urban holy, in which urban depravity contained seeds of spiritual renewal, in order to build Jewish law in the city. He turned foreign streets into sacred avenues. Halakhic man could now safely walk the urban streets, and would transform chaos into ordered reality. The physical space of the city materially informs Soloveitchik's Jewish practice and legal thought; and he, in turn, remodels the city into a creative space for legal fashioning. The Orthodox Jew can walk in the city, now reimagined as the urban holy. Jews construct their material selves in distinct places that shape the fashioning of legal discourse.

If theories of Jewish law "happen" in particular locales, as is the case in Soloveitchik's works, then all the more so for Jewish ritual practice. In chapter 4, I focus on Abraham Joshua Heschel's obsession with material things, and their relation to spiritual pursuits, in *The Sabbath* (1951) and *The Earth Is the Lord's* (1950). He struggles to identify objects that point to or enable spiritual experiences, and to distinguish them from other kinds of things that only arouse material consumption. The Sabbath weakens the hold of desirable things in physical space, and intensifies spiritual encounters and sacred wonder in revelatory moments of time. This bifurcation of the religious and the material recalls Robert Orsi's discussion of the Bronx Lourdes, in which Italian Americans drink and use city water from St. Lucy's grotto as if it were the miraculous holy water from Lourdes, France. Orsi's students are visibly agitated by this inadmissible mixing of the sacred and profane:

> The image of holy water being poured into car engines is especially disturbing to students, an instance of the general blurring of categories they want to keep distinct (sacred/profane; spirit/matter; transcendent/immanent; nature/machine) which occurs at St. Lucy's. What happens at the Bronx grotto is literally inadmissable [*sic*], intolerable, in a religion classroom, because it is not "religion," but defilement—the *other* of the sacred and of religion.[8]

Heschel harbors deep sympathies with this student view, for he also works in dualistic modes of holy and profane, time and space, spiritual and material. He recoils from categorical uncertainty, and works hard to keep matter where it belongs—in the spatial realm of social labor. But his obsession with things overwhelms his classificatory scheme, and things slip into the protective walls of holy time. For Heschel's Sabbath time does indeed contain walls, and not only metaphorical ones, in such evocative language as "tablets of every heart" or "bricks in the soul." As I read Heschel, material things go to the core of American Jewish identity. We are commanded, Heschel insists, to depose "the coveting of things in space for *coveting the things in time.*"[9] This is more than metaphorical prose: it is a language of display that exposes the inescapable features of material identity.

Heschel's material language introduces chapter 5 and its discussion of American Jewish literature. In chapter 4, I read Heschel against Heschel, revealing how his rhetoric undermines his categorical divisions. But the narratives explored in chapter 5 explicitly associate material objects with Jewish identity. In Anzia Yezierska's stories about immigrant Jewish women in the 1920s, a visual optics materially frames how her Jewish immigrants experience America. Yezierska's women literally see materially: they encounter America by gazing at clothes, furniture, dirt, and physical space. These materials are rarely symbols that represent or encode meanings; instead, they are inescapable physical things that make up and constitute immigrant Jewish experiences. Religious identity is not some essence, as some recent work has indicated, "given material shape and expression," such that it can be decoded by the researcher's gaze. Religion is neither "transcendent" nor "numinous," requiring a physical form to become a "materializing religion."[10] The religious characters in the Jewish literary works of this chapter rarely appear as ethereal essences in need of formal shape. Instead, they materially *enact* their identities in and through things. Material objects do not offer meanings to inchoate ideas; they instead embody religious identity. Reading a thing as meaningful symbol often leads to a quick dismissal of the thing itself, for the researcher has now "decoded" and thus reduced the object, in David Morgan and Sally Promey's felicitous phrase, "to another archival text."[11]

Instead of pursuing this linguistic model, students of material culture should focus on how people do things with things. This sense of material fashioning, in which things enact and expose the self, comes to the fore in the works of Cynthia Ozick, Philip Roth, and Bernard Malamud. I focus on Ozick's "Envy; or, Yiddish in America" (1969), and the ways in which she infuses language with material value that confers heritage, history, place, and obligation. In Roth's "Eli, the Fanatic" (1959), we read how the black suit fails as a meaningful signifier of Jewish inheritance. Suits and hats, in my reading, are only the material stuff of lived lives, and not profound indicators of deeper meanings. But these material clothes are no less valuable for their symbolic failure, and perhaps even more so because of it. Bernard Malamud's short stories from *The Magic Barrel* (1958), *Idiots First* (1963), and *Rembrandt's Hat* (1973) reveal characters chained to historical and cultural ghettoes. His dark images of confinement, touched with the tenderness of hope, revolve around things: the window shade in Rosen's apartment, Rubin's hat, Salzman's magic barrel, or Fidelman's text and Susskind's suit. These material things embody a scarred life rooted in a tragic past. For Yezierska, Ozick, Roth, and Malamud, material identity is a grounding feature of Jewish experience in America.

Yezierska discovers how American Jews cultivate visual practices. They see the world materially in ways that situate identity in and among things. Chapter 6 locates this optics in one particular gaze: the ways in which Jews imagine themselves as American Jews. I analyze three sites of this visual display: the magazine covers of *Lilith* magazine, Arnold Eagle's photographic collection of Orthodox Jews in New York City (1935), and the three film versions of *The Jazz Singer* (1927, 1953, and 1980). All three visual modes produce compelling images of cultural and religious heritage, exposing feminist visions of women's history (*Lilith* magazine), male nostalgia for the European ghetto (Eagle's stark photographs), and the choreography and aural techniques of becoming American (the three *Jazz Singer* films). The artistic mediums themselves—magazine covers, black-and-white photography, and film—display images of Jews as they wish to see and be seen. This form of visual Judaism is what David Morgan calls a practice, "something that people do, conscious or not, and a way of seeing that viewers share." These images do "cultural work," and I, like Morgan, explain less what the picture is than "what the picture does."[12] Material images do things for Jews in America, and one of those things is the creation of a visual heritage. Jews see their past in these magazine covers, photographs, and films. It is a productive gaze, a form of blending power with desire,[13] at once a visual practice and a display of material Judaism. The Jewish "act of looking"[14] produces Jewish material identity in America.

I have categorized these enactments of material Jewish identity into six rubrics that expose the subtle features of identity formation in America: self, past, place, presence, narrative, and gaze. Each rubric structures the analysis of identity in the corresponding chapter: Kaplan's performance of *self* in journal writing; Bernays, Liebman, and Fromm's struggle with the material *past*; the *place* of the city in Soloveitchik's account of Jewish law; the *presence* of things in Heschel's *Sabbath*; the *narrative* identity in the works of Yezierska, Roth, Ozick, and Malamud;

and the visual practice and *gaze* located in magazine covers, photographs, and film. Although thematic in structure, the chapters align in broad chronological order, and build a more robust thesis by drawing from previous chapters. The rubrics, to be sure, are neither exclusive nor entirely complete. They do, however, compose a trajectory of Jewish thinking about things, and the impress of those things upon Jewish identity. Although works in cultural studies tend to focus on gender and race (Freedman's *Klezmer America,* noted above, is but one example of this kind of writing), I have chosen to strategically engage these issues at pivotal moments in the book. Race works its way into two critical junctures: within Liebman's account of psychological maturity, and in the *Jazz Singer* films. Gender constructions are crucial to most chapters in this book: in Kaplan's performance of the male self, in Bernays, Liebman, and Fromm's gendered rhetoric, within the feminine allure of Heschel's things, in Yezierska's and Malamud's portrayal of female characters, and within the gendered gazes that construct Jewish material identity. Situating racial and gendered constructions *within* the thematic chapters holds the distinct advantage of intermixing: it enacts the point that gender and race are essential to material identity.

This book seeks to expand our notions of material culture so that Soloveitchik's theory of Jewish law, Heschel's account of the Sabbath, and even the utopian visions of an Erich Fromm become critical texts in cultural studies. Material culture, to be sure, is a vast field, and absorbs various disciplines and methods.[15] It can often devolve into sharp distinctions between popular and elite culture as it revives neglected voices and practices. Visual images, kitsch objects, clothing, architecture, and books on display become the stuff of scholarly research.[16] But we can also recognize journals, such as Mordecai Kaplan's diaries, as significant enactments of the material self. Although he ranks as an "elite" representative of American Jewish culture, Kaplan creates an "archival text" that still embodies material practices. Though not exhibited in a home or parlor, his diaries offer a broader account of visual display: the pageantry and spectacle of self-performance in and through a material object. Other Jewish "elites," such as Joseph Soloveitchik and Abraham Joshua Heschel, further expand the rubric of material culture, as do the literary works in chapter 5 and the neo-Freudian accounts in chapter 2. Rather than dismiss these voices to create a more popular "roots trip," we should instead reinscribe them within a more elastic and nuanced study of material identity. Objects and things come in many forms, and people, even Jewish elites, think about things in ways that inform our material gaze. Morgan and Promey suggest we examine what images and things *do*,[17] and they are right to emphasize these performative features. This book follows their model, but it also seeks to expand it. Material culture is broad enough to include how Jews in America enact their religious selves inscribed in journals, imagined through heritage, experienced during sacred moments of time, lived within cities, embedded in literary narratives, and seen through images. This is material Jewish identity in America painted on a broader, more diverse canvas.

The six rubrics that comprise this book propel us into a world of material Jewish practices enacted in America. I leave to the conclusion some accounting of what is Jewish, and what American, in this staging of identity. If these chapters persuade, as I hope they do, that material-ity lies at the core of Jewish thought and identity in America, then the conclusion only extends the contention of this book. For I argue there, finally, that we should be suspicious of the American–Jewish distinction because it often obscures lived realities of Jewish experience in this coun-try. The question concerning the Jewish or American quality of identity misses the point of material practices. When Jews work with and think about things, they do so in modes that undercut categorical distinctions between American and Jewish culture. As Jonathan Freedman makes clear, Jews enact multiple narratives, passions, ideas, and traditions in ways that complicate clear formulations of identity.[18] Things are messy, and working with them muddies us all. But this is a productive muck, as I hope the following chapters reveal. This book draws us into the mess, much like Orsi's urban holy, so that we arise, not cleaner, but more de-lightfully entangled in the webs of material identity.

ONE

The Material Self:
Mordecai Kaplan and
the Art of Writing

Mordecai Kaplan's diaries from 1913 to 1934 offer a window onto a tormented and lonely Jewish thinker. As a pioneering theologian, sociologist, and teacher of American Judaism in the twentieth century, Kaplan stood as a towering figure at the Jewish Theological Seminary in New York City (1909–1963), where he worked for a good deal of his very long life (1881–1983). Indeed, more than any other thinker of his generation, Kaplan tapped into and gave expression to enduring features of American Jewish experience. Yet even with the groundbreaking work, *Judaism as a Civilization* (1934), and his popular following, he felt marginalized and embattled throughout his life. To help manage and defend those professional conflicts, Kaplan turned to his journal[1] to record his personal struggles and anxieties. In this material thing, Kaplan discovered and created an American Jewish identity through the art of journal writing.

The editor of Kaplan's diary, Mel Scult, has compared this "universe of word" to Kaplan's penchant for mapping out ideas, and his reluctance to turn vision into practice. Words only, Scult argues, and not material things and projects, enliven Kaplan's life: "Kaplan's world was essentially a world of words, not things. . . . The words themselves become constitutive, become the totality. Once he had succeeded in stating the formulation, his task was completed." Those words could "rescue the self from oblivion," and even signify the heroic attempt to overcome human finitude. But Kaplan was still the prophet and far less the priestly builder of communities. The diary, Scult concludes, "is another dimension of his involvement in words, not things."[2]

Yet Kaplan personified his diary as a material friend through whom he could engage and explore his ever present desire to create something permanent. The very materiality of language offered Kaplan relief from the fear of creative failure, together with hope of securing a home in America. To rephrase Scult's critique, those words were Kaplan's things, and he embodied what he calls his "self-aspect" in the material script. Journal writing is Kaplan's performance of self in a material medium: the diary witnesses to the material existence of an engaged personality.

Kaplan's art of journal writing is a cultural strategy of belonging in America. By creating a distinctive personality in the diary entries, Kaplan employed the act of writing to perform and establish his American Jewish identity. Within those diary pages he would carve out space for expressive fulfillment: a performance of the self as a form of self-exposure. The journal allowed Kaplan to "externalize and render transferable" those most personal features of the self. Frustrated by repeated attempts to instill those features in his children, Kaplan instead turned to his journal as a material substitute. As he transferred his desires and fears to the journal, he created more lasting impressions of the self. In this way, disclosing the self in writing satiated his longing for a presence and home in America. Kaplan's readers become witnesses to his claim to America; the journal, in turn, serves as a material archive of Kaplan's life. Indeed, Kaplan believed that only his journal verified his life as a real and meaningful one—so much so that he worried the journal could be misplaced, or worse, never read and so quite easily be forgotten and discarded. As material object, Kaplan's journal became a commodity like any other thing. He could lose his American identity now inscribed in the material script.

This sense of displacement, expressed so frequently within the journal, parallels much of Kaplan's own personal history. Born the same year of the pogroms in Russia, Kaplan immigrated with his parents as part of the first wave of Eastern European Jewry to America in the 1880s. The anxious exposures of place, dwelling, and home, all so prevalent in Kaplan's diaries, echo much of the immigrant Jewish experience. The increasing nativism in America during the 1920s marked immigrants as foreigners, and was an overt attempt to protect American culture from dangerous outsiders. Feelings of displacement and loss surface from within the Jewish presence in America, as they do in Kaplan's journals.

But despite all this, immigrant Jews like Kaplan imagined a country open to their yearnings for a better life. Kaplan's passion for the diaries—they could fill twenty-eight volumes, each of 400–500 pages in length[3]—reflects his acute desire to archive the self in America: to create a permanent home and inheritance for himself and others.

The desire for presence in the journals exposes the possibility of failure: writing may not fully express the human personality, Kaplan might not recover his identity "from oblivion," and even more, the immigrant Jew could very well remain alien and homeless in America. Kaplan fears that his journal as material archive will be displaced by other forms and soon forgotten. This sense of self as a material commodity, one as ephemeral as products in the open market, haunts Kaplan's diary and his identity as an American Jew. A consuming culture might very well devour the archive and thus render the material self as absent rather than fully present. To better recover Kaplan's fear of material loss, and the importance of establishing a permanent dwelling in America, I turn to Derrida's understanding of the archive in his perceptive analysis of Yerushalmi's reading of Freud.[4] The ontological pressure to create a permanent thing—what Derrida calls archive fever—haunts Kaplan throughout his life, but nowhere more acutely than here in his journal. Kaplan's yearning for presence in a material thing exposes how Jewish identity is a performative act in material culture.

This story of arrival and loss is also a narrative about urban life in New York, where commercial interests, billboard advertising, leisure enticements, and the frenzied mix of cultures invade and become part of Kaplan's own American experience. Kaplan landed in America in 1889, a young boy who had lived his previous eight years in Lithuania, with the last year in Paris.[5] With his traditional upbringing in Jewish education, Kaplan would become the rabbi of an Orthodox New York synagogue, only to slowly, but ever steadily, move in more liberal directions in faith and practice. As a student and later teacher at the Jewish Theological Seminary, Kaplan developed what he hoped would become a reconstructionist program for the burgeoning Conservative movement in America. When the seminary proved too confining for his expansive program, Kaplan reluctantly gave shape to the new Reconstructionist movement that would establish its own rabbinical college, compose new prayer books, and build synagogues for an increasingly devoted community. But these creations would arrive after Kaplan's more foreboding thoughts in the 1920s and 1930s, when the concern for permanence and the anxiety of absence loomed large. Social historians of this period—Andrew Heinze, Jenna Weissman Joselit, and Riv-Ellen Prell chief among them[6]—can help situate Kaplan's works within this Jewish cultural moment in America. In so doing, they reveal how Kaplan's diaries remain part of the immigrant narratives in New York, when material consumption and social enticements carved out defining Jewish experiences.

Cultural tensions surface in Kaplan's writings because he displayed modernist and immigrant obsessions with self, place, and home in both his journal and his theory of civilization as aesthetic performance. Kaplan published his *Judaism as a Civilization* in 1934, and it promised a reconstruction of Judaism on a grand scale—one that would redefine how Jews lived in America and recognize their cultural singularity. As a practice of lived religion, Jewish civilization provided an artistic and material medium through which Jews could cultivate enduring Jewish sensibilities. Judaism would become a kind of Jewish art, offering an aesthetic model for the pragmatic and meaningful practice of a civilization. This practice, I want to argue, reflects Kaplan's concern with the performance of self.

Kaplan's journals disclose the central preoccupations of this book: the ways in which Jews think about materiality, and how Jewish identity is rooted in material things. Here we find echoes of what is to come: the material weight of the past on contemporary self-creation (the focus of chapter 2), Soloveitchik's urban motifs (in chapter 3), the abundance of material commodities that threaten Heschel's spiritual presence (chapter 4), the ways in which things ground and texture modern Jewish identity (the literary works of chapter 5), and finally, gendered invocations of civilization in the form of heritage production (chapter 6). Kaplan touches upon all these concerns, and more. In so doing, he has created a home and presence in America that even he could not have imagined. His burden, I believe, has become the heritage of American Jews as well.

But much of the interest in Kaplan has focused on his theological, philosophical, and sociological theories. To be sure, his disavowal of a personal God who commands, and his visceral denial of the special claims of a chosen people, have not won wide acceptance from American Jews, even from within the Reconstructionist movement. But rarely, if at all, have scholars turned to material culture to enliven and explore Kaplan's modernist dilemmas. This chapter attempts to draw cultural studies[7] into the orbit of American Jewish thought in order to enrich both material studies of religion and philosophical accounts of self-fashioning. The immigrant Jewish experience is a critical feature of Kaplan's material landscape, and significantly informs his work on Jewish civilization. Both his journals and published texts reflect immigrant and modernist preoccupations with personal meaning after the First World War, and the turn to aesthetics to retrieve a more genuine self. I want to focus on these cultural enactments of self to better expose how materiality and material culture constitute Jewish identity. As Kaplan searches for home, he relies on material products like his journal to create a space of belonging and authenticity. In this way, the art of civilization is a pragmatic cultural method for becoming American—to perform oneself, as it were, into the American material landscape.

THE JOURNAL PERSONIFIED

Autobiographical writing, as William Spengemann and L. R. Lundquist argue, produces a self by employing common cultural myths and images. The author "sees himself" through cultural categories, and so "creates for himself" a recognizable identity.[8] But as Elizabeth Podnieks observes, the boundaries between autobiography and diary writing have been obscured in the modernist era.[9] The diary, like autobiography, includes "internal closures and summations," provides "structural and thematic patterns," and is "a consciously crafted text." Rather than a secret, private work, the diary is a public text designed for a particular audience: it is a kind of "private-diary-as-public-text."[10]

Kaplan's diaries provide an illustrative example of journal writing as public performance, in which an author crafts a text as a spectacle for others to observe, interpret, and treasure. Kaplan edits his entries throughout the journal, often adding sentences in the margins, and even referring to other journal sections that relate to his present entry. His strong editorial hand—rewriting and repositioning sentences, correcting punctuation, including notes in the margins—reveals an author

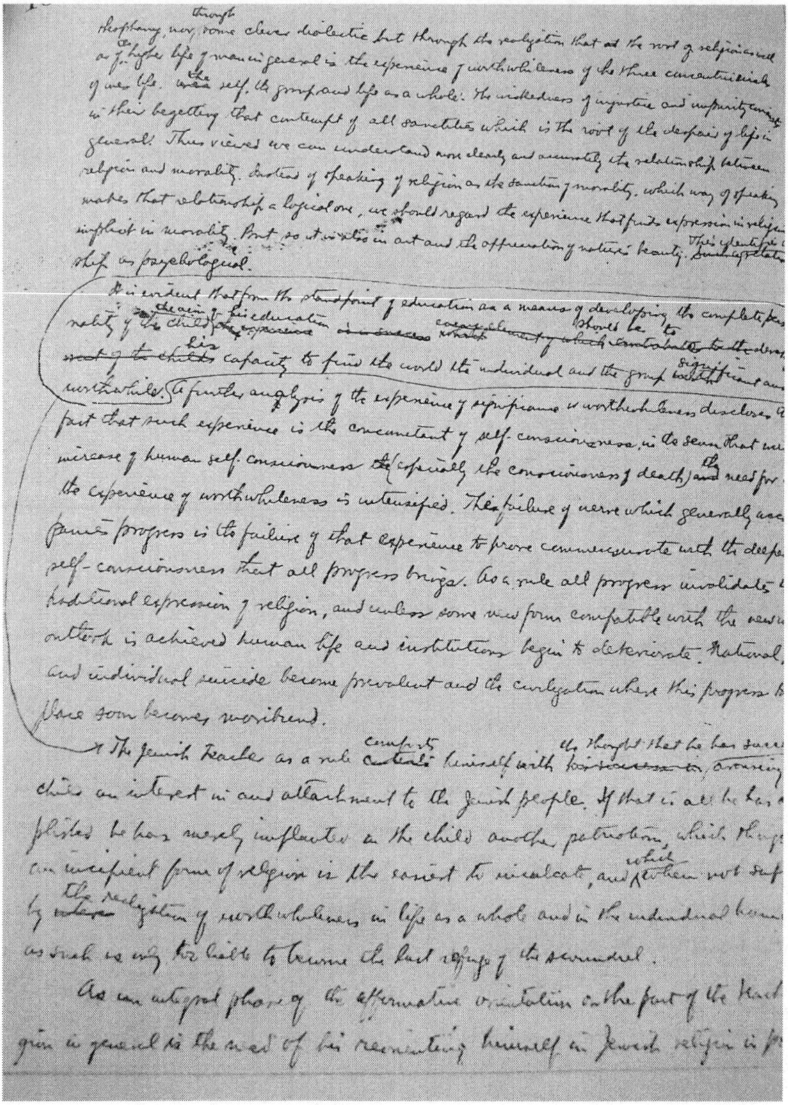

theophany, nor some clever dialectic but through the realization that at the root of religion and
of the higher life of man in general is the experience of worthwhileness of the three concentric circles
of our life, the self, the group and life as a whole. The wickedness of injustice and impurity consists
in their begetting that contempt of all sanctities which is the root of the despair of life in
general. Thus viewed we can understand more clearly and accurately the relationship between
religion and morality. Instead of speaking of religion as the sanction of morality, which way of speaking
makes that relationship a logical one, we should regard the experience that finds expression in religion
implicit in morality. But so it exists in art and the appreciation of nature's beauty. This identification [illegible]
ship as psychological.

It is evident that from the standpoint of education as a means of developing the complete personality of the child [illegible] should be to [illegible] his capacity to find the world the individual and the group significant and
worthwhile. The further analysis of the experience of significance or worthwhileness discloses the
fact that such experience is the concomitant of self-consciousness, in the sense that with
increase of human self consciousness especially the consciousness of death, the need for
the experience of worthwhileness is intensified. The failure of nerve which generally accompanies progress is the failure of that experience to prove commensurate with the deeper
self-consciousness that all progress brings. As a rule all progress invalidates the
traditional expression of religion, and unless some new form compatible with the new
outlook is achieved human life and institutions begin to deteriorate. National
and individual suicide become prevalent and the civilization where this progress took
place soon becomes moribund.

The Jewish teacher as a rule comforts himself with the thought that he has succeeded in arousing in the
child an interest in and attachment to the Jewish people. If that is all he has accomplished he has merely implanted in the child another patriotism, which though
an incipient form of religion is the easiest to inculcate, and which when not supported
by the realization of worthwhileness in life as a whole and in the individual human
as such is only too liable to become the last refuge of the scoundrel.

As an integral phase of the affirmative orientation on the part of the teacher to religion in general is the need of his reorienting himself in Jewish religion in [illegible]

FIGURE 1.1. Mordecai Kaplan journal entry, June 19, 1930 (Vol. 6). *The Eisenstein Reconstructionist Archives of the Reconstructionist Rabbinical College.* Courtesy of the Archives of Jewish Theological Seminary.

who understands his text as a public work to be read by others: this is, to be sure, a "consciously crafted text." Even more, Kaplan reviewed the typed copies of his handwritten diaries, and corrected those editions when stylistically necessary.[11] All this suggests a kind of private writing intended for public consumption that registered the diary as a material witness to the self. This public face of the diary emerged along with the self in Renaissance and Enlightenment currents, and became critical to the modernist preoccupation with self-fashioning.[12] Journals provided a material medium to render and create the self in words. Diaries were, to be sure, still cultural productions, and they expressed dominant images, anxieties, and desires to make sense of a life. As Kaplan's obsessive writing became increasingly haunted by insecurity and doubt, the diary captured his modernist desire for self-fashioning.

Kaplan had always admired those who wrote books, and even more those who secured each moment of the day for their professional duties. He would not defend work for its own sake, but rather valued a kind of dedicated engagement to material or "useful" practices. Surrounded by colleagues who churned out significant works in Jewish studies, or relatives who succeeded in business, Kaplan found little solace in returning to his diaries, again and again, to compensate for his lack of physical work or more lengthy written treatises. He chided his passion for diary writing as a leisurely desire, unbecoming of a serious academic scholar—and certainly not for one who aspired, as Kaplan surely did, to admired greatness and devotion from his students and congregants alike. Idleness, in the form of retreating to the diary, suggested failure. For Kaplan longed to create something of permanence, some physical and material reminder that he mattered—both to those he cared for and to future generations of American Jews. Journal writing became a conduit to explore this anxiety of presence, and the ways in which written words render the self visible and alive. The diaries confirm that he had created something durable and unique. This is why I call it a "performance," for Kaplan explores and fashions his identity through the material script, and enacts this identity through his writing on the journal pages. He struggles to reveal how the impressions of writing—the enduring markings on the page—could manifest a real, embodied personality of importance.

Kaplan turned to words to alleviate his sense of loneliness and failure. While on vacation at the Jersey shore in 1916, Kaplan recalled how much he enjoyed the fresh air and sunshine away from his home in New York City. He chafed at the material abundance and wealth of city life, and often associated the city with filth and cheap tastelessness.[13] But kitsch aside, the summer days on the shore offered health and a sense of leisure often missing from urban decadence. Kaplan shared much with other modernists who disdained the unhealthy working conditions of urban factories, and the suffocating reign of technology, bureaucratic rationality, and capitalist production in the city.[14] This was as much aesthetic critique as social commentary, for like other modernists, Kaplan sought some modicum of experiential meaning to counter the "technocratic promise" of Fordism that seemed to straightjacket self-fulfillment.[15] Yet distant from the oppressive urban air, Kaplan could still not fully enjoy his luxury—a recurring modernist anxiety. He complained of his "solitude and isolation" in what he imagined as a prison, where "the days and the weeks are passing by without my achieving anything." City life offered something else entirely: a community of speakers where Kaplan "at least [had] occasion to interchange a word with somebody."[16] So even as he imbibed much of the modernist rhetoric that resented urban decay, Kaplan still maintained a more hopeful view of city commerce and community, one that had deep roots in American Romantic thought.[17]

The city retains its appeal despite its filth and chaos. Away from New York, Kaplan admits, "I am all alone." It is noteworthy that Kaplan associates failure of achievement with the absence of discourse. Without "a human being who is interested in or troubled by problems similar to mine," Kaplan cannot produce a significant written or spoken word. Achievement means "to interchange a word with somebody";[18] failure is that sense of loneliness in which the productive word lies dormant. On that night at the Jersey shore, Kaplan turned to his journal for companionship, to engage "a word with somebody," even if that body became the journal personified. Scult notes Kaplan's propensity for describing his journal as a friend, reflected in this diary entry in 1929: "As on previous occasions I shall resort again to this diary as though it were an intelligent friend to whom I could communicate what I am struggling these days to formulate."[19] Historian Melissa Klapper notes that young women in the late nineteenth and early twentieth century also "treated their diaries as emotional confidantes," and often confessed their "inner feelings" in those pages.[20] Young girls personified their journals in order to relieve their loneliness, and they, like Kaplan, could explore and express themselves most fully in that material medium. For Sandra Rubin, fifteen years old in 1955, a journal captured her "true self," and she remained stubbornly loyal and committed to the diary.[21] This is certainly true for Kaplan as well. Trapped by the failure of work and the prison of isolation, Kaplan domesticated his diary as that embodied friend with whom a word is both possible and meaningful.

One senses the all-embracing seclusion of a writer yearning for meaningful words. Yet the journal proved a poor substitute for his friends in the city. Kaplan expresses profound ambivalence about journal writing and the significant time he devoted to the practice. He is admittedly ashamed of the diary as a compensatory substitute for human friendship. He often remarks of time better spent studying the Talmud than marking his journal.[22] The luxury of writing for (and perhaps to) oneself pales before the work of textual study. This ascetic tone echoes throughout Kaplan's diary entries, where he even expresses some remorse for his yearning for ice cream, and believes he should follow Gandhi's example, "and refrain from gratifying my want."[23] This intense focus on desires and the guilt evoked from them reflects some of the popular Freudian discourse that suffused America in the 1920s. It was everywhere: on billboard advertising, popular journals, and everyday discourse.[24] The practice of psychology became a fad and a "craze" to such an extent that "it became socially obligatory to develop complexes." Never before had the general public become so conscious about the unconscious. Freud's nephew, Edward Bernays, who pioneered modern public relations in America by invoking psychoanalysis at every turn (as we will see in the next chapter), relied on his audience to recognize the prejudices that moved them.[25]

Kaplan could not help but succumb to this popular Freudian discourse and desire, but he did so only after convincing himself that satisfying his urges would help advance his work.[26] As Joshua Liebman would argue some years later in his best seller, *Peace of Mind* (1946), it is better to express and recognize those impulses than to repress them. And through that recognition, greater economic opportunities would surely open for the expressive self.[27] Yet it is precisely these opportunities for self-expression that so burdened Kaplan: "Writing which records first hand experiences, however crude it be, it seems to me ought to have more value than formal writing in which we merely add to the endless discussions about this or that abstract concept."[28] That journal writing "ought to have more value" suggests it does not, both for Kaplan and his professional colleagues. Kaplan himself obsesses over his lack of production, and at forty-six years of age shamefully admits he does not have one significant book to his name—and blames his time with the journal for his professional infertility.[29] Three years later in 1930, while working on his *Judaism as a Civilization,* he returns to this trope and anxiety: "I am like a woman who constantly miscarries. Is it a wonder that I am green with envy when I see some of my younger colleagues spreading themselves out in numerous learned periodicals?"[30] *He* should be writing those texts, Kaplan believes, and return to the hard work of learning and academic discourse. But the journal serves as a source of comfort and friendship amid his jealousy, and it transposes his self into a material medium.

Kaplan tempers his jealousy, however, with biting critique. Although he miscarries often (to use Kaplan's gendered rhetoric), at least he does not prostitute himself by "spreading" throughout the learned periodicals. His manliness finds expression in his diaries—even as diary writing has been traditionally the literary outlet for women.[31] Though his colleagues publish often, they fail, in Kaplan's gendered division, to evoke that one essential male virtue: the production of the unique individual. Only Kaplan does this in his journal writings, for they expose the male desire to birth a reproduction of self. His colleagues spread themselves too thin, prostituting rather than producing the male self. He is still envious of his colleagues, to be sure, but Kaplan also reappropriates the male self as his own; personal experiences recorded in his journal really are more valuable for their intense "aura," as Walter Benjamin would call it.[32] His journal is no miscarriage: it is masculine writing that gives birth to the material self. Kaplan attempts to reclaim some notion of the unique (and male) personality in the material practice of journal writing.

This performance of the *male* self is of crucial importance for understanding Kaplan's journal. Kaplan was more the prophet than priest, more a man of words, as Scult would have it, than of things. But words were Kaplan's things: they were the permanent material objects of his creation. They embodied his thoughts, passions, and self. Yet Kaplan often complained of his failure to do "more permanent work"—the kind of work that makes lasting impressions.[33] Can the journal be that kind of thing? Can it retain the weightiness of permanent creation, of lasting mark and evidence of the embodied self? Kaplan is none too sure:

> I do not know why I find it so hard to write about myself. But as I think of it I really do know why. It is this terrible urge to do something worth while which leads me to regard as wasted every movement that I spend without improving my knowledge or mental power. I live inwardly as though I had but a short time to live and wanted to accomplish something substantial before it was too late. I suppose most people who combine mediocrity with inordinate ambition are always in a hurry.[34]

Here again Kaplan refuses the luxury of self-expression in diaries, and craves the status and respect of professional accomplishments. His ambitions lead beyond the journal to build communities and compose great academic works. The anxiety of writing, as expressed in this diary entry, is the anxiety of finitude itself: "It appears to me that even death makes no impression upon our type of people. And fool that I am I expect a sermon of mine to leave a lasting impression!"[35] To inscribe the self in this life is to leave an inheritance for others. Kaplan's journal is his material legacy, his construction of a "lasting impression," even if in a hurry, and even more in the failure to do something worthwhile.

That failure haunted Kaplan, and he suffered for it. He likened himself to Don Quixote, who in fighting imagined objects in battle, would still end up bested by those ghosts: "Beguiled by the delusion that I can help to render Judaism permanent, or even temporarily safe, I fight against windmills which always worst me. That is why I am the Knight of the long face, always grumpy, always in bad humor."[36] Turning to more worldly pursuits tempted Kaplan, and he discussed a career in the silk industry with his brother-in-law, Edward Rubin. Even as he romantically dreamed of "turning to the practical affairs of life," Kaplan still found industry "noisy, unsafe and unsanitary," and he lamented the "pitiless grind of the average well-to-do Jewish business man."[37] The sense of filth and disgust that Kaplan associated with housework finds it echo here in the city, and he instinctively recoils from it. He would not make his mark in what he called that "seething chaos of life"—a none-too-subtle allusion to the city that both repelled and attracted him—and he finally admitted, "I suppose I shall go on squirming and writing in spiritual agony for the rest of my days." Unable to work within the stench and disarray of city life, and yet unhappy with his "impotent spectatorship,"[38] Kaplan returned again and again to his diary to record his anguish and bad humor:

> And why can't I do what Julian Huxley did?[39] Because I haven't his heredity. . . . My ancestry consists of very ordinary folk who never achieved distinction in learning, business or saintliness. Why then do I not accept my limitations and try to lead a calm and peaceful inner life instead of forever boiling within like a volcano?[40]

To "render Judaism permanent" would enable Kaplan to stake a material claim in America—to become American through the fashioning of it. He would remold the city to enable a sturdier life, one less chaotic but no less seething. A desire for permanence in this sense is a yearning for place—a "calm and peaceful life" within, and a settled home in a new land. Fighting against windmills, and "boiling within like a volcano," witness to the anxiety of place as recorded in Kaplan's diaries.

I want to emphasize just how much of that fight occurred within Kaplan's journals. If he could not become that Jewish businessman, and so succeed in the more practical pursuits, then Kaplan would become the American male through inscribing his self within the diary. Indeed, Kaplan described his diary as "the struggle for self-expression by means of the written word."[41] This sense of exploring or mining the self in writing captures his imagination, and he finds solace that perhaps his own words may compensate for his failures in academic life:

> For the last hour and a half I have been writing aimlessly [in my diary] only to find some compensation for my frustrated hopes and ambitions. Would I not have employed that time to better advantage if I had worked on the paraphrase translation of the Midrash of Shir Hashirim [Song of Songs]? From one point of view the answer should be an emphatic yes. . . . On the other hand, no one but myself could write my diary. Whether what I have to say is wise or foolish, interesting or boring, it is the attempt of a personality to save itself from inarticulateness and oblivion by the mere skin of its teeth.[42]

Academic work attracts Kaplan for its prestige and admiration—qualities that Jewish men coveted from their co-workers and families. Kaplan's frustrated hopes and ambitions could be realized through intensive work in Hebrew translation. But he recognizes that "anyone who has a fair knowledge of rabbinic style and a sense of the English language could do that work." He could not inscribe or reveal his personality in that kind of writing. But in his diary, the self's "struggles are entirely its own and no other person in the world could know them and record them."[43] This is the self-made American male, the lonely individual before faceless conformists. It is the dream of the unique personality, created and determined by "no other person in the world." It is the wandering Jew who, in the very fashioning of home, has secured a place to rest. Saved from oblivion, Kaplan constitutes his identity within the written word that exposes the frustrations and hopes of a male Jew becoming American. The journal is Kaplan's own; it is his claim to America. A translation of Midrash captures some other self; journal writing fashions a home because it mimics the American practice of the individual, authentic self.

This helps to explain Kaplan's thrill when he chanced upon a reading by Bachya ibn Paquda. Kaplan read sections of ibn Paquda's *Duties of the Heart* (eleventh century) on a Sunday morning in May 1929. He finds comfort in ibn Paquda's reading of Ecclesiastes 12:11: "the words of the wise are like goads, and like driven-in nails are *ba'alei asuppot.*" Kaplan understands ibn Paquda's commentary to imply "that the written word is so much more valuable than the spoken word because it has permanence." What troubles ibn Paquda is the meaning of the Hebrew phrase *ba'alei asuppot,* left curiously untranslated in the Jewish Publication Society *tanakh,* but often awkwardly rendered as "the sayings of the masters of collections." Ibn Paquda leans on an earlier commentator to argue that the *ba'alei asuppot* are "the authors of compilations." Because "the books written about the various branches of wisdom endure and are of lasting value," they are likened to driven-in nails. Kaplan maintains little interest in ibn Paquda's exegetical struggle with the Hebrew linguistic meaning, and instead focuses on the "lasting value" of written words. And while ibn Paquda never mentions the spoken word, Kaplan introduces the distinction between it and the written text.[44] Vocal performances are momentary and fleeting; material writing creates permanent impressions.

The journal was not the only material medium Kaplan employed to establish his claim on America. Twice in his journals he mentions his interest in clay and sculpture, and both examples reveal a passionate desire to create a permanent, material object. In the fall of 1929, Kaplan recalls a need to "find relief from solitude and monotony" in his work on *Judaism as a Civilization*. While his journal offers the comfort and pleasure of a compassionate friend, academic writing provides no such amusement. So Kaplan lays down the pen, and reports that he "played with clay" to create a portrait of his brother-in-law Jacob H. Rubin.[45] After some ten hours of modeling the head, he finally molds a remote likeness to Rubin, and decides to carry the bust with him to Rubin's summer house for final corrections. But on the way, Kaplan has misgivings and considers turning back: "It seemed altogether too ridiculous for me to take this playing with clay so seriously as though I knew what I was about." But he continues nonetheless, and after lunch on Thursday begins to shape the bust into a "strong resemblance," and gains the confidence to continue working on it through the weekend. Kaplan appears quite obsessed with the clay piece:

> I worked on it Friday, Saturday night and Sunday till four in the afternoon. Outside of reading a number of *Moznaim* [a literary weekly] and fifty pages of Benet's *John Brown's Body* I did no intellectual work during the entire four days. The change from the effort to spin a Jewish Utopia out of the frailest cobweb of possibilities and the pleasure my attempt at modeling afforded every one of the folks in West End were extremely invigorating to me.[46]

Note how Kaplan compares the delight in modeling to the "effort" in composing an academic work. The intellectual struggle is tenuous and abstract, spun from "the frailest cobweb of possibilities." Work on *Judaism as a Civilization* does not consume him, and exposes only his deep anxieties of failure and incompetence. But creating a material object affords pleasure to others, even as it enlivens Kaplan's creative drives. To create something real—to mold a thing that actually resembles a human being—moves Kaplan in ways that "intellectual work" does not. We have witnessed this already in Kaplan's passion for journal writing. There, too, he discloses his desire for permanence and lasting significance. The clay piece and the journal are created material impressions, and those things as aesthetic objects captivate Kaplan's attention. They remove Kaplan from his intellectual world of "solitude and monotony," and surround him in a life of real objects to enjoy and create.

This sense of passionate enjoyment comes to the fore once again a few months later, in October 1929, when Kaplan describes his work on a bust of his father. He had showed the piece to the painter Joseph Tepper, who pointed out some minor faults with the figure. Only months earlier Kaplan had thought it ridiculous to play with clay. But now he bristles at Tepper's critique: "Faults or no faults before I started to remodeling it it bore a perfect resemblance to father." Kaplan set out to mold an exact likeness, and as he tells it,

> spent about twelve or thirteen hours on it. I was up till 3:30 in the morning. I simply could not tear myself away from it until I managed to retrieve the resemblance to father, and in this I succeeded only by restoring the very face lines that Tepper criticized most severely as not being human.[47]

There are surely deeper psychological issues at play in creating a likeness to one's father than mere fascination with material objects. Yet note Kaplan's arrival as master artist—not by dismissing Tepper's critique, but by materially revealing the critic's incompetence. For the bust only resembles Kaplan's father when he restores the lines that Tepper himself suggested he remove. Kaplan had it right from the beginning, and he stays up all night to prove himself more worthy, and artistically more perceptive, than the professionals (those other "fathers") about him. And it is precisely this sense of competence and superiority that Kaplan misses from his academic work. There he feels ashamed at his lack of scholarly publications, and considers what he has done only frail cobwebs amid more solid, sturdy pieces. But in creating a material object of stature and resemblance to the real, Kaplan underscores the divide between thought and things: "I wish my literary tasks and studies could have such a grip on me as this modeling."[48] Artistic work has this kind of grip on Kaplan because it is a material thing that retains a lasting impression. For Kaplan, academic studies are flights into Jewish utopia. But a clay model, or a journal that exposes the self, are permanent objects of enjoyment and passion. He discovers and enacts his manliness in creating material things. Kaplan need not succeed in business: his prestige and competence arrive through material productions. In short, Kaplan does things *with* things, and this material practice exposes a very different personality than the one who competes for academic distinction. Through art, Kaplan discovers his competence, loyalty, and a sense that he has arrived, despite what more established critics might suggest. He is at home in his art.

THE JOURNAL AS ART

Journal writing is for Kaplan a work of art. Art cultivates the expressive self and renders it in some material form. Kaplan has been reading Willa Cather's *Death Comes for the Archbishop,* and he empathizes with the archbishop's sense of futility, for "his work seemed superficial, a house built upon the sands." He recognizes much of himself in the archbishop, for Kaplan, too, is continually frustrated by "apathy and stupidity." However, he discovers in Cather's work a discussion on "the value of art," in no small part because Kaplan had just sat through a musical comedy at the Century Theatre before taking up the novel. As with his account of modeling, Kaplan describes how "this passage gripped me, or rather it enabled me to take a firmer hold on myself." Cather's novel offers a window into the function of art:

> The ancients had an idea that to know the name of a thing or person was to be in a position to exercise control over that thing or person. Somewhat akin seems to be the work of art. Its points describe and articulate the innermost aspects of the environment and of our own natures, thereby enabling us to put them under our control.[49]

To name the animals, as Adam had done in Genesis, is to rule over them. It is to act with authority and clarity of purpose. So too, Kaplan claims here, for the work of art. In aesthetic creations, the artist maps out natural and human terrain, and in so doing controls both the real world and the inner life. Art does not reimagine the world, or even the self, as some utopian possibility. Its power lies in adequately describing the nature of things.

Like Kaplan's clay pieces, art creates a "perfect resemblance" of the world and ourselves, and grabs us with its immediacy. Kaplan understands his journal in much the same way as a noble attempt "to save itself [the personality] from inarticulateness and oblivion." Journal writing is artistic work because it exposes the "innermost aspects" of the self, thereby giving expression to it. By exposing the self, the journal names and locates the human personality, and so enables its material expression. As Zachary Braiterman aptly describes this move, Kaplan gives "shape" to revelation. The self becomes what it is through Kaplan's description of it in his journal. It is an artistic mode of self-fashioning.[50]

Artistic works play a central role in Kaplan's understanding of Jewish experience. In *Art and Ethics* (1954), a text he wrote in Hebrew, Kaplan argues that art helps us achieve our deepest human strivings and goals, and that Judaism is a kind of artistic performance.[51] He explores these issues as well in *Questions Jews Ask*,[52] a text written in 1956 that responds with "reconstructionist answers" to contemporary concerns. Kaplan supports the arts as part of his program for an enlivened Jewish civilization. But he recognizes that some might consider this support "putting the cart before the horse." Should we not revive the Jewish spirit in order to invigorate the arts, rather than the reverse, as he suggests in this text? To justify the expansion of the arts for contemporary Jewish practice, Kaplan explains that "all art presupposes a deep emotional experience, of which it is the expression."[53] The Hasidic movement offers one telling example, for as a "popular religious revival of great emotional intensity, [it] left a permanent impress on Jewish culture in literature, music, dance, the theater and other arts." Note, to begin, the return of the "permanent impress" in Kaplan's discussion. Art retains a lasting imprint when it revives a strong emotional experience. But art also helps to strengthen that experience, and "stimulates emotions akin to those which produced it."[54] Emotions find their material expression in art, and in turn artistic works produce new emotions and experiences. In this way, Jewish art can enliven the Jewish spirit, even as it is produced by that spirit. Art becomes the expressive medium for cultural production and meaning.[55]

Kaplan harbors an expansive notion of the arts, one that includes literature, performance, and the plastic arts, as well as other cultural modes of expression. When asked what he means by the term "Jewish art," Kaplan responds with a spacious account:

> Though there is no Jewish art, from the standpoint of form, from that of content one may regard as Jewish art any creative expression, in any medium, of emotional experiences that grow out of Jewish life. Since it is the function of art to give significant and abiding expression to human experiences, whatever does that for Jewish experience may be considered Jewish art, whether the work be that of a Jew or a non-Jew.[56]

One could very well ask Kaplan what would *not* count as Jewish art? His functional view widens the capacity of the arts to become the emotional trigger of cultural life. Art creates lasting impressions for human experiences. Whatever does that for *Jewish* experience is Jewish art. But this functional account presumes that deep emotional experiences require an outlet. Without material expressions, those emotions "might otherwise subside and leave no permanent effect." The arts "keep alive those experiences," enable us to recognize them as our own, and help "stimulate new emotional responses."[57] We become fully human in and through the arts, and develop our emotional lives and experiences by creating lasting artistic expressions.

Yet Kaplan is attuned to public opinion, and the perception that Jews have never been keen on the arts, or for that matter very good at them. Why should contemporary Jews emphasize the arts when they "played a very subordinate role in Jewish civilization?"[58] Kaplan accepts this common prejudice,[59] even as he defends Jewish artistic expression in the modern world. In this, Kaplan echoes what Jewish cultural elites, in the years before and during the interwar years, had been pursuing with some fury. They had sought to "train the Jewish race in aesthetics" in order to cultivate Jewish creative artists, and perhaps most crucially, to transform Jews into cultural pioneers.[60] Undertaking this cultural agenda, Kaplan argues that in the past, religion had once unified Jews across cultural and political divides. All Jews, Kaplan claims, retained similar beliefs and practices. But those days had vanished, for "with freedom of thought, inevitably comes diversity of belief." How, then, can modern Jewry recoup this lost unity? Some "other influences must fill the vacuum" created by this loss of religious unity: "The spirit to animate the communal organism will derive from their cultural activities, among which the arts will have to figure prominently."[61] Modern art, as that preeminent cultural expression of human emotions and experiences, will "create a common intellectual and emotional content for Jewish life."[62] The "magic of art" lies in its capacity to unite disparate people and emotions in much the same way as religion functioned in the past. This is a material medium of lasting value.

Art is what Kaplan calls a modern "functional equivalent" to religion. Reinterpretation is a "process of finding equivalents in the civilization to which we belong for values of a past stage of that or another civilization."[63] One must identify basic human needs, and then discover how to satisfy them with a modern expressive form.[64] The arts are that form for modern Jews:

> By utilizing Jewish tradition and Jewish community life for the development of ethical standards and aesthetic content, Judaism can give the modern Jew a spiritual culture that would be the equivalent of what the Torah meant for his fathers.[65]

Like traditional religion, the arts unify the emotive experiences of Jewish life. As that common modern currency of cultural expression, art maintains the power to unite generations. Judaism as a civilization is a modernist aesthetic performance—for it too unites Jews across borders through cultural expressions of identity. To paraphrase Kaplan's famous closing lines of his *Judaism as a Civilization*: the Jew will have to save the arts before the arts will save the Jew.[66]

Journal writing, I now want to argue, is one way to save the arts for the Jews. In a fascinating journal entry in May 1931, Kaplan explores the same emotional terrain that underlies much of what will be published in 1934 in his *Judaism as a Civilization*. The question he posed in that 1934 text—how to transfer the emotional power of religious practices to future generations—foments in his diaries as well. Kaplan asks, in a rather stilted way, how "to render [the] self-aspect of our individual polarity transferable from our own bodies to other bodies."[67] It is a question concerning human finitude, and the desire for a lasting expression of the self:

> The desire that our children should cherish our traditions and ideals is essentially the desire to transfer to them our self-respect as well as bodily aspect, thereby assuring ourselves a form of survival which is as near to personal identity and continuity as is possible in the face of the fact of death.[68]

Personal identity expands through time, even after death, to include the lasting impressions created in our children. What lies behind these thoughts, however, is Kaplan's anxiety that his children will not "cherish our traditions and ideals." Indeed, he is bitterly disappointed with his Jewish life at home:

> I'm a failure not only in the Seminary and in the S.A.J. [Society for the Advancement of Judaism], but even in my own home. Despite all my yearnings to beautify Jewish life, to enrich it with song and poetry and dance, I do not get the least cooperation from any member of my family. I had hoped that Judith with her knowledge of music would bring the Shekinah [God's presence] into our household on Friday nights. I thought that my children would ask me to read or speak Hebrew with them. All these dreams of mine have proved to be nothing but illusions. It seems that I am doomed to live out the rest of my days in a sort of prison made for me by aspirations and tastes which separate me from my own wife and children.[69]

Kaplan's desire for survival—his need to render features of the self permanent and lasting—rubs against the apathy of his familial relations, and his children bear the brunt of Kaplan's frustrations. They are *his* children, after all, and should know better. One senses even professional embarrassment, as if the indifference at home only confirms the failures in academic life. Securing male prestige proves both maddening and futile "in a sort of prison." It is the kind of captivity that makes the fact of death certainly more real, and ever so personal. Yet it is nonetheless crucial that Kaplan's prison is an aesthetic one, informed by "aspirations and tastes" that seclude him in isolation. Domestic Judaism, "even in my own home," is an aesthetic experience of song, poetry, dance, and taste.

To relieve the pressure of these anxieties, Kaplan turns to the notion of a civilization, for it can transfer the "self-aspect" to future generations "without having to depend upon one's children to take it over." And it is especially the function of art, so Kaplan argues here, that "the self-aspect is externalized and then adopted by those to whom it appeals." If Kaplan cannot live through his children, then perhaps he can do so through other means. All too aware that he is "succeeding very little in getting my children to take over my self-aspect," Kaplan allows them to "have their way." He partially blames himself for this collapse, and claims "not

[to] possess the ability to externalize my personality by means of song, story, poem or painting."[70] Those kinds of artistic expressions do not fully materialize Kaplan's personality.

But his journal does precisely this kind of material work for Kaplan, for the journal becomes his artistic medium to transfer emotions and experiences to others: "In my frustration, I turn to writing in this journal as the only means left me to externalize and render transferable that aspect of my being I experience as my soul, self or reason."[71] Journal writing is Kaplan's performance of self to others. It is his art, his capacity to express personality in a material medium that creates lasting impressions. Judaism as a civilization harbors many forms of art that expose permanent cultural experiences. But Kaplan cannot fully express his self through song, painting, or some other artistic production. The journal is Kaplan's material medium through which his "self-aspect" becomes immortal. He can "render transferable" those constitutive features of his personality. As Kaplan realizes, "no one but myself could write my diary." Precisely so—for the journal cultivates the individual personality as an artistic, lasting, material presence.

THE JOURNAL AS MATERIAL ARCHIVE

Yet that sense of permanence, of transferring the self through journal writing, gave rise to the anxiety of finitude all the same. Kaplan exposes those fears when, on a train bound for Schenectady, he explores writing in the third person. His daughter Judith had tried this once, but she abandoned the practice when it came across as too superficial. But Kaplan takes it up here, and his reflections are acutely perceptive. He wonders why his craving to write "seized him like a madness." Without paper on the train, he grasped a blank part of a newspaper, and when he had filled up the page, he composed between the lines of the text. But this obsession belies a more ominous fear:

> After every such writing spell he would experience a sense of calm as though he had succeeded in accomplishing something that had permanence to it, something, therefore, that rescued his life from the vortex of time. But before long that feeling would vanish. "How insecure is our sense of security, how transient our experience of permanence" he said to himself.[72]

Why did the feeling of calm vanish? Kaplan suggests that even as his madness retreated, it would nonetheless reappear later, and so the craving would continue. And linger. He could never fully rescue his self "from the vortex of time" because it remained too embedded within it. The experience of permanence is momentary—a temporary calm before the maddening storm returns. This is, I believe, an intensely capitalist form of desire, in which Kaplan satiates his yearnings in a thing (the journal), only to heighten those desires once again in the very satisfaction of them.

The temporality of the commodity form continually excites Kaplan's desires. He expressed these on the eve of the Depression, when the spectral quality of commodities were in full force. His desire to experience permanence exposes the anxiety of material security. That desire is rooted, I will argue later in this chapter, in a process that Andrew Heinze has called "adapting to abundance." Seeking a home in America through consumption, Kaplan, like many of his fellow Jewish immigrants, believed that permanence could be had through material products. That faith, however, would vanish with the Depression. Yet the workings of the capitalist economy already suggest how material products are ephemeral. Could the self be yet another commodity form? On that train bound to Schenectady, the third person narrative suggests that the self can take on many styles—even impersonal and transient ones.

This sense of calm in the printed word, however temporary, eases Kaplan's anxiety about his failure "to beautify Jewish life" in the home. To be sure, the anxiety would return, again and again, as that sense of permanence in the material product inevitably disappeared. But the printed medium provoked this serenity in no small part because it was caught up in consumerism and mass culture, where it could reach beyond the household to influence countless others. This accounts for the widespread use of the press by religious groups in nineteenth-century America, when technological advances and access to new markets through better and faster transportation allowed print to influence regions beyond the spoken word.[73] The thoughts of one nineteenth-century Christian evangelical could very well have been Kaplan's own:

> What is written is *permanent*, and spreads itself further by far, for time, place, and persons, than the voice can reach. The pen is an artificial

tongue; it speaks as well to *absent* as to present friends; it speaks to them that are *afar off,* as well as those that are near; it speaks to *many thousands at once;* it speaks not only to the present age, but also to *succeeding ages.* The pen is a kind of image of eternity—it will make a man *live when he is dead. . . .*[74]

Writing confers immortality because it outlasts the self—or better, it carries the self forward and beyond. For Kaplan, the journal is not merely an "image of eternity," but is its very possibility.

So there is another sense of loss noted in the journal entry on the train: the material loss of paper. Kaplan describes a scene in which he frantically searches for scraps, even with texts filled to the edges, so that he could quiet his craving to write. But he could not silence this primal urge, for failure to write meant a loss of self:

> But I must keep up this diary. It is the only evidence I have that I have existed. I need it to counteract the feeling of blankness with which I am often seized. My past is as though it was not so that I feel forced to turn the pages of the diary to convince myself that I have lived. I sometimes feel that we don't have to die to know what death is—in fact, it is then that we don't know. The time that we know it is when we are alive and we try to keep our own past from dying; yet no matter what we do it dies on our hands.[75]

Driven to write ever more in his diary to prove his existence, Kaplan recognizes he could never do enough. His past will continue to die, even as he writes frantically and often. Kaplan is already dying, as it were, as he is unable to capture fully his own life experiences in his journal writing. The tight link between the absence of diary pages and the feeling of "blankness" tethers his sense of self to the material journal. If those pages are blank, then so is the self. The loss of material paper, then, is very much to the point. Without it, Kaplan remains imprisoned in a "feeling of blankness," and he cannot turn the pages to attest to a valuable life. The pages, like his self, are indeed blank without words. The material medium holds out some hope of permanence and continuity, as if Kaplan has invested the thing itself with an enduring presence. The self survives only if the material thing does too.

To counteract that "feeling of blankness," Kaplan creates an archive of the self in his journal. It becomes a material witness to a life lived.

The notion of an archive has fascinated modern commentators, especially those who recognize the importance of memory and technology in the production of meaning. Jacques Derrida's *Archive Fever* is, to my mind, a significant work in this area, and it can help us recognize the importance of material products for Kaplan's performance of self. Derrida critically appraises Yosef Yerushalmi's *Freud's Moses*,[76] but he also offers a fascinating account of archives along the way. In his typically masterful discourse, Derrida teases out multiple meanings, but claims that all material archives require a place of domicile "where they dwell permanently."[77] This dwelling marks a passage from the private to the public sphere. Among the many emotions that motivate the creation of an archive, one of them is the fear of death:

> There would indeed be no archive desire without the radical finitude, without the possibility of a forgetfulness which does not limit itself to repression. Above all . . . there is no archive fever without the threat of this death drive, this aggression and destruction drive.[78]

For Derrida, we create archives to limit forgetfulness, to hold back the threat of extinction. We desire permanence because we fear a deathly absence. This sense of the "trace," in which a figure of absence already lurks within the desire for presence, indicates the yearning to archive the self.[79] The threat of loss and forgetfulness conditions archive fever. We can certainly witness this in Kaplan's obsession with journal writing. He feels compelled to account for his life, not only for himself, but for others too. The journal provides that hope for a permanent dwelling within which his self remembers and overcomes a radical finitude. But it is a tenuous grasp on presence, for that "feeling of blankness" remains ever palpable and threatening. Kaplan yearns to transfer his "self-aspect" in the journal because, as archive, it witnesses to a "worthwhile" life. The journal exposes Kaplan's archive fever, and the fear of forgetfulness that informs it.

Kaplan demands a *material* archive as a compelling witness to personality. To witness, in this sense, is to offer some marker of testimony, some physical indication of existence and meaning. For Derrida, this appeal to testimony in a material archive reflects the desire for absolute presence. Yerushalmi had argued that if the Jews really did kill Moses, as Freud had indicated in *Moses and Monotheism*, then the murder would not have been repressed but recorded; that is, it would have been archived in some physical form. But how can Yerushalmi be certain that no archive exists? Why must an archive retain a material, written form, such that the historian can access and critique it? Could there not be virtual archives, or other such deposits hidden from the historian's gaze? According to Derrida, this is precisely what Freud has called for:

> Freud claimed that the murder of Moses *effectively* left archives, documents, symptoms in the Jewish memory and even in the memory of humanity. Only the texts of this archive are not readable according to the paths of "ordinary history" and this is the very relevance of psychoanalysis, if it has one.[80]

Archives create lasting impressions even if immaterial and in forms unrecognizable to the historian. There are traces and supplements, even surpluses of meaning that create their own archives of memory. But this worries Kaplan, and so he invests the material archive with a sense of permanence and transparency. Only the physical thing can transfer the self to others, in Kaplan's view. The very materiality of writing, and the physical presence of the journal, inspire (falsely, in Derrida's view) a sense of permanence and stability. Kaplan's religious faith begins with the hope that material things witness to the presence of a life, and those things transfer personality into the future. The material archive is the *only* archive for Kaplan that escapes the finitude of existence.

Yet as Kaplan discovered on the train to Schenectady, material things can disappear. If material archives remain the only human option to escape death, then Kaplan fears that even here, we continually die in archiving the self:

> In contrast with the extravagant waste of nature man is jealous of everything he produces. He projects his personality into whatever he creates, and he therefore experiences the agony of dying every time his creations have to be thrown into discard.[81]

For Marx, the value of our creations lies in the labor we invest in them. But not so for Kaplan, for that value resides in the personality, and we experience "the agony of dying" at the moment of material waste. This sense of material loss revives the anxiety of being itself, and the possibility of self-annihilation. Kaplan contends that more of us keep diaries because we no longer believe in personal immortality. Eternity can be had only in the transference of the self to others through the material journal. Kaplan even imagines a life flooded with diaries, "when the world will be cluttered with so much of this kind of writing that juries will have to be established to decide which diaries may be destroyed."[82] This idea shocks Kaplan, for it means some diaries will lose their permanent dwelling that, as Derrida reminds us, is constitutive of archive fever.

Kaplan's traumatic fantasy makes explicit what has been an underlying current in his self-reflections: personalities have become a kind of commodity to be discarded and wasted. We have become consumers of the self. In the engine of the market economy, consumption generates waste and overabundance. A consuming culture destroys the self—that "self-aspect" projected and enacted in journals. Like the publication of cheap paperbacks distributed easily and in bulk, Kaplan's journal might be "regarded like a newspaper, as something to be skimmed over and forgotten."[83] The book as commodity, so Janice Radway observes, focuses attention on a fickle consumer rather than a creative author. Here, too, the author disappears from view, silenced by the production of ever more circulating books.[84] Kaplan compares the process of "condemning the trashy" journals to "whether the victim of an incurable disease should have euthanasia administered to him." To lay waste to a journal is to kill a self: "I can't imagine that any one would have the heart to deliberately destroy a document in which the poor human ego flees as to the last refuge from complete death."[85] If this is a plea to his readers, then Kaplan begs for a permanent life in material form. Only his journal as permanent dwelling serves to archive his personality, and offers some consolation before death. Perhaps journals, and the performance of self within them, can cheat death after all.

Compare Kaplan's investment in the archive with Freud's *Note on the Mystic Writing Pad* (1925), a work composed around the same time as these excerpts from Kaplan's journal. Freud, too, fears the loss of memory, and believes as well that we can overcome forgetfulness through material deposits that recover memories without distortion. He searches for a medium that remains perpetually available to new inscriptions without erasing older ones. Freud wants a material archive that continually records the self through a permanent memory trace (*dauerhafte Erinnerungsspur*). The mystic writing pad (*der Wunderblock*) can do just that thing, in Freud's view, because it "provide[s] both an ever-ready receptive surface and permanent traces [*Dauerspuren*] of the notes that have been made upon it."[86] Derrida, in reading both with and against Freud, focuses on how the writing instrument performs erasures and supplements, "the double force of repetition and erasure, legibility and illegibility." He also alerts us to the technology of memory production, and the ways in which a material medium "founds memory."[87] This sense of presence and absence, together with the construction of memory, echo much that we have discovered in Kaplan's journal, for Kaplan recognizes the nearly apparitional quality of his journal in the way it both performs and hides the self. The ego flees to the journal, but that material object withholds the anchor of presence so coveted by the engaged personality.

Yet only aesthetic creations capture memories and produce archives, in Kaplan's view. Artistic works—poetry, dance, visual arts—produce selves of substance and "taste." Journal writing is Kaplan's artistic medium, and through it he externalizes his "self-aspect" for others. But Kaplan also worries that the ego really does flee to the journal—entirely, without remainder and distortion. This gives rise to the fear that the self is but another commodity in the open market, with all the possibilities of overproduction and waste. If the journal can produce the self, then the impersonal market can discard it. Kaplan's mystic writing pad exposes the spectral quality of commodities, and the selves marketed therein.

Kaplan imagines the day when we will literally lack the "breathing space"[88] to preserve all diaries, and will destroy the shoddy works in order to save the more expressive ones. Unable to turn the pages of those less fortunate archives of memory, we will inevitably practice the kind of forgetfulness that so troubles Kaplan, driving him to his archive fever—that all-consuming desire for presence. His journal must find a permanent dwelling for his personality to survive into the future. As Freud has taught us, virtual archives do not disappear. But material archives do, and so engender anxieties of finitude. Kaplan's journal is his art, his expressive desire to render inner emotions and experiences permanent and lasting. Without it, his personality "experiences the agony of dying" and the forgetfulness of a lived life. The loss of the material archive, so Kaplan believes, would mean a loss of self.

THE AESTHETICS OF JEWISH CIVILIZATION

The performance of self in art is a kind of archive fever, in which persons yearn for a material substance that exposes presence rather than spectral absence. Art reveals the emotional terrain of an engaged self. Artistic creations are material things in which persons invest their "soul, self, or reason." They enliven and give expression to cherished traditions and values, and inspire new experiences and ideals. Material archives compose the stuff of civilizations. Judaism as a civilization is a material archive of self-exposure.

Kaplan's idea of civilization is, of course, central to his reconstructionist program in Judaism, and has been the focus of a number of important studies.[89] But Kaplan was not the only thinker to employ civilization as a counter-cultural move. Gail Bederman notes that Ida B. Wells and Frederick Douglass coauthored (together with others) a pamphlet entitled *The Reason Why the Colored American Is Not in the World's Columbian Exposition* (in Chicago, 1893). In that essay they claimed "the truest American manhood and civilization were evinced, not by the white organizers, but by African Americans."[90] Kaplan adopted a similar strategy for Jews in America, arguing that Jews harbored the most robust, democratic, and expressive example of civilization, one that other Americans should emulate.[91] Yet Kaplan was certainly not alone in his turn toward building an American civilization. The term *civilization* was endemic to modernist conceptions of American identity, and exposed subtle racial distinctions between advanced and more "savage" (read "black") communities.[92] In the 1920s and 1930s, numerous published works focused on the nature of American civilization—*Civilization in the United States; Whither Mankind: A Panorama of Modern Civilization; Toward Civilization;* and Charles and Mary Beard's classic *The Rise of American Civilization,* to name only a few[93]—and distinctions between civilization and culture were widespread and crucial to the burgeoning American independence from Europe.[94] The "culture concept" became a focus of intense debate in this period among literary modernists and anthropologists,[95] with one historian arguing that Kaplan even linked

Jewish culture to whiteness.[96] By staking a claim in this debate, Kaplan situated himself within a modernist, racialized discourse. But as Warren Susman has observed, this discourse often turned into a referendum on modernist aesthetics.[97]

I want to highlight another form of this modernist turn: the ways in which civilization functions like art by locating the self within material productions. To be sure, Kaplan's notion of civilization is more than this, and captures a broad range of cultural acts. But one feature of civilization is the aesthetic performance of the self—the ideal of modernist expressions of self-fulfillment.

On a late Sunday night in March 1929, Kaplan once again had trouble sleeping, agitated, he tells us in his journal, by thoughts of a new book he will call *Judaism as a Civilization* (although he prefers the title *Whither Judaism?*, a clear reference to the modernist discourse on civilization). The opportunity to publish, finally, "a respectable piece of work," and one that could fashion a creative Judaism for the future, keeps Kaplan awake at night with "nervous tension."[98] As he meditates on how to save Judaism, Kaplan recognizes the need to generate "as many and varied aesthetic creations as possible." If he could round up a group of Jewish artists, poets, and actors, he would plan two initiatives: "Judaize the home," and "create new aesthetic forms for worship such as pageant, dramatic music, pantomime, the dance and music."[99] These artistic performances would tap into the collective emotional reservoir of Jewish experience and energize a cultural sensitivity to Jewish arts. Aesthetic performances reflect, even as they create, a Jewish collective life. Jews would participate in artistic works that both express their emotional yearnings and connect them to broader cultural experiences. In an earlier diary entry, Kaplan compares his notion of civilization to art and its singular ability to mold a collective life:

> I am interested in conserving and developing a civilization because in being the unique incarnation of the collective life of a people, it is as much an aesthetic object as any living thing or work of art.[100]

Kaplan's civilization functions like art: it fills a vacuum now vacated by religious unity, creates collective emotional experiences, and provides a material archive that leaves a "permanent effect" on future generations. Civilization is the material "dwelling," to adopt Derrida's term, for the cultural performances of a people—a dwelling, however, not with the Derridean erasure of presence, but with Kaplan's sense of full expressive performance. Judaism as a civilization is a work of art, a "living thing" that materially archives the self in America.

Scholars of modernism often distinguish historical modernism (between the two world wars) from a modernist aesthetic.[101] Works that focus on the interwar years tend to highlight the diversity and messiness of modernism, while those that reduce the movement to an aesthetic revolution will often minimize that diversity. Kaplan's work fits within both the historical schema and a particular form of high modernist aesthetic. Progressives such as John Dewey influenced Kaplan in ways that go beyond pragmatic philosophy. Dewey's *Art as Experience* (1934) was a critical player in what Susman called "an aesthetic movement" that offered "the opportunity for each man and woman to know some experience that was creative and satisfying."[102] Kaplan's turn to aesthetics is part of the cultural shift of the 1920s and 1930s in progressive politics. His civilization is an "aesthetic object" in the modernist sense of self-fashioning and creative performance. It is through the cultural products of a civilization that Jews would experience their "self-aspect," and in turn become American Jews through the play of aesthetic forms.

Kaplan makes this connection between art and civilization explicit in his *Judaism as a Civilization*. Artistic works, he claims here, are rooted in collective life, and establish an "inalienable relationship" with the "social life of the group."[103] As he would argue in *Questions Jews Ask* some twenty-two years later, Kaplan suggests how works of art express group emotions and "provide occasions for participating in them." Such works reflect and deepen collective sentiments, and impart the "rhythms into which the emotions of a civilization fall."[104] Art enhances and participates in collective life, aiding in the maintenance and persistence of civilizations:

> What is significant for the perpetuation of civilizations is that their characteristic ways of feeling are preserved only in the heightened forms and the accentuated rhythms of art. A civilization cannot endure on a high plane without the preservation and cultivation of its arts. The art creations become part of the social heritage which is the driving force of the civilization, and come to be the means of calling forth from the group the civilization's characteristic emotional reactions.[105]

In "calling forth" group emotions, art registers those sentiments in a cultural aesthetic performance. The rhythms of art map the emotional terrain of a civilization, and preserve those feelings as an inheritance for the future. That heritage is a material archive of the "characteristic ways of feeling" that distinguish Jewish civilization from other cultural productions. To preserve and cultivate the arts is to document the artistic personality that dwells within a civilization. In this modernist sense, Kaplan's civilization is an aesthetic performance of the self.

That performance comes to the fore in music, literature, dance, and the plastic arts.[106] But the "rhythms of art" also inform religious festivals like Sukkot—an autumn holiday recalling the temporary Israelite dwellings in the wilderness. Throughout his journal, Kaplan defends the Jewish fall celebration as a "return to the simple, the natural, the primitive and the primary sources of life." Sukkot is "an antidote and corrective to the ever growing complexity of civilization."[107] Kaplan really means the urban city when he writes of civilization in this early journal entry from 1917—a far different notion of civilization than the one he would later defend. But here he mimics Oswald Spengler's view, on the eve of the First World War, that the city symbolizes "the problem of civilization." Spengler supported the natural, organic life of the village that "lies completely fused and embedded in the landscape" against the artificial, rootless, "utterly land-alien" form of the city that "*denies* all Nature."[108] Like Spengler, Kaplan is alarmed by the "enormous growth of cities," and considers the urban landscape "fragmentary," "artificial," "sterile," and "parasitic."[109] Suggesting a Jeffersonian view of the city as a sign of European decay rather than American progress, Kaplan often considered urban life a kind of untamed jungle, in which Jews had to carefully navigate through and within.[110] Joseph Soloveitchik, the subject of chapter 3, holds a similar, (racially) tinged account of urban landscapes—one with significant implications for his account of Jewish law. But in Kaplan's ideal sukkah, Jews return to a collective simplicity much like Spengler's romantic village. It would be a kind of "teshuvah" [return] that preserves "plain living and high thinking" rather than urban "high living and plain, all too plain thinking."[111] In a 1928 journal entry, Kaplan considered Sukkot "a symbol of the simple life."[112]

Like Kaplan, a good many Jews in New York understood the sukkah as a traditional haven within a foreign land. Andrew Heinze quotes a reporter of the Lower East Side in 1895 who notes that "the noise of traffic and the tumult of the city made a deafening roar," but "up by the tabernacles on the reddened roofs all was peace and quiet."[113] Even the Yiddish press believed the Jews "have never had in any place such a comfortable, such a solid Sukkah."[114] Sukkot returns Jews to a very different rhythm than the one many experienced in the city. It could protect Jewish civilization from the chaotic and always present circulation of commodity forms, and limit the onslaught of urban expansion. Yet Kaplan was also critical of another popular understanding of Sukkot as a holiday to celebrate material abundance in America. Jews decorated their tabernacles with "the commodities of city life," and, as Heinze argues, Sukkot "seemed a good occasion for the appreciation of luxuries acquired by newcomers in the American city."[115] Kaplan, much like Abraham Joshua Heschel would do for the Sabbath (the subject of chapter 4), sought to distance the Jewish holiday from American capitalism by appealing to a simple and serene sukkah.

Kaplan revisited this notion of Sukkot as romantic *Gemeinschaft*— that sense of community and solidarity—days before the stock market crash on Wall Street in October 1929. On the first day of Sukkot that year, Kaplan preached about religion "as a means of fortifying ourselves against the insecurity and precariousness of modern life."[116] Only a few days after his sermon, that insecurity would play out in the economy. Kaplan transformed the traditional sukkah from a temporary, vulnerable dwelling place into a symbolic home of comfort, relief, and security. Jews could rekindle those desires for permanent dwelling, paradoxically, in the building of that provisional tent during Sukkot. The dislocating rhythms of urban life threatened Jewish civilization and its claim to a lasting, meaningful performance of Jewish identity. Some six months after the Bank of the United States had failed, an event that marked the beginning of the Great Depression for many New York Jews,[117] Kaplan defined civilization as "a heroic attempt to fit the confusion of human existence into the framework of a drama with a purpose."[118] Beth Wenger has argued that during the Depression, Jews like Kaplan sought to strengthen ethnic culture and community to fend off economic insecurity.[119] Kaplan's appeal to Sukkot is part of this Depression-era program, for Sukkot sustains Jewish community through the artistic rhythms of civilization. A "solid Sukkah" would cover over the insecurities of a rootless existence.

Kaplan was surely conflicted in his view of the city. On the one hand, when on vacation and away from town, he felt lost and isolated, yearning to return to urban life. Yet he also recoiled from the filth and bedlam that marked city living, and so retreated to his office, or sukkah, to restore an inner tranquility. This ambivalence also taps into features of the modernist aesthetic—mapping as it does the confluence among dominating technologies, urban expansion, anomy, and the retreat to romantic forms of overcoming and self-fulfillment. But these modernist tensions reflect another feature of Jewish civilization and its material products: securing a meaningful home in America. Sukkot works as a symbol for Kaplan because it reflects the American Jewish passion to remain, to attain status and respectability, to be integrated and whole on American soil. When the urban landscape threatens to undermine desires for tranquility and comfort, Jews can retreat to their folkways, and experience once again their return home. In more than one sense, a civilization that draws human experiences "into the framework of a drama with a purpose" is a civilization that creates a permanent dwelling for urban immigrant Jews like Kaplan. The aesthetic performance of the self, during Sukkot or within the various folkways of a civilization, is a cultural building of a home. If the city damages that structure, then urban Jews like Kaplan can restore it, again and again, in the material performances of Jewish civilization.[120]

FASHIONING JEWISH CIVILIZATION
IN THE AMERICAN JOURNAL

Andrew Heinze reveals how Jews consumed material products to become American and to secure a home in the nation. As immigrants to a new country, with a strange language and culture, Jews recognized how material goods could signify a changed identity. The study of immigrant consumption, in Heinze's view, reveals how groups adapt to new social conditions. Jews adopted "habits of consumption" that imitated American practices,[121] and Kaplan's journal fits within this paradigm of becoming American: it is an identifiably American journal. As Kaplan moves from immigrant to middle-class American, his journal marks his arrival and his claim to an American Jewish civilization and identity.

Surrounded by a variety of desirable goods, Jews, like most Americans, "expressed their hopes for advancement through the consumption of things that suggested a more secure social position."[122] The term *suggested* is important, for that security would be frustrated by a rising nativism that denied assimilation through consumption.[123] But many of these immigrants believed they had left nativism behind in Eastern Europe, and imagined America as a new promised land of opportunity. And savvy businessmen marketed those opportunities directly to immigrants. Installment plans allowed Jews to buy on credit those luxury items once thought to lie beyond affordable means. As more products became available, the possibility of "immediate acquisition" only hastened the transformation of desire into need.[124] Jews believed they could identify with America by becoming good consumers, and they could repeat this practice over and over again as new commodities came to the market. In this endless supply of circulating products, Jews appropriated those habits of consumption that would identify them as comfortable middle-class Americans.

Jews negotiated their anxieties to become Americans through the consumption of material products. Heinze recounts a "novel ritual" during Passover—"the dumping of household furnishings into the city streets"—as Jews improved their standard of living. Jewish immigrants would buy new Passover dishes and utensils, together with other products for the holidays, and then throw out the old items and simply use the new wares for the following year—when, presumably, they would eventually abandon the newer "old" items for yet another "Passover" set. Jews were "greening themselves out" by "upgrading their level of material life in the manner of urban Americans."[125] The purchase of the parlor organ, too, signified that Jews had made it in America.[126] Like the sukkah, the piano "could evince a sense of security and serenity that contrasted sharply with the insecurity and anxiety of city life."[127] The piano dominated the music scene well into the 1920s. Even as it corresponded with the rise of Tin Pan Alley and the marketing of sheet music, it also symbolized the values of hard work, domesticity, and moral integrity.[128] The piano enabled Jewish children, especially girls, to become refined middle-class citizens.[129]

Yet the anxiety always remained that, despite American assurances, consuming products would not transform Jews into Americans. Most

Jewish immigrants could not really afford a piano, although the install-ment plan allowed them to purchase one nonetheless.[130] And a piano barely fit within the small confines of most tenement apartments. The dumping of household goods in the streets during Passover, and the display of new clothes and furniture (in which, according to Heinze, the poor and the affluent participated), revealed that Jews invested their identity in material products, but those products could be wasted, lost, and discarded—much like Kaplan's fear of a journal destroyed. Jews, in other words, could fail to become Americans because, even as dedicated consumers, there were always more—more products, more desires, more anxiety. They might never consume *enough,* let alone what was required to live a decent life. Jewish consumption is an anxious performance of the self to become American.

Kaplan, too, is an American consumer, and we can see this in his journal writing. His intense desire to produce something of value, of per-manence, and of "lasting impression"—Kaplan's archive fever—remains part of this story of American consumption because Kaplan yearns for security among material products. If Heinze claims that Jews consume in order to become American, then Kaplan also creates products for others to consume—and in this he attempts to overcome his finitude and sense of failure. Those products—his journal and the cultural creations of a civilization—enable Jews to establish their home in America. Immigrant Jews, and Kaplan is one of them, invest their selves in the objects they live with and value. But as the market engine revs up, and commodities disappear only to be replaced by new ones, the anxiety of homelessness resurfaces. For Kaplan, the anxiety arises in his fear that we will destroy journals for lack of available "breathing space." Without such a place of dwelling, the self dies for a second time. Capitalist markets ensure that no thing can presume longevity and safe passage. As Jews consume products to identify as Americans, they become as insecure and ephem-eral as the commodity itself. The archive fever returns.

This anxiety of consumption lies at the heart of Riv-Ellen Prell's study of Jewish women and men in her *Fighting to Become Americans.* Prell's is a fascinating reading of Jewish stereotypes "with which Jews mapped their anxieties about Americanization and mobility onto the terrain of one another's lives." These gendered labels revealed deep Jew-ish ambivalence about acceptance within America, both in terms of their "hosts'" approval, and whether it was indeed worth all the trouble (and so Prell's subtitle: *Assimilation and the Trouble between Jewish Women and Jewish Men*).[131] Prell argues that just as Americans considered Jews "marginal, obsessed with money, uncivil, and unworthy of citizenship, Jewish men and middle-class Jews projected those very accusations onto Jewish women and the working class." She reveals, in fascinating and insightful ways, how class, gender, and race all shape Jews' attitudes to each other and to their place in America:

> The Jew was the alien to the nation, avaricious and aggressive. The woman was marked by her desire, in this setting defined primarily by consumer items of fashion and leisure. Her class was marked by the illegitimacy of that desire, wanting those things to which others, but not she, were entitled.[132]

Both Jews and non-Jews held these sentiments in twentieth-century America, and these stereotypes, to employ Heinze's phrase, reflect the anxiety and pressures upon an immigrant community adapting to abundance.

The image of the ghetto girl in the 1920s, who was "garish, excessively made up, too interested in her appearance, and too uncultivated to dress smartly,"[133] embarrassed both Jews and non-Jews. She would reappear under a different guise, and with altered names, throughout the century as "the Woman in Search of Marriage" and the "Jewish American Princess." And like those other incarnations, the ghetto girl's vulgarity reminded Jews that they might not be fully accepted by America's Protestant majority. Merely suggesting a kind of excess and unbounded desire "might more aggressively enforce their [Protestant] boundaries between insiders and outsiders."[134] Jews worried that they lacked refinement, and the ghetto girl's excessive and brash style exemplified the fear that all Jews were much like her. As Walter Benn Michaels has argued, "our America" would fast become a racial slogan that rebuffed assimilation through cultural practices—or, to put this another way, culture itself became a racial category.[135] Indeed, the ghetto girl enacted the "tragic flaw"[136] of immigrant Jewry: her consuming desires were illegitimate, for she revealed only her outsider status in becoming American through excessive consumption. To become American meant "to distance oneself from a vulgar, noisy Jewish woman."[137] In this, the ghetto girl "revealed the ways in which America beckoned and pushed away, forcing any single group of outsiders to fight among themselves as they Americanized."[138] The stereotype of the ghetto girl, or the Young Jewish Woman in Search of Marriage, and even the Jewish American Princess, are all defined by their excessive and crushing desires. They are dangerous to Jewish males who must supply what they demand. In failing to do so—and they could not but fail—Jewish men demonstrate "that they had not yet become Americans."[139] And if they could not do so, then the promise of material abundance was a cruel scam played on unsuspecting outsiders.

This sense of a con, I believe, haunts Kaplan's journal as well. America really was closed to Jewish aspirations and commitments. So Kaplan had to pry it open through archiving the self in cultural productions, in aesthetic performances, in a civilization that would remake America into a home for outsiders. It is a male performance to supply what the ghetto girl, and others like her, require. But Kaplan's civilization also witnesses to his own desire for home. To archive the self, as Derrida reminds us, is to assert oneself as present—to make an impression even on those who reject it. Kaplan's lifelong pursuit for something permanent, something to overcome human finitude and insecurity, belies a desperation to establish a home in hostile territory. The anxiety of journal writing itself (echoed in Kaplan's "I must keep this diary. It is the only evidence I have that I have existed.") reveals the very tensions that Prell and Heinze uncover in their cultural studies of Jews in twentieth-century America. Kaplan seeks a dwelling in America, for his journal and his civilization. But he buys a home aware that the cost might be too high. If the self lives for others in the journal, and in the cultural performances of a people, then the individual personality might become lost, or worse, rendered superfluous. If another journal, or some other cultural act, could take its place, then the self dies once again. Like the dumping of old Passover wares, a new material archive will simply replace the old, and the self as commodity becomes a relic of a distant past.

CONCLUSION

Material objects are constitutive features of personal identity. In a powerful article about the meaning things have for us,[140] Bill Brown reflects upon how "human subjects and inanimate objects may be said to constitute one another." Objects, Brown claims, hold the capacity "to materialize identity." In America, where the "abstract subject of democracy" always remains out of reach, the gathering of objects grounds that identity with "particular content." Brown recounts Mark Twain's grief at the death of his daughter Suzy, and the way in which Twain unites that death with the loss of a burning house: "Twain grieves her loss through its loss." In coupling the death of a child with the demise of a physical object, Twain illustrates, according to Brown, "the way objects touch souls."[141]

For American Jews, and certainly for Mordecai Kaplan, objects touched souls in ways that materialized Jewish identity in the accumulation and consumption of objects. In Kaplan, we recognize a Jew who thinks about things, and one who grounds identity in material objects. Jews negotiated their place in America through those objects, and invested things with their hopes and anxieties of a permanent, stable, and secure life. That possessions could vanish, as they did in the 1929 stock market crash, only witnessed to the very transient and vulnerable dwelling in which Jews resided in America. Kaplan understood this all too well. On a Monday night in May 1929, he attached a photograph of himself to his diary,[142] yearning once again for a material presence:

> I took this picture this morning on the way from Dr. Spivak to the library of the Union Theological Seminary. I suppose it is vanity that prompts me to have my picture taken or my bust made or to have a phonographic record made of my voice as I tried last Friday. But is there not also an innate desire to want to know more about oneself? Perhaps also the wish to snatch from the ravenous maw of Time something that might endure—if at least for a little while.[143]

A physical thing—a photograph, bust, or voice recording—reveals Kaplan's plea for immortality as material archive fever. The restlessness of American Jewry that Kaplan observed and sought to overcome only intensified the longing for an object that would, this time, make a permanent impression.

Kaplan wrote eloquently of this modernist unease in his journal, and his musings fit within a generational struggle for a sense of place. For the immigrant Jew, so Kaplan believed, this search proved especially difficult. Kaplan forever searched for home, and his concept of civilization

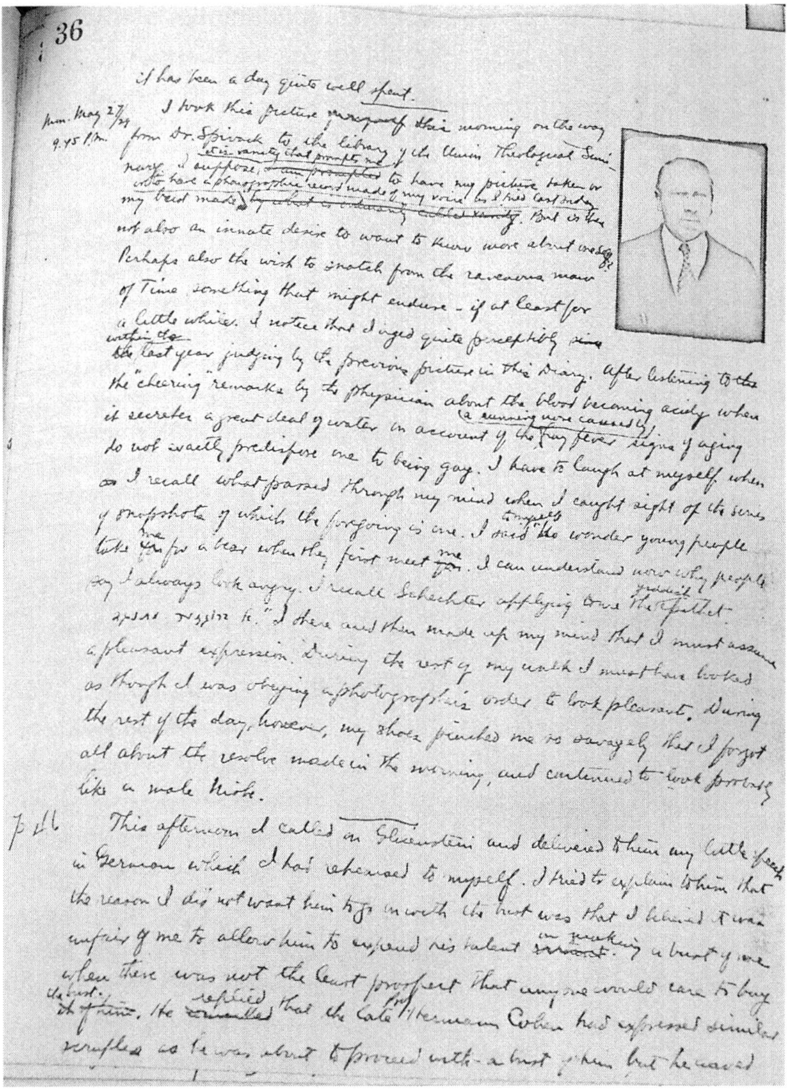

FIGURE 1.2. Mordecai Kaplan journal entry, May 27, 1929 (Vol. 5). *The Eisenstein Reconstructionist Archives of the Reconstructionist Rabbinical College.* Courtesy of the Archives of Jewish Theological Seminary.

marked one grand attempt to fashion it in America. Yet, as Kaplan well understood, the Jew in America could never quite be at ease:

> It is otherwise when I read a piece of Talmud, Midrash, medieval poetry or philosophy. Much of it is arid, barren, even ugly, but it is my cultural home, and this feeling of at homeness is more to me than the actual worth of the ideas or the beauty of their expression. I am utterly miserable when a long period of time elapses without my having an opportunity to read [a] Jewish text, and I am equally miserable when I do read it, because of the awful solitude in which I find myself. I feel like one who comes back to his home town and finds it completely deserted.[144]

A home in America is a tenuous thing. Kaplan attempted to find and secure it in his journal, and for others through a civilization, but he seemed homeless nonetheless.

That sense of modernist solitude, one that Ann Douglas attributes to the "terrible honesty" of the 1920s,[145] disturbs and consumes Kaplan's passions. His are the passions of a stranger in a foreign land who, after dwelling within it, can no longer fully return to his now deserted home. Kaplan finds himself in the classical Jewish texts, but those material books also uncover an "awful solitude" of wanderings and sterility. What I have called the performance of the material self is an ambiguous act of identity formation. It reveals both how Jews think about things, and the ways in which objects texture and inform the self. Yet those things can also consume the self to the point at which it dies continuously without identifying objects. Kaplan's journal, as a cultural and aesthetic act of writing, is a performance of self in and through a material thing. It represents his attempt to materialize his identity, to archive the self. The art of journal writing is to make a lasting impression upon the things and persons who constitute personal identity. Only through the writing will that awful solitude and sense of abandonment be relieved—if at least for a little while.

TWO

The Material Past: Edward Bernays, Joshua Liebman, and Erich Fromm

Sigmund Freud's height of popularity in America surfaced at two critical moments: after the war that should have ended all wars, together with the subsequent Roaring Twenties, and with the aftermath of the Second World War and the resultant triumphalism that swept America. In the 1920s and 1940s, Freud's theories of the self and society permeated cultural discourse, though often in mutated or simplified form, since very few actually read his works. Initially for urban elites in the 1920s, Freud's musings on the unconscious then inspired mass audiences following America's victory in Europe some twenty-five years later.[1] That Freud had visited America only once, in 1909, to offer lectures at Clark University, and that he had disdained the popular reception of his work in America, only heightened the distance between Freud's tragic European view and America's opportunistic progressivism.[2] Where Freud recognized trauma as indelible marks of a scarred life, his American interpreters discovered sources of liberation from a burdensome history. If Freud sought only a realist balance between the demands of civilization and the primal yearnings of the self, his readers in America jettisoned those pressures to better promote individual fulfillment and personal integrity.[3] And when Freud disparaged the blatant disregard for what he considered prudent application of his work, American psychoanalysts had no trouble recognizing the popular appeal of moving beyond the father, both literally and figuratively, after the wars in Europe.

For in translating Freud's guarded pessimism into an unbounded optimism for an American audience, the neo-Freudians (as they were often labeled as a group) could nurse a traumatized citizenry back to health, prosperity, and faith in an American future. To do so, these interpreters—some of whom published widely and reached mass audiences through radio and television programs—would reject a past now associated with European decay and childhood immaturity in favor of an open, mature faith in unlimited possibility. The past could weigh and tie the self down; yet Freud had provided keys to unlock the self from these moorings (or so his American interpreters believed), and could guide the self to personal and professional success. Tragic origins need not determine nor damage the self's capacity to flourish.

The meaning of human flourishing would vary widely among the American public in the 1920s and 1940s. But for the three American Jewish thinkers discussed in this chapter, human flourishing enabled personal growth unburdened by a debilitating past in ways that allowed Jews to become Americans. Each sought to disentangle a tragic and harmful past from the open possibilities of an American future, and each did so from distinctive fields of vision: Edward Bernays, the nephew of Freud and the founding visionary of public relations; Joshua Loth Liebman, author of the first best seller by an American rabbi *Peace of Mind* (1946); and Erich Fromm, the famed psychologist who integrated Freud and Marx to produce captivating visions of the self for an increasingly radical American audience. To think, feel, and consume according to one's own desires (Bernays), or to grow up beyond the confines of infantile wishes and parental demands (Liebman), and even more to become one's true self (Fromm) had special meaning for Jews in America, as it did for American interpreters of Freud and psychology. The work of Bernays, Liebman, and Fromm performed cultural labor for a Jewish public yearning to become American. They each recognized how the past constricts the self in ways that shackle free individual expression. None, to be sure, wrote for Jews alone, and perhaps not even primarily for Jews. While all three identified as Jews, with Liebman the most committed and Bernays the least, I suspect only Liebman, and to some extent Fromm, thought of their own work as Jewish in orientation.

Yet their visions of the self had particular resonance for American Jews who struggled to balance the burdens of the past, as Mordecai Kaplan had done, with the promises yearned for in the new American landscape. That Kaplan had failed to secure his home in America only heightened its cultural importance for his own generation and for those who followed. Bernays, Liebman, and Fromm were Jews who certainly wrote and spoke for Americans. But they were also Jews who exposed Jewish yearnings for self-fulfillment. If Kaplan never felt at ease in America, for he could never quite catch up with, nor make peace with his past, then perhaps it would be more sensible to let go entirely, and succumb freely to American dreams of the open frontier. Bernays, Liebman, and Fromm gave powerful expression to these dreams of Jewish belonging in America.

But the inherited past—whether psychological, religious, cultural, or ethnic—proved far more burdensome than these writers imagined or even suspected. They could not easily disavow that inheritance, nor could they fully adopt the American dream.[4] I choose to call a past that continually informs, textures, and even discolors notions of American progress "the material past," and in so doing I refer to something quite definite in the works of these three writers. One's inherited past has material effects in the present, but Bernays, Liebman, and Fromm each seek to alter those effects by renouncing inheritance and its authority over the self. In letting go of the past, I am neither referring to actual material objects that connect persons to a past, nor to the ways in which physical things, tethered to personal histories, limit and inform personal identity. In chapter 5, I will take up these issues in my readings of American Jewish literature, where I will explore the literary modes that conjure up the material object as an enduring presence for American Jewish identity. Here, though, I will focus on how Jews imagine the past as a material threat to self-flourishing.

In one sense, this claim seems rather mundane and facile, for surely any nostalgic memory or troubled heritage (pleasant or ugly memories of Friday night dinners at home, for example) will in part determine future conduct (observance of the Sabbath, or the lack thereof). Notions of the past are often tied to familial relations and perceptions. But the past for Bernays, Liebman, and Fromm obstructs selves from material success. For Bernays, honoring the past enforces a stupefying conformity to a herd mentality that restrains consumptive desires. For Liebman, reliving the past impedes the kind of maturity necessary for inner peace and economic prosperity. And for Fromm, ties to a past only enforce idolatrous worship of the wrong things, and forever mask the true self yearning to be set free through love and productive labor. Bernays, Liebman, and Fromm each claim, in very different ways, that personal histories destroy the self rather than help produce it. The past is a material past because it frustrates the acquisition of real material goods in the present: one cannot buy, love, relate, or possess the things that one should in order to flourish as an American self. The material past, in the sense that Fromm aptly describes it, is a form of idolatry for all three thinkers. In worshiping the wrong things, persons damage features of the self that enable human flourishing. An American humanism, one that does not sacrifice personal integrity to past authorities of any kind, will smash the idols of the past for more lucrative objects of the future.

A sympathetic, populist, and kinder Freud could show how to make this move from slavery to freedom, and all three of our Jewish thinkers appropriated psychological insights to better convince an American public of their destined triumph over history. Bernays is really a forerunner to Liebman in the latter's explicit revision of Freud. In his most influential works of the 1920s, Bernays reveals the power of psychology to refocus human attention and desires. As Americans recognize the sources that drive and manipulate their desires, they will free themselves from inhibiting, unnatural, and irrational cravings. Bernays associates those desires with an inherited "herd" mentality that enslaves personal freedom. The public relations counsel that Bernays established thus performed a vital public service by liberating the self from these repressive constraints. That this freedom also served the interests of Bernays's entrepreneurial clients is all for the better, in his view, for it weds the public good with private interests.

Liebman's *Peace of Mind* is a masterful work of Jewish polemic, as Andrew Heinze has rightly noted.[5] But to my mind, the brilliance of this text lies in what it *does* as a performative utterance. There are three distinctive moves in this act: 1) by revising Freud to fit a more optimistic, and even opportunistic, American context, Liebman enables Jews to prosper in America *as* Jews; 2) as American Jews buy into that prosperity, they simultaneously reject infantile religion (of the Jewish and Christian kind) that Liebman associates with European tyranny; and 3) by reimagining America *as* Jewish, Liebman empowers Jews to further their prophetic heritage in America. To achieve peace of mind in America, so argues Liebman, we all must become Jews in the image of the biblical prophets. Fromm, in more ways than one, appropriates this prophetic call for peace and justice, but seeks to disentangle it from all connections to a particular people, land, and history. He radicalizes Liebman's project, arguing that the prophetic critique of idolatry denies *all* forms of worship outside the self. Fromm's is a radical humanism that liberates the self from all coercive authority, recreates the self as fully present and responsible before others, and develops the self into a self-created, autonomous being. To be free means both a freedom *from* the past and a freedom *to* become a loving, responsible, ethical self.

In no way is this self recognizably Jewish to Fromm. But the material past that Fromm so passionately resists nonetheless returns to haunt him in ways that leave unmistakable scars, and Jewish ones at that. This is decidedly so for Liebman as well, and certainly true for Bernays, although his marks might not be Jewish at all. It is this tenuous and unending dance between denial and acceptance of a past that fractures their works: for Bernays, in the way he frees the self from conformity to inherited beliefs in *Crystallizing Public Opinion* (1923), only to manipulate those beliefs and solidify acceptance of them in *Propaganda* (1928); for Liebman, in his appeal to a mature religion that renounces parental influence even as it affirms Jewish prophetic visions; and for Fromm, in his deeply ambiguous account of love as both singular and universal, and in his own personal appeal to ancestors and their guiding influence.

This chapter tracks how Bernays, Liebman, and Fromm struggle to renounce inheritance. From within that struggle, I want to show how the material past still haunts their works by restricting the progressive openness of the neo-Freudian ideology. These three American Jewish thinkers imagined (and received) more than a Jewish audience for their works, and their influence certainly moved beyond Jewish circles. But theirs is an American Jewish story because they each reveal, in their own distinctive ways, the cultural strategies and options Jews faced in becoming American. Bernays, Liebman, and Fromm witness to the enduring need to both abandon and reclaim the material past in America.

EDWARD BERNAYS, PSYCHOLOGY, AND THE HERD

Edward Bernays lived an immensely long life (1891–1995), in which he developed the new field of public relations to better serve both the interests of American companies and the public welfare. Most have found his appeal to economic self-interest and the public good little more than a publicity stunt: a weak rationale for a man obsessed with power, manipulation, and success.[6] Yet even those more skeptical of Bernays find him a captivating figure, for he moved generations of Americans to think anew about material products. His brand of public relations was novel, well-informed, and explicitly based on the psychoanalysis of consumers. He simply inverted the pressures of consumption: "Under the old salesmanship the manufacturer said to the prospective purchaser, 'Please buy a piano.' The new salesmanship has reversed the process and caused the prospective purchaser to say to the manufacturer, 'Please sell me a piano.'" The public relations counsel (hereafter the PR counsel) manipulates various "stages" to mount this campaign of reversals. To begin, he sets out to influence architects to build music rooms with "a specially charming niche in one corner for the piano" in order to "implant the idea of the music room in the mind of the general public." A fanciful desire in turn becomes a need, for "the man or woman who has a music room, or has arranged a corner of the parlor as a musical corner, will naturally think of buying a piano." Purchasing a piano will thereby "come to him [the consumer] as his own idea."[7]

Bernays defends this crass manipulation as furthering both individual desires and progressive politics. He manipulates desires into needs by appealing to broad public trends. This imposes a "herd mentality" in which everything and everyone move the consumer to purchase a piano. The individual simply follows public sentiment in matters of consumption. But this also frees the self from a stultifying inheritance. By means of the PR counsel, the self is liberated from inherited desires, and so is free to adopt new, modern ones. In the process, however, the self becomes enslaved yet again to mass desires. To Bernays, this modern imprisonment is an enlightened one, in which the self desires consciously that which enables human flourishing. We really ought to want that piano, for it instills socially progressive values and sentiments, so Bernays asserts. The PR counsel engineers incentives to turn desire into public consumption, thus uniting individual desires with the social good.

Bernays's appeal to the psychological self, artfully contained in the pithy but revealing move from "please buy" to "please sell me," situates his work within the craze of psychological discourse in the mid-1920s. As noted in chapter 1, theories of the unconscious were widespread (more so in cities), and a general openness to psychoanalysis pervaded the professional classes.[8] Though relatively few English translations existed of Freud's work at this time, there were still popularized versions that reached a broad audience through such periodicals as *McLure's, Ladies' Home Journal, Good Housekeeping, Forum,* and *The American Magazine*.[9] Americans wanted to know more about the unconscious as they began to accept the irrational and sexual roots of their desires and longings. They appropriated these Freudian models of the self within American values of progressive optimism and hope. With regard to social and prison reform, mental hygiene, parenting, and treatment through psychoanalysis, Americans were steadfastly eclectic and positive. Freud was quite hesitant to approve this American version of his work, and according to historian Nathan Hale, "American open-mindedness had led to the watering-down of psychoanalysis, which, Freud believed, lost sight of essentials and reflected a lack of scientific rigor."[10] Freud's rather elitist views suggest just how widespread his work had become among the "lay public" in America. Mesmerism and other American spiritual traditions laid the groundwork for Freud's appeal by locating the source of divine–human communication in the unconscious.[11] But the perceived scientific rigor behind the popular Freudian works raised their level of authority among the general public.

Bernays took full advantage of this. Though not a psychoanalyst by training, he is rightfully considered by Larry Tye as "a psychoanalyst just the same, for he deals with the science of unconscious mental processes."[12] Though he wrote fifteen books and some three hundred articles in his life, his two most important works for creating the field of public relations, and for revealing his ambiguous attachments to a material past, are his *Crystallizing Public Opinion* (1923) and *Propaganda* (1928). His first book set out to describe the function and utility of the public relations counsel—the word *counsel* being a term that Bernays hoped would elicit the same respect conferred upon the legal profession.[13] Bernays mailed a copy of his work to his uncle, but Freud responded only that "as a truly American production it interested me greatly."[14] Freud and Bernays's relationship was both caring and fragile. Bernays offered to publish Freud's works in America to help his uncle's financial situation in Vienna, but Freud continually frustrated these ambitions. Still,

Bernays exhibited a fondness and respect for Freud, and clearly prized his familial attachment to him.[15]

But Freud was certainly right to call *Crystallizing Public Opinion* an American production. Bernays argued that the PR counsel could defend the public good by revealing an unhealthy reliance on the "herd" mentality—even if this counsel would secure new "herd" desires. No matter, for by liberating individuals from irrational conformity to inherited opinions, the PR counsel opened space for more progressive views to take shape that more closely aligned with modernity. The PR counsel would certainly do its job more effectively if the public recognized how its own unconscious drives had been manipulated by powerful group processes. Yet manipulation can work in both directions. To Bernays, propaganda is justified when it serves the public good. Lifting the accumulated weight of inheritance would free American consumers to form new and more authentic tastes allied to the progressive liberal visions of Bernays's PR counsel. It is this progressive optimism that runs throughout his *Crystallizing Public Opinion,* and justifies the engineering of public consent. The reemergence of the herd mentality, however, suggests that the material past remains in force to limit such progressive enthusiasm.

Much of Bernays's views of psychology derived not from Freud—whom he read quite infrequently, if at all—but rather from three well-known social psychologists of his time: Gustave Le Bon, Wilfred Trotter, and Walter Lippmann. Le Bon had originally published his French book *The Crowd: A Study of the Popular Mind,* in 1895, but it was quickly translated the following year, gathering a wide readership.[16] He exposed how individuals are transformed once they become members of the crowd. From rational, conscious agents they become "swamped by the homogeneous, and the unconscious qualities obtain the upper hand." From an isolated, cultivated individual, "in a crowd, he is a barbarian—that is, a creature acting by instinct."[17] Le Bon associates the individual with the perceived male values of reason, responsibility, and will, while crowds exhibit all that belongs to "inferior forms of evolution—in women, savages, and children." In short, a crowd is impulsive, irritable, irrational, sentimental, and, "like women, it goes at once to extremes."[18] What Bernays understood intuitively was the power of large groups to undermine individual interests. Le Bon was quite clear that even the most intelligent and well-educated male could easily succumb to the female allurements of the crowd.[19] If Bernays sought to return the American public to a self-empowering male individualism, then he could do so only by utilizing the debased femininity of communal perceptions. Gender images operated at the very core of Bernays's vision. He would manipulate the feminine crowd to free the male individual from the herd.

But Wilfred Trotter had argued, in part against Le Bon, that the allure of the crowd should be regarded "as a fundamental quality of man."[20] In his influential *Instincts of the Herd* (1916), Trotter closely aligned the burgeoning field of psychology with the established scientific discourse of biology and zoology to better shore up psychology in the eyes of the academy and the reading public.[21] Like Le Bon, he associates the crowd, now designated as "the Herd," with homogeneity. But rather than imagining a rational male individual who succumbs, unwarily, to the feminine crowd, as Le Bon had done, Trotter believes herd instincts are constitutive of the self: "The impulse to be in and always to remain with the herd will have the strongest instinctive weight. Anything which tends to separate him from his fellows, as soon as it becomes perceptible as such, will be strongly resisted."[22] For Trotter, the herd instinct manifests "not only in crowds and other circumstances of actual association, but also in his behaviour as an individual, however isolated."[23] So there is no retreat, as there is for Le Bon, to a prelapsarian state of male rationality. Individuals are completely subsumed within herd beliefs that appear entirely rational, even if they are, in fact, "totally false opinions." Only as Trotter reaches the end of his book does he hold out hope for "the intellect" to renew humanity in the wake of European destruction. Perhaps, Trotter suggests, the intellect might free itself from the oppressive grip of the herd mentality. Gendered rhetoric of male reason still holds sway, and so too the hope of male superiority before feminine enticements.

An independent, rational intellect was Walter Lippmann's hope as well, and Bernays adopted the title of Lippmann's masterful *Public Opinion* (1922) as his own (recall Bernays's title, *Crystallizing Public Opinion*). That Bernays would so closely align his own work, published just a year later, with Lippmann's sardonic piece on democracy and its failures, suggests an inheritance that Bernays actively cultivated. He believed that the PR counsel could do what Lippmann thought most essential: deliver essential, unbiased knowledge to a public incapable of making rational decisions on its own. Lippmann had powerfully argued, following Le Bon and Trotter, that the public remains the source of prejudice and misrepresentations. In order to act as rational political agents and build a reasonable picture of the world, individuals must maintain unmediated access to reality. But perception is always mediated by "the pictures inside the heads of these human beings, the pictures of themselves, of others, of their needs, purposes, and relationship." So individuals never achieve a clear vision of reality unencumbered by prejudice. For representative governments to operate effectively, the public requires "an independent, expert organization for making the unseen facts intelligible to those who have to make the decisions."[24] These disinterested experts would circumvent the inevitable distortions of group manipulation and public opinion. With his faith in rationality and science, and the accompanying disillusionment with the public sphere, Lippmann transferred Trotter's faith in the (male) intellect to a group of highly trained, neutral experts who could present clear facts to a public too sullied and mired within a (feminine) herd mentality.

Lippmann's "expert" would become Bernays's public relations counsel, however much Lippmann might have disdained this transformation.[25] There is ample evidence in *Crystallizing Public Opinion* that Bernays imagined his PR counsel as the rightful heir to Lippmann's vision. From his "Mr. Lippmann makes the same observation," to the many citations of Lippmann's work that run throughout the text,[26] Bernays leans on this tradition from Le Bon, Trotter, and Lippmann to carve out the public utility, and even the political necessity of the PR counsel. He shares with Le Bon a fear of the feminized crowd, even as he manipulates it to serve progressive ends. Like Trotter, Bernays recognizes the power of herd instincts to overwhelm individual pursuits. But it is to Lippmann that Bernays owes his transformative vision of the PR counsel, for he serves the public interests in the very manipulation of them. Indeed, it is this very dynamic—the appeal to individual desires, and the crystallizing of those desires within a "herd mentality"—that reveals the power of the material past to inform Bernays's thought. For the "herd mentality" is the psychological inheritance of the material past. The weight of tradition, of inherited customs and fashion, of proper consumption and savings, all burden modern selves with regressive desires. Bernays seeks to free the self from that inherited past, even if it means enslaving it to his progressive agenda.

But Bernays writes of this new enslavement as a form of self-revelation. These progressive desires are really trapped inside the self, yearning for self-expression. The PR counsel enables persons to liberate those inner longings. Michael North has perceptively noted how "Bernays did everything in his power to publicize Lippmann's ideas because it was necessary to his project that the public accept its own irrationality as an inescapable given."[27] If individuals succumb to the herd mentality, and fail to access the facts necessary to make informed, rational decisions, then the PR counsel can bring to light these hidden sensibilities obscured by unthinking conformity to the group. Bernays offers countless examples to justify the social utility of the PR counsel. He writes of a hair net company concerned that the new bobbed hair craze would destroy business. Only women who wear long hair would have any use for a hair net. This company hired Bernays's PR counsel, who discovered "club women" who actually preferred long hair. Their views "were given to the public and helped to arouse what had evidently been a latent opinion on the question."[28] In bringing to light this "latent opinion," the PR counsel helped to free other women from dominant fashion. They could now wear their hair according to their own tastes and desires, and not simply conform to herd judgments of beauty. Or witness Bernays's work for the Lithuanian National Council to increase Lithuania's visibility and respect among the American public. The PR counsel could provide "facts" to Americans "which gave them basis for conclusions favorable to Lithuania."[29]

Bernays focuses here, as in many other cases he describes, on the ways in which "the public relations counsel made articulate what would otherwise have remained a strong passive sentiment." He never worries about how the Lithuanian National Council benefits from such positive publicity, or that the hair net company's interest in fashion concerns only their bottom line. The PR council justifies its work by raising latent desires to consciousness that both serve individual interests and client business needs. For Bernays, if the latent-turned-conscious desires increase the profitability of his business clients, so much the better. The progressive ideals remain unchanged: the herd mentality thwarts authentic modes of personal expression. The PR council recognizes this, and encourages individual opinion to deviate from mass conformity so that it serves both the public good and the economic aspirations of American business. That such confluence forms a more powerful herd mentality rarely surfaces as a concern. Bernays focuses on the individual and political goods secured by the PR counsel. Simply, the herd represses desires; the counsel frees them. And this freedom liberates the self from the material past.

In this sense, as North suggests, the PR counsel will prove ever more successful as it reveals to the public how unarticulated desires motivate consumption. As Americans recognize unconscious drives and the means by which society quells and suppresses those motives, the work of the PR counsel becomes that much more effective:

> Bernays also relied on an explicit awareness in his audience of the very laws that were being used to move them. Thus psychoanalysis and public relations legitimate one another, as Bernays calls upon Freud to help make his audience not simply aware of but actively interested in its own manipulation.[30]

What North calls manipulation Bernays considers public service on both sides of the divide: companies thrive in selling their products to persons now freed from a debilitating constraint to mass suggestion. In *Crystallizing Public Opinion,* the PR counsel labors to uncover latent desires. The image is one of unconscious forces yearning for release, and the PR counsel, as both analyst and economic steward, enables their free expression. Americans want to be freed from their material pasts, and so permit a full exposure to their unconscious desires. This appeal to self-liberation is entirely missing some five years later in *Propaganda,* where Bernays speaks openly of manipulation and the manufacturing of human desires. But in 1923, when Bernays published *Crystallizing Public Opinion,* the sense of liberating the self from the herd is paramount. Yet as North argues, Bernays must convince the public of its own irrationality if it will actively work against the strong desire to roam with the herd. "Society must understand," Bernays tells us, "the fundamental character of the work he [the PR counsel] is doing, if for no other reason than its own welfare."[31] Bernays describes his work in public relations as a form of persuasion which integrates the client's interests with the public good.[32] He "calls upon Freud" so that the public can advance its own progressive ideals together with American economic success.

Bernays believes that most of us are imprisoned by judgments that impede the fullest expression of our inner desires. He accepts Trotter's account that divergence from centrist views of the herd is both painful and lonely. Human instincts tend to conform to the group, and so expand the "logic-proof compartments" that work against change and progress. As heir to Lippmann's expert, the PR counsel punctures those closed doors to free the self from tyranny:

> Mr. Lippmann says propaganda is dependent upon censorship. From my point of view the precise reverse is more nearly true. Propaganda is a purposeful, directed effort to overcome censorship—the censorship of the group mind and the herd reaction. The average citizen is the world's most efficient censor. His own mind is the greatest barrier between him and the facts. His own "logic-proof compartments," his own absolutism are the obstacles which prevent him from seeing in terms of experience and thought rather than in terms of group reaction.[33]

Bernays views the herd mentality as a form of irrational inheritance, in which persons unthinkingly accept all that is handed down to them. An "uninformed lay public" may too quickly condemn new medical discoveries that would ease suffering, or it might forgo real social goods because their views "are more often expressions of crowd psychology and herd reaction than the result of the calm exercise of judgment."[34] Bernays is certainly aware of potential abuses, and so he provides a code of ethics that will avoid "the propagation of unsocial or otherwise harmful movements or ideas."[35] But he understands the PR counsel as a higher calling, one that embodies "high ideals" and infuses "moral and spiritual motives into public opinion."[36]

This sense of public service permeates the very last sentence of *Crystallizing Public Opinion:* "It is in the creation of a public conscience that the counsel on public relations is destined, I believe, to fulfill his highest usefulness to the society in which he lives."[37] To actively destroy the herd mentality is to free the self for higher pursuits. It is to "discredit the old authorities or create new authorities by making articulate a mass opinion against the old belief or in favor of the new."[38] The old herd conformity must give way to a new self empowered by now fully conscious drives, all with the help of the PR counsel. But note how new authorities arise to replace the old. Mass opinion remains, but it now reflects "new" desires rather than "old beliefs." So even as Bernays frees the self to "discredit" all that the herd mentality, as the inherited past, has enforced on individuals, those same individuals appropriate new mass opinions that better align with Bernays's political (and economic) progressivism. Herein lies the dilemma and tension in Bernays's work: on the one hand, he renounces the past by overcoming the herd mentality; yet on the other, he seeks to reclaim that herd to support the progressive causes of his business clients. He at once disclaims and craves the *authority* vested in the material past.

The tension between denial and acceptance, so forcefully present in *Crystallizing Public Opinion*, is wholly absent in Bernays's next book, *Propaganda* (1928). Bernays still holds the same psychological model of the herd, in which individuals only think "by means of clichés, pat words or images which stand for a whole group of ideas or experiences." But the liberating politics has disappeared. The PR counsel has become a cynical propagandist: "By playing upon a [*sic*] old cliché, or manipulating a new one, the propagandist can sometimes swing a whole mass of group emotions."[39] At issue is political power rather than the public good. Mark Crispin Miller argues in the introduction to *Propaganda* that Bernays's work "is primarily a sales pitch, not an exercise in social theory."[40] It sells the political prowess of the PR counsel to manipulate public opinion.

What makes *Propaganda* read like a sales pitch, however, is the stark contrast between its social theory and the one pursued in *Crystallizing Public Opinion*. Note the opening sentence:

> The conscious and intelligent manipulation of the organized habits and opinions of the masses is an important element in democratic society. Those who manipulate this unseen mechanism of society constitute an invisible government which is the true ruling power of our country. We are governed, our minds molded, our tastes formed, our ideas suggested, largely by men we have never heard of.[41]

This invisible manipulation should neither be feared, overcome, nor even understood by the public. Instead, persons should passively work and live within a herd society. In *Crystallizing Public Opinion*, Bernays criticized this view, and offered the PR counsel as protectorate of individual desires and yearnings. Here, however, the PR council manipulates precisely what had previously repulsed Bernays some five years earlier. Instead of freeing individuals from the herd mentality, Bernays prefers that they remain seduced by public opinion so that an "orderly life" remains possible.[42] Bernays seems quite at ease with this social power: "It is the purpose of this book to explain the structure of the mechanism which controls the public mind, and to tell how it is manipulated by the special pleader who seeks to create public acceptance for a particular idea or commodity."[43] This "special pleader" no longer integrates individual interests with those of his clients. The PR counsel pleads only for the right to control and manipulate public opinion.

That Bernays still holds the PR counsel to ethical standards is certainly evident, even in *Propaganda*. His business is not "to fool or hoodwink the public," even if he still "functions primarily as an adviser to his client, very much as a lawyer does."[44] What has changed, however, is the way in which the PR counsel utilizes psychology to further his client's interests. In *Crystallizing Public Opinion,* the PR counsel could work only for a cause or client that furthered the latent but progressive desires of individuals. His job would be to read the subconscious yearnings of the public, and integrate them with his client's business.

But if Bernays revealed latent yearnings in *Crystallizing Public Opinion,* this is no longer the case in *Propaganda:* "The public relations counsel, then, is the agent who, working with modern media of communications and the group formations of society, brings an idea to the consciousness of the public."[45] As passive receiver and spectator, the public appropriates these visionary ideas from without, rather than from within the depths of the unconscious. Only in this way can "the public at large become aware of and act upon new ideas." Those ideas, in other words, do not originate within the self, but instead derive from "the active energy of the intelligent few."[46] In this sense, the PR counsel's disdain for the public mirrors Lippmann's "expert," for both trivialize individual autonomy and rational capacity within the herd. Bernays moves the herd to recognize new desires and to accept new products, but *as* a herd. He believes the PR counsel "has proved that it is possible," within limits, to answer affirmatively to this question: "If we understand the mechanism and motives of the group mind, is it not possible to control and regiment the masses according to our will without their knowing about it?"[47] This is to utilize psychology to enslave the self rather than to free it to pursue its innermost desires.

Some twenty-five years later, when Bernays recalls his work of the 1920s, he chooses to quote from the very last page of *Propaganda:*

> "If the public is better informed about the processes of its own life," I wrote in *Propaganda,* "it will be so much the more receptive to reasonable appeals to its own interests. No matter how sophisticated, how cynical the public may become about publicity methods, it must respond to the basic appeals.... If the public becomes more intelligent in its commercial demands, commercial firms will meet the new standards."[48]

This is no accidental rewriting, but a clear distancing of his earlier work from the kind of propaganda that permeated Germany at mid-century. In his attempt to distance his thought from the kind of manipulation warranted in *Propaganda,* Bernays instead highlights what is truly distinctive in this work. He certainly did quote his text accurately. But it is the only such writing in *Propaganda,* and it arrives far too late to make up for the blatant manipulation that Bernays advises on every other page in the text. This entry harkens back to the individual tenor and social concerns of *Crystallizing Public Opinion* (1923), but not *Propaganda* (1928). In the former text Bernays positioned the PR counsel as valiant defender of the free individual. But he has become, as he states emphatically in *Propaganda,* "the executive arm of the invisible government."[49] If Bernays once called upon Freud to resurrect unconscious motives to make them visible and effective for the individual and the public, he now opposes that transparency, fearing that, as Le Bon could have told him long ago, individual interests might not fully align with those of his clients. Once the protector of those interests against the herd, the PR counsel now engineers public consent by submerging the individual within the herd.

The significance of Bernays's work for understanding the material past lies in this tension between liberating the self from herd conformity and manipulating the self to conform to desired market trends. This dynamic between the exposure of latent desires, and the ability to manipulate those desires by outside forces, reveals the continued presence of the material past in Bernays's works. There are distinguishing scars here, and I wish to highlight a few of them.

The herd mentality absorbs inherited desires from the past, and subjects the self to them without concern for individual attachments.

In *Crystallizing Public Opinion,* Bernays sought to curb that inherited influence so that individuals could seek new comforts and express new desires that distinguished individuals from the crowd. The PR counsel denied the material past a voice in decisions made by individuals now fully aware of their unconscious desires. The problem was that persons made the wrong choices, aspired to the wrong goals, and consumed the wrong products because they could not recognize their true longings. Conformity to the herd mentality, to a past accepted as custom, damaged the self and its innermost cravings. Submitting to that past was to lose the self and individual freedom.

But the material past, as I have already suggested, leaves recognizable scars, and this is what we witness in *Propaganda.* The inheritance from the past, often viciously nurtured by the herd, cannot so easily be abandoned. Bernays's experts and progressive advocates move the individual *by means of* the herd. Certainly Bernays still believes in progressive social programming, and it is all true, as he claims in *Propaganda,* that campaigns against tuberculosis and cancer, together with research seeking to eliminate social diseases, advance the public welfare.[50] But his crusades manipulate rather than liberate public opinion. To be sure, there were certainly signs of this in *Crystallizing Public Opinion.* According to Bernays, women really did desire hair nets, but still fell victim to mass fashion; the PR counsel revealed those inner desires to consciousness. Hair nets would sell once again because women, now listening to their own desires, truly yearned for long hair. But this only fortifies the conformity to an inherited tradition. Bernays reinforces rather than subverts the herd mentality.

This dialectic between craving and renouncing authority is crucial to how Bernays confronts the material past. For the Bernays who frees inner desires, the material past forfeits its authority to command and persuade. Only unconscious motives, now brought to light by the PR counsel, determine consumption. Devotion comes *from* the self *for* the self, and not *because of* the past. The self becomes its own authority, replacing that of the herd and the material past it represents. But for the Bernays who manipulates those inner desires, the herd mentality now actively functions as a *new* material past, because it is already authorized, confirmed, and legitimated by the group. If Bernays persuaded women to smoke Lucky Strike cigarettes in public in 1929 as "Torches of Freedom," it was because he associated a new product with a material past that commands. The idea of American freedom, coupled with the feminist strivings of the 1920s, offered compelling incentives for women to smoke in public.[51] Bernays created a female desire that appropriated past American themes and inner feminist longings, all of which appeared to be a woman's "own idea." With the "Torches of Freedom" campaign, the individual acted in conformity to the herd without knowing it. A past had been reimagined to condone a new practice with all the authority and weight of the herd mentality. Believing they were overcoming the authority of the past, women were instead subjected to it.

In *Crystalizing Public Opinion,* Bernays sought to curb the impact of that authority by decoupling the individual from the herd. When individuals recognize their unconscious desires, they can dispute cultural fashion and values, and transform them to better suit their own needs. The herd mentality loses its influence over the psychological self. In this view, businesses can no longer rely on accepted fashions to sell their new products. They must, instead, understand latent desires, and position their products to fulfill those inner needs. In the model of *Crystallizing Public Opinion,* individual desires grow out of deep inner longings for self-fulfillment. These inner drives appropriate the authority once invested in the herd. The PR counsel merely expedites this process along, thereby liberating the self while advancing his client's interests. He furthers American material success and frees the self from blindly conforming to the past.

But a very different model develops in *Propaganda,* one that confers more authority and power upon the inherited past to inform individual desires. If Bernays once struggled to deny the influence of the past to rule market consumption, he now actively adopts it to further his client's agenda. The herd mentality, with all its inherited authority, determines how individuals recognize their desires. The tension between these two models suggests that Bernays, and the public he serves, seek to renounce authority, even as they crave for its return. The herd is a body to both admire and resist. If Bernays had once rebelled against the material past, he now recognizes its power to mold behavior and generate public support. Seeking to liberate the self from blind conformity, Bernays could not resist the power to establish new authorities to function as a material past.

JOSHUA LOTH LIEBMAN, MATURE RELIGION, AND A JEWISH AMERICA

Bernays struggled to situate the self within the economic prosperity of the 1920s. He sought to disentangle individual desires from conformist tendencies, only to reinforce those mass appeals to engineer public consent. I have understood this struggle as a problem of authority and its location. In *Crystallizing Public Opinion,* that authority resided in the psychological self who would appeal to inner motives to generate consumptive habits rather than conform to the herd. But in *Propaganda,* authority firmly rests within that herd mentality, and the PR counsel seeks to manipulate individual desires to support economic and business trends. If Bernays once appealed to a liberated self, he soon turned to mass psychology to engineer social conformity. The material past, in the form of the social herd, remains in force to enslave the self.

The problem of authority and its locale surfaces in somewhat different forms in the work of Joshua Loth Liebman (1907–1948). For Liebman, adults rarely wean themselves from childhood traumas, and so forever suffer from feelings of insecurity and impotence. To fully mature, persons must throw off the shackles of past authorities and develop into fully autonomous beings. But even in this radical freedom, Liebman still appeals to the wisdom of the Jewish prophets to turn America into the promised land. Psychology alone cannot authorize new beginnings. Americans, and especially American Jews, require the solace and comforts of a religious heritage.

Liebman published his best seller *Peace of Mind* in 1946, a time in which the American public sought relief from the horrors of the Second World War. It was also a time in which Americans fully embraced psychological explanations for trauma, depression, and the various anxieties plaguing an increasingly apprehensive public. Americans were inundated with psychological discourse: from psychological profiling during the war, notions of combat, and battle fatigue,[52] to the various popular magazines with articles on Freud and his theories, and even to movies and billboard advertising. Nathan Hale calls this era "the golden age of popularization" for psychoanalysis, and certainly it was for Freud as the scientific, European authority.[53] Americans, however, rejected Freud's more "sober vision," as Philip Rieff has described it. The psychoanalytic therapies appropriated by Americans would focus more on the "immediate releases of impulse" rather than on the constant negotiation between the demands of culture and instinctual claims.[54] Hale notes how articles in popular magazines "often simplified, smoothed, and exaggerated the versions psychoanalysts and psychiatrists already had created." Authors tended to reduce complex theory into more acceptable parlance.[55] In all these accounts, psychoanalytic treatment was inevitably followed by success. Echoing Rieff's critique of the therapeutic, Hale argues that the popularity of psychoanalysis legitimated the "importance of catharsis: 'once they get it off their chests, half their battle is won,' was a commonplace."[56] The American Freud was a popular one, sanitized from his pessimistic and ironic tone, and made to speak in an American key, with an "emphasis on therapeutic optimism, on moralism and simplification."[57]

Liebman's *Peace of Mind* is both a product of this popular Freudian culture in America and a producer of it. *Peace of Mind* set out to introduce Americans to basic Freudian tenets in order to combat personal loss and grief following the war. The American Freud of Liebman's book is the scientific researcher who uncovers inner secrets to liberate adults from their childhood traumas. The weary Freud, who brooded over inevitable psychic struggles, is missing in Liebman's upbeat, triumphalist narrative. From Freud, Americans could learn how to transform their destructive drives into "constructive, beautiful forms."[58] This was the triumph of psychology, American style, and one that Liebman knew well. While serving as a Reform rabbi for a pulpit in Chicago, Liebman had undergone psychoanalysis with Roy Grinker, a leading psychiatric theorist of the time. After moving to Boston to assume the pulpit of Temple Israel in 1939, Liebman continued his analysis with Erich Lindemann at Harvard Medical School. Liebman recognized his debt to both men for the success of *Peace of Mind*,[59] a book that outsold some of America's most famous works in this genre, including many of Norman Vincent Peale's writings (although not *The Power of Positive Thinking*), as well as those of Fulton Sheen and Harry Emerson Fosdick.[60]

In many ways, Liebman's only Jewish peer was Morris Lichtenstein of the Jewish Science Movement. Lichtenstein himself had published a book entitled *Peace of Mind,* and like Liebman, sought to curb the ill effects of the past on personal growth and maturity.[61] But the influence of Lichtenstein's work on Liebman's is difficult to assess,[62] though the convergence of titles points to a common mode of inspirational literature. Liebman, as much as Lichtenstein, sought a wide audience, and tailored his rhetoric to appeal to it. Like Peale, Liebman reached millions of listeners through his radio program, and many of those listeners were Christians.[63] Liebman absorbed the popular Freudian culture around him, and did much to disseminate it to other willing listeners. He was involved in interfaith work in Boston, and his charismatic and powerful oratory style reached those Americans yearning for a unified vision of faith and health. An abridged version of his chapter on grief in *Peace of Mind* was first published in *Reader's Digest* in 1947,[64] signaling an audience ready to listen to this Jewish preacher.

That audience had already been saturated with inspirational literature of this sort, and well prepared to accept it from a Reform rabbi.[65] There was already a burgeoning sense that much of middle-class life rested on a common "Judeo-Christian" cultural heritage.[66] But even more, Americans also inherited a tradition of "positive thinking" or "mind cure"—what came to be known, in part, as the New Thought tradition—that supported this modern ecumenical vision. This varied collection of movements and persons responded to the increasing rationalization and industrialization in the latter half of nineteenth-century America. Positive thinking awarded some modicum of personal power to those struggling against the dehumanizing and often reductive economy of industrial labor. As Americans felt increasingly like "cogs in complex organizational structures," they became ever more attracted to those who claimed that "states of mind" will lead to economic success and personal health.[67]

Positive thinkers argued that thought is a power that moves the world and has real material effects on others. These writers infused a sense of control, competence, and influence within those who had lost it in the urban industrial economy. But this sense of personal dominance was coupled with a passive acceptance of divine energy, or overflow, that worked through the mind to affect the material world. If one could just "let go," the divine overflow would then fill the mind with energy, abundance, and authority.[68] This influx or divine energy was everywhere, and one simply had to plug in and channel its power into correct thinking. Though not an essentially Christian practice, many writers imagined Jesus as the great mind-cure specialist who fully absorbed God's divine energy. But there was enough of that divine overflow for everyone, Jew and Christian alike. The central themes that Louis Schneider and Stanford Dornbusch discovered in their sociological study of inspirational works of this period bear this out. They examined forty-six inspirational best sellers published between 1875 and 1955, and found that after 1932, these works focused on emotional health (rather than wealth), psychological therapy, religious strategies to alleviate suffering, and, in concert with psychotherapy, the promotion of health and spiritual contentment.[69] Clearly, Americans sought psychological supports to withstand an increasingly dehumanized economy. Liebman could speak to Americans on these terms, even if he believed that Judaism retained spiritual resources missing from Christian practices. The Positive Thinkers opened a window of divine energy through which Liebman could air his own views of health and spiritual well-being.

Norman Vincent Peale's immensely popular *The Power of Positive Thinking* (1952) drew readily from this tradition, and it reveals just how prevalent and accepted positive thinking was at the time Liebman published his *Peace of Mind* in 1946. Peale's claims were certainly not original,[70] but they were extraordinarily effective in consolidating the positive-thinking tradition into a clear and concise program for living. He offered guidelines to transform good thoughts into effective deeds, and techniques to control behavior and channel bad thoughts away. Peale presented Americans a formula "of practical and workable techniques for living a successful life." That life could be subsumed into what he called "this great law" of positive thinking: "if you think in negative terms you will get negative results. If you think in positive terms you will achieve positive results. That is the simple fact which is at the basis of an astonishing law of prosperity and success. In three words: Believe and succeed."[71] Peale promised his audience everything in the very first sentence of *The Power of Positive Thinking*: "This book is written to suggest techniques and to give examples which demonstrate that you do not need to be defeated by anything, that you can have peace of mind, improved health, and a never-ceasing flow of energy. In short, that your life can be full of joy and satisfaction."[72] Offering more than Liebman's peace of mind, Peale promised the health and security of divine energy now channeled through the self. Positive thinking would direct this divine flow out into the world to create prosperity and success.

The "simple fact" that thoughts were forces was a central theme within the positive-thinking tradition. Ralph Waldo Trine's influential *In Tune with the Infinite* (1910) was perfectly clear: "In the degree that we love will we be loved. Thoughts are forces. Each creates of its kind." This power described an "immutable law" of the universe, one that channels the "Infinite Source" of divine energy through us so that "we are no longer slaves to personalities, institutions, or books." For Trine as well as Peale, being "in tune with the infinite" meant exchanging "weakness and impotence for strength; sorrows and sighings for joy."[73] Mary Pickford, in her popular *Why Not Try God?* (1934), appropriated Trine's tuning in metaphor, but captured it within images of electrical currents and connectivity: "All the Good that there is can be ours right now if we but tune in with God. And the only instrument with which we can tune in is our own thinking. But we can't get any more good out of the power of God unless we do tune in than we can get out of electricity if we don't turn on the switch." To make that "high voltage contact," one only need to connect: "God is a twenty-four-hour station. All you need to do is to plug in. You plug in with your thinking."[74] Radio technology had produced something extraordinary: connection without static; acceptance without fee. And like Trine before her, and Peale somewhat later, Pickford recognized how positive thinking empowered the self:

> Isn't it wonderful to realize that no one in the whole world, no government, no bank, no other person, no anything, can interfere with what each of us chooses to think! Like a radio, each one of us may tune in the good and instantly shut off the bad, or let in the bad and switch off the good.[75]

Thoughts, as Emmet Fox argued in his *Power through Constructive Thinking* (1932), "are things."[76] And as material things, thoughts rule a world now unsettled by industrialization, world wars, and psychological anxieties and traumas. Peale spoke to this world, as did Liebman before him. They both recognized how thoughts within could yield positive results without. Liebman and Peale promised peace of mind, and judging from the millions of books sold, Americans expected no less.

In the fall of 1947, Liebman hosted a conference on religion and psychiatry in Boston, only a year after the publication of *Peace of Mind*. He collected religious leaders in the New England area together with well-known psychiatrists and psychoanalysts. At their most advanced, Liebman insisted, both religion and psychology "lead us to an inner serenity and an inner maturity that will make us friends rather than enemies of justice and peace."[77] The central themes articulated here—the convergence of religion and psychology, and with it the "inner maturity" that follows—map closely to Liebman's concerns in *Peace of Mind*. His essay, "A Creative Partnership," together with his "Introduction" to the published volume of the conference papers, *Psychiatry and Religion* (1948), provide a helpful overview of his best-selling work. Liebman integrated what he calls the sanctuary (religion) and the laboratory (psychology), forming a "creative partnership" and making available "new resources for the good life upon this earth." Religion reveals the "moral goals" and "spiritual ends of our existence," while psychology offers tools to uncover hidden secrets of the self, such that "we cease being a mystery to ourselves, carrying around an unknown enemy, as it were, in our bosom." When we open ourselves to psychological investigation, "we are on the road to inner maturity."[78] Even more, Freud's work unveils a map of the human psyche:

> It was not, however, until Sigmund Freud arrived on the scene that humanity was given the brush with which to paint the detailed portrait of the mind. He has been the supreme cartographer of consciousness, the first scientist to draw a truly helpful map of the terrain of the psyche.[79]

The inner terrain is no longer mysterious or illusive. We can now navigate through our desires to rid ourselves of that "unknown enemy." Liebman's appeal to the laboratory is therefore quite appropriate, for he understands psychology as a science of the mind that discovers the facts of the inner life. God reveals truths anew in every generation, Liebman claims, and "some of the channels of this revelation in our day are in the healing principles and insights of psychology and psychiatry."[80] Psychology is a natural ally to religion.

With psychology as the new revelation, and a Freudian God as master cartographer, "religion, utilizing the newest discoveries of psychiatry, will aid immature men and women to achieve new depth and inner integration." With Freud's map before us, we can recognize the stumbling blocks to full maturity: "Why is it that we are so often immature? We all carry our infancy with us, our whole past histories, and many of us are still fighting the psychic battles of twenty or even sixty years ago." But we need not remain children all our lives, for psychiatry shows us that "a person does not have to be bound forever to a neurotic mother or a cruel father." We must learn to let go of our past and our infantile passions (even if, as Liebman reveals here, he succumbs to prevalent Jewish parental stereotypes). Still, Liebman admonishes us "to grow up psychologically."[81] The past holds us back, while limiting growth and success. Mature adults must learn to abandon that kind of material past.

One hears this refrain throughout his essays in *Psychiatry and Religion,* and even more so in *Peace of Mind.* Psychiatry, coupled with religion, enable persons to liberate themselves from the constricting demands and pressures of a past. Yet even as Liebman strenuously asserts the dual role of religion and psychiatry, one senses that all the growing up could be had with psychology alone. If Freud had discovered the psychic map, and Liebman translates that map into more accessible navigation, why do people still yearn for religion and its spiritual ends? Why recover some of that past in the form of religious ethics, if psychiatry enables the self to overcome past influences? Perhaps the claims of the past cannot be overturned so easily, nor dismissed so readily. The continued appeals to the past, even within the desire to abandon it, haunt Liebman's *Peace of Mind,* and suggest that achieving inner maturity may neither be as peaceful nor as wholesome as Liebman imagined it could be.

Peace of Mind offers techniques for looking inward so that more mature emotions and desires replace infantile fantasies. Like many within the New Thought tradition, Liebman protects the self from outside forces, such that an "inner equilibrium" maintains "a spiritual stability that is proof against confusion and disaster." This "shockproof balance," as Liebman describes it, can only be found within the self.[82] Freud is once again the expert cartographer who produces a "more dynamic map of man's troubled soul." This sense of mapping terrain, sequestering off dangerous byways and more ominous pursuits, appropriates images of the city to plot the inner dynamics of the self. The city imaginary was quite alive for Mordecai Kaplan, as noted in chapter 1, and became even more forceful in the work of Joseph Soloveitchik, whose work and its relation to the city is the subject of the following chapter. For Liebman, the image of mapping links psychology with the kind of awareness that arrives only with full exposure: as a "compass" of the soul, psychiatry helps to "guide individuals and nations through the hazardous channels ahead" in ways that "draw the picture of our own soul." With the inner terrain fully exposed, we only require the fortitude to gaze "steadily, unflinchingly, at our inward selves."[83] The outside world falls away here with such intense focus on the self. Social forces neither impinge nor misdirect the inner gaze: to see within is to perceive truly, clearly, and unconditionally. If the outer world, or more directly, the bustling city, offers only "confusion and disaster," then peace of mind can only be found through navigating and plotting its course from *within* the self.

Liebman's dynamic psychology seeks to replace the "technique of repression," which merely denies hostile desires. Rather than stifling those base motives, individuals must "bring the dark and uncomfortable aspects of their inner life to the surface." Through exposure, however, these "aspects" no longer control the self. They can be diverted either into "divine forms of art, science, beauty, goodness, and happiness," or they harmlessly escape into the ether: "Seal up even a small teakettle, place it over a flame, and it will wreck a house. But let the powerful vapors escape, and the kettle *sings!*"[84] A beautiful chorus follows the unveiling of repressed emotions that, if left untouched, would only oppress the self. But once released, these ominous feelings lose their force and appeal, and we just let them go. The acknowledgment itself frees the self from those baser drives: psychology "will remove only the *infantile* aspects of our fears, frustrations, and hatreds—leaving all that is strong and mature in us as the foundation for future building."[85] Liebman suggests that those baser motives simply vanish. They are not redirected into other channels: they require no mapping. The outer city has disappeared—as it did for those positive thinkers who tuned in and "shut off the bad."

Throughout *Peace of Mind,* Liebman associates the most sinister of emotions with infantile aggressions and fears. Achieving maturity and strength means to outgrow these older desires, and to live for a healthier, more peaceful future. Our past has, as Liebman aptly describes it, wrecked our house. To build a stronger one, we must disown our past to better fashion more "constructive, beautiful forms."[86] Navigating and controlling the self releases the harmful energies, replacing them with "divine forms" that protect the self from inner turmoil and outer disaster. A stronger self is achieved *against* a past.

Yet Liebman recognizes that psychology is only one of the "two great beacons" that guide the self to full maturity. The other "twin angel" is prophetic religion.[87] That Freud himself had a far more ambiguous relation to religion hardly concerns Liebman, who mocks Freud's "negative approach" as overly rational and too wedded to "his own bitter personal experience." Liebman summarily dismisses agnostics and atheists in similar fashion. However, religion, to be fully mature, must "make peace with Freud."[88] Liebman speaks of these two united beacons in messianic terms:

> Prophetic religion now has an ally in what might be called revealed psychology—a science that lays bare the secret diseases of man's troubled soul and provides a serviceable therapy for healing them. Fused together by terrible necessity, religion and psychology now bend forward, as one, to succor stumbling humanity, to lift it up, anoint its wounds, and fill its cup to overflowing with the oil of peace.[89]

The terrible necessity of the Second World War drew these two forces together. But that world tragedy has given birth to a new hope for the future: the cup overflowing with peace lies beyond the tragic past. Liebman's theological commitments surface here, as they do throughout *Peace of Mind,* to suggest how God's revelation is progressive. Psychology is indeed "revealed" because it exposes a new revelation of God's goodness:

> But wiser religious teachers today are coming to see the fallacy of identifying the truth with the frozen concepts of the past. They insist that whatever aids mankind in its quest for self-fulfillment is a new revelation of God's working in history, and that psychology's discoveries about conduct and motive are really the most recent syllables of the Divine.[90]

God now speaks through psychology in tones that silence the past. For religion to mature, it must "be humble enough to accept the tools of the psychological laboratory."[91] The "newest and sharpest tools"[92] for uncovering human motives lie within the province of psychology alone. What is left for religion to do outside the laboratory?

A religion mature enough "to make peace with Freud" rejects the domineering, oppressive father figure of the traditional God, and replaces him with the more relational, friendly deity of mature faith. Liebman's God becomes a copartner in the human quest for peace of mind: a journey of the soul toward inner quietude and harmony. Yet this mature religion "verifies" that which the Jewish prophets had always professed. Indeed, as Andrew Heinze has rightly argued,[93] Liebman transforms prophetic Judaism into a precursor of modern psychology. Liebman's Judaism is ancient psychology before it entered the laboratory:

> Traditional Judaism, as a matter of fact, had the wisdom to devise almost all of the procedures for healthy-minded grief which the contemporary psychologist counsels, although Judaism naturally did not possess the tools for scientific experiment and systematic case study.[94]

When Liebman refers to "traditional Judaism" he really means the prophets, for they (so argues Liebman) rejected the repressive father often associated with the Hebrew Bible. He blames Luther and Calvin, who follow Paul and Augustine, "all of whom were obsessed by the notion of man's wickedness."[95] They each created a "Divine Tyrant" who undermines human freedom and the possibility for future happiness.[96] A mature religion navigates a return to the "healthy-mindedness of Judaism."[97] Yet even in return, the recuperated past is one that always points to the future:

> A prophetic religion like Judaism is future-minded in placing its trust in the Messianic age to redeem the darkness and tragedy of present personal and social failure. Dynamic psychology underscores the intuitive wisdom of religion in stressing the future, because psychology maintains that the human ego lives and grows only when it has a hope for the future—only when there are seeds of new plans in the broken present.[98]

Prophetic religion as "mature faith" embodies "self-mastery and new integration."[99] A divinity that works in and for the self has now become the promise of revealed psychology.

This modern, divinely inspired psychology will help those who cannot "go home again" to ancient faiths and to outmoded notions of repression. But Liebman also directs this psychology at those who *should* not go home again, in the very real sense of returning to one's origins and parental care. Too often, Liebman warns, "the shelters of childhood become the prisons of maturity." Religions tend to encourage "those chains," and so help "keep men and women in subjection to their child-ish and adolescent conscience."[100] Many of us fail to escape this infantile period of development, and so "remain 'fixated' at an immature level of self-development."[101] This notion of stasis works against the forward thrust of Liebman's theological psychology. Human lives grow and de-velop, yearning always to achieve something new:

> The great thing about life is that as long as we live we have the privilege of growing. We can learn new skills, engage in new kinds of work, devote ourselves to new causes, make new friends, if only we will exercise a little initiative and refuse to become fixed, rigid, and psychologically arterio-sclerotic before our time.[102]

With an open future, the past only holds the self enchained in unhealthy inertness. Freud has taught us that early childhood experiences deci-sively influence future behavior. But those traumas need not impinge or damage the self. We are no longer children, after all, and should not choose to be so:

> Suppose we *were* unwanted or rejected by our parents? They do not ex-haust the whole world. There are others now in our present experience who want and love and admire us. Shall we, then, reject the present in or-der to remain incarcerated in the past? Let us look frankly into the mirror of our childhood and see how many of the fears and worries and distor-tions of our present existence come from that nursery level of life.[103]

Liebman presumes that most would prefer to grow out of, rather than stagnate within, the "nursery level of life." But he also believes that we can quite easily rid ourselves of that past immaturity to achieve peace of mind. For Liebman, we just have to grow up, and reject a past that weighs us down.

And it is always the childhood past that carries the greatest weight. Witness Liebman's callous dismissal of atheists and agnostics, who re-main simply too infantile to accept the basic goodness and abundance of life. Here at his most reductive, Liebman claims that skepticism of all kinds is "merely the reflection of the sufferer's own inner conflict, ag-gression and cruelty, projected upon the larger canvas of the universe." That inner conflict begins in childhood, when the atheist's "parents let him down catastrophically." Liebman can help patients recover from these infantile aggressions. He describes one case in which a patient's "atheism was merely the shifting of a grudge onto God because of his own understandable disappointment with his human father."[104] Scientists come out no better, for they are "repressed, ashamed of emotion, fearful of the consequences to themselves if their heart valves ever open to their fullest extent."[105] Liebman fully owns up to his pathological model to classify all these deformed faiths as "derivatives of childhood experience." He admits to "reducing the religious consciousness of God to some childish residue, some deposit of parental frustration or fulfillment, in the dregs of memory."[106] But the simplicity, even absurdity, of Liebman's critique magnifies the power of his psychotherapy: the past can be undone, it need not govern the future. The material past ought not to determine future success. We can relegate the past *as* a past that no longer incarcerates the self. To go forward we must leave home.

A mature faith is one that rejects the omnipotent God of our childish longings, and instead appropriates Mordecai Kaplan's notion of a God who enables human flourishing. Liebman quotes from Kaplan's works, and Kaplan himself read the manuscript before publication.[107] Like Kaplan's understanding of divinity, Liebman's approach to God is characteristically "dynamic, not static." It means, he tells us, "that we come to a *reconstructed* God idea."[108] As Andrew Heinze notes, "When Liebman wrote, 'I believe that God is the Power for salvation revealing Himself in nature and in human nature,' he was making a Kaplanian declaration of faith."[109] This divine power rejects the omniscient kind so readily ascribed to the childish God of immature faith. A reconstructed God builds "a predictable world, governed by law, [and] voluntarily surrenders something of His sovereignty."[110] A mature faith requires a mature God who, like us, is always open to the future and new possibilities. But this also means a more limited, if caring, God who acts more like a responsible co-worker,[111] a colleague who guides and offers hope. God is the psychological healer.

For those who remain of immature faith, a more ominous undercurrent surfaces in Liebman's inspirational writings. He tends to associate immature faith and experience with blackness. Heinze contends that Liebman was a "fighter for racial equality as well as an interfaith activist,"[112] and Liebman was sincere and committed to these areas of ethical justice. I seek only to reveal the ways in which lingering emotions, perhaps even traumas from the past, still haunt Liebman's peace of mind. At the conclusion to his dismissal of agnostics and atheists, and immediately preceding his "personal credo," Liebman describes those who believe in the "Green Pastures" idea of divinity (a reference to Marc Connelly's play of the same name in 1930). These persons believe that God should respond to every call and desire like "a cosmic bellhop." Liebman then continues:

> Many who smile at the childish credulity of the *Green Pastures* God, with all of its simple Negro symbolism, will, if they examine their own concepts honestly, find that there is very little difference between their god and Marc Connelly's picture of "De Lawd."[113]

Referring to Connelly's Pulitzer prize winning play *Green Pastures*, and the racial stereotypes of African American spirituality that it both portrays and advances, Liebman adopts the "simple" faith of "Negro symbolism" as the descriptive basis for immature faith. African Americans are emotional children in this schema, and we become like "them" the more we imagine God as "De Lawd." The Jewish tradition is, in contrast, a white heritage, with "the virtues of the patriarchs," and "the moral qualities of Moses."[114] Among the "commandments of a new morality," Liebman includes this one: "Thou shalt turn away from all supine reliance upon authority, all solacing slavery to an omnipotent social father."[115] If read together with Connelly's "De Lawd" reference, as I think it should be, one recognizes how color encodes a text to discriminate between children and adults. For Liebman, blackness marks childish immaturity, a failure to leave home, and a dangerous chaos, as in "the black forest of intolerance, sunless and fearsome for all who dwell in its shade."[116] Whites could regress too, and so passively accept enslavement to an omnipotent God. Becoming black further chains the self to a debilitating past. In this sense, *Peace of Mind* is a whitening of the self in which progressive psychology seeks to deny a black past. But that past, in the form of a black forest, remains ever ready to spread fear and danger. Scars from the past remain stubbornly present to impair one's peace of mind. The shadow of slavery darkens the peaceful whiteness of mind.

Liebman recognizes how the past controls the present, and he, too, understands its power. But his psychological technique enables Americans "to face them in full light, to disarm them, to triumph over them."[117]

In the racial language that at times surfaces in his writings, Liebman channels a black past into a white future. He hearkens back to Mary Pickford's imagery of the electrical switch, describing an adulterer who "must be shown *where the switch is* before he can control the powerful current being generated in his unconscious life." Persons can do more than manage their inner drives; they can navigate through them, even redraw the map of the self to excise the harmful circuits. The past and its "undesirable drives" can be surgically removed, magically turning "a person from an infantile weakling into a mature adult."[118] Psychoanalysis empowers the self to rewire its inner circuitry, to distinguish progressive from regressive switches, and to channel positive energy away from debilitating currents. The sense of liberation, of self-fulfillment and growth, overwhelm Liebman's prose. This is the Jewish preacher at work:

> Through looking fearlessly at all of his nature, he comes to see what actions are compatible with adult fulfillment. He faces ghosts of childhood and adolescence—ghosts which he had locked in unremembered chambers of the past—and as he faces them, they vanish. . . . He is free of haunting pain. Those moments of revelation have taken away the power of the past over him.[119]

Liebman calls this a "process of liberation": the ghosts of the past no longer haunt the self because psychotherapy frees it from those "chambers of the past." The current within flows in only one direction, and the inner switch blocks the past from carrying forward.

Release from the past triggers little if any guilt. This sets psychoanalysis apart from the Christian confessional, in Liebman's view. The religious confessional seeks atonement, whereas psychotherapy "does not require that you feel sorry for your sins so long as you *outgrow* them!" The confession only reinforces guilt, and inhibits "deep insight or permanent character change." It is "punitive religion" that "*simply has not worked!*"[120] But psychoanalysis offers liberation from guilt and childish fantasies, and a "newly won understanding" discovers the electrical switch of a more mature circuitry. Outgrowing the past also means abandoning outmoded forms of religious ritual. Like childish fantasies and desires, persons must exchange notions of sin, self-condemnation, and forgiveness for the newer psychological truths of growth, self-understanding, and fulfillment.

Liebman's critique of the confessional covered only a few pages of *Peace of Mind,* and could have easily been overlooked by readers more concerned with his discussions of grief, God, and self-acceptance. One reader who did not ignore this section, nor consider it trivial, was Fulton Sheen, a well-known and respected Catholic theologian who, only three years after Liebman's *Peace of Mind* came out, published a book (like other readers, I am inclined to call it a response)[121] entitled *Peace of Soul* (1949).[122] Sheen's critique highlights his own discomfort with Jews and Judaism in American culture, and so provides a useful foil to Liebman's progressive economic politics. The opening sentence marks Sheen's distance from Liebman's focus on the mind: "Unless souls are saved, nothing is saved." He reiterates this point on the very next page:

> Man now finds that he is locked up within himself, his own prisoner. Jailed by self, he now attempts to compensate for the loss of the three-dimensional universe of faith [earth, heaven, hell] by finding three new dimensions within his own mind.[123]

Sheen's work is a direct refutation of Liebman's, and should be read as such.[124] From his very title that distinguishes "soul" from "mind," to his critique of psychoanalysis, and certainly, as I will argue below, in his defense of the Christian confessional, Sheen responds to the challenges posed by Liebman's psychology for contemporary faith. In mounting his rejoinder, Sheen's blunt style contrasts sharply with Liebman's more fluent, conversant form of prose.

But Sheen seeks a higher calling, and believes the self has one too. Here he takes on Liebman directly:

> Sometimes there are mental or physical repercussions because of sin; *in these cases,* there must be peace of *soul* before there can be peace of *mind.* The two are not the same: peace of soul implies tranquility of order, with material things ordered to the body, the body to the soul, the personality to neighbor and to God. Peace of mind is subjective tranquility—a narrower thing. It requires great moral effort to attain peace of soul, but even those who are indifferent to right and wrong sometimes achieve peace of mind.[125]

If Liebman absorbed prophetic religion within the discourse of modern psychology, Sheen would abandon that language to salvage the soul and its religious yearnings. Liebman's psychology resides within the lowest order of existence, where material things interact with the body. One achieves peace of mind by repressing instincts and passions. While this can prove useful, it "can never give peace of soul, because this comes *only from* God."[126] Psychology is "a narrower thing," while peace of soul appeals to a divine inscription. Sheen's is a peace far removed from material things attached to the body.

Yet Sheen's hierarchy gives away too much, as if peace of mind leads to peace of soul. More often, Sheen ascribes a complete break between mind and soul in the tripartite division among the subhuman, rational, and divine levels. He compares these levels to a house, in which the first floor lies bare, the second contains some comforts, but the third is "orderly, luxurious, and full of peace." In this house, peace of mind resides on the second floor, but without access to the uppermost tier:

> And to suggest to those who live on the second floor of reason that there is still a floor above, where peace of mind becomes peace of soul, is to invite them to ridicule the supernatural order. Those who dwell on the second floor have no understanding whatever of the supernatural; they regard it as a pious extra, as unessential as frost on a windowpane or frosting on a cake.[127]

Sheen radically separates psychology from religion: "The supernatural, the third level on which we may live, is not an outgrowth of the natural, as the oak develops from an acorn. It marks a complete break, a beginning anew."[128] Only a conversion "brings the soul out of either chaos or this false peace of mind to true peace of soul."[129] Sheen's *Peace of Soul* supports a robust form of supercessionism, and one that, as I will argue below, permeates the anti-Judaism of his text. Peace of soul witnesses to a higher order, and is no mere frosting on a cake. The split between peace of mind and soul is absolute.

Sheen is careful not to indiscriminately condemn psychology as a modern science. He admits that psychotherapy cures many a sick person. But it "steps outside its legitimate area as a branch of medicine" when it pretends to be a philosophy of the self.[130] When psychology does so, it becomes demonic, for it closes the self to divine intervention and leaves it to wallow in its own filth: "One thing is certain—the modern soul is not going to find peace so long as he is locked up inside himself, mulling around in the scum and sediment of his unconscious mind, a prey of the unconscious forces whose nature and existence he glorifies." Nothing other than a "Divine invasion" can restore the person to health "when he is alone and in the dark."[131] The imagery of the debased, indecent self—full of "scum and sediment"—vividly portrays a modern soul attracted to filth yet incapable of rising above it. Those who attacked psychology often associated it with immorality and debased emotions.[132] With such powerful undercurrents that direct the self away from its higher calling, "no amount of hours or weeks or years spent on couches and being told one's fear of God's justice is due to a father complex will ever help."[133] If Liebman believes we must *outgrow* sin, Sheen argues that sin "is a reality all men know"[134] and, even more, cannot escape:

> Sometimes the blame for an abnormal mental condition is to be laid upon grandmothers and grandfathers, on cruel parents or clumsy kindergarten teachers; but let it never be forgotten that much more often the blame is more justly to be placed on oneself.[135]

To Sheen, Liebman has too easily shifted blame to parents. For psychology, "there is no God, there is no moral law, there is no final judgment." But with sin firmly in place, Sheen can appeal to "not mere psychoanalysis but Divine Analysis"[136] that breaks through the material human muck and raises the self to the third floor of divine abundance.

Liebman rejected the confession as divine analysis because, so argues Sheen, he had already denied God, and transformed guilt into a form of mental disease. But the "confession for peace of mind" cannot substitute for the Christian form: "When a man does wrong, he wants to avow it. Because he knows it to be a wrong, he will not tell it to anyone who happens by, but only to some representative of the moral order, for what he seeks is a pardon."[137] This appeal to the moral order, and the priest who represents it, lies at the heart of Sheen's defense of the confessional process. Psychoanalysis, so Sheen believes, makes no claim to a moral universe, nor does it seek to create one. The Catholic priest, through the institution of confession, underscores the depravity of the sinful person; but he also enables the confessor to restore proper relations with the world and God.[138] Confession allows a full release, a full mending of a broken soul with a compassionate God. It offers the means by which "the sick soul might be restored to moral health and union with

God." Psychoanalysis, on the other hand, "can offer no norm, no ideal, no motivation, no dynamism, no purpose in life; it has none of these to give."[139] Liebman offers release without redemption.

Sheen portrays the Catholic confession as the moral and religious counterpart to Liebman's form of psychotherapy. When Liebman wants to outgrow sin, Sheen seeks only to reinforce it.[140] Where Liebman returns to traumatic childhood experiences, Sheen uncovers the "seething lava of unrest" within the guilty individual. And if Liebman's psychotherapist offers insights and tools for self-fulfillment, Sheen's priest, and only him, mediates a healing through a divine invasion. This is positive thinking moderated by priestly power. Peace of mind, in Sheen's view, is not merely "a narrower thing"; it is a threat that must succumb to a higher order. It is like a past that must be whitened.

So too is Judaism. Heinze describes Sheen's views on psychoanalysis as a form of "Catholic polemic against a Jewish Freud," even as he suggests that it is also more than this.[141] Note, for example, how Sheen associates Judaism with filth and Christianity with clear waters:

> The Immaculate Conception and the Virgin Birth were to the beginning of a new humanity something like what a lock is to a canal, the former in a special way. If a ship is sailing on a polluted canal and wishes to transfer itself to clear waters on a higher level, it must pass through a device which locks out the polluted waters and raises the ship to the higher position. Then the other gate of the lock is lifted, and the ship rides on the new, clear waters, taking none of the polluted waters with it.[142]

Heinze notes the success with which Sheen attracted converts to Catholicism, in part due to the popularity of his weekly television show. Even here Sheen's anti-Judaism comes through: "The Old Testament is something like radio: a speech without vision." Love, Sheen continues, wants to see, and Jesus Christ transformed vision into revelation.[143] Just as television had replaced radio as the medium of communication in the 1950s, so too Christianity supersedes Judaism as it leaves the polluted waters behind. Sheen associates the filth of the unconscious mind with material Judaism. Psychoanalysis and Judaism are too polluted for the higher position that America protects and defends. The Jew has no claim to America as a land of Christian people. American waters must be cleansed of the material filth that pollutes Jews and Judaism.[144]

Sheen's critique of Judaism and psychoanalysis is important, indeed crucial, for understanding the dynamics of Liebman's *Peace of Mind,* for it suggests an acute anxiety about the social and economic status of American Jews in the late 1940s. Despite Liebman's call to unite psychology with religion, Sheen could only see a potential competitor (psychology) to the moral authority of Catholicism and its priests. He had to close the locks, as it were, to what appeared to be Jewish incursions into clean waters. This is significant because Liebman sought to open those doors, and his *Peace of Mind,* despite its rhetoric of internal harmony and self-liberation, fosters a path to economic well-being. Peace of mind within can yield material prosperity without: this was the very claim that Ralph Waldo Trine, Mary Pickford, and Norman Vincent Peale, among many others in the New Thought tradition, had all sold to the American public.[145] This would be true for Jews as well as Christians, but it surely held particular resonance for those Jews shut out from American prosperity. If Americans wean themselves from their debilitating reliance on their past, then the future holds untold possibilities for success. This is, to be sure, one of the many versions of the American dream. Sheen meant to close it for some; Liebman hopes to open it for all.

But Liebman's dream is dramatically gendered: material success for the male, relational and familial bliss for the female. He thrives in the public marketplace, able to return home a success and model for his male heirs; she remains at home and searches for nothing beyond it. So it would be more true to say that Liebman's *Peace of Mind* enables men to live well with material success, and counsels women to provide domestic tranquility for their prosperous husbands. This is clear in the many examples of male success in Liebman's text. When accounting for feelings of inferiority as a symptom of self-hate, Liebman offers this profile: "the man in business who is afraid to expand and grasp normal opportunities because he is convinced of his inevitable failure." Alongside this example, Liebman describes "the charming woman disparaging her social capabilities when measured by the yardstick of her neighbors." Or in learning how to choose among desires, most understand that "the man who wishes to achieve stature in the mature world will have to renounce many careers in order to fulfill one."[146] And surely this character is all too familiar as well:

> Take the woman who from infancy has been encouraged to feel helpless
> and dependent and was never taught self-reliance. Her life is miserable
> because she is constantly searching from one marriage to another for
> some magic helper, some omnipotent parent, some daily miracle.[147]

There are countless more stories in Liebman's *Peace of Mind* that articulate the same point: peace of mind offers material rewards for males, and relational happiness for females. While men fear success, women worry about love. All of this, Liebman predictably concludes, "is a hangover from that chapter in our life's story when we really *were* inadequate and inferior." Those childhood fears are "repeated again and again on the record of mature strivings."[148] Grown-up Americans are men successful in business, and women content to order the home.

Heinze has argued that, despite the lack of statistics, "there is reason to suspect that Liebman's message resonated with special force" for both women and Jews. He goes on to state that while "Liebman was not preaching feminism, neither was he preaching against it; his overriding theme—personal liberation from the psychological shackles of religion and culture—appealed as strongly to women as to men."[149] Heinze offers little evidence to support this claim; but if true, then these women either overlooked the heavily gendered rhetoric in the text, or were simply comfortable with it. Much of what Liebman offers men, and what he fails to provide for women, tend to support Prell's claim that Jewish men feared material success for their wives because they, in turn, would demand additional income from their working husbands to support their habits of consumption. Her material desires were illegitimate.[150] It may certainly have been true, as Heinze insists, that American women found comfort in Liebman's discourse on grief. But his stereotypical examples of male business executives and female homemakers are comforting models for the American male.

In drawing out these gender troubles, I want to stress how *Peace of Mind* offers distinctive goods for its readers. Transforming "a cottage into a spacious manor hall" offers one set of meanings for men, but quite another for women.[151] I take seriously the gendered language in Liebman's claim to the American dream: "I believe that man is infinitely potential, and that given the proper guidance there is hardly a task he cannot perform or a degree of mastery in work and love that he cannot attain."[152] For Liebman, men master and women relate. In this, he shares much with Morris Lichtenstein[153] and that other famous Jewish American male of this period, Erich Fromm (about whom I have much to say later in this chapter). In an essay with the provocative title "Sex and Character" (1949),[154] Fromm reproduces Liebman's division of gendered roles in American culture. He believes that "characterological differences" arise from the "respective roles of men and women in sexual intercourse." To satisfy the woman, the man must "demonstrate" his capacity for an erection. The woman, in order to appease the man, "needs to demonstrate nothing." From this it follows that "the man's position is vulnerable insofar as he has to prove something, that is, insofar as he can potentially fail." Male anxieties always refer to failure. But not so for women: "The woman's vulnerability, on the other hand, lies in her dependency on the man; the element of insecurity connected with her sexual function lies not in failing but in being 'left alone,' in being frustrated, in not having complete control over the process which leads to sexual satisfaction." Once again, males must perform, but women relate: "The man's vanity is to show what he can *do,* to prove that he never fails; the woman's vanity is essentially characterized by the need to attract, and the need to prove to herself that she can attract."[155] Fromm returns to these tropes in his well-known work, *The Art of Loving* (1956), in which he distinguishes the masculine qualities of "penetration, guidance, activity, discipline and adventurousness," from the feminine qualities of "productive receptiveness, protection, realism, endurance, motherliness."[156]

It might appear rather disingenuous, some fifty years later, to censor Liebman and Fromm for their gender biases, but I do not cite them to do so. Instead, I want to highlight how peace of mind, and the American success that comes with it, is neither universal nor innocent. We notice this in Liebman's discussion of "simple Negro symbolism," but it goes even deeper. America is open only to those more fortunate. This is equally true for peace of mind. The nature and quality of that peace might very well be determined by gender, racial, and economic ties. Those under the spell of the New Thought movement believed they could free themselves from those chains. But texts like Liebman's and Fromm's suggest that some roots are more securely attached than others. A material past surfaces to constrict sweeping notions of American success. So much of Liebman's *Peace of Mind* seeks to uproot that past, in part because he reimagines postwar America as a Jewish home for American

Jews. Like Kaplan before him, he had to pry open the doors to let the Jews in. But those doors had to be detached from a past too mired in Sheen's sinful soul.

Peace of Mind exudes an American triumphalism after the Second World War. America is uniquely positioned to herald a new culture of self-reliance, toleration, democracy, and freedom. Only Europe is weighed down by its past: "We Americans have had little of the feeling of helplessness and of dependence that characterized so much of Oriental and European religion."[157] The "we Americans" suggests that all, natives and immigrants alike, have made it in America. The roots have been shorn: the loving, tolerant, democratic American God has finally replaced the stern European father. It is as if Americans were born mature adults, without the tragic implications of childhood traumas. This, indeed, remains part of the American dream, where all individuals who seek can find success. Liebman's *Peace of Mind,* with its counsel to overcome childhood traumas, has left the shores of Europe for the "green pastures" of America.

This vision of inclusion draws from Jewish sources, so Liebman argues, for prophetic Judaism has long ago championed this mature God in contrast to the childish, "feudal" European deity. Judaism will flourish in America because America has become more Jewish:

> God, according to Judaism, always wanted His children to become His creative partners, but it is only in this age, when democracy has at least a chance of triumphing around the globe, that we human beings can grow truly aware of His eternal yearning for our collaboration.[158]

America has triumphed over Europe, and democracy over feudalism, because God's children have finally matured sufficiently to accept the Jewish God. America becomes more Jewish as it becomes more democratic, pluralistic, and tolerant. So America is not merely the proper home for Judaism and Jews; it is the *only* home within which Jews can flourish as mature, healthy adults. This reads like a counterhistory to Sheen's Christian triumphalism:[159] it is Liebman's prophetic Judaism that cleanses the world. America becomes more Jewish as it matures into a healthy, democratic, progressive society. The messianic image that captivated the Reform movement in nineteenth-century Germany does so again in twentieth-century America. American triumphalism, according to Liebman, is a Jewish story of success. Americans like Sheen must accept more than Freud; they must make peace with Judaism. *That* is what it means to have peace of mind.

A peace of mind of this kind sustains an ambiguous relation to the material past. On the one hand, that past damages material success in the future: a man fails in the open marketplace if he returns to the powerless childhood of his youth, and a woman undermines healthy relations with others if she relies continuously on her mother. Free, mature, American selves outgrow their pasts. But these pasts still maintain a claim upon us, and we see this in Liebman's appeal to prophetic Judaism. America requires the moral authority of Jewish ethics to develop into a just society. Judaism provides a kind of moral weight that situates American progressivism within a history of messianic longings. America overcomes one past (Europe) in order to recuperate another.

So too, then, for Liebman's *Peace of Mind*. It lays waste to the insecurity of childhood traumas, and replaces them with another, more forward-looking, past of the Jewish prophets. That these prophets sound more like Liebman's psychologists is neither coincidental nor insignificant. The peace of mind required in postwar America views the past as a mirror image to the present. That "traditional Judaism" could look so modern in its "procedures for healthy-minded grief" only shows that the map of the soul has been redrawn in ways to obscure more dangerous alleyways. Freud, Liebman's master cartographer, understood that rewriting the past does not obliterate it. Revisions, too, leave their mark, as they do on Freud's mystic writing pad discussed in the previous chapter. A material past altered, and thereby made safe to visit once again, underscores both its authority to control and to limit self-fulfillment. The force of Liebman's *Peace of Mind* lies in its capacity to trace the sources of authority, and the means by which mature adults both overcome and surrender to the material past.

ERICH FROMM AND HUMAN FREEDOM

Liebman updated the prophets to appeal to the psychic needs of an American culture. Even as he renounced European dependence as a childhood overcome, he returned to innocent visions of the past and to a prophetic Judaism cleansed of its ritualistic moorings. He had marked the prophets as *his* Jewish heritage. What is so remarkable about Erich Fromm's corpus, beginning with his *Escape from Freedom* in 1941, and straight through to *You Shall Be as Gods* in 1966, is the force with which he rejects all ties to a past. To become truly human, to accept freedom rather than escape from it, means to completely uproot the self from physical and social ties to a past, and to accept the open possibilities of the future. Fromm's freedom is radical, and it drives Liebman's vision of human self-fulfillment to its limit (however much Fromm would deny this association with Liebman). Fromm arrived in America after fleeing Nazi Germany, and became one of the foremost interpreters of Freud in the 1950s and 1960s. Indeed, according to Robert Fuller, Fromm practically embodied the neo-Freudian movement:

> Virtually every theme that distinguishes the "American psyche" from its Freudian predecessor appears in Fromm's writings: the importance of the present (or existential) situation of the individual rather than his or her past; consciousness and willed freedom rather than intrapsychic determinisms; the continuing openness of the personality and its responsiveness to new experiences as opposed to fixed character structures; and rejection of the biological homeostasis in favor of belief in the forward-moving progressive tendency of the unconscious.[160]

Fromm spoke to a generation of seekers, and though he lived in Mexico from 1950 until 1973, he considered himself an American, and Americans considered him theirs as well.[161] Yet as it did for Bernays and Liebman, the past still retained some appeal to Fromm, however much he wished to deny its influence. Unearthing the sources of conflict in Fromm's relation to the material past once again exposes its power upon those who most wished to suppress it.

Fromm's ascension as spokesperson for the American neo-Freudian movement began with the publication of his most famous work, *Escape from Freedom* (1941). The book surveyed the various ways moderns remain unfree, despite the many social and political gains of the twentieth century. Freedom from a feudal past did not foster a "freedom to" realize human dignity and self-expression. Even though liberated from the past, a modern person still feels "isolated" in contemporary society, and faces two stark choices: "either to escape from the burden of his freedom into new dependencies and submission, or to advance to the full realization of positive freedom which is based upon the uniqueness and individuality of man."[162] The backdrop to all this, of course, is the rise of fascist regimes in Europe, and Fromm's work extensively probes the appeal of Nazi Germany to those seeking escape from freedom. We must sever the "umbilical cord" to what Fromm calls "primary ties" in order to become fully independent, rational beings. But we too often return to the security of those ties by means of new forms of domination and dependence. We escape from freedom by subjecting ourselves to modern varieties of oppression.

Fromm outlines two central themes that will preoccupy him for a lifetime: the capacity of primary ties to deform the self, and the search for new dependencies to replace the lost security of those formative relations. The original ties provide security and orientation to the child dependent upon a "mother, the member of a primitive community with his clan and nature, or the medieval man with the Church and his social caste." While natural, these primary ties also inhibit individual growth:

> The primary ties block his full human development; they stand in the way of the development of his reason and his critical capacities; they let him recognize himself and others only through the medium of his, or their, participation in a clan, a social or religious community, and not as human beings; in other words, they block his development as a free, self-determining, productive individual.[163]

Individuals must orient themselves in the world (they must grow up, in Liebman's terms) and achieve security in ways that do not slide back to those primary ties. But human beings often do return to their roots, either by failing to mature or by grasping onto new authoritarian rule. This "new bondage," as Fromm labels it, differs from the primary enslavement only in this: "the escape does not restore his lost security, but only helps him to forget his self as a separate entity."[164] In sliding back into the security of primary ties, or in leaving them for new forms of slavery, the self is trapped within the material past.

These twin themes of freedom *from* the primary ties that bind, and freedom *to* develop as an independent self, suffuse Fromm's discussion of the self in *Psychoanalysis and Religion* (1950). This text is, to my mind, the most crucial for understanding Fromm's account of the material past, and the self's relation to it. Originally a set of lectures delivered at

Yale University during the winter semester of 1948/49, *Psychoanalysis and Religion* confronts Liebman's "attempts to reconcile psychoanalysis and religion," as well as Sheen's opposition. Fromm seeks a third way, although much of what he provides only intensifies Liebman's approach. But to Fromm, the differences between his approach, and those of Sheen and Liebman, are dramatic:

> There are no prescriptions which can be found in a few books about right living or the way to happiness. Learning to listen to one's conscience and to react to it does not lead to any smug and lulling "peace of mind" or "peace of soul." It leads to peace *with* one's conscience—not a passive state of bliss and satisfaction but continuous sensitivity to our conscience and the readiness to respond to it.[165]

Fromm offers no easy prescriptions, no sense that "peace of mind" can be discovered, packaged, and then directed straightaway to happiness. For him, existence is "felt as a problem," and so requires a continual responsiveness and alertness to "becoming aware."[166] Fromm here repeats a critique he leveled at Liebman from an earlier work. In *Man for Himself* (1947), Fromm recognizes that many readers expect prescriptions for a "peace of mind." But his work will do nothing of the sort; instead, Fromm desires only "to make the reader question himself rather than to pacify him."[167] He repeats similar criticisms in *The Art of Loving*, mocking the notion of God as partner as really meaning, "make God a partner in business, rather than to become one with Him in love, justice and truth."[168] Fromm believes that his own work seriously engages human finitude and strivings, whereas Liebman and his ilk only mollify readers with their catchy phrases and unlimited promises. Fromm sets out to diagnose a problem, and to offer visions of overcoming dependence on the past. To Fromm, Liebman and Sheen read as reworked forms of totalitarian dependence, in which persons leap for security, expecting to find the happiness of their youth, but instead subjugate themselves once again to new forms of slavery.

Though Fromm seeks to uncover nuanced tensions in individual development, his rhetoric often yields stark choices: either return to an enslaved youth, or develop as an independent self; either take hold of freedom to become who you really are, or be controlled by others; either love actively, or passively receive, and thus depend upon others to love you. In the end, one is independent and thus wholly free, or determined by others and so enslaved.

All notions of dependence ultimately point back to ancestor worship, a form of devotion that Fromm associates with incest. Human progress, he argues, "is the development from incest to freedom," and the love for a spouse "is dependent on overcoming the incestuous strivings." We must leave home to mature as individual, free adults. Yet Fromm thinks we must entirely reject that past influence in order to flourish as individual persons:

> But while we have traveled a long road toward overcoming incest, mankind has by no means succeeded in its conquest. The groupings to which man feels incestuously tied have become larger and the area of freedom has become greater, but the ties to those larger units which substitute for the clan and the soil are still powerful and strong. Only the complete eradication of incestuous fixation will permit the realization of the brotherhood of man.[169]

This demand to sever ties to the past is the main theme of "all great religions," so Fromm believes, and especially so for the texts in the Hebrew Bible. God commands Abraham to leave his country, and Moses, too, abandons his family to live with strangers in Egypt. But Fromm is no Zionist reader of texts: "The condition for Israel's mission as God's chosen people lies in their leaving the bondage of Egypt and wandering in the desert for forty years. After having settled down in their own country, they fall back into the incestuous worship of the soil, of idols, and of the state."[170] The Prophets, too, fight against "this incestuous worship," preaching instead universal ideas of truth, love, and justice for all. As primitive religions develop into more bureaucratic organizations, they "take over to some extent the place of family, tribe, and the state." Religious social elites tend to "use the incestuous ties which keep a person in moral bondage to his own group to stifle his moral sense and his judgment."[171] Modern religions have thereby lost their moorings by reinforcing them: rather than abandoning family, land, and the group as the primary texts demand, they instead seek to reinforce these primary ties, and so enslave rather than free "the growth of reason."[172]

Incestuous ties to a past are a form of idolatry. Fromm concludes his *Psychoanalysis and Religion* with a fervent appeal to combat idolatry with the force of the Jewish prophets of old. Idolatry, as "the deification of things, of partial aspects of the world and man's submission to such things," stands in contrast to "the highest principles of life, those of love and reason." Fromm is an unabashed humanist who seeks the greatest power of the self with the least dependence on outside material forces. Idolatry signifies an unacceptable displacement of human power upon "such things" that limit human freedom: "Words can become idols, and machines can become idols; leaders, the state, power, and political groups may also serve. Science and the opinion of one's neighbors can become idols, and God has become an idol for many."[173] Fromm cannot imagine how authoritative persons, communities, or material things could *enable* human flourishing if these authorities falsely appropriate the freedoms that ontologically reside in the self. Although Fromm appreciates human frailty and finitude, he nonetheless distinguishes the recognition of that finitude with the worship of it:

> Indeed, man is dependent; he remains subject to death, age, illness, and even if he were to control nature and to make it wholly serviceable to him, he and his earth remain tiny specks in the universe. But it is one thing to recognize one's dependence and limitations, and it is something entirely different to indulge in this dependence, to worship the forces on which one depends. To understand realistically and soberly how limited our power is is an essential part of wisdom and of maturity; to worship it is masochistic and self-destructive. The one is humility, the other self-humiliation.[174]

Words are idols if they are not *my* words, if they are spoken to me rather than from within. The notion of an obligation imposed upon the self from without inhibits self-fulfillment.

But note that all forms of humble dependence in Fromm's list are physical—death, age, illness, and nature. None refers to existential relations to a past or future. Individual identity can and ought to be formed independent of a past. But when that identity relies on some external factor, then individuals become members of the herd, in which "actions are determined by an instinctive impulse to follow the leader and to have close contact with the other animals around him." As Le Bon had argued, communities swallow the individual whole. To Fromm, there is, on the one hand, *"the orientation by proximity to the herd,"* and, on the other, *"the orientation by reason."* In his Kantian view, reason demands "full freedom and independence," while subjecting reason to external commands is a form of enslavement.[175] The self must be free, and to achieve that freedom it must worship only itself as an independent, powerful being.

Fromm's account of humanistic religion echoes Feuerbach's critique of Christianity a century earlier. Just as Feuerbach believed that God's qualities reveal, in an alienated form, truly human virtues, so too does Fromm distinguish between alienated worship and human dignity: "While in humanistic religion God is the image of man's higher self, a symbol of what man potentially is or ought to become, in authoritarian religion God becomes the sole possessor of what was originally man's."[176] Rather than project unto God the most cherished of human values, we should instead recognize those goods as originally ours. But "authoritarian religion" inscribes human qualities onto an all-powerful, majestic tyrant, turning free human beings into enslaved sinners. These tyrants come in many forms, so Fromm believes, and not only divine ones. Whether they resemble the Hitlers or Mussolinis of his time, or the domineering God that sometimes appears in the Hebrew Bible, tyrants all seek to dominate the self in order to create complacent subjects. Reverence for these new authorities is idolatrous worship.

The real conflict, in Fromm's view, lies not in the struggle between religious faith and atheism, but between humanism and idolatry. He finds warrant for this in Exodus 3:13–14, when Moses asks God to reveal God's name. In Fromm's reading, God responds, "My name is NAMELESS."[177] Those like Maimonides and Meister Eckhart recognized the power of this negative approach, Fromm argues, for it means "no man can presume to have any knowledge of God which permits him to criticize or condemn his fellow men or to claim that his own idea of God is the only right one."[178] So Exodus really speaks out against idolatry as the great challenge to religious belief. Fromm transposes this religious view onto a radical humanism, appropriating the religious fight against idols as a battle against dehumanizing powers. Much like Liebman, but without the softer language, Fromm's god appears like a human copartner: "Inasmuch as humanistic religions are theistic, God is a symbol of *man's own powers* which he tries to realize in his life, and is not a symbol of force and domination, having *power over man*."[179] Whatever furthers human strength is humanistic, just as whatever leads to human weakness is idolatrous. In a reading that Fulton Sheen would undoubtedly label as "nice," Fromm appropriates Jesus' precept that "the Kingdom of God is within you" as a "simple and clear expression of non-authoritarian thinking."[180]

Fromm empowers the self to rise above the chains that bind it to the past, and to remain free from all forms of coercion and dependence. The future is open to human pursuits, decoupled from the shackles of an enslaved past. This image of radical human freedom has proved remarkably powerful to Fromm, and he returns to this theme again and again in his many works of the 1950s and 1960s. In *The Sane Society* (1955), Fromm distinguishes between "natural" and "human" roots: we must dispense with the former to achieve the latter. Those natural roots include blood relations, the clan, and later the state, nation, and church. Natural history is a story about incest relations, but *human* history begins "with the expulsion of man from paradise, from the soil in which he was rooted." To flourish as a human being over against a natural one, persons must cut "the ties with nature and with Mother," and set a new goal "of being fully born, of being fully awake, of being fully human; of being free."[181] Freedom requires a rebirth into unlimited human potential: only then is a sane society possible. A year later Fromm would publish another classic, *The Art of Loving*, in which he yet again associates human progress with "the emergence of man from nature, from mother, from the bonds of blood and soil."[182] Note, too, this claim in *The Heart of Man* (1964):

> The person bound to mother and tribe is not free to be himself, to have a conviction of his own, to be committed. He cannot be open to the world, nor can he embrace it; he is always in the prison of the motherly racial-national-religious fixation. Man is only fully born, and thus free to move forward and to become himself, to the degree to which he liberates himself from all forms of incestuous fixation.[183]

This mother complex with its attending fixations conflict "with the opposite tendency—to be born, to progress, to grow." Fromm returns to these themes with clarity and conviction in his *You Shall Be as Gods* (1966): "The aim of human action is the constant process of liberating oneself from the shackles that bind man to the past, to nature, to the clan, to idols." Human freedom, in contrast, "is based on the achievement of liberating oneself from the primary ties that give security, yet cripple man." Fromm even interprets the binding of Isaac story in Genesis as a "command to cut the ties of blood to the son." The command to sacrifice Isaac means "man must be completely free from all ties of blood."[184]

This is a characteristic transition in Fromm's work: to move from the son's blood to "all ties of blood." He tends to universalize from particular circumstances, such that personal ties are only a subset of more general, binding relations. Fromm fails to distinguish, as some contemporary moral philosophers do,[185] between ethical obligations to those most dear and loved, and more general moral duties to all persons. Instead, he continually devalues personal ties, and ferociously asserts commitments to universal fellowship.

But in his account of love as a performative art form, we witness Fromm struggling to account for an individual, erotic love that obscures, or more likely overcomes, universal brotherly love. Here we begin to see how the material past continues to press upon him. In all of Fromm's works, claims to the universal trump commitments to the individual. Indeed, to be fully human means to renounce kinship ties and to accept all humankind as one's family. And yet, as Fromm's biographer Rainer Funk tells it, Erich Fromm fell madly in love with Fromm's third wife, Annis Freeman, and their "experience of their love made its mark on *The Art of Loving*," a work published only three years after their wedding in 1953. Funk's work is more hagiography than biography, and he defends Fromm's "ability to love" as "extraordinary" (Fromm had divorced his first wife in Germany, and his second wife died in June 1952).[186] Recall that in *The Art of Loving* Fromm promises no prescriptions in the manner of Peale or Liebman, but instead demurs that "to love is a personal experience which everyone can only have by and for himself."[187] The problem for Fromm is that personal experiences do not translate very well into his form of radical humanism. How can I erotically love only one other when all others deserve my love? Personal moments tend to bind the self to "primary ties" in ways that a progressive freedom does not.

We witness Fromm struggling with this tension in his account of erotic and brotherly love. In his tripartite division, love can be brotherly (loving all in equal measure), motherly (loving the helpless), or erotic (exclusively loving only one other). Of the three, brotherly love is "the most fundamental kind of love," for "if I love my brother, I love all my brothers; if I love my child, I love all my children; no, beyond that, I love all children, all that are in need of my help." Once again, Fromm moves from the particular to the more universal case, as his radical humanism demands. Loving is a character trait as an "attitude toward everybody," a list that includes family and friends, but also professional and business associates.[188] Yet in contrast to both motherly and brotherly love, erotic love is "the craving for complete fusion, for union with one other person. It is by its very nature exclusive and not universal; it is also perhaps the most deceptive form of love there is." Its deception lies in my belief that I can *only* love one person, or that I cannot expand erotic love to include all others: "If I truly love one person I love all persons, I love the world, I love life. If I can say to somebody else, 'I love you,' I must be able to say, 'I love in you everybody, I love through you the world, I love in you also myself.'"[189] As I read these sentences, Fromm's "you" tends to evaporate among the many other objects of love. The expression, "I love you" is a performative utterance in which I am really loving myself, the world, everybody. Although erotic love is exclusive, "it loves in the other person all of mankind, all that is alive," and in this vital sense is equivalent to brotherly love.[190] The essential particularity of erotic love, in the end, vanishes before Fromm's more universal commitments. Fromm recoils from an erotic love that is singular and exclusive, replacing it for the more universal dimensions of passion.

But Fromm cannot entirely dismiss the peculiar singularity of erotic love, as his own biography attests. When he does admit to the unique attractions of individual selves, his prose becomes strangely dispassionate:

> Inasmuch as we are all one, we can love everybody in the same way in the sense of brotherly love. But inasmuch as we are all also different, erotic love requires certain specific, highly individual elements which exist between some people but not between all.[191]

When persons fall in love, I doubt they do so over "highly individual elements," for those elements are simply not charged enough to account for erotic love. Fromm is stuck, in my view, between his claim to "love everybody" and his experiential knowledge that not all loves are equal. But a love with singular preferences holds too tightly to primary ties. The mature person must abandon those ties, and the erotic love associated with them, for more universal, brotherly ones. Yet even Fromm recognizes the power of primary ties to transform brothers into erotic lovers. Fromm's biography is revealing in this case, for I doubt he could have read the Isaac story in the way that he did if, in fact, Fromm had fathered children of his own: he simply could not have equated Abraham's love for his own child with the love of others. The force of the story lies in Abraham's devotion to *this* child (even if, as some midrashim suggest, Abraham loves Ishmael equally). If love is, in part, the capacity to emerge from narcissism "and from the incestuous fixation to mother and clan,"[192] then the art of loving is also a commitment to the ties that bind. It is a commitment, in other words, to Fromm's account of erotic love. And if I have read him correctly in his discussion of love, Fromm understands this too. The sense of primary commitments is more than an acceptance of physical death, age, and illness. It borders on that sense of idolatry in which one succumbs to an erotic power beyond the self. Perhaps Fromm would prefer to call this humility rather than idolatry, but in both cases the self recognizes an erotic power that limits its own. Human freedom is bound by primary ties, and Fromm's account of erotic love attests to that fact.

CONCLUSION

In *You Shall Be as Gods,* Fromm describes the goal of radical humanism "to be that of complete independence, and this implies penetrating through fictions and illusions to a full awareness of reality." The question posed in this chapter has been whether a "full awareness of reality" requires "complete independence." A deep ambivalence lurks within the works of Edward Bernays, Joshua Loth Liebman, and Erich Fromm, especially in the ways they establish ties to what I have called the material past. That past is one that carries material influences into the present, such that the persons we love, the things we buy and consume, and the homes we build all are rooted in what Fromm has called "primary ties." Even as Bernays, Liebman, and Fromm all deny the authority of the past to control human flourishing in the present, that past continues to haunt and enliven their work.

Recall Fromm's claim from *You Shall Be as Gods,* in which he seeks a radical freedom and independence from primary ties. With all that he has written on the subject, this claim is hardly surprising. But it is rather startling that Fromm admits to those very ties as he introduces his book:

> Although I am not a specialist in the field of biblical scholarship, this book is the fruit of many years of reflection, as I have been studying the Old Testament and the Talmud since I was a child. Nevertheless, I would not have dared to publish these comments on Scripture were it not for the fact that I received my fundamental orientation concerning the Hebrew Bible and the later Jewish tradition from teachers who were great rabbinical scholars. . . . Not being a practicing or a "believing" Jew, I am, of course, in a very different position from theirs, and least of all would I dare to make them responsible for the views expressed in this book. Yet my views have grown out of their teaching, and it is my conviction that at no point has the continuity between their teaching and my own views been interrupted.[193]

Fromm's dilemmas are not his alone, although he seems most burdened by them. He seeks unique vision (he alone is responsible for views developed through "many years of reflection") together with continuity with a past. Fromm claims an individual freedom, but one still moored to past authority. This tension comes to the fore in his tortured description of a text: is it the Old Testament, Scripture, or Hebrew Bible that claims Fromm's attention? He employs all three terms, and each carry weighted meanings and associated inheritance with them. What is that text to Fromm? What kind of authority is it? How does an Old Testament, Scripture, or Hebrew Bible identify Fromm as a free, liberated self?

The answers to these questions would reveal how material pasts inform personal identity. But Fromm rejects obedience to past authority as a form of enslavement and idolatry. Yet clearly he is drawn to his ancestors, and yearns for continuity, perhaps even acceptance, from a heritage that has grown distant from his own radical humanism. He recognizes that his text is no longer the Hebrew Bible of his forbears. This troubles him, for as the text slowly transforms from the foreign "Old Testament" to the ambiguous work of "Scripture," and finally to the sacred "Hebrew Bible" and "Jewish tradition," Fromm seeks the authority vested in his Jewish heritage. But he recovers his inheritance not from a foundational text, but from universal "teaching," such that the message, rather than the book, confers acceptance and continuity. Though not a "believing" Jew, his views and "their teaching" maintain an uninterrupted contact to secure Jewish continuity. So long as that foundational text supports a humanist vision to combat idolatry and external authority, Fromm can appeal to it as Bible, Scripture, or Testament. The universal thrust is still very much evident here in Fromm's agonizing prose: call it what you like, but accept its message of human freedom and progress. One can adopt the text as sacred without being enslaved to it.

Even more, Fromm argues that his generation is uniquely positioned to understand the true meaning of ancient texts:

> If it is possible to discover the seeds of radical humanism in the older sources of the Bible, it is only because we know the radical humanism of Amos, of Socrates, of the Renaissance humanists, of the Enlightenment, of Kant, Herder, Lessing, Goethe, Marx, Schweitzer. The seed becomes clearly recognizable only if one knows the flower; the earlier phase is often to be interpreted by the later phase, even though, genetically, the earlier phase precedes the later.[194]

Fromm has reversed the inheritance, such that his generation recognizes, in ways that his predecessors could not, the underlying meaning of an earlier text. Fromm now owns his past, and it becomes *his* heritage, much like Bloom's strong poet who denies past influence by rewriting it.[195] Yet by subjugating the past to such radical revision, the poet also reveals its influence upon him. And so it is with Fromm: even as he overcomes inheritance by privileging the flower over the seed, he nonetheless craves the authority of the Bible, and the great rabbinical scholars of his youth. These ancestors sanction his radical humanism. The roots of primary ties are strong indeed.

This ambivalent relation to the past, in which Fromm both renounces and craves its authority, burdens Bernays and Liebman as well. Bernays sought to liberate individuals from mass conformity to inherited desires. He appropriated insights from psychology to encourage persons to leave the herd, and discover within themselves the passion to identify new objects of consumption. I take seriously, as Bernays did, the social progressivism of his public relations counsel, and its work to remake individuals out of the herd. Yet even as Bernays cherished the public utility of his PR counsel, that counsel could so easily manipulate individual desires to serve business needs and trends. This only reinforced the power of the herd to oppress individual freedoms. Bernays stood on both sides of this complex dynamic, drawn as he was to self-liberation and manipulated acceptance. Perhaps even more than Fromm, Bernays recognized the human desire to both renounce and crave authority.

Liebman, too, confronted this dilemma in his vision of religious and psychological maturity. The psychic scars from childhood need not influence self-development; indeed, early traumatic experiences could be wiped clean of their power. Fulton Sheen understood this better than most, for he recognized how Liebman denied the inheritance and power of sin to inform identity. The past had no claim on the future, Liebman had argued, and so America could be remade as a Jewish home worthy of the messianic times. To adopt Fromm's imagery, America would blossom as a healthy, open flower out of Jewish prophetic seeds. But as it was for Fromm, so too for Liebman: those seeds were tied to Jewish roots. He could not imagine an American future divorced from a Jewish prophetic past, and he leaned on that past to liberate the self from slavery and tyranny. Authority, for Bernays, Fromm, and Liebman, resides in a past that provokes an anxiety of influence.

This past is a material one when it informs the various contemporary enactments of identity. The meaning of those performances, and the kind of self created by them, distinguishes Bernays's individual consumer, Liebman's mature and successful adult, and Fromm's liberated self. Those selves have real goods to win in America: for the consumer, the satisfaction of inner longings through appropriated objects; for the adult, the achievement of peace of mind through mature growth; and for the humanist, the liberation of the self through the denial of idolatrous objects and authority. But a material past still informs these claims to personal satisfaction, achievement, and liberation. It continually threatens, even as it enables, various modes of human flourishing. Jews were certainly not the only ones to confront the material past in America. But that they did so, I believe, was inevitable. As Bernays, Liebman, and Fromm attest, the more that persons deny past influence, the greater the inherited burden is upon them. This was, of course, Freud's more despairing vision of the human condition. American Jews attempted to slay that father too, and transform him into a more progressive optimist suited to the postwar triumphalism. But if past inheritance, as both burden and blessing, is as inescapable as I think it is, then it will always be part of material identity in America for Jews, and not only them. Identity is a tense brokering of resistance and accommodation to an inherited past in all its many forms. This is what I take to be one of Freud's great insights. It is also what Bernays, Liebman, and Fromm worked so hard to deny. But in and through that labor, they protested too much. Their work testifies to the power of the material past to identify selves as scarred by inheritance.

THREE

Material Place: Joseph Soloveitchik and the Urban Holy

In the previous two chapters, I located material Jewish identity in America within two broad thematic rubrics: the material self and the material past. Though each touches upon specific concerns and tensions for Jews in America, both reveal how material culture lies at the heart of Jewish thought. For Kaplan, it arises in the journal as material archive—a claim to permanent status and acceptance within his new American home. For Bernays, Liebman, and Fromm, the material weight of the past informed their visions of American progress, despite their eagerness to deny that inheritance. Both *self* and *past* are material because physical things, experiences, and persons constitute the meaning of American Jewish identity and heritage. Even more, Kaplan, Bernays, Liebman, and Fromm all reflect about the nature of things, and their Jewish thought is material to the core. In this chapter, I will focus on how this kind of material thinking is situated within a physical place, and constitutes a thinking about place. Urban space is material in precisely the two ways outlined here: it is a physical space that informs Jewish identity, and Jewish thinking about it shapes the very nature of that place. This dynamic interplay between thought located in place, and thought materially inflected by that place, emerges most powerfully in the work of the great American Jewish thinker, Joseph Soloveitchik.

To recognize the physical contours of Soloveitchik's Jewish thought, imagine the American middle-class Victorian home as a segregated, domestic space. The more open, public homes of colonial America were gradually giving way to multiple-room lodgings in which each space held its own specialized purpose and use. Cultural critics even persuaded the less wealthy to divide their interior spaces into simple but well-defined living quarters, bedrooms, and cooking areas. As one ascended to economic prosperity, the home took on more complicated shapes: the living room divided into a formal parlor for guests and an informal sitting area for family.[1] The hall leading into the sitting areas contained, among other things, a hallstand with coat and hat racks, a mirror, and for guests who wished to leave impressions after their departure, a card receiver. The hallstand communicated to guests not only who resided at home, but also revealed the social status, cultural relations, and the "mood" of the household.[2] These nineteenth-century architectural revolutions secured privacy as a necessary, specialized area for home life, one that mirrored the industrial specialization of trades in the public sphere. The change in architecture conditioned new social arrangements, as children were sequestered from adults, and servants from family members. For the child who mistakenly found herself in father's study, the specialized room was "alien territory."[3]

The orderly boundary markings and crossings that made up this Victorian household, in both physical shape and social practice, contrasted with the perceived chaos of the city. Where the home reflected clear markings of status, identity, and leisure, the city appeared all too mercurial, strange, and dangerous. Indeed, Americans often thought of their home as a private refuge from the vulgarity and seething turmoil of the American urban landscape.[4] Leisure time would occupy orderly space, and the city would retain, at least within this private sphere, its foreignness at a distance.

Joseph Soloveitchik's modern Orthodox theology reproduces this Victorian sensibility in navigating Jewish halakhic life in the city. Soloveitchik (1903–93) did more than appropriate dominant images of urban life as chaotic, foreign, and untamed. His vision of the wild and primitive city also depicted, and so constituted, urban space as a site of religious transformation, where the dirty, contaminated, and profane could become clean, pure, and sacred. These fantasies of the city landscape converge into what religious historian Robert Orsi calls the "urban holy": those images of "urban desolation, primitivism, alienation, depravity,"[5] coupled with salvific presence and spiritual renewal. Even as this urban imaginary glosses over the inner dynamics and tensions of city life, it still provides a powerful trope of religious conversion. The cityscape as urban holy locates where "God is encountered with special intimacy,"[6] for amid the suffering and ruins one can lay down paths to holiness. Soloveitchik's theory of Jewish law and practice (*halakhah*) is rooted in this urban imaginary: the committed Jew turns ruptured paths into more directed avenues of holiness. Halakhic man walks the urban streets in order to transform them into sacred byways. Like those earlier Victorian Americans who erected secure houses to ward off urban chaos, Soloveitchik fashioned a theology of *halakhah* to transform chaos into structured reality, and thereby keep alien forces at bay. His was a thought located in place, and one that organized and created that place into an urban holy.

Soloveitchik built his halakhic house *in* the city, and so he could not comfortably insulate the Victorian private home from public view. *Halakhah* would have to *transform* the city, and mold it into a conducive space for Jewish Orthodox practice. This dual sense of the depraved, primitive city, and its native capacity to be transfigured into a sacred space, reveals the powerful effect of the urban holy in Soloveitchik's Jewish thought. Like the sequestered and functional rooms of the Victorian home, the city could be mapped and controlled by the creative *Halakhic Man*. Halakhic man would define the pathways to holiness and produce a religious cartography within which American Orthodox Jews could walk securely and without fear. If Joshua Liebman had mapped the psyche of the soul to liberate the self, then Soloveitchik would invert that map to produce urban roads to holiness. There would be neither wrong turns, nor daughters turning up in their father's den: Soloveitchik would provide order where there was once chaos, impose boundaries upon unlimited terrain, and define markers of identity among the diversity of city dwellings. Like God in the Genesis account, halakhic man would create order through boundary maintenance. As a guide for the Orthodox Jew in the city, Soloveitchik's halakhic thought channeled anxious perplexity into orderly and recognizable practice.

Soloveitchik's theory of *halakhah* enables a particular kind of Jewish urban experience, and reveals how physical space both informs and is created by Jewish practice and identity. In Barbara Kirshenblatt-Gimblett's important article, "The Future of Folklore Studies in America: The Urban Frontier," she argues for new perceptions of urban practices that evoke distinctive identities and social structures. In search of a "sense of the city" that is fashioned rather than discovered, she asks: "How do people use expressive behavior to personalize and humanize the urban environment?"[7] I want to pose similar questions to Soloveitchik's works. How does *halakhah* as expressive behavior Judaize the urban landscape, such that Jewish walking transforms city strolls into religious practice? Along that walk in the city, how does urban space enable particular modes of Jewish behavior? To explore these questions in depth, I will turn to several of Soloveitchik's works, especially his magisterial *Halakhic Man* (1944), a text that challenges modern Jews who prefer his more existential work, *The Lonely Man of Faith* (1965). Jewish thinkers have struggled mightily to unite these disparate works, and I too will suggest how they can be read together—for *The Lonely Man of Faith* reproduces many of the urban concerns first articulated in *Halakhic Man*. I also want to employ what is, to my mind, Soloveitchik's most beautiful piece on suffering, "Kol Dodi Dofek" ("It is the Voice of My Beloved that Knocketh," 1956) as yet another textual witness to the urban holy. Together with the article "Confrontation" (1964) on Jewish–Christian dialogue, and *The Halakhic Mind* (published in 1986), Soloveitchik offers testimony to the impact of urban landscapes on Jewish thought. Geography grounds material identity, providing physical textures and locations for Jewish practice. Soloveitchik traversed the urban frontier through the markings of *halakhah*, and in remapping the city, he turned the foreign into a welcoming space for Jewish expressive behavior. That space, as the imagined urban holy, materially conditions Jewish religious observance.

When East European Jews came to America, they overwhelmingly settled in cities. The populations of U.S. cities surged after the civil war, with New York City alone rising from 515,500 in 1850, to more than three million in 1900. That number then increased with the enormous rise of immigrants to America between 1880 and 1920, with Jews accounting for more than 2 million of some 20 million settlers. And those immigrants dominated the urban landscape: in 1890, 62 percent of foreign-born Americans lived in cities, and in 1910, still 41 percent of those living in urban America were foreign-born.[8] But the rise in urban growth also came from those seeking industrial work and a better future. Between

1910, when 89 percent of African Americans still lived in the south, and 1940, more than 1.5 million blacks traveled to northern and mid-western cities to settle, and 5 million more arrived between 1940 and 1970.[9] Hence, when Jews encountered America, a majority viewed it through urban frontiers, with its ethnic mix, racial "in-betweenness," and cultural vibrancy.[10] America had become an "urban nation" by 1920, and even the suburban outflow of the 1950s failed to halt the founding visions fashioned in the city. The *goldeneh medinah,* an image of America treasured by many immigrant Jews, really evoked the "golden land" of cityscapes.

Americans have always been fascinated with their cities. As that "City on the Hill," America for the Puritans became a figure of new hope that could certainly remain untainted by European decadence. Even Ralph Waldo Emerson, no supporter of the city, recognized the social benefits of urban centers for aesthetic and intellectual promise.[11] Images of the city in twentieth-century America were dynamically related to patterns of immigration. As the city became predominantly immigrant enclaves of ethnic communities, it challenged long-held assumptions about American identity. Even more, as the migration of African Americans to the city joined that immigrant mix, visions of the city were inextricably tied to race and class stereotypes. America as an urban nation was not the same America of its founders. Much of Jewish thought reflects this urban sensibility, where images of America were no longer assumed but challenged, where ethnic identity was imposed as much as lived. What would America mean to those shaped by city life, and for those who envisioned religious practice within the city?

For many nineteenth- and twentieth-century Protestant elites, the city represented all that was foreign to America. It diverged in almost every way from those "fundamental categories of American reality—whiteness, heterosexuality, domestic virtue, feminine purity, middle-class respectability,"[12] and instead was figured as dark, unconstrained, shameless, vile, poor, and rootless. It would have to be tamed, ordered, and inhibited—the city must be "saved," as much of the religious literature noted. Young Protestant evangelicals and Catholic missionaries turned to the city as new territory for spiritual renewal—a place sunk so low as to require divine guidance and rebirth. They returned in great numbers to the city, reversing the trend of their parents who had found security in the suburbs. Robert Orsi relates the story of Brother Giles, a Franciscan friar who "reclaimed abandoned buildings, cleared ground, and planted gardens." Here, amid broken-down rubble and dilapidated buildings, Brother Giles claimed, "This is where I will find God." He had plans to build a park next to the friary that visually recalled the sacred narrative of the urban holy: "New Christians would begin their spiritual journeys amid the debris of the old world/lost Eden/the South Bronx in disrepair, and then move through the waters of rebirth to the garden— and a revitalized South Bronx—beyond."[13] This is the language of the urban holy: a depraved place transformed into a beautiful, regenerated garden. Brother Giles finds God in the lost Eden, for Giles seeks a redeemer to resurrect a broken city. It is a journey through chaotic depths into clean waters. The city offered "signs of hope and transcendence amid the devastation,"[14] for one could rise higher after sinking so much lower. The very allure of paradise lost energized the cityscapes with spiritual force for Brother Giles, and, as we shall see, for Soloveitchik as well.

Orsi charts the course of many religious types who came to the city to purify themselves and those disfigured by urban depravity. This vision of the perfected, resurrected city became public spectacle at the 1893 World's Columbian Exposition in Chicago. The show included the "White City" as a model for urban planning and a vision of the American city. But with its formal collections of buildings, and its "elegance, order and restraint," the exhibition imagined an "ordered urbanism" utterly divorced from the reality of American urban experience. According to Orsi, the White City "seemed to be the alternative Americans had long sought to the threatening messiness of the immigrant city."[15] Cultural fears of the foreign, dark-skinned, and alien city were subsumed under the controlling brilliance and beauty of the White City.[16] New streets and highways physically imposed an ordered beauty that created geometric grids to efficiently navigate through the city. The foreign other could be left alone in its urban messiness, invisible to the patterned mappings of ordered urbanism.

These images and fears of the city—as the source of desire, the primitive, and the unrestrained that required the ordered, patterned mapping of efficient navigation—influenced Soloveitchik's view of his new homeland. As he was an immigrant to the American city, his life and work reflect the impact of urban religion and the ways in which landscape informs material identity. He, too, sought to control the perceived excesses of urban culture, and he offered "religious cartographies"[17] to better enable Jews to find their way in America. Soloveitchik came to the United States in 1932 after studying for his doctorate in Berlin for six years. His dissertation focused on the Jewish neo-Kantian Hermann Cohen—a topic he pursued after abandoning his earlier desire to write on Maimonides and Plato. Upon arrival in Boston, he became the chief rabbi there, and so followed his father and grandfathers before him as the halakhic authority of traditional Jewish practice. That pedigree of great Lithuanian talmudic rabbis, so focused on legal practice and textual study, shaped Soloveitchik's loyalties. He is often read as a staunch defender of the *mitnagdim* who, like the Gaon of Vilna and Hayyim of Volozhin in earlier centuries, defended Lithuanian rabbinic legal and textual traditions before the charismatic, populist, and mystical leaders of Hasidism.[18]

Upon reading his *Halakhic Man* (1944), one easily recognizes Soloveitchik's defense of the scholarly student of law so entrenched within the Lithuanian tradition. He describes halakhic man as an ideal type who combines features of "cognitive man" and "*homo religiosus,*" but is nonetheless a "singular, even strange" creature. Like cognitive man, the halakhic type searches for clarity and precision; he creates laws and establishes fixed principles of action and judgment. His cognitive approach aligns him with science and the logic of mathematics. But like *homo religiosus,* halakhic man "is devoted to God and of a world view saturated with the radiance of the Divine Presence."[19] Halakhic man embodies these "two opposing selves," but he is not, Soloveitchik insists, "some illegitimate, unstable hybrid." He must actively engage these conflicts to achieve a higher unity:

> On the contrary, out of the contradictions and antinomies there emerges a radiant, holy personality whose soul has been purified in the furnace of struggle and opposition and redeemed in the fires of the torments of spiritual disharmony to a degree unmatched by the universal *homo religiosus.*[20]

Like the many Christian evangelists and Catholic leaders who emerged from the dangers and chaos of city life to redeem both themselves and those who remained in the city, so too does halakhic man lower himself into "the furnace of struggle" and the "fires of the torment of spiritual dis-harmony" to rise up, victorious, cleansed, and more holy for the struggle. This, too, is the language and vision of the urban holy. The "antinomies" serve a higher purpose, as the holy arises out of despair and turmoil. The more fractious the elements, the stronger the forged unity.

It is within the ravages of the city that "God is encountered," and this is the place where one transforms "ruins into the ground of holi-ness." Soloveitchik describes this movement in much the same way as the monks and nuns of the South Bronx who recognize "signs of hope and transcendence amid the devastation."[21] In his powerful article on the Holocaust and suffering, "Kol Dodi Dofek" (1956), Soloveitchik reiterates this urban motif of purified dross:

> Afflictions come to elevate a person, to purify and sanctify his spirit, to cleanse and purge it of the dross of superficiality and vulgarity, to refine his soul and to broaden his horizons. In a word, the function of suffering is to mend that which is flawed in an individual's personality. . . . From out of its [the world's] midst the sufferer must arise ennobled and refined, clean and pure.[22]

This theology of suffering draws its psychological power from the urban holy. Afflictions purify and even transfigure the self. A redeemed soul is a refined one, like the precious metals forged through the ancient prac-tice of alchemy. The urban imaginary is a lost soul awaiting redemption through patient care and transformative struggle. It is here in the city that halakhic man discovers his religious calling, and transforms that city into the urban holy. He becomes that much stronger and more whole by passing through the urban tests and torments. The city is not to be shunned or cordoned off; it is, rather, to be transformed, reshaped, and cleansed. If, as the talmudic text Avot 5:23 states, "in accordance with the suffering is the reward," then, as Soloveitchik adds, "in accordance with the split the union!"[23] In this way, Soloveitchik is less the harsh defender of Lithuanian legal practice than a creative unifier of legal and experiential Jewish traditions. He bridges the expressive dimensions of Hasidic Jewry with the halakhic centrality of his Lithuanian forebears. Conflict and suffering provide opportunities for an elevated unity within which halakhic man accesses new spiritual dimensions. He recreates the city landscape into the urban holy.

Positioning Soloveitchik's thought within material culture and urban terrain, as I do, uncovers new trajectories of his Jewish thought. It moves his philosophy away from theological or ideological concerns, and instead situates it within an urban culture. To recognize the implications of this material move, note how David Singer and Moshe Sokol understand *Halakhic Man*. In their influential article on Soloveitchik's "conflicted personality" between the Litvak rationalism of *Halakhic Man* and the Hasidic emotionalism of *Lonely Man of Faith,* Singer and Sokol discover the seeds of that split in *Halakhic Man,* but find it emerging more fully in *Lonely Man of Faith.* Though Soloveitchik raises the issue of a conflicted religious type in the first book, he diffuses the inner tensions throughout the main body of the work, and does not fully develop them until the latter one.[24] Singer and Sokol recognize that halakhic man emerges purer for his struggle in the "fires of spiritual conflict." But this "positive value" that enables "religious growth" still does not fully develop the "conflicted nature of halakhic man."[25] Soloveitchik represses this inner conflict, so Singer and Sokol claim, until some twenty years later with his *Lonely Man of Faith,* where he exposes it once again.[26] Soloveitchik appears torn between the rational, practical thinking of halakhic man, and the anxious, seeking dynamics of existential struggle—the concern of *Lonely Man of Faith.* The expressive union achieved through the urban holy, in which halakhic man "emerges a radiant, holy personality whose soul has been purified in the furnace of struggle and opposition," rarely surfaces in Singer and Sokol's reading of Soloveitchik.

The conflict in *Lonely Man of Faith* is not as radical as Singer and Sokol claim it to be, and it is not even present in *Halakhic Man.* Singer and Sokol misunderstand how the spiritual opportunities for glory (the urban holy) underlie the struggles of city life. The conflict lies less *within* halakhic man than *between* him and the religious type (*homo religiosus*) who seeks escape from this world into some other supernal realm. To be sure, halakhic man shares much with *homo religiosus* who "thirsts for the living God." But with regard to the city, "they travel in opposite directions":

> *Homo religiosus,* dissatisfied, disappointed, and unhappy, craves to rise up from the vale of tears, from concrete reality, and aspires to climb to

the mountain of the Lord. He attempts to extricate himself from the narrow straits of empirical existence and emerge into the wide spaces of a pure and pristine transcendental existence. Halakhic man, on the contrary, longs to bring transcendence down into this valley of the shadow of death—i.e., into our world—and transform it into a land of the living.[27]

There are no wide spaces in the city for *homo religiosus* to walk. Rather than transform the "narrow straights" into purer pathways, he recoils in horror to seek more pristine existence.[28] This his Victorian ancestors did before him, building shelters to keep the "vale of tears" where they belonged: out of the house and in the city. It is also what Abraham Joshua Heschel finds so disturbing about "islands" of religious practice where politics have no force, as I discuss in the following chapter. But halakhic man lives in "concrete reality," in "our world," and traverses the city in order to transform death into life. He visualizes the city as an urban holy: as the "shadow of death" in need of religious transformation. *Homo religiosus* transcends as halakhic man descends into the fiery furnace. This is so because the urban holy still retains its allure for halakhic man. The city entices him as it becomes an imagined space of transfigurative potential. It awaits the straightened paths of halakhic practice; the city is halakhic man's clay, and he molds it into a recognizable "land of the living." The city takes shape so that he can practice the rules and patterns of halakhic discourse. For Soloveitchik, spiritual torment gives way to the promise of redemption—for both the individual and the concrete reality surrounding him.

Urban torments surround halakhic man as they persistently challenge his faith in reason, logic, and law. He must navigate a straight and narrow path through the dangers of urban exposures and desires, and not merely renounce the otherworldly yearnings of *homo religiosus*. For if *homo religiosus* seeks to escape to a more distant, solitary world, halakhic man firmly roots himself in the "real world," in the life of community and practice, in order to bring that ideal law of *halakhah* to earth. Like Moses, he approaches reality from Sinai, with Torah in hand. And like cognitive man, he is "well furnished with rules, judgments, and fundamental principles."[29] With his Torah as guide, halakhic man is armed and strengthened to face the uncertainties of urban life:

When he approaches the world, he is armed with his weapons—i.e., his laws—and the consciousness of lawfulness and order that is implanted within him serves to ward off the fear that springs upon him. Halakhic man does not enter a strange, alien, mysterious world, but a world with which he is already familiar through the a priori which he carries within his consciousness. He enters into the real world via the ideal creation which in the end will be actualized. . . . Why, then, should he be afraid? Such concepts as nothingness and naught, chaos and the void, darkness and the abyss are wholly foreign to him.[30]

If one were to replace "world" with "the city," for indeed the world *was* the city for most American Jews, this sense of urban warfare would be hard to escape. Even Soloveitchik has the city streets in mind when he continues to describe the entrenched positioning of halakhic man: "He is unfamiliar with the dark back streets of defilement, nor does he ever go astray in the blind alleys and narrow pathways of the world's emptiness and chaos." The world is the city for Soloveitchik, as it is for his Jewish community in Boston. Fortified with Torah from Sinai, Jews navigate the city with a religious map that wards off darkness and the abyss. In his Hebrew essay, *u-Vikashtem mi-Sham* ("But If You Search from There"), Soloveitchik explores how Jewish law "sequesters mystery" and "plans a new world."[31] With proper measurements, boundaries, and pathways, halakhic man classifies and orders, creating for himself a White City within the strange and alien.

But halakhic man does more than segregate the profane from the sacred, as the White City had set out to do. Instead, he turns "blind alleys" into beautiful pathways of order. Soloveitchik compares this halakhic creativity to God's fashioning the world in Genesis, where "chaos and the void" become recognizable and hospitable space and time. Just as God distinguishes and carves out boundaries, so too does halakhic man transform the abyss into marked borders. He does not abandon the city for more orderly terrain, as many middle-class Jews did in the 1950s. Rather, he converts the city into "familiar" halakhic spaces. Aviezer Ravitzky notes this parallel between creation and halakhic activity, and argues persuasively that, like creation, *halakhah* "implies construction and formation by means of quantification and definition, distinction and separation. In sum, creation is a 'halakhic' occurrence, while halakhic activity is a 'creative' occurrence."[32] The city is truly "chaos and the void," as the world once had been. But unlike *homo religiosus* who seeks escape through transcendence, or the Victorian types who retreat to physical shelters, halakhic man carves out meaning from within the abyss, and marks out domains of the sacred amid the ruins. He turns mystery into awareness, and fear into familiar acceptance. The urban holy becomes so through the creative activity of halakhic practice.

More than a few commentators have recognized how geometric models govern Soloveitchik's theory of halakhic activity.[33] Soloveitchik himself invites this comparison, for he often likens halakhic creativity to scientific and mathematical thinking. David Hartman has usefully described the "normative framework" through which halakhic man perceives reality. Like the scientist–mathematician who views nature through "conceptual constructs, so too does halakhic man perceive reality through the mediating framework of halakhic norms."[34] The incisive point here is that perceptions of reality transform reality itself. When halakhic man witnesses a sunrise or sunset, he dwells neither on its beauty nor its radiance, but instead subsumes the aesthetic within legal categories. Dawn and sunrise "obligate him to fulfill those commandments that are performed during the day," and so too sunset requires fixed performances for the night. When coming upon a majestic mountain, halakhic man is less overwhelmed by its grandeur and more concerned to utilize "the measurements which determine a private domain."[35] As Lawrence Kaplan rightly argues, "the natural-sense world is only of interest to the halakhist insofar as it is possible to apply halakhic categories to it."[36] The world really looks different to halakhic man, or better, he makes it look different: "Every contact with nature that might inspire aesthetic enthusiasm is channeled through the functional halakhic question: What mitzvot, what new obligations does this phenomenon awaken?"[37] The world looks less strange or chaotic, and so becomes an experiential opportunity to determine "fixed laws and principles" of halakhic observance. Halakhic man does not approach the world with a clean slate, but with normative precepts to apply and determine. Kaplan states the issue nicely, for halakhic norms create "modes of perceiving and organizing space," and are "a prism through which one sees, perceives the real world."[38] Halakhic man builds a world that is recognizable and orderly—one that mirrors the forming acts of God's creation and the laws from Sinai. This "a priori yardstick," in the Kantian language that Soloveitchik employs throughout his text, determines the very possibility of perception. The sun or mountain would fail to register as such without these halakhic perceptual guides. Halakhic man would be lost in the city without these norms in view; yet with them, he transforms chaotic structures into organized space—the very movement and structure of the urban holy.

To minimize urban terror, Soloveitchik arms halakhic man with weapons to fight anomy and suburban flight. He knows that, despite all of halakhic man's creative endeavors, the world stubbornly resists order and limits. Halakhic man is more ideal type than practicing Jew, and so too the halakhic framework is more unified theory than practical guide. Indeed, Soloveitchik appears to take flight himself, much like the maligned *homo religiosus*. The concept of the Day of Atonement, or the night of Passover, are "ideal constructions" revealed to Moses on Sinai. They can never be fully enacted in a world bereft of the Temple service. But halakhic man "sees" those days as if he were once again with God and Moses at Sinai, and "'forgets' temporarily" that he lives in a time "devoid of all that holiness and glory."[39] Elliot Dorff has criticized this view of Jewish law as a "bad mistake," in part because it "exists in a transcendent world unaffected by empirical realities." Jewish law exists within human history, so argues Dorff, and "any approach which ignores that is to that extent simply false."[40] Hartman, in his defense of Soloveitchik, suggests that he never intended to portray an "empirically accurate" account of *halakhah* or those who live by it. Instead, Soloveitchik develops "a phenomenology of what he sees as an ideal halakhic type."[41] In this view, Soloveitchik desires only intelligibility, and not a practical description of halakhic observance. It is the kind of religiosity associated with the Brisker–Lithuanian tradition of Soloveitchik's father and grandfather.

But neither Hartman nor Dorff seems to recognize that the terrors of this world inform how halakhic man constructs ideal legal codes. Soloveitchik's legal reasoning is neither an ideal phenomenology unexposed to material culture, nor an esoteric theory without practical effect. Worldly terrors really do influence creative legal discussions. We can see this in Soloveitchik's account of Maimonides, the great Jewish medieval philosopher, and his portrayal of the Passover seder. Soloveitchik's account appears initially to support Hartman and Dorff's claim that his ideal types (Hartman) have little practical import (Dorff). But a more careful reading suggests how terrors of this world inform legal reasoning. Maimonides, as Soloveitchik claims, "pays no attention to the cruel and bitter present" in his description of the Passover night. He appears as the ideal halakhic man, who constructs reality through the prism of divine laws. Maimonides transposes Sinai to his present world as a timeless, almost mythic presence. But Soloveitchik qualifies this transcendent vision:

> However, from time to time he bestirs himself from his ideal dream and romantic vision and finds himself confronted with an exile filled with nightmares and terrors, with physical oppression and spiritual degeneration, and he states: "In the present time he does not say, 'tonight it is all roasted,' for we no longer have any paschal offering, etc." . . . In other words, the present time is only a historical anomaly in the ongoing process of the actualization of the ideal Halakhah in the real world, and there is no need to elaborate about a period which is but a temporary aberration that has seized hold of our historical existence.[42]

Despite the "nightmares and terrors," Hartman is right to say that *halakhah* is normative and guides the perception of reality. Only through it can halakhic man distinguish an aberration from an ideal type. And Dorff exposes just how peripheral "historical existence" seems to be in Soloveitchik's reading. It is as if halakhic man has already witnessed a sunset, or confronted a mountain, before he really does so. He has already perceived them, as it were, in a priori time and space—in that mythic realm of Sinai. Encounters with historical events are merely opportunities to apply these a priori concepts. Nothing can truly disturb the sense of rightness that dominates the halakhic framework. Aberrations are temporary anomalies that eventually succumb to the force of halakhic determinism.

But this serene vision can last only so long. The "nightmares and terrors" still persist, and this Soloveitchik cannot ignore as easily as Dorff suggests. It is hard to escape the notion that, in writing about Maimonides' time, Soloveitchik also reflects upon his own. Not only Maimonides, but Soloveitchik, too, confronts "an exile filled with nightmares and terrors, with physical oppression and spiritual degeneration." And though he struggles mightily to curb those terrors, Soloveitchik fears such "concepts as nothingness and naught, chaos and the void." The abyss is certainly not foreign to him, despite his labored protests.

True, halakhic man "does not despair," nor does he "kick against his lot and fate."[43] But the nightmare of chaos, even if a historical anomaly, can still turn back the borders and boundaries that halakhic man has created with such care and accuracy. This, too, is the point of creation: to keep evil at bay so that it will no longer overwhelm the sacred order. God does not eliminate chaos, as Jon Levenson has argued, but rather "confines" it, and must continue to do so to protect human life from "the onslaughts of chaos and anarchy."[44]

Soloveitchik reads the beginning of Genesis as a divine act of separation, in which God "engraved and carved out the world." Much like halakhic man in the city, God "separated the complete, perfect existence from the forces of negation, confusion, and turmoil and set up cosmic boundaries, eternal laws to keep them apart."[45] But those forces of dissolution remain, and continually threaten "to plunge the earth back into chaos and the void." Their foreboding presence endangers the established boundaries of an ordered and coherent life. This is a cosmic battle, one that spills over into the streets:

> This relative "nothingness" is plotting evil, the deep [hatahum] is devising iniquity, and the chaos and void [ve-hatovu u-havohu] lie in wait in the dark alleyways of reality and seek to undermine the absolute being, to profane the lustrous image of creation.[46]

Beyond the boundaries of creation and the halakhic city lie the profane, dark, and chaotic world of nothingness. Only the law "holds them back and bars the path before them."[47] Halakhic man must act like his creator, and determine lawful boundaries that prevent ruptures, breaches and overflows from the dark alleyways. One can transform chaos into order, but only partially. For the terror that remains beyond, structures of containment limit fear and anomy.

To continue God's role as covenant partner, halakhic man must fashion sacred space from within the city. But like God, his mastery is fragile, for the Leviathan of creation could overwhelm the "cosmic dikes,"[48] and the "dark back streets of defilement" could overshadow the light of halakhic practice. My point is that Soloveitchik *must* create an ideal halakhic type to better confine these darker visions, and, like God, must continually reassert halakhic authority to keep the nightmares at bay. It is not, as Dorff claims, that Soloveitchik is stubbornly "unaffected by empirical realities." To the contrary, he is all too aware of them. Halakhic man lives in the city, after all, and will not take flight, like *homo religiosus,* to the suburbs or to other transcendent spaces. If Soloveitchik designs his work, as I have argued, for urban Jewish observance, then he cannot abandon the defiled city, but instead must recreate it in the image of God's creation. Terror and dark alleyways still remain, but they are now confined to walled areas at the outskirts of the halakhic map. Soloveitchik provides a guide for Jewish city life, one that relegates mystery to the periphery of perception. One can still sense, even feel its force. But within Soloveitchik's religious cartography, halakhic streets confine and subdue terror; only when "the ideal world will triumph over the profane reality" will it finally be annulled.[49]

The *halakhah* as boundary marker also curbs the dark streets within the self. Soloveitchik worries about a "subjective religiosity" that overflows into transitory practices, and so never establishes fixed principles. With its source in "inner experiences," subjective religion "surges and swells like the waves of the sea, then pounds against the shore of reality, there to shatter and break." Soloveitchik here describes the experience of *homo religiosus,* who is moved by transcendent moments of ecstasy, yet must finally succumb to the everyday world of matter and sense. *Halakhah* transforms these "qualitative features of religious subjectivity" into "firm and well-established quantities" that "no storm can uproot from their place."[50] Referring to "nails well-fastened" in Ecclesiastes 12:11—the very same text in which Kaplan recognized the permanence of the material script—Soloveitchik understands the inner life as mirror to the urban holy: moving into the depths of qualitative, subjective experiences, halakhic man transforms those experiences into fixed, determined, and meaningful practice. Like Liebman's psychological remapping of the self, Soloveitchik replaces mystery with clarity. Instead of chaotic overflow, a patterned roadmap guides the self:

> The Halakhah sets down statutes and erects markers that serve as a dam against the surging, subjective current coursing through the universal *homo religiosus,* which, from time to time, in its raging turbulence sweeps away his entire being to obscure and inchoate realms.[51]

Soloveitchik fears those "inchoate realms" in the self and in the urban streets of religious practice. *Halakhah* reshapes "the amorphous flow of religious experience," and turns chaos into "a fixed pattern of lawful-ness."[52] In short, Soloveitchik's *halakhah* is a form of boundary con-struction, in which amorphous feelings or boundless spaces become precise and clear. This is the urban holy now embodied within the self. Mimicking God's creative designs in Genesis, halakhic man delineates and divides the self in the image of the well-ordered city. There he is safe from both internal and external threats.

Soloveitchik reiterates this sense of a subjective urban holy in *The Halakhic Mind* (1944),[53] a complicated and technical text written in the same year as *Halakhic Man,* though not published until 1986. Students had expected *The Halakhic Mind* to contain a discussion of Soloveitchik's philosophy of *halakhah.* But by the time the book appeared in print, it of-fered something quite different. The essay focused on how to *reconstruct* the "subjective" religious consciousness according to "objective" norms, texts, and practices.[54] Soloveitchik's reconstruction would be altogether distinct from Mordecai Kaplan's famous vision of a reconstructed Juda-ism. In Soloveitchik's view, religious practice always contains a subjec-tive, qualitative dimension, and an objective, quantitative order. But one cannot access inner experiences directly; instead, one travels through objective, material things to uncover their subjective qualities. So even as these subjective qualities undergird their objective expressions—in a kind of idealist movement from the inner spirit to a manifest, material practice—the researcher must still reverse this process to access the "subjective background." Reconstruction means, in this phenomeno-logical account, a method by which one apprehends inner experiences that lie behind and within embodied practices:

> The starting point in any analysis of subjectivity must be the objective order. It is impossible to gain any insight into the subjective stream unless we have previously acquired objective aspects.
> The analysis of a work of art or an ethical maxim is synonymous with the act of retracing the route along which objectifying creativity moves. Eliminate the objective criteria, however, and entrance to the enchanted sphere of subjectivity is immediately barred.[55]

To help explain this process, Soloveitchik discusses Plato's philosophy and the process to reconstruct "the subjective aspects of his creativ-ity." One must go through "the printed pages of his work" to discover the hidden "subjective phenomena," and reconstruct, for example, the uniqueness of Plato's character in relation to cultural forces, or the social construction of his psyche.[56] There is no causal connection, Soloveitchik emphasizes, between the subjective aspects and their objective correlates. Those subjective qualities remain forever "inscrutable" and mysterious.

What, then, does a reader like Soloveitchik actually reconstruct if he can never fully reveal the dynamics of an inner spirituality? The process of reconstruction functions as a technique of conversion, in which Soloveitchik redefines the qualitative features of subjectivity into quantitative, measured units. If *homo religiosus* moves according to chaotic surging passions of inner religious experience, it is because subjectivity is lawless, unregulated, and terrifying. But cultic features of religion arrive "to freeze subjective religiosity into solid and stable forms": subjective religious experiences are "crystallized into forms of ritual."[57]

Yet in hardening those unstable forms, Soloveitchik actually *replaces* the original qualitative experience with a patterned, quantitative structure that correlates more accurately with the objective order of things. There are really two subjective "orders," so Soloveitchik claims, "the antecedent, sensuous variety A_1 and the reconstructed structural aspect A_2. The objective additive order A lies between these two orders."[58] The researcher begins with A (the objective order) to better reconstruct its subjective correlate (A_1). But he replaces that "antecedent, sensual variety" with the more structured quantity A_2. This new, "reconstructed" inner experience is now "the objectified expression of some more primitive subjectivity [A_1]," such that there is now a "definite causal relation between objective A and reconstructed A_2."[59] This reconstructed correlate (A_2) contains features that mirror the objective order: regularity, marked boundaries, and quantitative measures. A sense of "objectification," as Soloveitchik labels it, defines the practice of halakhic activity:

> Halakhah is the act of seizing the subjective flow and converting it into enduring and tangible magnitudes. It is the crystallization of the fleeting individual experience into fixed principles and universal norms.
>
> Halakhah frequently operates with quantitative standards. It attempts not only to objectify religiosity, but also to quantify it. The act of measurement is a cardinal principle of Halakhah, and the religious experience is often quantified and mathematically determined.[60]

Halakhah substitutes order where there had once been chaos, and "reconstructs" that chaos into defined patterns of mathematical precision. The urban holy reconstitutes religious experience as well.

Note the adjectives Soloveitchik employs to describe the subjective order A_1: it is ephemeral, elusive, enchanted, chaotic, lawless, unregulated, transient, esoteric, fleeting, and above all amorphous. The reconstructed subjective matrix A_2 offers something quite different: it is solid, stable, enduring, tangible, and yields "fixed principles and universal norms." Soloveitchik's method of reconstruction exchanges chaos for order, mystery for logic, and indeterminacy for structure. Religious experience is no longer enchanted, but instead is regulated, controlled, and delimited. Lawless subjectivity can yield stable principles and norms through halakhic reconstruction. In *u-Vikashtem mi-Sham*, Soloveitchik inscribes the body with sanctifying potential, such that the "halakha is the law (Torah) of the body," and through bodily discipline, Jewish law "elevates life to the heights of eternity." Fortunate, indeed, is the one who meets God "on the pathways of the world."[61]

Those pathways have been forged by a *halakhah* that reconstitutes amorphous bodily experiences into quantitative, recognizable structures. In this, Soloveitchik inscribes the urban holy within the self, for the dark regions of subjective experience are transformed into enduring patterns of religious ritual and practice. As halakhic man transforms the city into an urban holy, so too he reconstructs the inner self as an urban holy space of renewal. The self exists as a site of halakhic manipulation, in which the chaos and void within convert to tangible and fixed norms in the "objective" world. Subjectivity is dangerous, unformed, and ambiguous, much like the city imaginary that so captivates Soloveitchik's account of halakhic discourse. Yet just as Jewish law transforms the winding streets into sacred, straight pathways, so too does Jewish law convert inner experiences "into enduring and tangible magnitudes." The streets have become safe, and so too the self.

In providing this safe haven from terror and anomy, both within and outside the body, Soloveitchik has also protected his halakhic man from rebellious desires. Divine commandments conform to his own wishes, as if the halakhic norms originated "in his innermost self." Where *homo religiosus* rages against this norm, halakhic man accepts it as "an existential law of his very being": "We do not have here a directive that imposes upon man obligations against which he rebels, but delightful commandments which his soul passionately desires."[62] Dorff recognizes the oddity of this approach, for rabbinic sources also praise those who desire to transgress the law but do not do so. This signals reverence for God, rather than some inner rage to conquer and destroy.[63] But Soloveitchik has less the rabbis in mind, and far more Kant's distinction between heteronomous and autonomous laws: the one commands from an external authority and binds the will, the other reveals true human freedom to act according to the will's directives. Halakhic man is free in this Kantian sense, protected from the shock of uncertainty:

> When halakhic man comes to the real world [read "the city"], he has already created his ideal, a priori image, which shines with the radiance of the norm. The real world does not impose upon him anything new, nor does it compel him to perform any new action of which he had not been aware beforehand in his ideal world. And this ideal world is his very own, his own possession; he is free to create in it, to arrive at new insights, to improve and perfect.[64]

God's city "is his very own" because he comes to the real world ready to impose the boundaries and limits of the halakhic norm. The real world is the urban holy, at once a home for religious practice and a space awaiting perfection and improvement. When halakhic man walks in the city, he performs his human freedom by transforming profane confusion into sacred order. If *homo religiosus* flutters "to and fro," and thereby suffers from "spiritual anguish,"[65] halakhic man is, like "nails well-fastened," rooted in the city:

> The Halakhah is not hermetically enclosed within the confines of cult sanctuaries but penetrates into every nook and cranny of life. The marketplace, the street, the factory, the house, the meeting place, the banquet hall, all constitute the backdrop for the religious life.[66]

Halakhic man creates in the city, establishing cosmic boundaries that maintain order and clarity in the midst of chaos and darkness.

We can now recognize just how much the urban landscape critically informs Soloveitchik's theory of Jewish law. According to city planner Kevin Lynch, three conceptual models govern our thinking about the city: the cosmic, the practical, and the organic.[67] The cosmic city is "stable and hierarchical—a magical microcosm in which each part is fused into a perfectly ordered whole."[68] Witold Rybczynski, summarizing Lynch's view, describes the cosmic city as one that symbolically represents particular rituals or beliefs (an example would be Washington, D.C.). The practical city grows according to material needs, and is imagined as a "machine for commerce" that often employs grids for quick and easy navigation (New York City is this kind of city, although neither quick nor easy!).[69] Lynch describes the practical city as "made up of small, autonomous, undifferentiated parts, linked up into a great machine. . . . The machine is powerful and beautiful, but it is not a work of magic or a mirror of the universe."[70] Suburbanites navigate through the practical city in order to use, rather than to live in, the urban environment.

The third model of the city, and the one most crucial for Soloveit-chik's halakhic approach, is the organic type that appears "natural rather than man-made."[71] This is so because the organic city arose, according to Lynch, in the late eighteenth and early nineteenth century as a reaction to "industrialization, gigantic new cities, and the unprecedented leaps in technology."[72] Rybczynski argues that this organic model can be discovered much earlier, within cities whose streets "vary in width, they are rarely straight, and they wind sinuously throughout the town." Medieval cities were often built in this way, but so too was London and Los Angeles. Soloveitchik's forbears lived in or near organic cities, as did Soloveitchik himself when he came to America and settled in Boston. Founded in 1630, Boston is notorious for its "winding, narrow streets, irregular plots, [and] vaguely defined public spaces."[73] Dark and winding alleyways abound in Boston, and suggest the kind of mystery and chaos that halakhic man masters and subdues. As an organic city, Boston is the urban holy, with all its allure, mystery, and possibility for revival. Halakhic man searches out every "nook and cranny" of the streets, and transforms them into holy sites of religious practice.

Soloveitchik's theory of *halakhah* transforms the organic city into a practical one so that it becomes a cosmic city. Halakhic man enters the marketplace and the factory, and travels down the countless one-way Bostonian streets, all to better transfigure chaos into cosmic order. Organic cities are dangerous, as Soloveitchik's ancestors well knew, for their seductive enticements and promise of excess. American cities, in this sense, are no different than the cities of Europe. Andrew Heinze has argued that immigrant Jews were particularly well-suited to adapt to the

American urban environment because they maintained a "cosmopolitan outlook."[74] That outlook, in the language employed here, is the ability to navigate through the organic city. But Soloveitchik wants to *live* in the city, and to do so he transforms the organic landscapes into cosmic ones. He makes the city pliable to halakhic practice. Soloveitchik wrote *Halakhic Man* before he traveled weekly to New York City to teach at Yeshiva College. But even then, he could not but recognize the differences in city planning between New York and Boston, and the ways in which Jews traverse within the urban landscape. That landscape would now contain halakhic markers, and so turn winding streets into sacred, straightened paths. The organic city becomes a cosmic, American home for halakhic man.

When Soloveitchik published his *Lonely Man of Faith* in 1965, many readers were shocked, if not by the title, then by its profound exposure to existential crisis that appeared so at odds with the confident tenor of *Halakhic Man*. If in that earlier work Soloveitchik had cordoned off a protected realm of halakhic practice, that sense of security had apparently been shattered in the intervening twenty years: "The nature of the dilemma can be stated in a three-word sentence. I am lonely. . . . I am lonely because, in my humble, inadequate way, I am a man of faith. . . ."[75] Halakhic man confronted neither the religious perplexity nor the loneliness that haunts the divided self in *Lonely Man of Faith*. In this latter text, Soloveitchik compares the inner conflict of the man of faith to the two Adams in Genesis, the one created in the image of God, the other (in Genesis two) formed of dust. Adam the first, as Soloveitchik calls him, follows the dictates of his creation: in God's image, he too is a creative being, seeking to dominate nature and use it for his purposes. Created together with Eve, Adam the first lives in community and desires a dignified, responsible life of freedom. Adam the second, however, confronts the mystery of creation, and rather than create a world that functions for him, as Adam the first does, he instead "studies it with the naïveté, awe, and admiration of the child."[76] Seeking redemption rather than dignity, Adam the second yearns for fellowship, and finds it with other lonely souls in the covenantal community of "I, thou, and He."

The man of faith is caught between these two personality types. Both Adams reside in each of us, Soloveitchik claims, and forever remain in dynamic conflict. And it is this conflict that suggests a rupture between Soloveitchik's two works. Commentators have struggled to unify the discordant images of *Halakhic Man* and *Lonely Man of Faith*. Some argue that each text focuses on separate concerns (David Hartman and Aviezer Ravitzky), while still others, most notably Lawrence Kaplan, suggest that Soloveitchik intended *Halakhic Man* (originally in Hebrew) for a Jewish audience with its "insider" perspective (and so represents, the argument continues, Soloveitchik's stronger religious convictions). *Lonely Man of Faith,* published in English, reflects Soloveitchik's ambivalent relation to Western thought and culture.[77] David Singer and Moshe Sokol reduce the conflict to Soloveitchik's own split personality and his desire, on the one hand, to defend the traditional Lithuanian view of his forefathers, but on the other, to give expression to a very different, existential (even Hasidic) mood. But clearly all Soloveitchik's readers puzzle over the sharp divide between the majestic, cognitive certainty of halakhic man, and the existential angst of the man of faith.

Indeed, this divide appears to be sharp and irredeemable. From the beginning, the second Adam recognizes his "ontological incompatibility with any other being."[78] This is true even in his relation to Eve, because his "I" is singular and "cannot be repeated, imitated, or experienced by others." Adam the second requires a new kind of "faith community" in which "one lonely soul finds another soul tormented by loneliness and solitude yet unqualifiedly committed."[79] Hartman draws out the very different movements for the first and second Adams. Where Adam the second recoils in an act of defeat before mystery, Adam the first controls space, and powerfully engages the world. The one retreats; the other confronts the world and makes it his own. To Hartman, only Adam the second "makes room for a God who can address man."[80] Adam the first simply absorbs too much space. When faced with dangers, he seeks others to protect him. But Adam the second has no others to find, and must confront God in his singular experience. His existential loneliness is radical: neither friendship, communal solidarity, nor creative acts relieve his crisis. Insecurity and loneliness, apparently, go all the way down.

But if Adam the second shares so little with halakhic man, then Adam the first shares even less. It would be a mistake to reduce Adam the first to the scientific, mathematical thinking of halakhic man. Although they share a creative, constructed approach to the world, their differences reveal far more.[81] Soloveitchik calls Adam the first a "surface personality," for he craves companionship and honor from his worldly endeavors. He associates dignity with fame, and those around him "feel his impact." Adam the first is a social being, so God created him with Eve—they emerged together, for "Adam the first exists in society, in community with others." The "surface" features emerge, however, in the fear of being lonely. Adam the first resists the dignity of "the silent person, whose message remains hidden and suppressed in the in-depth personality."[82] Halakhic man, in contrast, maintains a deliberative, steady approach to practical activity. He worries neither about fame nor prosperity, but creatively translates halakhic norms into urban practices.

If halakhic man shies away from the egoistic, "surface" features of Adam the first, he also differs from that other Adam the second who, as the character with depth, witnesses to the loneliness of faith. Soloveitchik writes of religious loneliness rather than halakhic order. He recovers the in-depth personality of Adam the second, and his estrangement from social practices and political life. Adam the second is thereby doubly silent. Unable to express in words the awe and amazement he registers before the mystery of creation, he is also silenced by the public, communal, and active life of Adam the first. Like cattle, Adam the first shares "the primordial urge to come together in face of opposition."[83] This Adam the second cannot do, for he is existentially lonely. Soloveitchik thus appears to leave us with three incompatible types: the surface, communal personality of Adam the first, the existential awe and bewilderment found in Adam the second, and the boundary-making creativity of halakhic man.

Yet it is this recurrent move to overcome mystery that draws Adam the second into the orbit of *Halakhic Man*. Adam the second must withdraw to a profoundly internal loneliness in order to rise up more exalted and redeemed. His body morphs into the urban holy, where mystery and awe give way to a redemptive life. Halakhic man mapped out the city to ward off chaos and anomy, and in so doing transformed urban terrors into redemptive pathways of holiness. Adam the second faces this mystery in the depths of his personality, but cannot remain defeated and lost. It is through that defeat, as Hartman astutely points out, that one discovers an "intensive intimacy" with God.[84] Soloveitchik will not allow

Adam the second to remain lonely, silenced, and insecure. He must, like halakhic man, move from doubt to confidence, self-absorption to intimate relations, from anomy to meaningful existence. Adam the second discovers his self within the boundaries erected by the covenantal faith community. His soliloquy now "manifests itself in a threefold personal union: I, thou, and He."[85] The "tortuous paths of creation" are no longer mysterious, for God's "footprints" now reveal an ordered world.[86] Adam the second had once asked, "What is the purpose of all this?" With the new borders of community in place, "the covenant, not the cosmos, provides him with an answer to his questions."[87] God's footprints provide a religious mapping of the cosmos. The world has been ordered and secured. It is safe to walk again.

Mystery turns into revealed order in the covenantal community—"*Deus absconditus* emerges suddenly as *Deus revelatus*," just as "*homo absconditus* sheds his mask and turns into *homo revelatus*."[88] The God who could suddenly vanish "into the recesses of transcendence"[89] now becomes fully revealed to Adam in the covenantal community. This revelatory presence, in turn, opens Adam to new forms of expression and friendship. Within the "I, thou, and He" structure, Adam reveals his "passional experience" to others. The covenantal community offers "the opportunity to communicate, indeed to commune with, and to enjoy the genuine friendship with Eve."[90] That Adam could shed "his mask," with all its attendant fears and insecurities, reveals that his existential loneliness never went all the way down. Too timid or afraid to seek out others within the mystery of the cosmos, Adam the second requires surer footing and markers to navigate the streets. God's partnership in the covenantal community remapped the terrain, and allowed Adam to remove his mask, as Moses had done, in order to confront God face-to-face. Within this kind of divine "meeting," the cosmos turns into a divine and human colloquy, and the organic city becomes cosmic in its order, power, and beauty.

The divine colloquy moves across the ages, linking Adam the second to the past and future. Here, a passionate sense of continuity and legitimacy emerges as one takes part in an ageless drama: "Within the covenantal community not only contemporary individuals but generations are engaged in a colloquy."[91] The burden of loneliness dissipates in the covenantal community as it spans the many Adams who search for companionship. That colloquy can be found in the streets, but also in the texts that speak to and within the covenantal order. Situated within a community of interlocutors, Adam the second overcomes his existential loneliness. These conversation partners speak in tones that position Adam the second within a sacred hearing. To be sure, the "element of the tragic" remains, for "the steady oscillating between the majestic natural community and the covenantal faith community renders the act of complete redemption unrealizable."[92] Yet even if Adam the second cannot wholly immerse himself in "covenantal awareness," he is no longer lonely and conflicted. Even more, the mystery of the city streets slowly turns into something far more friendly and discernible: "I would say that the norm in the opinion of the Halakhah is the tentacle by which the covenant, like the ivy, attaches itself to and spreads over the world of majesty."[93] Ivy absorbs and contains, but it also creates pathways of order and direction, even for the lonely man of faith.

This divine–human dialogue captures the notion of prophecy, on the one side, and prayer, on the other. When God speaks and Adam listens, it is prophetic utterance. But the roles reverse in supplications to God: "In the prayer community the initiative belongs to man: he does the speaking and God, the listening. The word of prophecy is God's and is accepted by man. The word of prayer is man's and God accepts it."[94] Adam the second is neither alone nor lonely. Prayer, Soloveitchik emphasizes, is merely "the continuation of prophecy." It connects Adam the second to his prophetic ancestors, and maintains "the intimate companionship of God." The end of Jewish prophecy did not mark the closure of "the covenantal colloquy." Instead, the burden shifted from God to Adam, "from the level of prophecy to that of prayer."[95] But there are noble and nefarious appeals to God, and persons must learn how to pray with "covenantal awareness of existential togetherness."[96] The boundaries of community belong not only to the streets, but also to those who walk them:

> Only Adam the second knows the art of praying since he confronts God with the petition of the many. The fenced-in egocentric and ego-oriented Adam the first is ineligible to join the covenantal prayer community of which God is a fellow member.[97]

Existential togetherness travels only so far. Sometimes borders arrive to protect the holiness within. The divine colloquy silences rather than modulates the profane, creating protected fences of seclusion. This the biblical Job had discovered, for his prayers "remained unheard," and he "met with catastrophe and the whirlwind uprooted him and his household." In Soloveitchik's reading, the book of Job depicts a conversion narrative in which Job learns how to pray as Adam the second. Job's prayers are left unanswered so long as he remains outside the fences of the covenantal prayer community. He must overcome those barriers and rise up as Adam the second. Only through catastrophe does he learn of "the great covenantal experience."[98] One must be cleansed by the whirlwind to land in sacred spaces. For Soloveitchik, the urban holy resides in Job's world too.

Adam the second finds his place in the city, much like halakhic man. Both transform their worlds into recognizable urban landscapes. The once mysterious cosmos becomes rich with divine instruction and navigational signs; a loneliness turned inward blossoms into a colloquy of passionate words and committed relations. Adam prays with others to the Other, and discovers a covenantal community of committed believers. However singular and unique, he speaks to God, and God responds. Adam finds other committed souls, and they form communities across generations; he reads the sacred texts, and he debates with Rashi and Maimonides. As this Adam walks the streets of the city, he finds halakhic man already there, paving a way to holiness. Wrong turns must bend to the right, narrow pathways yield to wider avenues, and alluring side streets become opportunities for transformative practices. Adam the second confronts the urban holy as a sacred image of redemption, and he has traveled a rather long road—one marked with secure borders of halakhic rules and norms. The lonely man of faith discovers God in the city.

Soloveitchik frequently refers to his Lithuanian ancestors in *Halakhic Man,* and underscores the expansive sense of a covenantal community. Those ancestors lived in the Jewish shtetl, where markers of difference were everywhere in force. But they lived, too, like Soloveitchik, in the city, even if they often sought to avoid its dangers. Meir b. Elijah, the grandnephew of the Gaon of Vilna, spoke fervently of city dangers, and noted the strength required to survive in urban terrain:

But any person who must carry upon his shoulders the burden of earning his living, and who must therefore be surrounded by women—especially a person who must go out into the marketplace and public streets and big cities—such a man requires great zeal and strength.[99]

Most American Jews lived in "the marketplace and public streets and big cities," and they required defenses to overcome urban seductive lures. Soloveitchik's philosophy of *halakhah* offered such weapons. His halakhic man could navigate the city with "great zeal and strength," armed with a priori laws from Sinai. Religious boundaries, even for the man of faith, were secured in covenantal communities that prevented incursions from more sinister forces. To expand Soloveitchik's metaphor, the ivy moves in only one direction—from covenantal community out toward unclean and impure lands. Ever expansive boundaries make over the organic city into a pure, cosmic one. Jews can live in the American city because chaos remains on the other side of halakhic practice.

Soloveitchik's typological discourse relies on a bounded–unbounded distinction, a theme that runs throughout his essays and books. Both halakhic man and Adam the second require borders and limits, whereas Adam the first reflects the capitalist entrepreneur who searches for ever new markets to dominate and control. He reaches beyond, but never confronts the tormented loneliness within. *Homo religiosus* too is boundless, and exhibits the kind of restlessness and unease unknown to halakhic practice and pathways. The power of Soloveitchik's thought lies in the drawing of secure boundaries that enable the movement of the urban holy *within* these limited borders. We confront this vision—in which halakhic man sinks lower only to rise higher within fixed boundaries— in Soloveitchik's other important works as well. Building a well-constructed, ordered Victorian house *in* the city requires continual vigilance and border maintenance.

Boundary construction is the focus of Soloveitchik's important essay "Confrontation" (1964), in which he marks out the limits of interfaith dialogue between Jews and Christians—especially Catholics influenced by the Second Vatican Council (1962–65) and its concern for Jewish–Christian relations.[100] Here he writes of "natural man" who is "unbounded, merging harmoniously with the general order of things and events." Natural man becomes the modern aesthete who seeks only "unlimited aesthetic experience."[101] Beauty seduces (in the guise of the feminine), and natural man remains blind to the forces that dominate him. He can "deny himself nothing," and appropriates beauty only as "a source of pleasure rather than one of frustration and disillusionment."[102] In Zachary Braiterman's reading, the aesthetic "takes the form of un-ethicized, unredeemed beauty."[103] Natural man remains a prisoner to his own desires, imagining that experiential immediacy overcomes physical borders. But clearly Soloveitchik believes in the reality principle: natural man must eventually encounter "something wholly other than his own self, an outside that defies and challenges him."[104] This "objective order" limits the exercise of his power, and natural man confronts the reality of restrictions and borders. A redeemed beauty would then be an ethics with fitting borders. Braiterman is right in one other respect as well: for Soloveitchik, beauty must be redeemed, and to be so, it must fit within the patterned universe of halakhic pathways. Abraham Joshua Heschel offers a similar account (discussed in the next chapter), in which beauty reveals itself as a signifier to holiness. But Soloveitchik is less concerned, as Heschel certainly is, with experiential encounters of transcendence. Instead, Soloveitchik seeks to delimit and confine human freedom and desire. We already live within confined spaces, so Soloveitchik argues here, and *halakhah* creates "the boundary line between a finite idea and a principle nurtured by infinity."[105] Jewish law remaps the borders into beautiful cosmic highways.

Soloveitchik had earlier, in 1956, appealed to this sense of navigation in "Kol Dodi Dofek," an essay on human suffering and the Holocaust. A stirring and moving text, it remains an important theological statement that links the Holocaust to the state of Israel. Just as halakhic man must "arise ennobled and refined" from within the depths of suffering,[106] so too the state of Israel emerges out of European disaster and death. I want to focus, however, on another feature in this work: the transformation from passive to active existence. In what would become a crucial paradigm for later modern Jewish thinkers, Soloveitchik distinguishes two types of existence: the existence of fate [*goral*] and the existence of destiny [*yi'ud*]. The nature of fate is compulsion, a life "devoid of meaning, direction, purpose." In this existential state, suffering has no significance: "afflictions appear shadowy and murky, like satanic forces, the offspring of the chaos and the void which pollute the cosmos."[107] The borders and limits created by God return to a primordial "chaos and the void." Proper and life-affirming boundaries disappear, and the "all-encompassing framework of being" recedes from view. But the existence of destiny is altogether different. Within this mode persons move from mechanical passivity to an "active mode of existence":

> Man's task in the world, according to Judaism, is to transform fate into destiny; a passive existence into an active existence; an existence of compulsion, perplexity, and muteness into an existence replete with a powerful will, with resourcefulness, daring, and imagination.[108]

Persons cannot but fail to understand suffering within the existential fate experience: when confronted by its radical mystery, they turn silent, stifled by the weight of the unknown. But those within the community of destiny act to transform chaos into order, and deny suffering its capacity to suffocate the self. Judaism reshapes, in Soloveitchik's phrase, the camp (fate) into a congregation (destiny), turning fear imposed by fate into active love demanded by a holy nation.[109]

Only a congregation, and not a camp, functions in the city. A camper faces the world alone, and is struck dumb by the overwhelming presence of unexplainable suffering and the destruction of meaningful frameworks. Just as Adam the first turned to others for protection against unknown and uncontrollable forces, so too the camper "grasps his own helplessness and joins with his fellows both for protection from and victory over the enemy." For Soloveitchik, the camp is born "out of the dread of extinction and annihilation."[110] Fear reigns in the camp, and the camper passively accepts his fate. One must be protected from the city, and like the American Victorians of the nineteenth century, create physical markers to ward off chaos and harm. But the congregation lives in the city because the congregation actively transforms the streets into religious pathways of holiness. Congregants face the city not as individuals but as members of a community. They reshape the city landscape to further God's creative acts in Genesis. They are "witnesses" to "events that are long since past, and to a wondrous future that has not yet arrived."[111] Within a bounded and regulated community, they move from passive to active existence, from fate to destiny, from the depths of despair to exalted redemption.

This is the sacred movement of halakhic practice. Jewish law transforms, activates, distinguishes, and marks boundaries of sacred space. It is a move from the Victorian suburbs *back* to the city. But in that return, the physical barriers remain. The congregation may indeed remap the city, but like the camp, it also creates protective boundaries. To live in the city requires a double movement: a transformation of chaos into order, and the building of fences to ward off chaos yet unredeemed. Jews like Soloveitchik confront the city as a congregation in the midst of the urban holy.

CONCLUSION

In Soloveitchik's reading of First Kings in *Lonely Man of Faith*, Elisha becomes the typical Adam the first, a prosperous farmer "centered around this-worldly, material goods," and focused on "economic success" and "material wealth."[112] He is the Adam of the majestic world who values efficiency, practical work, and rational execution. So distant is Elijah, that other prophet of the covenantal community, who "walked as a stranger through the bustling cities of Shomron . . . negating the worth of all goods to which his contemporaries were committed." Yet suddenly "the mantle of Elijah" was cast upon Elisha, and he experienced the "transforming touch of God's hand." The "old" Elisha vanished, and in his place stood the "new Elisha" who renounced all possessions, family, and place in the majestic world. Like Elijah, he became a wondering, homeless prophet. But he did not succumb to an all-too-easy withdrawal from the world. Instead, he returned "to society as a participant in state affairs, as an adviser of kings and a teacher of the majestic community." Never losing courage or faith within the world he once prized, Elisha "found triumph in defeat, hope in failure." Still lonely, but no longer alone, Elisha "met the Lonely One and discovered the singular covenantal confrontation of solitary man and God."[113] Once the typical Adam the first, Elisha had rediscovered his place in the world as Adam the second. He could walk once again in the city.

To be sure, Soloveitchik's account of Elisha offers a beautiful defense of modern Orthodoxy in America. Refusing to withdraw into insular ghettos, the committed Jew courageously engages the world as a man of faith. He begins in the majestic, economic world of success, but ends in the covenantal community of sacrifice, dedication, and partnership. Yet Elisha's story is more than this. It is also a narrative about how committed Jews navigate in and through the city, and transform it into a home for religious practice. In Soloveitchik's retelling, Elijah is the foil to Elisha's triumph. It is Elijah who abandons the urban landscape and retreats, finally disappearing "under a veil of mystery." He is the "solitary covenantal prophet" who remains the stranger in "the bustling cities."[114] Elisha made a similar move of retreat, but having "arrived at the outer boundaries of human commitment, he came back to society."[115] Indeed, he came back. He lives in the city, seeks to remodel it, and encounters the urban holy as a sacred space of triumph and hope. He would rise higher by sinking lower. Transforming pathways into clear religious journeys, sequestering chaos to the margins where it loses its seductive force, Elisha lives in the city as a man of faith. But this is not the city that Elijah encountered and rejected. It is the city as the urban holy: a place of sacred mappings, of sparks of transcendence, of religious renewal and energy. The city is the only arena within which Elisha *can* live. The wandering Jew has arrived home.

American Orthodox Jews are no longer, if primarily, city dwellers as they have moved beyond urban limits to suburban frontiers. I have argued that Soloveitchik's Jewish thought was profoundly influenced by the cityscape, and even more so by the notion of the urban holy. How well his urban thought translates into suburban Orthodox practice is an open and pressing question. It requires a new look at contemporary Orthodox theology and halakhic discourse. But this rethinking should be rooted in material culture and suburban landscapes, as Eitan Diamond's work on Orthodox Jews in suburbia makes clear.[116] It must reveal how suburban material culture, if there is one, informs and is created by halakhic norms. Soloveitchik wrote and lived when Jews were just beginning to move, en masse, to the suburbs. Perhaps this accounts for some of his loneliness and existential concern, for he wanted to remain *in* the city, and to rise cleansed and more holy by doing so. As a guide for Jews living in the city, Soloveitchik translated the cityscape into clear pathways of sacred space. The urban imaginary in *Halakhic Man* and *Lonely Man of Faith* (and not only these works) produced a material space of transformation and renewal. Committed Jews could live in the city because the city was a halakhic site awaiting the patterned grids of limits, borders, and clear markings. By remapping the urban landscape as cosmic city, Soloveitchik created in the image of his

God. Halakhic man fashioned a city, as God did the world, in order to practice Jewish law.

The urban imaginary is seductive and powerful in Soloveitchik's Jewish theology, and reveals the dialectical relations between Jewish thought and material practice. The cityscape, in the ways it is both imagined and configured, radically informs Soloveitchik's Jewish thought. No Victorian edifice need shelter the Jew from terrifying surroundings, for *halakhah* can build structures of meaning. But like the Victorian child who knows where to hide and which rooms to enter, halakhic man traverses only well-trodden paths of orderliness and comfort. But those paths must be continually maintained and protected. If Soloveitchik remaps the city, it is only because the city has already become a site of halakhic observance. It lies expectant and waiting for structure and redemption. The urban holy is the halakhic city—a Victorian home of sacred space and boundary maintenance. Here Soloveitchik meets his God, perplexed and lonely no more.

FOUR

Material Presence: Abraham Joshua Heschel and *The Sabbath*

A reading of Abraham Joshua Heschel's *The Sabbath* (1951) typically goes like this: in this poetic and lyrical text, Heschel carves out holiness in the experiential moments of time amid the materialism of physical space. The Sabbath is Judaism's response to the excess of mass media, marketing, capitalism, and the enslavement to material possessions. The seventh day allows us to use things, yet we remain free of their allure. Rather than being exploited by consumer culture, we should seek an "inner liberty" to live in the world, but not of it. Even more, the tranquility of Sabbath time realigns our notions of success and material wealth, for the six days of the week become "a pilgrimage to the Sabbath." The things in space fade away, but the holiness experienced in Sabbath time remains eternal. That taste of eternity within the rhythms of the Sabbath transcends spatial limits, and moves us to encounters with God. In short, "material things are our tools; we work with them; the Sabbath reminds us that in the midst of that work our heart should be set on eternity."[1]

This standard reading, reproduced in a good many secondary works, is nonetheless quickly jettisoned for Heschel's more "philosophical" texts—*Man Is Not Alone* (1951) and *God in Search of Man* (1955). There has been increasing interest in Heschel's *Torah min-Hashamayim* (1962), in part due to Gordon Tucker's masterful translation of the original Hebrew into English.[2] And there are important studies of Heschel's view of the Holocaust and his interfaith work.[3] But Heschel's "Philosophy of Religion" (*Man Is Not Alone*) and "Philosophy of Judaism" (*God in Search of Man*) have born the brunt of academic scrutiny. To be sure,

The Sabbath has remained popular, but for professional academics, its lyrical beauty betrays a lack of intellectual rigor and focus. It is what one might call a pleasant reading that inspires, a testimony to the spirit of Sabbath observance rather than a rational defense of it. Indeed, critics have tended to view Heschel's entire oeuvre as more inspirational than philosophical in program and intent.[4] *The Sabbath,* in this view, is just more of the same: eloquent, engaging, and a prophetic witness to a spiritual reality hidden within the commerce of modern society.

Yet *The Sabbath,* together with Heschel's *The Earth Is the Lord's* (1950), remain the most insightful contributions by an American Jewish thinker to the conflicting dimensions of material identity. In these texts we witness a Jewish theologian thinking about things—their seductive power, their potential to reveal holiness, their capacity to provoke idolatrous worship. Things are ambiguous figures: markers that reveal false and authentic gods. By coupling these two works together, as Heschel himself did (there is even a published volume with the two texts printed together),[5] one recognizes how the "typical" reading barely recovers Heschel's obsession with things and their power to define the self. For it is simply not true that material objects reside in the world of space while banished from the holiness of sabbatical time. Heschel's Sabbath is full of things, and he often appeals to material images when describing the nature of the Sabbath.

In *The Earth Is the Lord's*—Heschel's phenomenological reconstruction of the East European Jewry of his childhood—the opening sentence introduces the attractive power of things: "Most of us succumb to the magnetic property of things and evaluate events by their tangible results." Those things move us because they "are displayed in the realm of Space,"[6] a physical area in which we live and work. In Heschel's nostalgic roots trip, he imagines an East European Hasidic Jewry steeped in Jewish lore and law, spiritually beyond the attractions of the material world of space. Yet even as he seeks to distance this mystical heritage from things, the "magnetic property" of objects continues to entice and lure him as things nestle within his prosaic accounts of Hasidic spirituality. For what does Heschel mean when the words of the commandments, having just been shattered by Moses at Mt. Sinai, "still knock at our gates as if begging to be engraved 'on the Tablets of every heart'"? Or if the Phoenicians could erect temples to God, how do Jews "lay bricks in the soul"?[7] What *kind* of things are bricks of the soul, and how do they differ from those structural materials? Is this just metaphorical language, as Edward Kaplan has argued, in which its "suggestiveness" points "to a fuller realm of being"?[8] Even Kaplan worries that phrases such as these contradict Heschel's "axiomatic opposition to spatial analogies of the holy."[9] Do things only reside in space and not also in the soul?

I want to read Heschel against Heschel, as it were, in order to recover his account of things that also witnesses to the constitutive presence of objects in Jewish identity. In and through this deconstructive reading, I seek to capture the power of things—their seductive presence and absence—to disclose just how much Heschel's thought is rooted in things. This could very well lead to critical analysis of metaphor, idolatry, or even Heschel's strong dualistic, ahistorical thinking. These are crucial matters, but they diverge from the central preoccupations of this chapter. For my deconstructive reading is not meant to weaken Heschel, and thereby to dismiss his overwrought prose. Instead, I want to expose the centrality of things for his Jewish thought, and to communicate how Heschel is perhaps the most penetrating modern Jewish thinker on the nature of things. Though Heschel continually erases the presence of things, his very labor testifies to their material power over him. We need to dig deeper into the materiality of his thought to better understand how things are inescapably part of the Jewish self.

As the direct descendant of his namesake, the Apter Rebbe, and closely related to many of the charismatic Hasidic Rebbes (holy leaders) of Eastern Europe, Heschel might appear aloof to the worldly temptations he discusses in *The Sabbath* and *The Earth Is the Lord's*. But his mystical vision, fully present in these and his many other works, always engages the particular circumstances of material existence. Heschel never retreated to the inner halls of spiritual contemplation; his politics in support of civil rights, his outspoken criticism of the Vietnam War, and his interfaith dialogue with the Vatican all witness to the expansive scope of his philosophical practice. Born in Warsaw in 1907, and raised to succeed his father as leader of a Polish Hasidic community, Heschel still set out to Berlin for university training, receiving his doctorate in 1935 after writing his dissertation on the prophets (an expanded version in English would appear in 1962). A year after leaving Germany in 1938, he received an invitation to teach at the Hebrew Union College in

Cincinnati—though he did not arrive in America until the following year. Not until 1945 would Heschel move to New York City to accept his appointment as Professor of Jewish Ethics and Mysticism at the Jewish Theological Seminary, where he lectured until his death in 1972. Arnold Eisen has argued that Heschel exemplified the life of Jewish observance more fully than he could successfully argue for it,[10] and the lasting image of his protest march with Martin Luther King Jr. in Selma, Alabama (1965) reinforces this sense of activist scholar and prophetic witness. Heschel's politics should alert us to the way he engaged the world, and even more, to how he imagined the material world relates to the self. For even if his Hasidic forbears, so Heschel claims, "carried deep within their hearts a contempt for the 'world'," such cannot be said of Heschel himself. To be sure, he shared with the Hasidic Rebbes their distrust of worldly "power and pomp"; but he also exalted a practice "in deeds" that moved beyond the confines of Jewish communal life. If Heschel prayed with his feet in 1965 with Dr. King, then he also lived in a world of things that informed his sense of self.

Heschel's discourse on things in *The Sabbath* and *The Earth Is the Lord's* reveals the inescapable presence of things in the construction of human identity. But the nature of a thing is a rather complex notion, and I will spend some time unpacking how Heschel thinks about things and what they do. This is more an unpacking, a depth reading to match Heschel's depth theology, to better expose how Heschel thinks about things. Heschel certainly holds some troubling accounts of the primitive mind, theories of metaphor, and idolatry, but I engage these issues for what they tell about the nature of things, and not to decide whether such theories are appropriate or true. I will subsequently turn to how persons relate to things, with particular focus on the aesthetics of that relation, and the problem of idolatry. Throughout this analysis, I will explore the links between things and the Sabbath in order to understand why Heschel "seeks to displace the coveting of things in space for *coveting the things in time*."[11] He struggles with this concept of "things in time," in part because he is both repulsed and seduced by things in space. As I read Heschel against Heschel, things seamlessly move between space and time to debunk the rigid dualism between the goodness of space and the holiness of time. Things are ever present and always there during all seven days of the week.

More than a study of things, Heschel's work performed cultural labor as well, for he wrote *The Sabbath* at a time when the Jewish Conservative movement sought to buttress Sabbath observance among suburbanite Jews. The 1950s promised increased material wealth for many Americans, and Jews desired to decorate their homes and holidays with beautiful things. Heschel was not immune to these consumerist pressures, even as his critique of the Sabbath takes on this capitalist anxiety. That anxiety comes to the fore in two particular kinds of consumer products: Jewish observance manuals (especially *The Jewish Home Beautiful*) and the woodcut engravings by Ilya Schor that accompany *The Sabbath* and *The Earth Is the Lord's*. These visual texts saturate Jewish observance with beautiful things, and intensify the material weight of Heschel's Jewish thought. *The Jewish Home Beautiful,* together with the engraving on the cover of *The Sabbath,* contain all the markings of cherished things that render the self as a material identity—in physical space and sabbatical time.

WHAT IS A THING?

The creation story in Genesis includes a panorama of created things—from natural vegetation to lights in the heavens. God sanctifies only the Sabbath day with holiness; the rest of creation is merely good. In the prologue to *The Sabbath,* Heschel asks this rhetorical question: "Now what was the first holy object in the history of the world? Was it a mountain? Was it an altar?" That Heschel considers the Genesis account a "history of the world" suggests how he reads the biblical text, but his central point is clear enough: despite the abundance of creative things, only the seventh day is made holy. And this day alone owns it all, so Heschel warns: "There is no reference in the record of creation to any object in space that would be endowed with the quality of holiness."[12] Note, to begin, that Heschel refers only to "any object in space." He leaves open the possibility, to be discussed later in this chapter, that objects in time, if we could call them that, might contain some sense of holiness. But all objects we touch and see—and Heschel associates those senses with things of space[13]—might be good, but they are never holy. To Heschel, the Hebrew word *qadosh* represents "the mystery and majesty of the divine." Holiness points to an intangible feature of the divine: something more and beyond that nonetheless inhabits within the world. We cannot see or touch mystery, but we can experience or confront its presence. Yet things in space fail to reveal this majesty to human perception or contact. Things are not created with such holiness in them, nor do they readily signify beyond themselves to that sense of majesty. The "mythical mind"—or what Heschel might think of as popular religion—would expect holiness to reside in particular places like mountains or springs. We embark on pilgrimages to sacred spaces and worship in sanctuaries that promise greater divine energy and presence. But for Heschel, "when history began, there was only one holiness in the world, holiness in time."[14] The monotheistic God creates a singular and exclusive day in which holiness rules alone and unchallenged.

Though he claims "not to deprecate the world of space," nor to "disparage space and the blessing of things in space,"[15] Heschel privileges the holy over the good. This hierarchy of value reinforces Heschel's classic rhetorical prose: meet the reader where she stands (ethics), but move her slowly to recognize divine features of experience (holiness).[16] Most of us operate with a "mythical mind" that expects God's presence in spatial things. Heschel also deploys this critique of spatial theology to challenge Israel as a holy national center. Nation-states of all kinds claim an eternal validity deserving loyalty from their citizens. But only a divinity in time can rightfully command that kind of allegiance. Objects, too, can become fetishes of desire as we transform them into personalities with passions and power. God did not create things with divine substance, yet we imbue them with such energy all the more.

The temptation to transfer personal power to created things is strong, and Heschel knows this. The Israelites in the desert, after all, "succumbed to the temptation of worshipping a thing, a golden calf." Even more, they built a Tabernacle soon thereafter as a holy thing in space. But God ordered the world by hallowing time before the Israelites consecrated space: "The sanctity of time came first, the sanctity of man came second, and the sanctity of space last. Time was hallowed by God; space, the Tabernacle, was consecrated by Moses."[17] Heschel maneuvers gently between his strong claim that objects in space remain good but not holy, and the Exodus text that specifies a thing (the Tabernacle) as "holiness in *space*."[18] He argues only that "in the record of creation"—that is, in Genesis—do objects lack "the quality of holiness." Yet that is even true for spatial things. God did not erect the Tabernacle as a holy object. Moses consecrates the thing, and in so doing registers the very absence of divine authority.

What, then, is the qualitative difference between the Tabernacle and the golden calf as spatial things? Heschel labels the calf a mere "thing," but the Tabernacle is "holiness in *space*," a kind of thing that suggests "the mystery and majesty of the divine."[19] Yet Heschel also emphasizes that "in the Bible, no thing, no place on earth, is holy by itself."[20] The Tabernacle, as a mere collection of physical materials, stands without inherent supernatural qualities, and so is very much like the golden calf. For the Tabernacle to gain majesty and mystery, Moses must ascribe holiness to the structure in a way that points beyond the thing itself. The Israelites worshiped the golden calf alone, as a thing with inherent protective powers. The Tabernacle is not that kind of thing, but could always devolve into a fetishized object. This helps to explain why Heschel worries about sight and touch as senses most conducive to false worship. By seeing and touching things, we easily imagine a world replete with powerful objects, and miss the holiness in time:

> In our daily lives we attend primarily to that which the senses are spelling out for us: to what the eyes perceive, to what the fingers touch. Reality to us is thinghood, consisting of substances that occupy space; even God is conceived by most of us as a thing. The result of our thinginess is our blindness to all reality that fails to identify itself as a thing, as a matter of fact. This is obvious in our understanding of time, which, being thingless and insubstantial, appears to us as if it had no reality.[21]

Thinginess can surely be good, but it can never lead to holiness. If the Israelites worship the Tabernacle in its "thinginess," then it becomes even more dangerous than a golden idol. But as a thing endowed with "holiness in *space*," the Tabernacle suggests the real mystery of holiness in time, and is transformed into a special kind of thing.[22] Thinghood, as it were, is self-referential; holy things, like the Tabernacle, refer beyond the physical object to a spiritual reality. We do not touch or see them as things, as a "matter of fact," but as pointers to the ineffable. Heschel observes that from the viewpoint of Jewish tradition, the six days of the week serve the Sabbath, and progressively lean toward holiness in time.[23] So too holy things in space—merely good on their own, they nonetheless become holy by revealing a world without things.

A thing only has spiritual value, then, if it points beyond itself to a "thingless" reality of time. For Heschel, "there is a world of things and a world of spirit." Things are good, but spirit is holy:

> To the philosopher the idea of the good is the most exalted idea. But to the Bible the idea of the good is penultimate; it cannot exist without the holy. The good is the base, the holy is the summit. Things created in six days He considered *good,* the seventh day He made *holy.*[24]

Base things are superficial, lower in the hierarchy of value to the holy summit. Holy things become markers for something higher and more worthy. Yet all things are fleeting and ephemeral if they fail to point beyond themselves. They do not possess eternity in space, but can expose eternity in time. Holiness in time thus enables things to become more than they are. But to be more also means to be less—for things lose their bodily "thinginess" to become spiritual markers of mystery and majesty. In shredding their material presence, these markers of spiritual reality become the very opposite of a fetishized object, emptied of all inherent power and value. The Tabernacle does not contain holiness in space. If Moses thought it did, then he adopted that view from some other religion:

> Holiness in space, in nature, was known in other religions. New in the teaching of Judaism was that the idea of holiness was gradually shifted from space to time, from the realm of nature to the realm of history, from things to events. The physical world became divested of any inherent sanctity. There were no naturally sacred plants or animals any more. To be sacred, a thing had to be consecrated by a conscious act of man. The quality of holiness is not in the grain of matter. It is a preciousness bestowed upon things by an act of consecration and persisting in relation to God.[25]

In consecrating the Tabernacle, Moses bestowed holiness upon a thing. But for Heschel, the thing itself is not holy; it becomes so only when the thing persists "in relation to God." In this sense, holiness describes a kind of relation rather than a quality of substance. Things are holy only in the sense that they maintain a relation to mystery and grandeur. But once in that relation, these objects lose the "thinginess" that marks them as spatial things. There is, indeed, a world of things and a world of spirit. When the former persists "in relation" to the latter, things cast off their self-referential, material status. They become things in the image of God.

That holiness does not inhere in things suggests an enchanted world of spiritual relations. Heschel's critique of centralized worship, in which local spaces become special abodes of divine presence, explodes the alliance between religious elites and divine sources. Instead, we all live in a world in which any thing can refer to something beyond, and point to the mysterious and ineffable quality of divine encounter. This is the point of Heschel's discussion, in *Torah min-Hashamayim*, of the *Shekhinah* and its presence in the world. In Heschel's view, Rabbi Akiva (the first- and second-century Jewish sage) contained God's presence (*Shekhinah*) in a particular place, claiming that "the *Shekhinah* abides in the west, that the west is its preferred locale." But this would mean that God's presence "is spatially bounded" (*bamakom mugbelet shekhinato ke'ilu*). The "as if" (*ke'ilu*) hints at Heschel's support for Akiva's contemporary rival Rabbi Ishmael, and his opposing view that "the Shekhinah is everywhere," and so "transcends place." Heschel calls this view the "spiritual-intellectual conception" that establishes God's presence above spatial limits. Heschel also reads the Midrash in the Mekhilta of Rabbi Ishmael (a biblical commentary on the book of Exodus from the school of Ishmael) to show how the rabbis removed spatial metaphors that delimit God's presence. According to Heschel, the Midrash transformed a verse "that apparently pins down a specific location for the Divine Presence" to mean that "God is present in every time and place."[26] Every spatial location, in Heschel's reading, becomes a spiritual locale and occasion to encounter God. The world is alive with spiritual presence, and material things can provide conduits to the divine.

Yet even with this sense of mystery and enchantment in the physical world, Heschel denies the capacity of any one thing to capture holiness or divine presence. This leads him to malign physical objects as mere things that harm spiritual selves. The epilogue to *The Sabbath* reads as an extended battle against the worship of things. Though pagans imagine their God as a "visible image" or a "thing of space," Moses accepted the two tablets of stone received on Mount Sinai, yet "broke them before their [the Israelites] eyes."[27] Following the Midrashim that suggest Moses shattered the tablets not out of anger but from the desire to instruct, Heschel reads this Exodus scene as Judaism's rejection of material things. "The stone is broken," Heschel relates in *The Earth Is the Lord's*, "but the Words are alive," begging to be engraved "on the tablets of every heart."[28] My point here is not to highlight Heschel's misguided view of pagan ritual and belief. Instead, I want to emphasize how the nature of things is closely tied to his critique of paganism. We live in space, Heschel informs us, but we must move beyond it: "things are the shore, the voyage is in time."[29] Material things and their attractions await only pagan eyes.

Spiritual dimensions lie on the far side of physical boundaries—a constant theme in Heschel's philosophy, and one that he vividly portrayed in *Man Is Not Alone:*

> The search of reason ends at the shore of the known; on the immense expanse beyond it only the sense of the ineffable can glide. It alone knows the route to that which is remote from experience and understanding. Neither of them is amphibious: reason cannot go beyond the shore, and the sense of the ineffable is out of place where we measure, where we weigh.
>
> We do not leave the shore of the known in search of adventure or suspense or because of the failure of reason to answer our questions. We sail because our mind is like a fantastic sea shell, and when applying our ear to its lips we hear a perpetual murmur from the waves beyond the shore.[30]

Throughout his many works, but especially in *The Sabbath,* Heschel reiterates this sense of a voyage beyond physical experience and rational accounting. The "sense of the ineffable" belongs not to space; it is, literally, "out of place." Pulled from the murmur "beyond the shore," and decentered as "citizens of two realms," persons must hear the voice of the sacred to be fully human.[31] In conjuring up this spiritual awakening, Heschel also protects it from the spaces measured and the things weighed. For things to allude to a spiritual reality beyond the shore, they too must be "out of place" in that divine encounter. The two tablets at Sinai offer visual markers and aids to conjure the divine. But they have no place in the spiritual voyages to the ineffable; as spatial things, the tablets remain citizens of only one realm, both primitive and pagan.

This is how it must be in Heschel's taxonomy, for if God's presence (*Shekhinah*) dwells in all places at all times, then it really exists in no *place* at all: "monuments of stone are destined to disappear; days of spirit never pass away." The *Shekhinah* lives in eternal time, always "beyond our grasp," and reveals the immense "distance that lies between God and a thing."[32] Thinginess lives and dies in space:

> It is the world of space that communicates to us the sense for temporality. Time, that which is beyond and independent of space, is everlasting; it is the world of space which is perishing. Things perish within time; time itself does not change. We should not speak of the flow or passage of time but of the flow or passage of space through time. It is not time that dies; it is the human body which dies in time. Temporality is an attribute of the world of space, of things of space.[33]

Spatial things fail to surpass this permanent border to eternity; instead, they witness to the mortality of physical existence. These things are not holy things: they fail to point beyond themselves to spiritual dimensions, but rather stop at the shore, unable even to hear the remote echoes of eternity. We encounter God in time, Heschel maintains, but "things created conceal the Creator."[34] This world no longer appears enchanted.

And a disenchanted world is a dangerous one where feminine things seduce and destroy the self. In *The Earth Is the Lord's*, Heschel speaks of the "magnetic property of things" to attract, or worse, to distract us from "the genuinely precious" in time. Displaced objects move persons through their form and allure, and they must continually do so to maintain human interest. Yet "moments of the soul endure even when banished to the back of the mind." Eternity is most ours, Heschel claims, because feelings, thoughts, and "moments of the soul" live within us. Things as possessions, however, "are alien and often treacherous to the self. To be is more essential than to have."[35] Things entrap persons within a foreign and dangerous world of displayed objects. They deny essential features of the self. Humans simply cannot "be" with things. The desire to possess and use them overwhelms those "moments of the soul," and persons yearn to possess that next thing on display. Heschel rarely genders spatial objects, but he does associate them with culturally dominant notions of the feminine: things are seductive, treacherous, alluring, and material, yet always illusory. A disenchanted world is a space replete with feminine things that undermine spiritual lives. To be holy is to be male, and men "deal with things" but live beyond them. A thing is a temporal, feminine object of space that obstructs encounters with the divine.

Heschel's works offer two divergent accounts of things as 1) physical objects that point to a world of mystery and grandeur; and as 2) fallen materials that seduce our visual senses, and excite our desires to have rather than to be in the presence of God. He navigates through this tension by distinguishing base from special things, such that things without "thinginess" refer to the divine, while common things only attract us to their visual display. Edward Kaplan, a keen reader of Heschel's rhetorical language, recovers Heschel's distinction between a "real symbol" and merely a "conventional" one. The real symbol, argues Kaplan, presumes that "the Divine resides in it or that the symbol partakes to some degree of the reality of the Divine." This kind of symbol attracts the pagan mind. It acts like a treacherous thing that constrains the ineffability and mystery of the divine. But the conventional symbol only "represents to the mind an entity that is not shown." By not visually portraying the divine, the conventional symbol merely "suggests that entity."[36] This conventional representation functions like a thing that refers to the divine without delimiting it within space. Kaplan argues that Heschel evades the real symbol in his prose, for his "poetics of faith" enliven concepts (or things) to surpass themselves. Heschel's language, in "its suggestiveness, points to a fuller realm of being."[37] As another commentator on Heschel's account of symbol argues, "objects of art are solely functional, for they have no religious meaning by themselves, nor do they have an independently valid religious existence."[38] There are strong indications that Heschel's account of symbol is less nuanced than it needs to be.[39] But my concern is not with Heschel's truncated view of symbolic meaning, nor Kaplan's reading of it. Instead, I want to reveal that Heschel's "real" and "conventional" symbols map onto his account of things: the former is a feminine, deceitful kind of thing, whereas the latter is an iconic indicator of spiritual presence. Things are instruments, in this "conventional" view, that point beyond rather than at themselves.

Yet Heschel's prose remains forever stuck in the materiality of things. He suggests, almost reluctantly, how the "magnetic property of things" is inescapable. Indeed, the more Heschel attempts to free himself from the physical things that restrict God's presence, the more he finds himself within the things that bind the soul to space. Barbara Kirshenblatt-Gimblett alerts us to this propensity in Heschel to distinguish spiritual features from the concreteness of physical details, even as he "made objects metaphors for tangible and inexpressible features of an unseen though fully experienced inner world." Heschel enacts this very project in *The Earth Is the Lord's,* she argues, for he seeks (in Heschel's own words) "to ennoble the common, to endow worldly things with hieratic beauty." Kirshenblatt-Gimblett reads Heschel's metaphorical language as a heritage project that recaptures an imagined past for survival into a Jewish future.[40] Heschel's work is certainly this and more: even as he protects a spiritual core for survival after the Holocaust, his works testify to the concrete embeddedness of those spiritual encounters. The tablets of stone still exist—engraved and marked—in the inner dimensions of the heart. Protected from the allures of sight and touch, the written commandments still move us, perhaps even more so because they now reside within the self. The unseen and fully experienced inner world is cluttered with special kinds of holy things. The real and conventional symbol is a false distinction because the presence of things underlies both physical and spiritual worlds.

But Heschel writes as if that distinction remains in force. He distinguishes sacred from spatial things by uncovering objects that point beyond their "thinginess" to some other ethereal dimension. Though things are inescapable features of human experience, not all things are mired in space. Heschel's prose, then, however exposed to spatial imagery, still alludes to *holy* things, or things that refer beyond themselves. One has to read Heschel against Heschel, as I have done, in order to see that "thinginess" goes all the way down, penetrating his real and holy symbols. But Heschel seeks to convince us that this is not true, that some things still remain unsullied by spacial limits and feminine enticements. This is a recovery of a spiritual heritage untouched by material death. A thing, like a soul, can lead to eternal time.

We witness this move to recover a spiritual heritage in Heschel's account of Jewish texts. These books are sacred things that act like conventional symbols leading to the divine. He wistfully describes the Jews of Eastern Europe as those who "lived more in time than in space. It was as if their soul was always on the way, as if the secret of their heart had no affinity with things." This "as if," reminiscent of the same phrase in *Torah min-Hashamayim,* grounds Heschel's nostalgia in the physical contours of everyday life. For though East European Jews lived more in time, they still lived in space. In searching for a sensibility "more suggestive of their essence," he compares these Jews to a book "whose pages are constantly turning." This book mimics the Jewish soul "always on the way"; it is a book in time but not space, a book on a journey—a book, in other words, that is not a thing in space. Heschel contrasts this "Jewish" text to an "open book" that contains "a static picture of uniform lines with a definite proportion of text and margin."[41] Where the one remains fixed and stable, the "Jewish" book forever churns forward into new configurations. The open book, with its consistent lines, clear borders, and fitting proportions, conforms "to classical standards of beauty." It perpetuates its "thinginess" in its stable, conventional, and pleasant forms. The Jewish book, however, is "unique": valued by other standards of taste and beauty, it moves beyond the "definite proportion of text and margin" to suggest a singular journey to the ineffable.

Heschel carries over this distinction between the open and "constantly turning" book to the differences between Sephardi and Ashkenaz books—yet another hackneyed dualism so often found in Heschel's works. I am less concerned with the plausibility of this distinction (it makes no sense to me), but I am interested in the account of material things that underlies it. Heschel's argument here is part of a broader polemic, to be discussed below, concerning American Jewish affinities to Ashkenaz culture, and the ways in which American Jews have evaded this heritage. To recognize the value of that Ashkenaz heritage, Heschel wants to show how Sephardi books function like open ones, but Ashkenaz texts behave like those "Jewish" books that incessantly move beyond and threaten to burst through the seams. Heschel overturns the long-standing appeal of Sephardi heritage for liberal, modern European Jews who were embarrassed by the perceived legalistic history of Ashkenaz Jewry.[42] For Heschel, Ashkenaz books remind one of Rembrandt—"profound, allusive, and full of hidden meanings." They exude "the tension of dialectic," while the Sephardi texts (more like Raphael paintings, so Heschel believes) "favor the harmony of a system." Like the open book, the Sephardi style reveals a "balanced solemnity," and its texts a "mastery of expression." Yet note the contrast to the Ashkenaz "impulsive inspiration": "[The strength] of the Ashkenazim [lies] in the unexpressed overtones of their words. A spasm of feeling, a passionate movement of thought, an explosive enthusiasm, will break through the form."[43] Ashkenaz books behave neither like things with a proper form, nor as a harmonious, balanced system like their Sephardi counterparts. Just as special things point beyond themselves, so too do Ashkenaz books suggest a world of eternal time:

> Sephardic books are like neatly trimmed and cultivated parks, Ashkenazic writings like enchanted ancient forests; the former are like a story with a beginning and an end, the latter have a beginning but frequently turn into a story without an end.[44]

Books without end, I submit, are not books as spatial things, with "trimmed and cultivated" boundaries and margins. Instead, they are special kinds of books that surpass the "thinginess" of spatial objects. They "break through the form" to suggest something other. Heschel calls time an "otherness, a mystery that hovers above all categories."[45] As books in time but not space, Ashkenaz writings are not things but moments: not physical objects, but rather experiences of the divine. One does not read Ashkenaz texts so much as live them.[46]

This is all the more true of the Torah and the Talmud, for Jews did not enslave themselves to physical texts, but rather lived within them. Heschel recalls how "in almost every Jewish home in Eastern Europe . . . stood a bookcase full of volumes; proud and stately folio tomes together with shy, small-sized books." These texts remain physical objects as things on display within private dwellings. Yet books prove to be more: they are "timeproof receptacles for the eternally valid coins of spirit." Even with all their splendor, the sacred texts did not seduce Jews into becoming "the People of the Book." That would mean a book as a possession in which the Jew, entranced by the beauty of the material, simply desires to accumulate more things. But East European Jews "did not feel that they possessed the 'Book,' just as one does not feel that one possesses life. The Book, the Torah, was their essence, just as they, the Jews, were the essence of the Torah."[47] Heschel conflates Jews and the Torah into one body that surpasses physical markings: they both are "life"—an experience in time rather than a thing in space. The Jews live Torah not as a thing to possess, nor as a book to see and read, but as an "otherness" of exposure. In their wrestling with this experiential text, Jews "were able to feel heaven in a passage of Talmud."[48] As "timeproof receptacles," Jewish sacred texts might look like things, but they did not act that way. Instead, Jewish books channeled the divine into lived experience. They were not things but holiness in time.

Yet Heschel could hardly escape the material quality of Jewish sacred texts. Even as these books channeled the divine in time, they still did so within physical space. Note the architectural images Heschel employs to describe these medieval commentaries:

> The Ashkenazim rarely composed books that stand like separate buildings with foundations of their own, books that do not lean upon older works; they wrote commentaries or notes on the classical works of olden times, books that modestly hug the monumental walls of older citadels.[49]

Heschel offers a vivid portrait of how medieval Jews imagined their writing and its place within traditional exegesis (commentaries "hug" rather than "lean upon" classical sources). Readers like Edward Kaplan would surely argue that Heschel's language is metaphorical, such that walls and citadels merely conjure up the sense of a commentary in "the structure of metaphor." To think that books really act like buildings is to miss the tenor and "poetics of piety" of Heschel's prose.[50] Yet when Heschel calls the Sabbath "our great cathedrals,"[51] Kaplan recognizes that he "comes perilously close to contradicting his axiomatic opposition to spatial analogies of the holy."[52] Even analogies such as these can become alluring commodities.

But I wonder how Heschel could escape these spatial analogies, here and in the many other examples from *The Sabbath* and *The Earth Is the Lord's,* when he appeals to physical things to explain holiness in time. Jewish books signify transcendence, yet they do so as everyday things:

> But drunkards were rarely seen among Jews. When night came and a man wanted to pass away time, he did not hasten to a tavern to take a drink, but went to pore over a book or joined a group which—either with or without a teacher—indulged in the enjoyment of studying revered books.[53]

Reading sacred texts became an enjoyable pastime, a communal practice to "pass away time." One took pleasure in books, as others did in drinks at the local pub. Jewish works are certainly not frivolous things, but they are things all the same. And one senses that enjoyment comes not only through reading texts, but through reading texts with others. Books serve to heighten communal solidarity through the pleasures of play: exhausted by "their day's toil," Jews could still hear "the austere music of the Talmud's groping for truth." These are neither Ashkenaz or Sephardi texts, nor are they conventional or real symbols, but books to treasure, love, engage, and touch. These East European Jews, at least, could enjoy their books as sensual things of beauty.

AESTHETICS AND THINGS

As Jeffrey Shandler has noted, Heschel often ridicules aesthetics even as he appeals to beauty and grandeur.[54] It becomes increasingly clear, however, that Heschel's view of aesthetics tends to follow his account of things: he maligns beauty for its own sake, but admires it as a conduit of the holy. Those Jews who indulge in reading revered books recognize a kind of beauty that "hugs" the eternal. But all other kinds of aesthetic enjoyment are far less honorable:

> An esthetic experience leaves behind the memory of a perception and enjoyment; a prophetic experience leaves behind *the memory of a commitment*. Revelation was not an act of enjoyment. God spoke and man not only perceived but also accepted the will of God. Revelation lasts a moment, acceptance continues.[55]

Beauty and pleasure do not force commitment, but prophetic experiences do. For Heschel, "this world acquires flavor only when a little of the other world is mingled with it." We should enjoy beautiful things when they offer a taste of eternity. But when we seek pleasure in the "thinginess" of things, our flesh "is full of darkness."[56]

Compare, for a moment, Heschel's view of aesthetic experience with Mordecai Kaplan's notion of aesthetic performance, discussed in chapter 1. For Kaplan, working with things discloses beauty. We noticed this in Kaplan's play with clay, and even more in his journal writing. Material products were the stuff in and through which selves performed and cultivated their American identities. This performance materialized, in the thing itself, the presence of an engaged personality. But not so for Heschel: performance must signal transcendence beyond the physical markings of experiences and things. Aesthetic beauty, like special things, must partake of holiness in time; otherwise beauty, again like things, seduces the soul into spatial darkness. Kaplan's aesthetic performances are good, so might argue Heschel, but they fail to engage transcendence.

The experience of beauty in Ashkenaz books derives from this transcendent contact in and through a thing.[57] If the Sephardi text represents a harmonious system, with its "balanced solemnity" and "mastery of expression," together with "neatly trimmed and cultivated" borders, then the Ashkenaz book suggests "the tension of dialectic" and "impulsive inspiration." These more "Jewish" books transcend the physical limits of the binding through "a spasm of feeling, a passionate movement of thought, [and] an explosive enthusiasm." Beauty is constantly on the move, turning into a "story without an end." It is "profound, allusive, and full of hidden meanings." But the "Raphaelesque paintings," like the Sephardi books, lack this unbounded energy and high trajectory.[58] The "mythical mind" revels in the spatial characteristics of things—"striving after measure, order, and harmony."[59] A system might yield coherence, but it does not count as beautiful.[60] Even more, Heschel associates notions of beauty with democratic societies that favor the "naturalness of the humble mass." Sephardi cultures, so Heschel believes, were shaped by an elite. In contrast, Ashkenaz societies were grounded upon "the archaic simplicity" and "imaginative naïveté" of the masses.[61] Heschel praises the great medieval exegete Rashi who, as an Ashkenaz Jew, "*democratized* Jewish education, he brought the Bible, the Talmud, and the Midrash to the people. He made the Talmud a popular book, everyman's book. Learning ceased to be the monopoly of the few."[62] Aesthetic beauty is spontaneous, dynamic, and available to all—just like those holy things that immediately transcend space to access eternity.

Reading sacred texts marks one kind of transcendence "from the boundaries of here and now." It also defines the aesthetic experience:

> Learning was essentially nonutilitarian, almost free of direct pragmatic designs, an aesthetic experience. They [the East European Jews] delved into those parts of the lore that had no relevance to daily life no less eagerly than into those that had a direct bearing on it. Detached in their learning from interests in mundane affairs, they grappled with problems which were remote from the banalities of the normal course of living.

Let the Lord grapple with "mundane affairs"; the Jewish "aim was to partake of spiritual beauty." There, in the sacred text, the Jew found "holiness . . . in their wrestling with the Lore."[63] Heschel called this kind of reading and studying an "artistic act," but one that did not employ things like "stone or bronze, but the mystic substance of the universe."[64] I am none too sure what kind of holy substance that might be, but I doubt it is a physical thing. When Heschel's Jews wrestle with Torah, they do not struggle with a physical, material book. Aesthetic beauty and pleasure are not to be found in things, but in that "mystic substance" that taps into spiritual forces. Studying Torah opens an experiential window to another reality—and only there can one partake of spiritual beauty. Like Jews, sacred texts "often lacked outward brilliance, but they were full of hidden light."[65]

In appealing to the aesthetic charm of books and their capacity to move readers, Heschel draws upon the cultural tastes of middle-brow culture. Janice Radway suggests that middle-brow readers of the 1920s actively distinguished their literary tastes from those of high-brow or academic discourse. The term *middle-brow* evokes a professional, managerial readership who "wanted desperately to present themselves as educated, sophisticated, and aesthetically articulate," but also one who viscerally recoiled from the sterile, objective, and passionless reading practices of the elite. Though defenders of high culture dismissed this middling tradition as popular and vulgar, middle-brow readers yearned for books that reflected their own conflicted and emotional lives.[66] By immersing themselves within the texture and narrative of cheap novels, middle-brow readers discovered a transformative experience "with greater force and fervor than one might be permitted in ordinary daily life." Radway insists that books with this kind of emotional power captured selves within the world of material things, even if books linked them "to something beyond the self."[67] This account of middle-brow readership fits nicely with Heschel's notion of an aesthetic beauty that facilitates moments of transcendence, and explains why many academics dismiss his works as inspirational, trendy literature. Ashkenaz texts characterized as popular, sentimental, and democratic echo the emotional style so beloved by the middle-brow readership. These "Jewish" books, too, had "decorative value" that ennobled the self. And as middle-brow readers harnessed books to travel beyond the self, so too did Ashkenaz works tie transformative moments to material beautiful things.

When reading Heschel, one senses his desire of return: that sense of retrieval in which Ashkenaz sources reawaken spiritual encounters. Scholars often describe *The Earth Is the Lord's* as a eulogy for the lost world of Heschel's childhood.[68] Yet the text is a heritage project of spiritual importance. Rashi, after all, appears akin to an *American* hero. Heschel refashions his own East European heritage in images that American Jews can recognize and honor. This is a world familiar to them: it really is *their* world, their democracy, and their culture—only a forgotten one. American Jews can relive Rashi's world because it has become so close to their own. But Jews have traveled far, and in America they have abandoned their spiritual roots. In Eastern Europe, Heschel tells us, Jews created literature "about Jews, and for Jews. They apologized to no one . . . and they wasted no energy in refuting hostile opinions." There, but not in America, "the Jewish people came into its own. It did not live like a guest in somebody else's house, who must constantly keep in mind the ways and customs of the host."[69] Cultural amnesia replaced Rashi with far more timid teachers and bashful students. American Jews were seduced by foreign, even treacherous "ways and customs." Beautiful cultures require authentic roots: the earth might be the Lord's, but America is for Ashkenaz Jews.

Heschel recognizes that America is more, and less, than its passion for democracy. He notes how "a civilization that is devoted exclusively to the utilitarian is at bottom not different from barbarism." American Jews must recapture the more noble pursuits of the "unpractical spirit," for "the soul is sustained by the regard for that which transcends all immediate purposes."[70] But material things create public spectacles that dazzle and seduce. Visual displays of fashion emphasize physical things rather than an inward spirit. As spectacle, a thing seduces the eyes into false worship and forgetfulness: "Dazzled by the lights of the metropolis, we lost at times the inner sight. The luminous visions that for so many generations shone in the little candles were extinguished for some of us."[71] The Sephardi Jews secured beauty in proper forms and fitting lines: they did not dazzle, but they still created beauty in things. Ashkenaz Jewry, however, detached the pleasant and the beautiful from physical appearances, and discovered the object's allure instead in the "hidden light." To repeat, I do not want to condone Heschel's distinction between Ashkenaz and Sephardi culture. I find his discussion banal and grossly inaccurate. What fascinates me, here and elsewhere, though, is the account of material things underlying this very imprecise account of complex cultures. Here again we find seductive things among luminous, holy possibilities. Vision misdirects the soul toward outward spectacle and those alluring things. A *hidden* light, after all, cannot be seen, but it may be experienced. Aesthetic beauty is more experience than substance, in Heschel's view; it lies neither within the self nor the object, but in the relation between self and other.

The Sabbath puts us in a right relation with other things, and thereby endows them with beauty. Rather than banishing material products to the other six days of the week, Heschel reorientates our vision to see things differently—in the light of Sabbath time. This is no "cult of domesticity," in which the Sabbath enables more efficient labor during the week by setting aside time for rest and recuperation.[72] Heschel situates the Sabbath at the center so that other days more effectively serve it. In this way, the Sabbath reawakens aesthetic enjoyment: "Unlike the Day of Atonement, the Sabbath is not dedicated exclusively to spiritual goals. It is a day of the soul as well as of the body; comfort and pleasure are an integral part of the Sabbath observance."[73] The comforts associated with commercial success have been co-opted by a day of rest that offers competing delights. Although the Sabbath diverts the self from commercial hungers, it nonetheless satiates these hungers by other means. In this sense, one need not sacrifice aesthetic enjoyment for Sabbath observance. On the day of rest, "the soul cannot celebrate alone, so the body must be invited to partake in the rejoicing of the Sabbath."[74] Things used during six days of the week become holy during the Sabbath. Material objects are beautiful on the seventh day as things in time rather than in space.

Heschel labors to explain how a thing in time might appear. He draws heavily from architectural models, even if this requires him to emphasize spatial imagery more than he would like. But when Heschel calls Jewish ritual "the art of significant forms in time, as *architecture in time*," and then describes the weekly Sabbaths as "our great cathedrals,"[75] a reader could easily import spatial images into the holiness of time. For those attuned to American architectural history, the reference to "our great cathedrals" would certainly conjure up commercial department stores like John Wanamaker's in Philadelphia,[76] as well as the Woolworth building in New York City—built in 1913 and itself called the "Cathedral of Commerce." But unlike Cass Gilbert, who designed the Woolworth building (at that time the tallest in the world), Jews build "a *palace in time*."[77] What kind of representational image is this? What work does it do? Edward Kaplan, who has written extensively on Heschel's poetics, describes the structure of metaphor in this way:

> The metaphor is a concrete image that alludes to another reality, based upon some analogy between the two terms. The "vehicle" of the metaphor is the term (or image) that appears in the text, alluding to the "tenor," the absent reality or concept.[78]

If we take "our great cathedrals" as a metaphor for the weekly Sabbaths, then the cathedral is "the concrete image" and "vehicle" that alludes to the Sabbath as the "tenor." But a metaphor works only if a common quality exists between the vehicle and the tenor (what Kaplan calls its "ground"), for only then will the comparison make sense. So for Heschel's metaphor to elicit a sense of holiness in time, he must play on conventional cultural notions of grandeur. A cathedral has to be the kind of thing that typically evokes awe and wonder for those culturally aware to make that connection; otherwise, the correlation between it and the Sabbath breaks down. In Josef Stern's terms, the metaphorical sense has to capture some feature of the literal:

> The literal/first meaning of the words must "remain active in the metaphorical setting." Whatever turns out to be the exact nature of the dependence of the metaphorical on the literal, knowledge of the literal/first meaning of words is necessary on the occasion of utterance itself in order to determine what they metaphorically make us notice, that is, their metaphorical interpretation.[79]

Readers require specific cultural knowledge to recognize and accept Heschel's metaphor as a provocative one. Heschel seeks to convince us that the Sabbath evokes a sense of awe in a stronger, even deeper way. But to do this, he trades off that "literal/first meaning" of a physical cathedral in space. If, as Kaplan warns, the metaphor acts as "*understatement,* for the vehicle of language can never completely express the divine tenor,"[80] then things in time conjure up holiness more directly than physical buildings. How things in time do this we do not know, and Heschel offers little to help us "tell it to our minds."[81] But some knowledge of cathedrals "makes us notice" Heschel's metaphor as a powerful one.

Sabbaths as our great cathedrals: the metaphor suggests that we commonly recognize things in space as something more than material objects, something that can provoke emotional responses. It trades on the notion that spatial things are indeed sublime. Yet the point is not to understand the Sabbath as a great cathedral, but rather to experience it as such. It would mean exposure to mystery and awe on a scale beyond the site of skyscrapers or magnificent palaces. Even so, the ambiguity in metaphorical thinking persists: does the "tenor" (the Sabbath) reconfigure the meaning of the "vehicle" (cathedral), such that we experience buildings with more profound awe; or does the concrete image overdetermine the sense of the ineffable, so that we cannot but imagine the Sabbath as an awesome structure? The metaphor "depends" on the literal, as Stern points out, but the nature of that dependence remains unclear. How much, I want to ask, does the spiritual depend on the material?

To avoid such religious dilemmas, some thinkers turn to negative theology, indicating what God is not, as a means of minimizing false and irresponsible images of the divine. For students of this theological practice, all positive linguistic descriptions constitute false belief, for language is intrinsically deficient. Heschel, who wrote an extensive book on Maimonides (himself a master practitioner of negative theology), certainly understood the risks of comparing the Sabbath to physical objects. Indeed, Heschel appeals to negative theology when defending the many abstentions of Sabbath observance: just as "we can never say what He is," we should honor the day "by the silence of abstaining from noisy acts."[82] As I indicated earlier, Edward Kaplan thinks Heschel came "perilously close" to a spatial analogy of the holy when he likened the Sabbath to a great cathedral.[83] Yet Heschel cultivated his metaphors to move readers to experience the "hyphens between heaven and earth." He conceived of the biblical text in this way, as words that "became a live wire charged with His spirit."[84] Something of this charge transfers over to his metaphors of cathedrals and palaces. Heschel employs his metaphors to elicit a charged experience of the divine that is analogous to, but substantially different from, the experience of awe before a magnificent building. It is a kind of experience that he believes Jews encounter every day. For Jews do not build cathedrals or synagogues, Heschel tells us; instead, they build "bridges leading from the heart to God."[85] The Jew, as "an architect of hidden worlds," experiences the divine without things.

And yet things surround the Jew as they do all other persons living in the world. Here as elsewhere, Heschel distances things from the sense of holiness, but must appropriate them in metaphor and notions of aesthetic enjoyment. Jews cannot escape the "thinginess" of things during the Sabbath. Things are everywhere present as markers of beauty, awe, and mystery. Put simply, one cannot imagine things in time without juxtaposing them to things of space. In their very absence, things remain stubbornly present on the day of rest. Even as Heschel claims that "there is no quality that space has in common with the essence of God," he nonetheless appeals to spatial things to conjure up divine mystery: "The art of keeping the seventh day is the art of painting on the canvas of time the mysterious grandeur of the climax of creation."[86] If there is no "ground," as Edward Kaplan would call it, between space and God, then the metaphor of a painted canvas fails as a representational image. There would not be enough commonality between the vehicle and the tenor for the metaphor to do its work. Intimations of the holy must hold some relation to aesthetic acts for Heschel's metaphors to provoke meaningful experiences. And Heschel seems all too aware of this:

> For all the idealization, there is no danger of the idea of the Sabbath becoming a fairy-tale. With all the romantic idealization, the Sabbath remains a concrete fact, a legal institution and a social order. There is no danger of its becoming a disembodied spirit, for the spirit of the Sabbath must always be in accord with actual deeds, with definite actions and abstentions. The real and the spiritual are one, like body and soul in a living man.[87]

Some eleven pages earlier in *The Sabbath,* Heschel had described an object's "thinginess" as a "matter of fact." Here too, the Sabbath is "a concrete fact" in its cultural, social, and institutional locations. If the Sabbath reveals holiness in time, a day that acts like a hyphen between heaven and earth, then it is also a matter-of-fact kind of thing. And it could not be otherwise. Things that point to some beyond—to mystery, awe, and aesthetic beauty—do so precisely as material things. An aesthetics in time cannot escape bodily practices in space: the real and the spiritual, after all, are one. Material culture and identity, as Heschel unwittingly testifies, is an inescapable feature of Jewish practice and experience, even on the Sabbath.

IDOLATRY, IDENTITY, AND THINGS

Though persons cannot escape things, they can certainly avoid worshiping them as holy objects. Heschel's move from things of space to things in time is meant to do just this. Even if the metaphor of a cathedral in time conjures up a spatial building, it still prevents the veneration of a physical thing. The negative commandment not to covet things of space is "correlated with the unspoken word: *Do covet things of time.*"[88] Space and time implicate each other, such that things of space allude to things in time. Yet venerating spatial things is a form of idol worship, whereas honoring things in time serves God. What kind of idolatry troubles Heschel? What is lost or misdirected when one venerates a physical object? Moshe Habertal and Avishai Margalit have artfully catalogued four conceptions of idolatry in religious traditions: 1) as betrayal and rebellion; 2) as a theoretical error; 3) as a form of magic; and 4) as erroneous practice.[89] When Habertal and Margalit discuss Maimonides and the second form of idolatry, they suggest that "the problem with iconic representations . . . is not that they are mistaken representations but that they are improper representations."[90] The image offers a poor depiction of divinity—it is inappropriate more than it is wrong, disrespectful more than mistaken.[91] Heschel holds something like this view with regard to the veneration of things. But he also shares the biblical notion of idolatry as betrayal and rebellion.[92] Heschel associates false worship with forgetfulness—a form of betrayal of personal relations and historical continuity. To worship a thing is inappropriate because one forgets the obligations that bind persons to holiness.

The Sabbath as a day of holiness draws us away from the instruments of space. The "idols of technical civilization" reinforce and propel the capitalist engine, and transform material devices into "weapons of destruction." These tools damage personal sanity and communal sharing. Heschel associates these things of space with "the vulgar," and the Sabbath returns us to more tasteful pursuits. The indecency and gaudiness of material consumption texture Heschel's view of things in general: "In regard to external gifts, to outward possessions, there is only one proper attitude—to have them and to be able to do without them. On the Sabbath we live, as it were, *independent of technical civilization.*"[93] The "as it were" implies that we cannot divorce ourselves completely from material concerns, but should live as if that were the case. Again, Heschel slides between dismissing material things altogether and seeking to find the right relation to them. The Sabbath decodes material products as vulgar things—as those objects unworthy of human veneration. They are filthy, soiled, and distasteful: they harm the self rather than exalt it. Even more, things dissociate persons from others, such that we forget to share, and learn only to possess: "Through my ownership of space, I am a rival of all other beings; through my living in time, I am a contemporary of all other beings." In this sense, a thing "is that which has separate or individual existence as distinct from the totality of beings. To see a thing is to see something which is detached and isolated."[94] We become the mirror image of our possessions: unhitched from communal attachments, we become isolated individuals. To worship a thing is to debase the self.

Yet Heschel also worries about the relation of that self to the Jewish historical community. Idol worship is both improper and an act of betrayal. As persons rely on material things for comfort and satisfaction, they lose sight of their obligations to the past: "We have helped to extinguish the light our fathers kindled. We have bartered holiness for convenience, loyalty for success, wisdom for information, prayers for sermons, tradition for fashion." The "we" in this text are those American Jews who, in their "passion to advance," have lost the "ability to believe."[95] They have become idol worshippers, replacing a religious heritage with vulgar things. In that fourth sense that Habertal and Margalit outline, these Jews worship in the wrong way: their error is not metaphysical but practical. Yet their error compounds the predicament of detached souls, for "a world has vanished" together with connected beings. Idolatry becomes a form of forgetfulness:

> We of this generation are still holding the key. Unless we remember, unless we unlock it, the holiness of ages will remain a secret of God. We of this generation are still holding the key—the key to the sanctuary which is also the shelter of our own deserted souls. If we mislay the key, we shall elude ourselves.[96]

Habertal and Margalit make much of the biblical command to remember, relating it to personal loyalty and its rival, intimate betrayal. To remember is to maintain personal relations with God, but to forget is to betray a covenant with all its personal obligations.[97] Heschel appeals to this notion of betrayal when he criticizes American Jews who forget their ancestral obligations. Devotion to things in space has replaced loyalty to one's heritage experienced in time. This act of betrayal and forgetfulness can be reversed ("we of this generation are still holding the key"), but until that time, we "elude ourselves" and "the legacy of ages."[98] Only the Sabbath, Heschel warns, "teaches all beings whom to praise."[99]

The stakes are high, as they were in ancient times when a passionate God demanded absolute loyalty. Heschel concludes his *The Earth Is the Lord's* with a call to arms:

> The time for the kingdom may be far off, but the task is plain: to retain our share in God in spite of peril and contempt. There is a war to wage against the vulgar, against the glorification of the absurd, a war that is incessant, universal. Loyal to the presence of the ultimate in the common, we may be able to make it clear that man is more than man, that in doing the finite he may perceive the infinite.[100]

Worshiping a thing glorifies the absurd and the vulgar. It misidentifies the proper being to praise, and thus betrays the loyalty demanded and deserved by God. Heschel turns to the Sabbath to liberate "man from his own muddiness" in space. Idol worship appears only in material form: in the technological world of commerce with money as "the world's chief idol."[101] Yet the "key to the sanctuary" does not return us to an insular Sabbath in time. To perceive the infinite in the finite, one must engage the world of space and things. Heschel will not "wage war against the vulgar" by retreating to the "islands of stillness"[102] of the Sabbath day. As Arnold Eisen has argued, Heschel offers a more expansive notion of the commandments then he himself was prepared to follow: he "opened wide a door through which he declined to walk."[103] But he did march through nonetheless, and step-by-step expanded Jewish responsibility "to include public activity on behalf of civil rights, Soviet Jewry or cessation of the Vietnam war."[104] If Heschel prayed with his feet, he did so not in Sabbath time but in the messy, vulgar world of spatial things. You do not smash idols in time but in space. To be loyal to ancient traditions, and to remember covenantal obligations, one must leave the Sabbath to engage things in all their unseemly filth.

But the filthy things weigh us down such that we "surrender to space" and are enslaved by things. Ensnared by these "forgeries of happiness" and the "Frankensteins of spatial things,"[105] we lose our selves in "the acquisition of things of space." We become and act like a thing: "Many hearts and pitchers are broken at the fountain of profit. Selling himself into slavery to things, man becomes a utensil that is broken at the fountain."[106] Idol worship transforms the self into an image of the venerated object. If the object is a "treacherous" or "alien" thing (a kind of Frankenstein), then it will capture the self within a world of freakish monsters. Heschel recognizes the need to live in this dangerous world, but not to be entranced by it. The self, too, can become a monster of spatial things. When Moses smashed the two tablets "before their eyes," he broke "the most precious object that has ever been on earth."[107] Those tablets could have easily become "forgeries of happiness," as the golden calf surely was for those who danced around it. Artistic works, like music, can both elevate and deform the self.[108] All things, Heschel implies, are potential monsters who torment the self. To personify things in this way only adds to their allure as possible idols. Spatial things are dangerous because we become akin to the things we embrace.

Heschel discloses a profound anxiety about things in this world and how best to relate to them. At times he would rather shut them out altogether, and retreat to the secure and serene experience of Sabbath time. Yet we also find Heschel engaged and strongly attached to spatial things. The borders between time and space remain far more porous than Heschel sometimes admits. He pleads against "enslavement to things," in part because he also dreads the "thinginess" of things. Even as he desires "not to deprecate the world of space," nor "disparage space and the blessing of things of space," he still fears things even as he works with them. This anxiety mirrors his account of words as either descriptive of real, physical things (a chair or table), or indicative of more sublime, hidden meanings that "draw a person to an understanding of the realities which they indicate."[109] Heschel values the indicative capacity of words to hint at mystery and grandeur, but he worries that such words will easily slide into mere descriptions of things to venerate. The allure of secure, descriptive words are all too powerful, as all idols surely are.

This anxiety about things in the world arises most powerfully in Heschel's allegorical reading of Shimeon ben Yohai's challenge to the

Roman empire and its great works.[110] In Heschel's retelling of this talmudic story, three rabbis sit together in Palestine in the year 130 CE to discuss political power. Rabbi Judah ben Ilai admires the Roman roads, market places, bridges, and bathhouses. Rabbi Jose remains silent, but not Rabbi Shimeon: "All that they made they made for themselves. They made roads and market places to put harlots there; they built bridges to levy tolls for them; they erected bathhouses to delight their bodies."[111] Upon receiving word of this argument, the Romans exalted Rabbi Judah, exiled Rabbi Jose, and put to death Rabbi Shimeon "who reviled our work." To escape his punishment, Rabbi Shimeon took his son Rabbi Eleazer, hid in a cave, and studied Torah and prayed together for twelve years. When informed of the emperor's death and the annulment of the decree, Shimeon and Eleazer finally emerged from the cave. But upon seeing laborers plowing fields, they exclaimed: "These people forsake eternal life and are engaged in temporary life!" Whatever they gazed upon was consumed by fire, and a "voice from heaven" responded: "Have ye emerged to destroy My world? Return to your cave!"[112] After twelve more months underground, Rabbi Shimeon and his son returned to see "an old man carrying two bundles of myrtle in his hand." When asked about the significance of the herbs, the old man replied, "they are in honor of the Sabbath." At that moment, the story concludes, "both found tranquility of soul."[113]

Heschel's reading instructs on a number of levels. He associates Rome with America, for both represent great nations at the height of their power (Rome in 130 CE and America after the Second World War). Like Roman civilization, American culture has "attained a high degree of perfection in the technical arts. In all her provinces, signs of immense progress in administration, engineering and the art of construction were widely visible." Public life functions in the city, where citizens remember their heroes, and fallen soldiers attain immortality through monuments that bear witness to the past. The city becomes eternal by means of these physical markings of memorialization, and the city-state deserves the adoration of its populace.[114]

America appears much the same as Rome, with its technological sophistication, its highway projects and engineering savvy; indeed, after the war America, too, recognized its dead through public monuments. Yet to Rabbi Shimeon, "these triumphs were shocking, hateful and repulsive. He disparaged the calculating, utilitarian spirit of Roman civilization." So too did Heschel despair of American utility and veneration of false idols. He clearly shares with Shimeon a disgust for inverted values, where building roads and market places that serve the flesh uproot spiritual progress. For both rabbis, the Romans and then the Americans "forsake eternal life and are engaged in temporary life!" If Shimeon fled to the cave "in order to endow life with a quality of eternity,"[115] then Heschel returns to the Sabbath to find holiness in eternal time. Indeed, Shimeon's existential commitments seem very much like Heschel's own:

> To Rabbi Shimeon eternity was not attained by those who bartered time for space but by those who knew how to fill their time with spirit. To him the great problem was *time* rather than *space;* the task was how to convert time into eternity rather than how to fill space with buildings, bridges and roads; and the solution of the problem lay in study and prayer rather than in geometry and engineering.[116]

The talmudic story becomes, in Heschel's prose, a proof text for the reversal of values instituted by sabbatical time. Immortality arrives in time but not space, and those "captivated by the things of the earth"[117] worship false gods.

But God condemned Rabbi Shimeon's rejection of the world, and the cave became a prison of confinement rather than a shelter for spiritual pursuits. Shimeon actually destroys the world by denying it, as fire consumes all that his eyes envision. Heschel, like that voice from heaven, renounces this kind of retreat to a safe haven.[118] Reflecting on the state of interfaith dialogue, Heschel objects to "religious isolationism" as a "myth": "No religion is an island," Heschel warns, for "parochialism has become untenable."[119] In a stunning admission some seventeen years after writing *The Earth Is the Lord's,* Heschel sought to revise his postwar retreat:

> A good many people in our midst still think in terms of an age during which Judaism wrapped itself in spiritual isolation, an age which I sought to relive in a book called *The Earth Is the Lord's.* Nowadays [1967], however, for the majority of our people, involvement has replaced isolation. The emancipation which has brought us to the very heart of the total society, has not only given us rights, it has also imposed obligations. It has expanded the scope of our responsibility and concern. Whether we

like it or not, the words we utter, the deeds we perform, affect the life of the total community. It is necessary, therefore, to clarify our position in relation to the general community.[120]

Writing these words in 1967, when he battled discriminatory racial practices, and would soon speak passionately against the Vietnam War, Heschel alerts us to the historical and cultural moment that shaped *The Earth Is the Lord's* and *The Sabbath*. It was a time of retreat, of returning home (or, for many Jews, for moving to the suburbs) to discover tranquility after the horrors of the Second World War. Jews, like other Americans, turned inward, and Heschel provided them a day to recover their forgotten spiritual connections to the ineffable. The tumultuous sixties, however, reinforced the sense that obligations go beyond the self. If those like Rabbi Shimeon could flee the city to study and pray in the 1950s, by the 1960s they had to learn to pray with their feet.

Yet even in 1951, Heschel agreed with the voice from heaven that Shimeon must cultivate the self through worldly pursuits. How did Heschel understand the relation between spiritual wholeness for the self, and material justice for all? To Shimeon, "there is only heaven and nothing else." But to Heschel, "the world this side of heaven is worth working in."[121] While the rabbi and his son denied the world, Heschel forms a tentative truce:

> This, then, is the answer to the problem of civilization: not to flee from the realm of space; to work with things of space but to be in love with eternity. Things are our tools; eternity, the Sabbath, is our mate. Israel is engaged to eternity. Even if they dedicate six days of the week to worldly pursuits, their soul is claimed by the seventh day.[122]

Heschel believes Shimeon and his son Eleazer also make peace with the world, for they found "tranquility of soul" in the end. But Heschel reads into the text far more than the text itself can bear on its own. For those rabbis do not see "worldly pursuits" when they reemerge from the cave; instead, they meet an old man who, in carrying myrtle in his hand, honors the Sabbath. Jews now exist, these rabbis understand, who do not entirely forsake eternal life. But this still does not give us a responsible life dedicated to worldly pursuits. Heschel's interpretive gloss reveals a more engaged approach to material life, even if things are merely "tools" for our use rather than objects of pleasure, meaning, and value. Things certainly have their place in our lives, but we should neither love nor venerate them as anything more than practical items. If Kaplan understood a civilization as the fullest expression of a people's spirit and culture, then for Heschel it is a "problem" to negotiate and resolve. In order to live in but not of the world, we should recognize our spatial boundaries, even as we surpass them on one day of the week.

Yet engaging the world fully, without recourse to a protected time for spiritual nourishment, makes us lose sight of obligations to self and God, together with the religious traditions that sustain them. Jewish practice too easily devolves into a form of idol worship. For Heschel, the Sabbath provides a time and, I would argue, a space too—in the home, synagogue, or community—within which Jews reconnect to their spiritual sources. Repeatedly Heschel warns against trivializing space and things. God saw "it was good," and we should too. But nothing more. The Sabbath limits our worship of things to "use value." The allure of idol worship is indeed strong; the Sabbath functions as a weekly protector against enslavement.

I do not wish to suggest that Heschel, like Rabbi Shimeon, would prefer to seclude himself in the cave while excluding worldly pursuits. To argue that would impart both a misreading of his texts and his life. But this should not blind us to the palpable anxiety in Heschel's works over the meaning and value of material things. Heschel does admire Shimeon's dedication to time, holiness, and eternity. The great problem in reality is time and not space, study rather than engineering, prayer but not consumption. When injustice becomes intolerable, as it did in the 1960s, Heschel leaves the security in time for the muddiness in space, and he does so with integrity and passion. But to love the things in space, to devote oneself completely to them, is a form of idol worship that destroys the self, and makes one evade commitments to other goods. Israel, Heschel concludes, "is engaged to eternity," but not to things as "our tools."[123] We work with things of space out of necessity, not out of love. Eisen believes that Heschel "possessed both the pessimism necessary to evoke his labors and the optimism needed to sustain them."[124] This may indeed be true, but it misses that sense of unease with which Heschel writes about spatial things, and his preoccupation with them. This disquietude surfaces throughout *The Sabbath* at moments like this: "The six days stand in need of space; the seventh day stands in need of man. It is not good that the spirit should be alone, so Israel was destined to be a helpmeet for the Sabbath." Heschel compares this union to a betrothal in which he genders the Sabbath, "bedecked and perfumed," as a bride who "comes to Israel lovely and perfumed." This is an exclusive marriage, situated only in time without "need of space." Yet things continue to linger in time, for the groom, too, "is dressed in his finest garments."[125] My point is simply this: things are inescapable in Heschel's *The Sabbath* and *The Earth Is the Lord's,* yet Heschel imagines a pristine moment of spiritual experience in which this is not so. *Ke'ilu*—as if things did not attach so strongly to the self.

THINGS IN TIME

Heschel's texts witness to the material features of identity even when he most vehemently asserts its spiritual character. I have focused on *The Sabbath* and *The Earth Is the Lord's* because these works, more than Heschel's many others, attempt to carve out an unspoiled experience of temporal solitude, distant and protected from a consuming, spatial culture. Persons have spiritual needs, Heschel maintains, and these can be gained only by a disencumbered self:

> In the tempestuous ocean of time and toil there are islands of stillness where man may enter a harbor and reclaim his dignity. The island is the seventh day, the Sabbath, a day of detachment from things, instruments and practical affairs as well as of attachment to the spirit.[126]

Heschel yearns for such quiet islands, but he knows, too, that he cannot remain there. Still, one reclaims dignity from within, and Heschel imagines that the seventh day enables spiritual progress without worldly attachments. Religious work is personal, relational, yet insulated. Coveting "things of time," as Heschel suggests we should at the close of *The Sabbath,* rewards the self with a return to spiritual goods utterly divorced from everyday materialist practices, "teaching man to covet the seventh day all days of the week."[127] Craving things in time provides a different kind of consumption: it recovers internal goods of the spirit. Heschel carves out this time from within space in order to redirect our desires. Coveting things in time opens new channels of experience where we seek relations with the ineffable rather than possessions of a product. The dilemma, as I have posed it here, remains how to imagine things in time without conjuring up things in space. Can we experience special kinds of spaceless things without importing more vulgar, materialist objects?

Heschel thought we could, and even more, believed human dignity and religious experience required it. Too much has been conceded to space and material consumption, so Heschel believed, and this at the expense of the self. We recognize this when we compare Heschel's view of Sabbath time to that other current then sweeping America in the 1940s and 1950s: the advice literature concerning Jewish holiday observance. Jenna Joselit has shown just how much that advice was directed at Sabbath home observance, and the desire, especially among Conservative Jews in America, to rekindle Sabbath observance for a lax and rather lethargic laity.[128] Numerous published books, by academic and other cultural elites, detailed the practice, history, and beauty of the Jewish Sabbath. The Conservative movement even launched a "National Sabbath Observance Effort," and its law committee condoned Saturday car travel in order to increase synagogue attendance and commitment.[129] Directed at suburban Jews who no longer lived in close proximity to Jewish institutions or to other Jews, "the driving teshuvah" conceded to material needs in order to foster spiritual goods.[130] It was an uneasy marriage, to be sure. Joselit believes the Conservative rabbinate "misread the popular attitude toward ritual performance," for the folk accepted the Sabbath only "on their own temporal terms" and within "the rhythms of their household."[131] But there were spiritual worlds to win too, and sometimes compromises to material reality offer the best hope of renewed religious commitment. Heschel brokered a peace with material goods as well, but one quite different than was to be found in the Sabbath advice literature.

Nowhere is this more pronounced than in the cultural icon of that time, *The Jewish Home Beautiful*.[132] Together with other home observance guidebooks (*The Three Pillars; The Rites and Symbols of the Jewish Home;* and *The Jewish Woman and Her Home*), *The Jewish Home Beautiful* targeted young wives and mothers who sought a more Jewish and committed home in the suburban landscape. Many of these second- or third-generation women from immigrant homes had not grown up in observant households, and with kosher kitchens becoming more prominent and popular in the 1950s, they sought advice on "the particularities of kashrut and the rhythms of the Jewish calendar." These home manuals, which had been popular as early as the interwar years, offered welcome advice, even if they portrayed "an idealized portrait of the Jewish home."[133] *The Jewish Home Beautiful* had begun as a pageant at the New York World's Fair in 1940. The Women's League of the United Synagogue of America, a Jewish Conservative group, had presented the spectacle not "as a museum piece, as something to admire and then to forget," but rather as a work of art "to urge every mother in Israel to assume her role as artist, and on every festival, Sabbath and holiday, to make her home and her family table a thing of beauty as precious and as elevating as anything painted on canvas or chiseled in stone."[134] These are not metaphors of holiness, nor are they Heschel's "painting on the canvas of time."[135] They are instead descriptions of beauty that rival other aesthetic practices.[136] The Sabbath family table can be a beautiful thing too.[137]

The Jewish Home Beautiful as a published book provides a "narrative" and a "dramatic" version of the pageant, together with "production notes" that would help stage the event in other venues. The authors suggest that the pageant "is very effective for a Mothers and Daughters Day program," when the mother lights the candles and the daughter "reads the description of the holiday represented by their table."[138] There are seven or eight tables altogether, each associated with a major Jewish holiday, and each "meticulously set with choicest linen, china and silver table service." The elaborate performance begins with a reader who explains the various rituals and foods associated with the holiday, includes a choir to sing melodies special to each festival, and introduces actors who perform the ceremonies. The stage direction for the Sabbath is thoroughly choreographed:

> Off-stage choir sings "Sholom Aleihem" softly as woman dressed in taffeta dress, wearing a soft white apron and a white lace scarf over her shoulders, walks slowly to Shabbat table. She covers the two Sabbath loaves with a Hallah cover, lights the candles, covers her head with white scarf, and as singing off-stage is concluded, raises her hands and recites the blessing for the kindling of the Sabbath lights in Hebrew and then in English.[139]

With elegant black-and-white photographs that reveal exquisite table settings, a "suggested list of songs and Zemirot," a page with the blessing over the candles (in Hebrew and English), a Jewish calendar, and, of course, a cookbook with "special holiday foods and delicacies," *The Jewish Home Beautiful* provided a compendium of ritual observance for American suburban households in the 1940s and 1950s.

As an immensely popular book, *The Jewish Home Beautiful* tapped into a desire by many middle-class Jews to adapt "the secular patterns of consumption to Jewish ceremonial life."[140] It conflated, in Heschel's terms, things of space with the holiness of time. Clearly, Heschel sought to limit this consumptive habit from trespassing upon the sanctity of Sabbath observance, and to reacquaint suburban Jewry to their spiritual foundations. There were, to be sure, candles and food on Heschel's Sabbath table too. But note the tenor and mood of Heschel's preparation for the Sabbath:

> When all work is brought to a standstill, the candles are lit. Just as creation began with the word, "Let there be light!" so does the celebration of creation begin with the kindling of lights. It is the woman who ushers in the joy and sets up the most exquisite symbol, light, to dominate the atmosphere of the home.
>
> And the world becomes a place of rest. . . . People assemble to welcome the wonder of the seventh day, while the Sabbath sends out its presence over the fields, into our homes, into our hearts. It is a moment of resurrection of the dormant spirit in our souls.[141]

The lights refer less to material consumption than to the light of creation, rest, and the soul. Material things serve other purposes, or witness to spiritual experiences beyond the physical object. For Heschel, things enable other spiritual realities to take the place of material possession. We use things to advance and enliven other spiritual pleasures. But for *The Jewish Home Beautiful,* the thing itself mediates beauty, consumption, elegance, tradition, and holiness. And according to the manuals and guidebooks of the 1940s and 1950s, one takes pleasure in things: the Jewish home, in its very "thinginess," is holy and beautiful. As Betty Greenberg, one of the coauthors of *The Jewish Home Beautiful,* reminds each of her readers, ethical and historical lessons "have been as deeply impressed upon many a youthful mind by memories of unique foods and symbolic ceremonies round the family table, as by books and teachers."[142] We recall experiences *with things* to access the holy, according to these home guidebooks. These moments do not appropriate secular patterns of consumption onto sacred traditions, as Joselit suggests; rather, they tend to undermine the false dualism between consumption in secular space and religious experience in sacred time. Heschel labored tirelessly against the *Home Beautiful* approach, for he defended the pristine values associated with the holy. To him, the Sabbath "has blown the market place away."[143] His memories are of a very different kind than those Jews who, as Joselit aptly describes them, "enjoyed a leisurely Friday-evening dinner with challah and much conversation, and then went about their business."[144]

Heschel's business, I have argued in this chapter, reveals an anxiety provoked by guidebooks like *The Jewish Home Beautiful* that stress the beauty of things in and of themselves. Yet his anxiety has mined the complex relations between material culture and Jewish identity. Like Bernays, Liebman, and Fromm, who labored to deny the material past, Heschel protests too much. Material things infiltrate holy time. Both *The Sabbath* and *The Earth Is the Lord's* include wood engravings by Ilya Schor in their published editions.[145] In *The Earth Is the Lord's,* Schor's work includes idealized images of shtetl life in Eastern Europe, and evoke a "romanticized folk-past."[146] But I would like to briefly focus on one wood engraving in *The Sabbath* that both adorns the cover and the opening prologue of the book. It is an engraving of a cathedral in time, with an inscription from Exodus 20:8—"Remember the Sabbath day, to keep it holy." Above the cathedral sits a man at the Sabbath table, with lights kindled, and what appears to be a raised cup to recite the blessing over the wine. The cathedral itself is decorated with a number of beautiful ornaments associated with Jewish ritual holidays: a shofar (Rosh Hashanah), lulav and etrog (Sukkot), the two tablets representing the Ten Commandments (Shavuot), and so on. For a book dedicated to protecting holy time from the material encroachment of space, what are all these things doing here? As Nahum Glatzer recognized almost sixty years ago in his review of *The Sabbath*, "only partly do the illustrations fit into the sphere of the volume. They might very easily serve to distract the reader from the acuteness and immense actuality of the text."[147] Do we require these visual things to remember the Sabbath day? What is the relation between material images and holiness in time? I do not pretend to know the answers to these queries, but I do take them to be serious questions indeed, as Heschel surely did as well.

FIGURE 4.1. Wood engraving by Ilya Schor from *The Sabbath* by Abraham Joshua Heschel. Copyright © by Ilya Schor. Reprinted by permission of Farrar, Straus and Giroux, LLC.

Heschel proposed a sharp dichotomy between holiness in time and things in space. But he also revealed a strong ambivalence about the value of material things and their place in time. For readers of *The Jewish Home Beautiful* and viewers of Schor's engravings, this ambivalence suggests a more profound attraction to and need for material objects of beauty. Things do not just enrich our lives; they constitute essential features of personal identity. We experience holiness in and through things, and revivify the sacred by recalling the things intimately associated with it.[148] Things can be both trivial and vulgar, and Heschel anxiously worried about our enslavement to debased objects of desire. But he cannot escape the tyranny of things even in his well-protected cathedral in time. Heschel's anxiety will persist so long as the false dichotomy between sacred time and secular space governs the discourse on material things. And this, so I have argued, we learn by reading Heschel against Heschel. To covet things in time, finally, means only that things are inescapable for selves who live in cathedrals, palaces, or any other kind of thing in space and time.

FIVE

The Material Narrative: Yezierska, Roth, Ozick, Malamud

Things entrance, seduce, and for some, even harm selves with higher callings. Abraham Joshua Heschel's denials of material presence invoked this very allure and power. Yet a deep ambivalence lurked within Heschel's works, for material things could both undermine and enable holiness in time. The Jewish narratives discussed in this chapter evince none of this ambivalence, but instead offer robust accounts of identities immersed in material objects. If Heschel feared objects, the stories of Yezierska, Roth, Ozick, and Malamud actively engage them. One cannot imagine Malamud's dark but hopeful characters without the material objects that define and limit their human possibilities. Nor can one account for the vacuousness of suburban Jewish identity in Roth's "Eli, the Fanatic" without the presence of the black suit. For Ozick, language is a material embodiment of culture, tradition, and history. And Yezierska's characters see the world materially. Her narratives of immigrant struggles expose a visual materiality in which American newcomers recognize others through dress. These are narratives of exposure that root American identity in material presence. While Heschel uncovered the material dimensions of holiness despite his fear of idolatry, these Jewish writers celebrate the intimacy between material culture and Jewish identity.

American Jewish literature is a broad, even cumbersome field. Literature can do many things, and its various performances have become the material stuff for academic English departments. In recent years, moral and religious philosophers have turned to literary narratives to recover the ethical dimensions of lived lives. The very best work reveals how literary styles invoke imaginative portrayals of the good life. Literature now crosses many borders of inquiry, and helps to soften the frontiers among reading professionals. Still, debates linger about the nature and scope of Jewish literature, and its relation to other ethnic writings. Now there is talk "about many Jewish American literatures," rather than one unified field of texts.[1] Even the terms *Jewish* and *American* are in dispute, implying moving targets rather than fixed identities.[2]

I do not intend to take on these and other disciplinary arguments. My purposes are far more modest regarding material culture and Jewish identity. Through an analysis of carefully chosen short stories and novels by American Jews, I want to expose how these works advance my reading of Heschel as outlined in the preceding chapter. The works discussed here reveal the inescapable allure and presence of material objects for personal identity. To uncover these roots of material presence, I have selected texts, from the 1920s through the 1970s, that fruitfully engage notions of materiality. The list is neither exhaustive nor extensive, for I prefer close readings to broad strokes of analysis. Neither Saul Bellow nor Chaim Potok are included, though they could be, and so too numerous others. The choice has been strategic and ruthless: select those texts that serve to illustrate and develop the argument of this book. I take these works to be Jewish, even though the authors themselves may not accept that claim. For utterly divergent reasons, both Cynthia Ozick and Bernard Malamud, for example, refuse the appellation "Jewish" writer—Ozick because the abyss between art and the commandment against idolatry is too great, and Malamud because it cheapens his stature as creative artist. But their short stories find their place in this study, as do the works of Anzia Yezierska and Philip Roth, because their texts explore dimensions of material culture and Jewish identity in America.

Literary narratives often develop characters in relation to the richness of the material world. Narratives can build a scene in which actors work and identify with things. They trace the presence of objects in lived lives, and reveal how objects texture and inform human identity. The narratives of Yezierska, Roth, Ozick, and Malamud uncover the depth and presence of things in human lives. Their stories represent well how American Jews visualize a material world, and their place within it.

In Yezierska's short stories and novels, persons interact with and through objects, especially dress, to define borders and expectations. They act materially because they visualize dress as primary visual stuff—it is the first thing they see. Immigrant Jewish culture is visual, and materially so. This is also true for Roth and his portrayal of suburban Jewish life after the Holocaust. Eli, Roth's representative fanatic, becomes entangled with the "greenie" who dons a black suit. But as I read this powerful short story, the suit resists nostalgic allures to Jewish tradition and practice, and instead exposes the vacuity of American Jewry. Material things fail as meaningful signifiers; they simply are the stuff of lived lives. This is certainly not the case for Cynthia Ozick, who burdens material products and language with meaningful content and depth. In her "Envy; or, Yiddish in America," Ozick invests language with material richness and obligation. Language uncovers the material links and roots that bind people to history. We find this obligatory weight of history in the work of Bernard Malamud as well. In his short works, especially "The Last Mohican" and "The Magic Barrel," Malamud explores the intricate relations between things and human destiny. Though his characters yearn for a life of new possibilities, they are trapped by the objects that control their fate. For the Jews in these texts, a life lived is a material narrative in which objects constrain the limits of human flourishing.

But these are also Jewish narratives that expose the limits of belonging and acceptance in America, and echo many of the themes already explored in this book. The materials in these stories curb Jewish acculturation and prevent an American homecoming. Dirt and bad style prevent Yezierska's immigrant young women from becoming equals before their American peers. Eli Peck dons his black suit because it materializes his sense of difference and exclusion in suburbia—even if that sense of difference is vacuous and empty. As Jews left Soloveitchik's city for the open spaces of suburban life, the grid of observance and identity became more difficult to trace. The Yiddish language in Ozick's poignant story encodes a double loss: death through translation, or death through neglect. Either way, this *mamaloshen*, like many foreign tongues, inhibits a full presence in America that Kaplan so desired. For Malamud, too, things constrict, confine, and imprison souls in the mundane but hopeful workings of everyday life—a far more tragic vision than Heschel's mystical sensibilities. Malamud's characters yearn for more, always receive less, and are forever tied to objects that identify them as tragic souls. America beckons, as Riv-Ellen Prell warns, but too often pushes away.[3] These stories from Yezierska, Roth, Ozick, and Malamud are certainly more than Jewish tales, for they speak to immigrant narratives of arrival, loss, and hope. But they are still all the more Jewish as they recount how material things identify Jews as different—weighed down by a material inheritance that Fromm, Liebman, and Bernays desperately sought to evade. That sense of material avoidance, most pronounced in Heschel and the neo-Freudians, rarely surfaces in these Jewish narratives. In its place we discover material Jewish identity in America.

SEEING DRESS: YEZIERSKA AND ROTH ON CLOTHING

The rediscovery of Anzia Yezierska's work of the 1920s began with Yezierska herself, in her semi-autobiographical piece *Red Ribbon on a White Horse* (1950).[4] At that time, she was some thirty years removed from a very public career that witnessed her rise from the ghettoes of Hester Street to literary and movie fame for her moving portrayals of immigrant life in *Hungry Hearts* (1920),[5] *Salome of the Tenements* (1923),[6] and *Bread Givers* (1925).[7] Yezierska (1880?–1970) recalled those moments of hunger, desire, success, and loneliness in *Red Ribbon,* and once again captured her audience in a world of immigrant yearnings for an American life. The republication and interest in her works, beginning in the 1970s, by Alice Kessler Harris, Katherine Stubbs, and Magdalena Zaborowska, among others,[8] only heightened her appeal, especially among feminists, as a gifted writer who revealed how Jewish women experienced immigration and participated in American practices.[9] Two biographies, both published in 1988, provided strikingly different accounts of her life and work. The one (published by her only daughter), offered a vivid portrayal of this "Hester Street Cinderella";[10] the other exposed how Yezierska's intense affair with John Dewey became a "foundational scene" in her narratives of an emotional, passionate immigrant woman and a placid, rational American man.[11] Much, indeed, has been made of Yezierska's overwrought prose and recycled characters. As one reader ventured: "once her autobiographical heroines move out of their neighborhoods and into their new tailored suits, the author loses the Yiddish pungency that was her trademark."[12] Donald Weber is closer to the truth, I believe, in his assessment that Yezierska evoked "the emotional costs of Americanization upon her vivid assortment" of characters.[13] Yet even with the loss of the "Yiddish pungency" as the price paid for entry into the new land, at least one thing remained vividly present: the tailored suits. If Weber is right, and I think he is, that Yezierska "literalizes" hunger such that ethnic foodways and table manners become the sites of generational struggle,[14] then clothing, too, is an inescapable feature of immigrant experience and identity. But clothing is not a "site" where things happen. It is an inescapable feature of the visual landscape: a material thing that attracts because it is always on display.

The temptation to read clothing as a symbol or representation for something else is strong, and it often reveals important insights into American Jewish culture. But in so doing, one often loses the material force of the dress itself. By moving to what the garment signifies, rather than sticking with the material substance, readers dismiss the cloth, and in its place resides a series of significations. Instead of a material thing that attracts, one finds a symbolic object in search of a meaning.[15]

Note Katherine Stubbs's engaging article, "Reading Material: Contextualizing Clothing in the Work of Anzia Yezierska." Stubbs locates Yezierska's work within the American garment industry, and the growth of ready-made clothing at the turn of the century (together with the sweatshops and factories that made them). Garments that had once been fashioned at home, or purchased only by wealthy consumers from professional dressmakers, could now be owned by the urban poor. By the end of the nineteenth century, "every type of women's clothing, including undergarments, was available in a ready-made version."[16] Easily reproducible, standardized styles meant that everyone could afford new clothing. Even with the advance of the haute couture design that helped preserve class distinctions, mass-produced copies of couture were everywhere.

But Stubbs focuses her attention less on this material excess, and far more on how clothing "functions" in its "conflicting signification"—and so the need to "read" materiality.[17] Engaging not the thing itself, and so recognizing its material presence, she reads dress as a text, decoding its signifying meanings. In *Salome of the Tenements,* Stubbs argues, "clothing is used as a vehicle to engage in a fascinating attempt to transgress and transcend forms of economic and social hierarchy."[18] As a vehicle, garments function to dissolve boundaries, as Stubbs and others who "read" dress make clear.[19] I find her argument quite persuasive *as a reading*, but not as an exhaustive account of material identity. Stubbs moves too quickly from the material thing itself (clothing) to its various significations. When Yezierska comments in *Red Ribbon on a White Horse* that, "even now when I no longer had to search through bargain basements, now that I had money enough to shop at the best stores, perversity made me cling to my pushcart clothes," Stubbs believes "her 'pushcart clothes' can be read as an effort to signify her class and ethnic background." Reading and signification work together to expose underlying meanings in dress. Stubbs decodes dress, immediately revealing root meanings and associations. One of Yezierska's characters desires new clothes, yet as a sewing machine operator she refuses to become a designer because "my hands are sick from waists." All of this carries important symbolic meaning for Stubbs:

> The narrator's relation to clothing has undergone a shift from that of a consumer's relation to a highly desirable commodity (her dream of herself in "new American clothes") to that of an exploited worker's relation to the symbol of her oppression, the "waists" which signify the entire sweatshop system.[20]

For Stubbs, clothes reveal systems of meaning. Yet all these significations obscure the material "thinginess," as Heschel had called it, that so attracted American Jews.

By tracing the underlying symbolic import, Stubbs fails to highlight what her work has made so impressively clear: clothes were everywhere as they surrounded the visual and material scene of the immigrant American. Yezierska's characters could not escape clothes, either as consumers, producers, or wearers. These garments certainly held various meanings, but they also rooted the immigrant Jew in an inescapable visual landscape of material things. The presence of things exposes an American Jewish visuality. Instead of reading clothes as meaningful signs, I want to *see* dress as constitutive of a visual material culture.[21]

Clothes play a central role in the immigrant material landscape in *Hungry Hearts* (1920), Yezierska's noted collection of wrenching short stories that Hollywood's Sam Goldwyn adapted into a feel-good movie. The opening story, "Wings," portrays how the immigrant Shenah Pessah falls in love with the well-dressed, professional John Barnes. A sociologist conducting field work for his academic thesis, Barnes seeks to live on the East Side "to get into closer touch with his subject" on Russian Jewish education. To him, Shenah Pessah is a "splendid type for his research," for she has little contact with "Americanizing agencies," and Barnes is the first to introduce her to libraries and the world of books. Even as he pities her suffering, seclusion, and hunger, he is curiously drawn to his subject, and in "an impulse of compassion," he kisses Shenah Pessah on a romantic stroll at the pier. That kiss carries far greater weight for her than it does for him, and as Barnes apologizes for his "passing moment of forgetfulness," Shenah Pessah, in her shame and anger, leaves him to contemplate his rejection of her. Barnes quickly realizes that, despite the demands of his research to go native, he must vacate the apartment: "No matter how valuable the scientific inquiry might prove to be, you can't let the girl run away with herself."[22] But Shenah Pessah is far more resourceful: she understands that Barnes opened a new world for her, and she will fight to be his recognized equal. The wings of her soul must soar beyond the ghetto to new frontiers.

Much that would engage Yezierska over the next five years can be gleaned from "Wings": the immigrant, passionate girl who confronts the cool, rational, American male; the mutual allure of passion for reason, and intellect for desire; the yearning to move beyond the ghetto, and the American fascination to return to it; the power of wealth, and the enslavement of poverty; and finally, the role of education to transform outsiders into American insiders. Clothes, no doubt, play an essential role in negotiating the various meanings in Yezierska's text. But they are also visually present in ways that demand attention. Note Yezierska's description of Shenah Pessah's first encounter with Barnes:

> The bell rang sharply, and as she turned to answer the call, she saw a young man at the doorway—a framed picture of her innermost dreams.
>   The stranger spoke.
>   Shenah Pessah did not hear the words, she heard only the music of his voice. She gazed fascinated at his clothes—the loose Scotch tweeds, the pongee shirt, a bit open at the neck, but she did not see him or the things he wore. She only felt an irresistible presence seize her soul. It was

as though the god of her innermost longings had suddenly taken shape in human form and lifted her in mid-air.[23]

Mirroring what Yezierska's readers do to material things, Shenah Pessah immediately moves from a fascinating gaze "at his clothes" to the representation of his dress. Rather than "see him," she instead imagines a different "shape," one that lifts her away from the stifling ghetto. But though she fails to listen or see, she nonetheless absorbs minute details of his dress: the materials, patterns, and style of work. Shenah Pessah intuitively understands the symbolic power of that dress. But my point is that her gaze falls immediately on the physical clothing. She registers only its details, and in this she reveals her knowledge of fashion and design, even if, as Yezierska imagines the scene, she did not see "the things he wore." But Shenah Pessah cannot frame her picture without that initial gaze. Clothing, in this sense, is not just a physical marker or signifier. She does not "read" his clothes in order to decode meaning. This scene manifests, first and foremost, Shenah Pessah's visual knowledge as an abiding, physical presence. Rather than offering referential meaning, her gaze maps out a material culture.

Clothes continue to surround Shenah Pessah, from her "greenhorn shawl" to the ostentatious dress and hat she buys to impress Barnes.[24] She notes, too, as she enters the library, "the librarian's simple attire." The visual display of clothes surrounds immigrant Jewish women. This is palpably clear in the opening scene of "Soap and Water," in which the college dean, Miss Whiteside, withholds the narrator's diploma:

> She told me that my skin looked oily, my hair unkempt, and my fingernails sadly neglected. She told me that I was utterly unmindful of the little niceties of the well-groomed lady. She pointed out that my collar did not set evenly, my belt was awry, and there was a lack of freshness in my dress. And she ended with: "Soap and water are cheap. Anyone can be clean."[25]

The narrator recalls the teacher's eyes scrutinizing her dress on every office visit: "I watched her gimlet eyes searching for a stray pin, for a spot on my dress, for my unpolished shoes, for my uncared for finger-nails." As Miss Whiteside sits as "one of the agents of clean society, delegated to judge who is fit and who is unfit to teach," the narrator still remains "unconscious" of clothes until she enters college.[26] This cultural failure, however, is more stubborn resistance than unconscious act:

While they condemned me as unfit to be a teacher, because of my appearance, I was slaving to keep them clean. I was slaving in a laundry from five to eight in the morning, before going to college, and from six to eleven at night, after coming from college. Eight hours of work a day, outside my studies.

Often as I stood at my board at the laundry, I thought of Miss Whiteside, and her clean world, clothed in the snowy shirtwaists I had ironed. I was thinking—I, soaking in the foul vapors of the steaming laundry, I, with my dirty, tired hands, I am ironing the clean, immaculate shirtwaists of clean, immaculate society. I, the unclean one, am actually fashioning the pedestal of their cleanliness, from which they reach down, hoping to lift me to the height that I have created for them.[27]

Whiteness in these passages, to be sure, harbors the symbolic power to reveal economic injustice. But we should not overlook the physical density of "slaving in a laundry." Mired in material attire, the narrator sees the world through and within the grotesque conditions of laundry sweatshops.

The narrator of "Soap and Water" abandons her "sweatshop childhood" for college, but there, too, she finds clothes an essential physical feature of her material landscape. "One glance at my shabby clothes," she tells us, and she feels "condemned" all over again.[28] Clothes, she admits later, "form the basis of class distinctions," even if Miss Whiteside "never looked into my eyes. She never perceived that I had a soul." Stubbs, for one, has brought that insight to the fore. But clothes also form the basis for the way the narrator visualizes the world: "the whole clean world was massed against me. Whenever I met a well-dressed person, I felt the secret stab of a hidden enemy."[29] Yezierska's narrator does more than signify how clothes materially identify persons: she herself identifies persons materially. This narrator confronts America through clothes, even if that America "never looked into my eyes. She never perceived that I had a soul."[30] The true self hides because it can never be seen. Materiality blocks access to deeper meanings.

We can learn from Yezierska, before we move to second-order reflections about meaning and signification, just how materially imbedded an American life is, both for new immigrants and established middle-class professionals. All see and are seen through material cloth: this is what it means to identify materially. Shenah Pessah first records Barnes's dress, and then seeks more ethereal dreams. But that initial register of visual material is inescapable: she must take stock of his clothes before she can swoon before her god. It is as if, despite herself, she *must* fantasize this way: Shenah Pessah does not dream unless she first sees materially. This sense of the inescapable material runs throughout Yezierska's work, and not only in relation to clothing. In one quite dramatic scene in *Bread Givers* (1925), Yezierska describes how her main character Sara can now afford, with her school teacher's salary, a clean, bright, apartment of her own. She had left her parents and their Hester Street filth to attend college, and she now celebrates her freedom:

> I furnished my room very simply. A table, a bed, a bureau, a few comfortable chairs. No carpet on the floor. No pictures on the wall. Nothing but a clean, airy emptiness. But when I thought of the crowded dirt from where I came, this simplicity was rich and fragrant with unutterable beauty. . . . I celebrated it alone with myself. I celebrated it in my room, my first clean, empty room. In the morning, in the evening, when I sat down to meals, I enjoyed myself as with the grandest company. I loved the bright dishes from which I ate. I loved the shining pots and pans in which I cooked my food. I loved the broom with which I swept the floor, the scrubbing brush, the scrubbing rag, the dust cloth. The routine with which I kept clean my precious privacy, my beautiful aloneness, was all sacred to me.[31]

Sara's space may indeed be sacred, but it is not empty. Clean, to be sure, but still full of things: pots and pans, dishes and brooms, brushes, rags, and chairs. Sara celebrates with her things, and she is alone with them as they beautify her life. Things do not disappear; instead, she wipes away the "crowded dirt" of her Hester Street home.[32] Sara loves the dishes for their brightness, the pots for their shine, the broom and brush and dust cloth because they really do clean her room. When Sara left home for college and a professional career, she yearned for that sterility that Miss Whiteside protected. Becoming American meant becoming clean. But material things did not disappear, nor did Sara's capacity to see materially. An ordered, sterile, and clean life is still a material one. And those things have become so embedded in Sara's life that she can, without a hint of irony, celebrate "alone with myself." If the narrator of "Soap and Water" could be "unconscious" of her clothes, and Sara of her fine things, then perhaps it is because, so immersed in things, they no longer see these objects as sources of inner referential meanings. These things inhabit their visual landscape as material necessity: they make possible a certain mode of seeing. Things function less as signifiers, and far more as embodiments of a visual practice.

Seeing clothes as an indicator to some deeper, existential meaning is part of what Stubbs implies by "the performative function of clothing."[33] We signify to others the kind of persons we are, or wish to be, through dress. Commentators often read Philip Roth's "Eli, the Fanatic" in precisely this way.[34] First published in *Commentary* in 1959, and again that same year in Roth's collection *Goodbye, Columbus*,[35] Roth's essay describes lawyer Eli Peck, who parades through the downtown streets of quiet suburban Woodenton wearing a black suit once worn by a Holocaust survivor (the "greenie"). The clothes take on "the performative function" of exhibition: the lawyer who seeks comfort and anonymity with his Protestant neighbors discovers that even the Holocaust, and through that horror his own Jewish heritage, mark him as other. That this "greenie" lives in a yeshiva on the outskirts of Woodenton, one that houses eighteen children with Leo Tzuref as their Talmud teacher, terrifies Ted, Artie, and the other assimilated Jews who hire Eli to represent their interests. Concerned that their Protestant neighbors will associate "modern Jews" with this "hocus-pocus abracadabra stuff,"[36] the Jews of Woodenton ask Eli, on the pretense of accusing the yeshiva of violating zoning regulations, to send these "crazy people" back to the city where they belong—echoing the very notions of urban chaos discussed in chapter 3. Their anxiety stems from the greenhorn's appearance in suburbia: with his black hat and black suit, he attracts the attention of (and by) the wrong sort. So Eli offers his two best suits, confident that if the "greenie" could wear modern dress, Ted and the rest would leave him alone. But the "greenie" returns the favor, and leaves his bundle of "blackness" on Eli's front steps. Eli, in turn, parades through the streets wearing the black suit and hat, mimicking the greenhorn's own performance, as he marches to the hospital to visit his—Eli's—newborn son. Like the other residents of Woodenton, Ted believes Eli is "flipping" (as he had done twice before), and so asks the doctors to inject a sedative to help relax the confused and distraught new father. Roth concludes the story with the memorable line: "The drug calmed his soul, but did not touch it down where the blackness had reached."[37]

As Hana Wirth-Nesher rightly notes, any reading of Eli "will have to offer an interpretation of this 'blackness' that is located so deeply within Eli that it is immune to the 'treatment' that his American society administers."[38] For most readers, this blackness is indistinguishable from the material dress itself: when Eli dresses in the greenhorn's black suit and hat, he takes on "this 'blackness'." Wirth-Nesher is especially attentive to the meaning of blackness in Roth's story—a meaning she now recognizes as both culturally and historically located. Yet she continues to read "blackness" as a signifier of Eli's "authentic Jewish self."[39] Wirth-Nesher has taught both in the United States and Israel, and she observes how Americans accepted while Israelis rejected the conflation of Jewish authenticity with a Holocaust survivor. Yet both still read the story *as* an allegory, in which Eli chooses "a visible Jewish identity and a commitment to collective memory."[40] To be sure, Wirth-Nesher retains good company in reading Roth's story in this way. For Sol Gittleman, Eli "discovers the roots of his own Jewishness in the box of clothing," and he "has to show the world: I am a Jew." As a performance of self, Eli's appropriation of black dress signifies his "transformation into an East European Hassidic survivor of Hitler's slaughter." In his short story, so Gittleman contends, Roth "made his benchmark on what it meant to be a Jew."[41]

In discovering meaning through the appropriation of "blackness," Roth's interpreters argue that the performance of dress reveals, indeed must reveal, Jewish content. I want to resist this kind of symbolic reading, and not merely because it covers over the tactile qualities of clothing, as interpreters of Yezierska had done. For Eli, blackness simply fails as a meaningful signifier. The sedative does not touch where the blackness had reached because its meaning is forever inscrutable. This is not so, however, for all the other characters in the story. For Ted, Artie, Miriam (Eli's wife), nurses at the hospital, Harriet Knudson (Eli's neighbor), and even for the mayor's wife, Eli's performance through dress signifies insanity. Eli dismisses their reading with an appeal to personal will: if you choose to be crazy, as he had done, then you could not be flipping. At one point, Eli hesitates, considers returning home to dress in his old clothes, and only then sets out for the hospital. His Woodenton neighbors would soon forgive his momentary lapse, rather than label him as insane. But to do so, Eli claims, "would be to go halfway."[42]

But halfway to what? Eli cannot answer this question, even though his interpreters do so for him. That Eli takes on an identity through blackness is, I believe, clear. But the meaning of that identification—its character, history, and value—is just as inscrutable as the very title of Roth's story: to whom, for whom, is Eli a fanatic? Silences like this often invite allegorization, as Wirth-Nesher suggests, and the allure of meaning is indeed strong. Dress often functions as symbol, or as performative signifier. But in "Eli, the Fanatic," dress is a constitutive, material feature of identity that resists symbolic content. Eli does not perform his identity through clothes so much as inhabit it. He sees identity *in* the material dress; but the meaning of that visual practice never touches where the blackness has reached. Eli's performance in black dress is inscrutable as public exhibition because his Jewish identity lacks all content and meaning.

The symbolic power of blackness in "Eli, the Fanatic" confronts the reader immediately. When Eli first meets Tzuref, the wise old Talmud teacher, he correlates darkness with the traditional, ancient traditions of the Jewish yeshiva, and lightness with modernity and the claims of an assimilated Jewish community. The white column from which Tzuref emerges to meet Eli stands out of place in this dark, "sagging old mansion." Both Tzuref and Eli sit together in a "dim room" illuminated only by candlelight ("the lamps had no bulbs"), and hear the Yiddish chatter of schoolchildren—to Eli, they are "half-dying shouts," and the children's play appears like a "tribal dance." Upon leaving, Eli "walked carefully down the dark tomb of a corridor to the door." Blackness testifies to a foreign past, a decaying urban community, and to traditions and languages well left behind. To preserve an enlightened, progressive sensibility, the town of Woodenton opposes darkness with light. As Eli views the suburb from the mansion's door, he sees "the street lights blink on in Woodenton": "the stores along Coach House Road tossed up a burst of yellow—it came to Eli as a secret signal from his townsmen: 'Tell this Tzuref where we stand, Eli. This is a modern community, Eli, we have our families, we pay taxes. . . .'"[43] When Eli first views the man "wearing the hat, that hat which was the very cause of Eli's mission," he sees "only a deep hollow of blackness." Indeed, the man with the hat is covered in darkness:

He was stopped by the sight of the black coat that fell down below the man's knees, and the hands which held each other in his lap. By the round-topped, wide-brimmed Talmudic hat, pushed onto the back of his head. And by the beard, which hid his neck. . . .

To counter this black shadow, "the town's lights flashed their message once again: 'Get the one with the hat.'" Eli, so Roth tells us, "hurried toward the lights."[44]

To Ted Heller, Artie Berg, and Harry Shaw—the three Woodenton Jews who hire Eli to chase out these "Goddam fanatics"—the black hat symbolizes all that they left behind in the city. Their anxieties focus on the hat and its signifying power:

> "And the guy with the hat, you saw the guy with the hat?"
> "Yes. He was sleeping."
> "Eli, he sleeps with the *hat*?"
> "He sleeps with the hat."
> "Goddam fanatics," Ted said. "This is the twentieth century, Eli. Now it's the guy with the hat. Pretty soon all the little Yeshivah boys'll be spilling down into town."[45]

Eli understands that "if he'd take off that crazy hat everything would be all right," and all would return "to Normal" in the "calm circumstances of their domestic happiness."[46] Even Tzuref recognizes the symbolic power of blackness. Eli suggests a compromise: the yeshiva can stay, so long as the "greenie" enters the town of Woodenton, "attired in clothing usually associated with American life in the 20th century." Tzuref's response to Eli's proposal—"the suit the gentleman wears is all he's got"— indicates that he has lost everything in the Holocaust, and the black suit and hat materially witness to that loss. Its presence reveals a tragic absence. But Eli, of all the characters in this story, fails to appreciate the symbolic import of dress:

> "I offered a compromise, Mr. Tzuref. You refused."
> "Refused, Mr. Peck? What is, is."
> "The man could get a new suit."
> "That's all he's got."
> "So you told me," Eli said.
> "So I told you, so you know."
> "It's not an insurmountable obstacle, Mr. Tzuref. We have stores."

"For that too?"

"On route 12, Robert Hall—"

"To take away the one thing a man's got?"

"Not take away, *replace*."[47]

As Tzuref catalogues the man's loss—his parents, wife, children all dead—together with the medical experiments performed upon him, Eli still cannot see the suit as anything but a piece of cloth. He offers Tzuref money to buy a new one, and only then, as he reaches for his wallet, does he understand the symbolic import of the black suit: "'Oh . . .' Eli said. He moved away along the wall. 'The suit is all he's got then.' 'You got my letter,' Tzuref said."[48]

For both the Jews of Woodenton and the Holocaust survivors of Tzuref's yeshiva, the black suit and hat signify deeper meanings, and the "greenie" performs those meanings through dress. They read those meanings differently, to be sure. For Ted Heller, the hat provokes backward images of the East European shtetl, and Heller fears that these yeshiva boys will soon bewitch his daughters. For Tzuref, it is the sole reminder of a beloved past now tragically lost. But Eli does not "read" dress for meaning. For him, the hat is merely a material thing, easily discarded and replaced: it simply fails as a meaningful signifier. Although Eli finally understands Tzuref's claim ("The suit is all he's got then"), he accepts it only as Tzuref's intended meaning, and not his own. Instead of decoding a meaning, Eli situates the material thing within his visual landscape. Instead of meaning, Eli sees the presence of things. He replaces symbolic import with material rawness.

Despite Tzuref's insistence that one cannot merely replace the hat and suit, Eli searches through his own winter suits for worthy substitutes. Eli acts as if his compromise remains in force: the "greenie" will now wear twentieth-century attire whenever he walks the Woodenton streets. When Eli's wife, Miriam, shows concern for his mad search (she fears he is "flipping"), Eli responds by actively suppressing deeper meanings: "[I am] getting clothes for the guy in the hat. Don't tell me why, Miriam. Just let me do it." To Eli, Miriam always proposes "fancy reasons" for his eccentric behavior. She sets out to explain, understand, and forgive. But Eli recoils from these insights, regarding them as "a trap," and complains that Miriam radiates with "a goddam New School enthusiasm for Sigmund Freud."[49] Miriam, like the other Roth characters in this story, sees *through* the clothing to uncover personal meanings and anxieties. But Eli halts his gaze *at* the material cloth: "Damn it, Miriam! I'm giving this guy a new suit, is that all right? From now on he comes into Woodenton like everybody else, is that all right with you?"[50] As it turns out, it is not all right, and Miriam directs her anger at Eli who must offer *his* suits, even his favorite Brooks Brothers outfit. She quickly returns, however, to the more personal meanings that clothing signifies: "'Eli, I'm going to have a baby. Do we need all *this*?' and she swept the clothes off the sofa to the floor." But Eli refuses to go there, immersed as he is in the material details. Gleefully he responds to his wife, as he looks at the suit's lining, "it's a J. Press."[51] For Eli, it is about the suit, not about blackness.

Eli leaves his package of two suits and a hat at the yeshiva's steps, and the following day the Holocaust survivor returns to Woodenton in Eli's green suit. Ted is amazed: "He's walking straight up Coach House Road, in this damn tweed job. Eli, it worked. You were right." When Eli finally spots the "greenie" (a description that now takes on additional meaning), he describes a man who "looked as if he belonged."[52] This, of course, is what Ted and the rest had desired all along. But Eli did not expect the "greenie" to package his own black hat and suit in the same box left for him on the mansion steps, and offer it to Eli as a tempting gift.

This is a pivotal scene in the performance of blackness. For here, as some argue, Eli first recognizes the claims of Jewish tradition upon him.[53] Eli certainly sees blackness upon removing the box top, but the objects within lack referential meaning:

> The shock at first was the shock of having daylight turned off all at once. Inside the box was an eclipse. But black soon sorted from black, and shortly there was the glassy black of lining, the coarse black of trousers, the dead black of fraying threads, and in the center the mountain of black: the hat. He picked the box from the doorstep and carried it inside. For the first time in his life he *smelled* the color of blackness: a little stale, a little sour, a little old, but nothing that could overwhelm you. Still, he held the package at arm's length and deposited it on the dining room table.[54]

Note, to begin, how Eli immediately dissects the eclipse into parts. Blackness is not all of a piece: Eli sorts out the "glassy" from the "coarse" from the "dead" blackness, and soon recognizes "the mountain of black: the hat." He discovers *things*, not meaning, in the box. And those things have textures, sizes, shapes, and even smells. As Eli absorbs the smell of blackness (stale, sour, old), it is curiosity, rather than repulsion, that moves him. But those smells fail to draw him into Jewish tradition, or signify something more than material odor. Blackness retains qualities of touch, sight, smell, and taste, but still lacks the referential memories and anxieties that confront others such as Ted, Miriam, and Tzuref. These clothes make no existential claim upon Eli, and once again fail as signifiers to some larger meaning.

To fully appreciate how Eli recognizes these clothes only as consumable material products, one has to read further:

> Twenty rooms on a hill and they store their old clothes with me! What am I supposed to do with them? Give them to charity? That's where they came from. He picked up the hat by the edges and looked inside. The crown was smooth as an egg, the brim practically threadbare. There is nothing else to do with a hat in one's hands but put it on, so Eli dropped the thing on his head.[55]

From an eclipse of blackness, the clothes transform into wasted material. This is not a tempting gift, but a deposit of used clothing. He no longer inspects blackness, and beholds instead a collection of disposable things. Eli resents being used as a storage dump, and would rather get rid of the material altogether. Even the hat loses any signifying power: that "mountain of blackness" turns into a basic "thing" that one puts on a head ("there is nothing else to do with a hat"). After donning the hat, Eli undresses, gazes at his body in the mirror—"what a silly disappointment to see yourself naked in a hat"—and begins to feel "the terrible weight of the stranger's strange hat."

At this point, as with his conversation with Tzuref, Eli begins to understand the symbolic import that all ascribe to the hat and the dark suit. As he removes the rest of the clothing from the box, he notes how "it smelled deeper than blackness" (the text is unclear: is "it" the box, the jacket, the trousers, or all of it?). Slowly Eli discovers the one white garment remaining, and without recognizing it as an undergarment worn by religious Jews, slips it over the hat and onto his chest. Yet just at this moment when the symbolic reading seems most convincing, for perhaps

Eli truly has taken on, physically and spiritually, the Jewish traditions, Eli himself seems most confused: "And now, looking at himself in the mirror, he was momentarily uncertain as to who was tempting who into what. Why *did* the greenie leave his clothes? Was it even the greenie? Then who was it? And why?"[56] The text implies that Eli slowly descends into a nervous breakdown. The suit attracts Eli, and tempts him, but the import of that temptation remains unclear. If the suit functions as a conduit to a more robust Jewish identity, then Eli lacks the cultural and religious knowledge to accept it as such. The white garment remains a white garment, rather than a *tallit katan* worn by observant Jews. For Eli, it fails as a meaningful religious signifier.

How one interprets Eli's first reactions to blackness significantly informs the possible meanings of his appearance before his neighbors in the black suit, his eventual stroll down Coach House Road en route to the hospital, and finally the relief of the needle that calms Eli's soul but does not reach the blackness. If the symbolic power of blackness carries over to the suit itself, and Eli accepts his Jewish heritage in the wearing of it, then it seems reasonable to assert that Eli performs his newly discovered identity through dress. The needle slides under the skin, but it cannot touch the blackness of Eli's recovered Jewishness. But if, as I have argued, Eli never attributes these meanings to the black suit, then the significance of his public exposure is altogether unclear. In this case, the needle calms his soul, but cannot illuminate the inscrutability of personal identity, nor can it reveal referential meaning through public performance.

What, precisely, is Eli *doing* when he wears the black suit? Even the "greenie" remains unsure of this. Before his stroll down Coach House Road, Eli runs toward the yeshiva in search of acceptance. Seeking recognition—"Please, just *look* at me," Eli repeats twice—he still considers the suit a piece of used material: "'We'll moth-proof it. There's a button missing'—Eli pointed—'I'll have it fixed. I'll have a zipper put in . . . Please, please—just look at me.'"[57] The "greenie" will not respond, dazed and confused, and is perhaps sickened by what stands before him. When Eli grabs the black hat and shouts, "Look, look, what I've done *already*," the gravity of Eli's performance still remains unclear. But the "greenie" suggests what he *should* do, and Eli interprets his hand gesture in the direction of Woodenton as a request to walk through its streets wearing the black suit. Now everyone would gaze at "the man in black," and believe that "Eli's having a nervous breakdown."[58]

The black clothes reveal deep symbolic meaning for the residents of Woodenton, but not for Eli. If the clothes signify insanity, or fanaticism, or some authentic Jewish identity, then Eli himself fails to attach these meanings to the black material. Instead of revelation, Eli discovers acceptance. When he finally arrives at the hospital to see his newborn son, he marks the suit as a material embodiment of difference:

> Well, now that he was here, what did he think he was going to say to it? I'm your father, Eli, the Flipper? I am wearing a black hat, suit, and fancy underwear, all borrowed from a friend? How could he admit to this reddened ball—*his* reddened ball—the worst of all: that Eckman [Eli's psychologist] would shortly convince him he wanted to take off the whole business. He couldn't admit it! He wouldn't do it! . . .
>
> No, even Eckman wouldn't make him take it off! No! He'd wear it, if he chose to. He'd make the kid wear it! Sure! Cut it down when the time came. A smelly hand-me-down, whether the kid liked it or not!
>
> Only Teddie's heels clacked; the interns wore rubber soles—for they were there, beside him, unexpectedly. Their white suits smelled, but not like Eli's.[59]

Blackness signifies a difference so deep that not even a needle can touch it. But this difference retains little if any substance. Whether the kid likes it or not, he will come to recognize difference with all its smell and color. But the *fact* of difference does not yield the *claims* of difference. Eli's Jewish identity, if he has one, is utterly vacuous. But Roth's characters, as do his interpreters, see *through* the blackness to hidden meanings. They do not rest with a material gaze, but seek to look beyond and behind it. Drawing from a cultural storehouse of associations and images, the Woodenton residents link blackness to insanity, while readers identify blackness with authenticity. But Eli never inscribes blackness with meaningful content. At best, he can only pass a smelly hand-me-down to his son. The black material carries an altogether different smell than a white one, but Eli can neither explain nor clarify that sense of difference. This is not a passing on of authentic heritage or recovered identity, but its very failure: Eli's son inherits a suit that smells, not a tradition that inspires. Dress imparts difference, but its meaning and significance remain inscrutable. The power of "Eli, the Fanatic" lies in the contrast between the lived reality of the material life, and the various symbolic readings of it. The suit's symbolic import never fully reveals the basic claim to difference that Eli associates with the material, nor the felt loss of a lived life by the "greenie." In these and other ways, "Eli, the Fanatic" resists symbolic readings.

Roth vividly captures how a material substance, in and of itself, yields vibrancy and force, even if it fails as symbolic performance. He recaptures this notion of material force in *Patrimony* (1991),[60] an exceedingly moving portrait of his dying father. This is a passionate and troubling book, with recollections that reveal a defiant but very human father, and an equally tenacious son. In one touching scene, Herman Roth recovers from the biopsy of his brain tumor at his son's house. Unable to defecate for days, Herman drinks and eats laxatives to help his dietary system. After some four days, Roth discovers his father in the shower stall, covered in feces. The stench is overwhelming, and Roth describes the scene in lucid detail: "The shit was everywhere, smeared underfoot on the bathmat, running over the toilet bowl edge and, at the foot of the bowl, in a pile on the floor. It was splattered across the glass of the shower stall from which he'd just emerged, and the clothes discarded in the hallway were clotted with it."[61] Roth helps his father recover, and then sets out to erase the incident, and memory of it, from the bathroom. As he carries all the soiled clothes to the trunk of his car, Roth takes stock of his father's legacy:

> And *why* this was right and as it should be couldn't have been plainer to me, now that the job was done. So *that* was the patrimony. And not because cleaning it up was symbolic of something else but because it wasn't, because it was nothing less or more than the lived reality that it was.
>
> There was my patrimony: not the money, not the tefillin, not the shaving mug, but the shit.[62]

Roth had previously voiced his desire for some material inheritance. Those items were precious—especially the shaving mug—but none were as raw or basic as bodily waste. Roth asks not what the patrimony means, but only understands that it is, that it is his, and that it is experienced as a lived reality. The prose actively resists symbolic readings. Its meaning lies not in "something else," but only in "that it was." This is the lived reality of the material life: not weighted signification of bodily performance, but the smell, touch, and physical sensations of things.

OZICK'S MATERIAL LANGUAGE

If Roth's *Patrimony* viscerally connects sons to their fathers, eschewing grander insights of meanings, then Cynthia Ozick's work actively searches for metaphorical power and significance. Indeed, her writing is often compared (favorably) to Roth's more gritty, suburban, and sexed prose.[63] As Ruth Wisse astutely notes, Ozick is "an intellectual writer whose works are the fictional realization of ideas. Her reader is expected, at the conclusion of her stories, to have an insight, to understand the point of events rather than to respond to their affective power."[64] Ozick has written brilliant theoretical essays that others have found both enticing and revealing of her Jewish views, despite her warning not to read her polemics as keys to her fiction. Elisa New aptly describes Ozick as "a writer of extraordinary verbal resource, acute intellect; and a program."[65] That program tends to focus on idolatry, and the temptations to worship, as artists often do, imaginative human creations. Readers often cite her piece, "America: Toward Yavneh" (1970), in which she calls for a "New Yiddish" to emerge, like the "Old Yiddish," as "the language of a culture which is centrally Jewish in its concerns and thereby liturgical in nature."[66] Liturgical prose thwarts idolatrous worship. Her biting polemic of Harold Bloom's theory of poetry pits her Jewish liturgical writing against Bloom's "anti-Judaism." Bloom's strong readers, as idol worshipers, seek to undo what is, for Ozick, the foundational reading practices of Jewish tradition: "[For Jews] there is no competition with the text, no power-struggle with the original, no envy of the Creator. The aim, instead, is to reproduce a purely transmitted inheritance, free of substitution or incarnation."[67] The second commandment against idolatry, Ozick warns, "runs against the grain of our social nature, indeed against human imagination," but it is "nevertheless expressive of one of the essential ideals of Judaism."[68] Ozick's sharp distinctions between imagination and memory, experience and history, the natural world and Judaism, idolatry and pure devotion, can at times overwhelm her essays, where her style is "precisely goatlike—omnivorous, frisky, and ever ready to lower its horns."[69] She is a demanding writer who provokes strong judgments, intellectual rigor, and disciplined reading.

Ozick is, to my mind, most provocative and insightful when she uncovers the material features of language. Her "Envy; or, Yiddish in America" (1969), is a brilliant exploration of language as a material medium that anchors and delimits identity. First published in *Commentary*,[70] and then included in her *The Pagan Rabbi and Other Stories* (1971),[71] "Yiddish in America" tells the story of Edelshtein, a man who yearns for a translator in America for his Yiddish poetry.[72] He is consumed by envy for Ostrover, who of all the Yiddish poets found glory and success because he required translators: "Though he wrote only in Yiddish, his fame was American, national, international."[73] Even as some read her essay as a critique of "Yiddishkayt," Ozick claims otherwise:

> I wrote it as an elegy, a lamentation, a celebration, because six million Yiddish tongues were under the earth of Europe, and because here under American liberty and spaciousness my own generation, in its foolishness, stupidity, and self-disregard had, in an act tantamount to autolobotomy, disposed of the literature of its fathers.[74]

To reclaim that heritage requires translation, and therein lies the rub and creative tension of Ozick's story:

> It seemed to me, in any case, that translation was at best a hoax and at worst a false lure, and that translation would never, never engender the splendor and richness and dearness and idiosyncrasy of Yiddish to my own generation and to the next, and to the next; and that if we did not come to the heart and bones of the language itself we would only betray it and ourselves, becoming amnesiacs of history.[75]

Ozick herself had translated Yiddish poems for the *Penguin Book of Modern Yiddish Verse*, many of them originally composed by Jacob Glatstein. She made these comments about "Yiddish in America" in honor of Glatstein, who to her great sorrow had misunderstood her story. What makes this particularly tragic is Elaine Kauver's suggestion that "in her [Ozick's] translation of 'Yiddishkayt,' Ozick inhabits Glatstein; in creating Edelshtein she becomes Glatstein."[76] Although Ozick models Ostrover on Isaac Bashevis Singer, Glatstein appears to be the creative source of Edelshtein's envy. Glatstein had published savage critiques of Singer's work in tones that echo Edelshtein's attack on Ostrover.[77] Edelshtein belittles Ostrover's whimsical pieces that play well for the non-Jewish world. He ridicules his stories as "insanely sexual, pornographic, paranoid, freakish." And yet, Edelshtein admits, "I want to be a Gentile like you!"[78] His envy runs deep, for though he despises Yiddish in translation, he also yearns for it.

Yet if Ozick appropriates Glatstein's voice to enliven her art, she also refocuses his critique to better suit her own. For the problem of translation touches upon betrayal, memory, and history. We betray language, and so ourselves, when we forget its "heart and bones." Within that amnesia, history loses its cultural force and no longer compels future generations to adopt the richness of a now dead "literature of its fathers." Ozick cares deeply about obligations to history, and soon after publishing "Yiddish in America" she admitted to her own idol worship: "I am in thrall to the history of the Jews. It is the history of the Jews that seizes me ultimately, and with the obligation of *kavanah* [intention]. History is my master, and I its servant. . . ."[79] To worship history means to stand in judgment before it and to perpetuate its cultural legacy. A sense of legacy that obligates, binds, and memorializes lies at the heart of Ozick's meditation on language in "Yiddish in America." A "New Yiddish" must absorb this inheritance, "attentive to the implications of covenant and commandment."[80] But that language will be English in America, Ozick makes clear, and venturing "toward Yavneh," toward a renewed Judaism, requires an act of cultural and linguistic translation. Can language function as a carrier of obligations, loyalty, history, and memory for American Jews?

This is but one of the central questions that confronts a reader of "Envy; or, Yiddish in America," and I want to explore it through the categories of this book: material identity that is located in place, experienced as a presence, and embedded in a past. What if we consider the material past, place, and presence of the self through language? How does language embody, locate, delineate, and inform material identity? Ozick's "Yiddish in America" offers penetrating analysis of these issues, and expands the material features of the self to include the "heart and bones" of language. Yiddish is a material medium that defines American Jews as inhabitants of a different world—a world without presence and allure, and a world that commands through history and memory. It is not only, as Jeffrey Shandler argues, a "postvernacular" language of symbolic recovery and cultural retrieval.[81] Yiddish also accrues material weightiness and texture. If Sanford Pinsker complains of Ozick's "crankiness" that surfaces in many of her essays,[82] it is because so much is at stake: as Edelshtein laments, a betrayal of Yiddish "courts amnesia of history." Yet the alternative offers little consolation: "Yiddish! Choose death or death. Which is to say death through forgetting or death through translation."[83] Betrayal comes in many forms, but here it emerges through language. The death of Yiddish signals the death of a particular kind of self that remains committed to a material past. However vigorously polemical Ozick surely is in her critical essays, her story of Edelshtein's passion for language, and the cultural richness that Yiddish both engenders and evokes, is a fiercely nuanced study of linguistic material identity.

For Edelshtein, Yiddish resides in the East European shtetl. Even as he yearns for a translator, and so freedom from the ghetto into "the world" (to be a gentile like Ostrover), he recognizes the inevitable death of a language anchored to place. This tragic sensibility lures the young Edelshtein to a Russian "red-cheeked little boy,"[84] Alexei Kirilov, who offers the promise of escape. Edelshtein recalls his youthful passion for Alexei, who belonged to a wealthy Jewish family in Kiev. Embracing the culture of the Soviet Union, the Kirilovs changed their last name from Katz. To Edelshtein, now reflecting on his youthful passion, Alexei represented all the promise of the world outside the Jewish ghetto: beauty, wealth and learning, together with the material goods (as seen in his German-made toys) of the West.[85] Alexei lived in the gentile world, while Edelshtein with his Yiddish remained apart. The Kirilovs still maintained ties to their Jewish roots, and all (except for Edelshtein's father) would call Alexei by his more familiar name, Avremeleh. Though his father had been hired to teach Alexei Jewish texts, Edelshtein would drill the young pupil as his father dozed. Ozick hints at Edelshtein's pedophilia, for the Kirilovs dismissed his father as tutor because, apparently, Edelshtein had kissed Alexei on the stairs, "where I once saw the butler scratch his pants."[86] Edelshtein's love for the boy, for "the face of flame," ignites his passion to be free of the self-imposed prison of his Yiddish. In that sexual desire resides the allure of Ostrover's "world" with the gentiles.

Edelshtein's desire for Alexei provokes the dilemma of place and locale of the Yiddish language. This tension arises in the boy's name (Alexei or Avremeleh?) and his political status: "Avremeleh had a knack of getting things by heart. He had a golden head. Today he was a citizen of the Soviet Union. Or was he finished, dead, in the ravine at Babi Yar?" Would that golden head mark him as a gentile among others, or would his "Ukraine-accented Yiddish" force a quite different fate? When Edelshtein returned from Kiev to his home in Minsk, he recalled "every coveted screw of the German toys." Alexei's world was one of order, cleanliness, and anonymity. But the train carriage home "reeked of urine and the dirt seeped through their shoelaces into their socks."[87] Does Alexei belong among the comforts of the world, or does the filth and stench of the ghetto pull Avremeleh back to a different, separate, and ultimately destroyed world? Ozick asks the same question of Yiddish: does it reside in the world "out there," even if translated, or must it die its lonely death in the ghetto?

Ostrover is only a "make-believe Gentile" who plays at being a Jew in order to sell his works and, equally important, to be and reside among "them."[88] He abandons the place of Yiddish for the "spaciousness" of the gentile world. But clearly Alexei cannot play with such casual disregard for future consequences. And neither can Edelshtein, for he imagines Alexei's fate to be intimately tied to that of Yiddish in America. If Alexei could make it, then perhaps so too Yiddish. Edelshtein yearns for the Alexei of the Soviet state, only to recall "the little corpse of Babi Yar"; the one resides in fantasy, the other confronts a brutal historical legacy. Edelshtein yearns for a translated Yiddish in America, but he knows it's "death or death." In the end, Babi Yar awaits his Yiddish too.

Ozick portrays this harsh fidelity to history in Edelshtein's letters to Hannah—the young niece of Vorovsky, one of Ostrover's many translators. She holds out the promise of a translated Yiddish, for she had learned the language from her grandfather in America. Perhaps she, like no other, could save Yiddish and "be like a Messiah to a whole generation."[89] For Edelshtein, Hannah symbolizes a possible future for Yiddish, and nothing more. In his first letter, he only knows Hannah "as an abstraction," as "an incarnation of the Future." She barely exists as an embodied person, for Edelshtein only hears "the sound of a dead language on a live girl's tongue!" It is only her "strong mouth" that attracts Edelshtein, and the possibility of "translation in America!"[90]

But Edelshtein soon awakes from this fantasy, and his second letter to Hannah reveals a more sober vision: "You made no impression on me. When I wrote you before at Baumzweig's I lied. I saw you for a second in a public place, so what? Holding a Yiddish book. A young face on top of a Yiddish book. Nothing else." Edelshtein's callous dismissal turns quickly vindictive of those "American-born" writers who pretend they know a little Yiddish phrase here and there. But he remains "indifferent" to Hannah "and her kind." He was merely seduced by her knowledge of his Yiddish poetry, and admits his attraction to youthful promise: "Riding in the subway once I saw a beautiful child, a boy about twelve. A Puerto Rican, dusky, yet he had cheeks like pomegranates. I once knew, in Kiev, a child who looked like that. I admit it. A portrait under the skin of my eyes. The love of a man for a boy. Why not confess it?"[91] Edelshtein entangles images of Hannah and Alexei: as Vorovksy's niece represents the promise of translation, so too does Alexei embody the beauty of the gentile world. Translation converts Edelshtein into one of "them." Hannah becomes his messiah in his quest "to reach."[92] He even harbors a love for Alexei that mirrors his envy for Ostrover and his desire for Hannah. For the beautiful young boy, the "Pig" Ostrover, and the twenty-three-year-old speaker of Yiddish all represent Edelshtein's tragic yearning for unattainable acceptance:

> Mechanical. Alexei Y. Kirilov, engineer. Bridges, towers. Consultant to Cairo. Builder of the Aswan Dam, assistant to Pharaoh for the latest Pyramid. To set down such a fantasy about such an important Soviet brain . . . poor little Alexei, Avremeleh, I'll jeopardize your position in life, little corpse of Babi Yar.[93]

Alexei is the Israelite or Jew who creates magnificent modern structures for advanced civilizations, but only as a consultant or assistant, for to tread more assertively in that world would only "jeopardize your position." Like Yiddish, Alexei does not belong in that world—he remains a little corpse in Babi Yar. Yiddish, too, is alive only in Hannah's disembodied "strong mouth." Unless Hannah becomes a builder of civilizations, Yiddish will likewise die a gruesome death, another corpse without a place to settle. Languages, too, are rooted in a material place.

Hannah understands linguistic roots, and desires a life free from Edelshtein's gruesome fantasies. She is not, as some argue, a simple-minded "American-born Jewish youth" who too easily renounces Jewish distinctiveness.[94] Hannah is more nuanced and perceptive than Edelshtein believes. Indeed, she exposes narrative tensions that other interpreters, especially Elaine Kauver, seek to exploit.[95] For her part, Hannah believes Yiddish forever resides in the ghetto, and she will not be overtaken by that history: "'Bloodsuckers,' she said. 'It isn't a translator you're after, it's someone's soul. Too much history's drained your blood, you want someone to take you over, a dybbuk—'." Edelshtein recognizes the word *dybbuk* as "Ostrover's language," but he nonetheless accepts Hannah's description: "'All right, I need a dybbuk, I'll become a golem, I don't care, it doesn't matter! Breathe in me! Animate me! Without you I'm a clay pot!' Bereaved, he yelled, 'Translate me!'"[96] Hannah refuses to play God's role to breathe life into dead matter. She will not be Edelshtein's messiah. Like his fantasy of Alexei, Edelshtein imagines a gentile Yiddish, a language unmoored from its ghetto origins. Yet as a "corpse of Babi Yar," Alexei also exposes the limits of acceptance. Hannah only reinforces those borders:

> Hannah said: "You think I have to read Ostrover in translation? You think translation has anything to do with what Ostrover is?"
>
> Edelshtein accused her, "Who taught you to read Yiddish?—A girl like that, to know the letters worthy of life and to be ignorant! 'You Jews,' 'you people,' you you you!"
>
> "I learned, my grandfather taught me, I'm not responsible for it, I didn't go looking for it, I was smart, a golden head, same as now. But I have my own life, you said it yourself, I don't have to throw it out. So pay attention, Mr. Vampire: even in Yiddish Ostrover's not in the ghetto. Even in Yiddish he's not like you people."
>
> "He's not in the ghetto? Which ghetto, what ghetto? So where is he? In the sky? In the clouds? With the angels? Where?"
>
> She meditated, she was all intelligence. "In the world," she answered him.[97]

Edelshtein understands Ostrover's place all too well: "Very good, he's achieved it, Ostrover's world. A pantheist, a pagan, a goy." Exactly right, Hannah responds, for Ostrover is a "contemporary" as "he speaks for everybody."[98] The world belongs to the goyim, for those with "a sensibility" and an intelligence; in the ghetto resides those enslaved to a past who require the life of others to exist. Though Hannah mimics Alexei's "golden head," she belittles Edelshtein's fantasy of translation. Ostrover never required translation "to reach"; he was already "in the world," even in Yiddish. He had already accepted the amnesia of history as the price of being one of "them." Edelshtein's Yiddish, too caught up in its place of origins, cannot be translated in America.

Hannah and Alexei represent the promise and inevitable failure of translation. To give up on a translated Yiddish is to abandon Hannah and Alexei. It is to renounce all that is contemporary, alive, and beautiful. But it is also to forego a life without substance. This is how Edelshtein, resentful to the core, now envisions the world:

> What he [Edelshtein] understood was this: that the ghetto was the real world, and the outside world only a ghetto. Because in actuality who was shut off? Who then was really buried, removed, inhabited by darkness? . . . An infatuation! He was the same, all his life the same as this poisonous wild girl, he coveted mythologies, specters, animals, voices. Western Civilization his secret guilt, he was ashamed of the small tremor of his self-love, degraded by being ingrown. Alexei with his skin a furnace of desire, his trucks and trains! He longed to be Alexei. Alexei with his German toys and his Latin! Alexei whose destiny was to grow up into the world-at-large, to slip from the ghetto, to break out into engineering for Western Civilization! Alexei, I abandon you! I'm at home only in a prison, history is my prison, the ravine my house. . . . Avremeleh, when you fell from the ledge over the ravine into your grave, for the first time you fell into reality.[99]

Edelshtein has not surrendered his envy, despite his reversal of values. He still yearns for a translator, even begging Hannah, after brutally cutting her lip, to breathe life into his poetry. Edelshtein has always known that Western civilization is "his secret guilt," his passage away from history, the ghetto, and Yiddish. The ghetto is not the world; but it is the only world for Yiddish. Western civilization, as Edelshtein soon discovers, belongs to "the beautiful sacramental English of our Holy Bible," as the Christian evangelist tells him on the phone. Hannah resides in that world, but not Edelshtein. He talks with a "kike accent," and so must forever be a "kike" and "Yid."[100] Language defines place, and place delimits identity. Ostrover strives against this association, and at least for Hannah, succeeds in writing a Yiddish beyond the ghetto. Yet like Edelshtein's joke about some Esperanto scholars, who after delivering learned talks on international language speak Yiddish among themselves, Ostrover, too, only plays the part of the gentile. He yearns to be "one of *them*," but even his "spinster hack" translator claims Ostrover's success as her own.[101] To her, Ostrover's Yiddish simply "doesn't matter," for she makes him modern, and creates the gentile out of the Jew by translating Yiddish into English. Even Ostrover's Yiddish remains in the ghetto.

Ostrover is aware of this, and has given up on Yiddish as a holy language. Like Hannah, he strives for a "sensibility" that "speaks for everybody." Note Ostrover's judgment of Edelshtein: "It doesn't matter what you speak, envy sounds the same in all languages."[102] Though Hannah believes this to be so, readers should not. As Joseph Lowin suggests, Ostrover distinguishes linguistic content (envy) from its form (language)—the very fantasy of Esperanto. Yet even the Esperanto scholars return to Yiddish, in Edelshtein's joke, and this because languages are material expressions tethered to place. One cannot cleanse a language of its material filth, as it were, so that it "speaks for everybody." Only translation can do that, and as Ostrover's spinster hack reveals, this means that "whatever's in Yiddish doesn't matter."[103] Despite Hannah's protest, Ostrover really does live in the ghetto because Yiddish does too.

Reclaiming Yiddish as a ghetto language, staking its place there, denies it a presence in the gentile world. Here I am not referring to Kaplan's notion of material presence, in which he stakes a claim in the American landscape. In the context of Ozick's narrative, presence confers life: it conveys an experience, a sense of repose, an attentiveness to "being present." Recall Abraham Joshua Heschel's notion of the Sabbath as a presence, an awareness of awe and wonder that shatters limiting borders and worship of place. Language, too, can maintain a sense of presence when it evokes universal experiences or sensibilities, when it is open and alive to the future rather than closed and harnessed to a past. But Yiddish lacks all presence in Ozick's story, and she associates this lack with death:

> And the language was lost, murdered. The language—a museum. Of what other language can it be said that it died a sudden and definite death, in a given decade, on a given piece of soil? . . . Yiddish, a littleness, a tiny light— oh little holy light!—dead, vanished. Perished. Sent into darkness.
>
> This was Edelshtein's subject. On this subject he lectured for a living. He swallowed scraps. Synagogues, community centers, labor unions underpaid him to suck on the bones of the dead. Smoke. He traveled from borough to borough, suburb to suburb, mourning in English the death of Yiddish.[104]

Like the subject of his lectures, Edelshtein hovers and glides through space like smoke as he witnesses to a linguistic death. Extinguished and lost, Yiddish as a "little holy light" has been "sent into darkness" without place or presence. Though he tells jokes to blunt his embarrassment, Edelshtein knows that "to speak of Yiddish was to preside over a funeral." As Sarah Cohen observes, Edelshtein is less the "stand-up comedian" and far more the "stand-up mourner" as "he laments the premature loss of a precious child."[105] Edelshtein never fathered children, and the notion of impotence and infertility haunts him: like Yiddish, he has no future. He witnesses to the same anxiety that plagued Mordecai Kaplan and his archive fever to cultivate an American home for his children and community. After his wife's seventh miscarriage, Edelshtein's bitterness overwhelms his despair: "'*My* sperm-count?' he screamed. '*Your* belly! Go fix the machine before you blame the oil!'" Without a publisher and translator, without sons or daughters, Edelshtein lacks a life of presence. He embodies the death of Yiddish.

Ostrover's "spinster hack" translator recognizes how translation confers presence. Although Ostrover "keeps all his translators in a perpetual frenzy of envy for each other," her work opens a world: "I know you call me hack . . . with Ostrover on my back I'm something else: I'm 'Ostrover's translator.' You think that's nothing? It's an entrance into *them*."[106] That portal into the gentile world is also an exit from obscurity, a breath of life safe from the smoke of incinerated bones. Ozick, who admits to the impact of the Holocaust on her work, and who has written eloquently about it,[107] no doubt evokes images of death, burial, smoke, and light to situate Yiddish within a cultural and historical locale. Yiddish can only escape the death camps when it is no longer Yiddish, when it is translated into and for "them." Ostrover, too, understands that his fame rests on escaping his Jewish roots. Edelshtein screams "out loud like a Jew," but not so Ostrover: "I'm one of *them*. You too are lured, aren't you, Hersheleh? Shakespeare is better than a shadow, Pushkin is better than a pipsqueak, hah?" Lurking in dark corners like a shadow, Edelshtein believes too much in Yiddish, too much in holiness.[108] In this, Yiddish has become Edelshtein's idol, and he infuses it with all the powers that Ozick associates with pagan worship.[109] But Yiddish cannot bring back the dead, nor confer presence on what has gone up in smoke. Ostrover "was free of the prison of Yiddish"; he had become that "pagan, a goy" who "doesn't stink from the ghetto."[110] The burnt stench that is Yiddish smoke lacks a physical presence in the world because it is forever burdened by a past. America, in stark contrast to Europe, promises a natural life of ease and sentimentality that satiates "the desire to escape history." But Jewish history, Ozick argues in one of her polemical essays, "offers the hard life," and the Jew chooses history over nature.[111] That history burdens Yiddish with a lack of presence in America; it literally has no place there. Rooted in a past place, Yiddish hovers like a deathly smoke in America, without a live presence and denied a future.

Tethered to a deathly past, Yiddish retains its filth and stench, as well as its "little holy light." It bears the scars of its heritage. Hannah rejects this past, and pursues an American future unencumbered by a vampish history. Like Ostrover's other admirers, Hannah considers him modern and American, a "contemporary." The contrast with Edelshtein is stark: Ostrover tells witty jokes to a young audience, while Edelshtein's jokes prove stale even to "the painted old ladies" attending his talks. Translation offers youth and the opportunity to project a modern "sensibility": "Now he examined her. Born 1945, in the hour of the death-camps. Not selected. Immune. The whole way she held herself looked immune—by this he meant American."[112] Impervious to the effects and pull of history, Hannah distinguishes between the "old" Jews who wallow in their own suffering, and those "new" Jews, like herself, who believe suffering is "unnecessary" and "history's a waste."[113] Edelshtein painfully, slowly, understands that Hannah's Yiddish is not his own. They both passively absorbed the language as children.[114] But Edelshtein proudly accepts Yiddish as the bearer of ghetto stench, the death-camps, and the weight of history, denying Hannah the right to adopt it as her own:

> "Forget Yiddish!" he screamed at her. "Wipe it out of your brain! Extirpate it! Go get a memory operation! You have no right to it, you have no right to an uncle, a grandfather! No one ever came before you, you were never born! A vacuum!"[115]

What is dead is dead, so Edelshtein claims, and if Hannah denies the suffering history of the past, then she must also relinquish the language that witnesses to it. Yiddish evokes memories, familial relations, and a thicker air of sounds and smells. Hannah's Yiddish lies dormant, in a vacuum without history or presence.

To Hannah's more open and lighter spirit, Edelshtein and her uncle Vorovsky are lecherous parasites who restrain her ambitions. She wishes they would all "hurry up and die," and "give somebody else a turn!"[116] With too much history, suffering, and depth, these "old socialists" deny what she prizes: magic and imagination, sensibility and lightness, youth and experience. She recognizes neither Edelshtein nor Yiddish as bearers of a meaningful past, but as barriers to her self-fulfillment. Hannah finally refuses to translate Edelshtein's poetry because she finds him "boring," and even more to the point, uninteresting:

> "Business. I'll pay you," he said.
> "No."
> "Because I laid a hand on you? Forgive me, I apologize. I'm crazier than he [Vorovsky] is, I should be locked up for it—"
> "Not because of that."
> "Then why not? *Meydeleh,* why not? What harm would it do you? Help out an old man."
> She said desolately, "You don't interest me. I would have to be interested."[117]

Hannah judges Edelshtein and Yiddish by the American categories she knows well: utility, interest, and personal advancement. Edelshtein finally abandons Hannah and his fantasy of translation, for his Yiddish is too burdened, too burnt and scarred to withstand the judgment of utility and interest. His sense of responsibility and concern ring hollow for the "allrightnik's children" like Hannah.[118] Edelshtein's Yiddish bears the responsibility of a tragic and beautiful heritage. With its death on a "piece of soil," Yiddish cannot migrate to America and still witness to a past. America is too clean, too immune from the burdens of history. Hannah has her own life to live, unshackled by past constraints—the very promise of youth. Yiddish is an old language, heavily worn and marked by suffering.

Edelshtein bears the markings of the Yiddish past. He witnesses to a linguistic material self—rooted in place, history, and memory. These are inescapable and material markings of his Yiddish. Despite Hannah's protest, languages have stories to tell, and Yiddish as *mamaloshen* recalls both a past and those shaped by it:

> *Mamaloshen* doesn't produce *Wastelands*. No alienation, no nihilism, no dadaism. With all the suffering no smashing! No INCOHERENCE! . . . Also: please remember that when a goy from Columbus, Ohio, says "Elijah the Prophet" he's not talking about *Eliohu hanovi*. Eliohu is one of us, a *folksmensh,* running around in second-hand clothes. Theirs is God knows what. The same biblical figure, with exactly the same history, once he puts on a name from King James, COMES OUT A DIFFERENT PERSON. Life, history, hope, tragedy, they don't come out even.[119]

This is linguistic material identity: *Eliohu* in second-hand clothes, with a tragic history who nonetheless confers wholeness and familiarity. Elijah is a different person altogether. Theodor Herzl, so Edelshtein claims, published in German, "but the message spread in *mamaloshen*": if you speak "their language," he continues, "you will become like them."[120] Yiddish is the common language, the idiom of the *folksmensh,* a jargon "with a littleness, a familiarity, an elbow-poke" that "was still pieced together out of *shtetl* rags."[121] It is a material language tethered to a history and place, and its speakers become the bearers of this linguistic heritage. Hannah rejects this inheritance, and so Edelshtein revokes her right to "know the letters worthy of life."[122] The responsibility to a past, the demands of inheritance, and the rags that bind generations are themes that haunt and consume Ozick's prose, and not only here in "Yiddish in America." Material identity is linguistic in these senses, for the languages we speak tie us to place and past, and inform our ethical duties as witnesses to heritage. Ancestors obligate their descendants in the languages they speak and live, even in America.

IDENTIFYING MATERIAL: THE TRAGIC
CHARACTERS OF BERNARD MALAMUD

Ozick masterfully appropriates American Yiddish inflections into her story, remaining faithful to a literary tradition that includes Henry Roth's *Call It Sleep* and, above all, the works of Bernard Malamud. Malamud's prose characteristically interweaves American Yiddish locutions with magical accents of the bizarre. Alfred Kazin once quipped that Malamud "writes, a little, the way Chagall paints," for both capture the fantastic in the ordinary and commonplace.[123] Malamud transposes the humdrum into the extreme, and "tends to the bizarre, the contorted, the verge of things that make you shiver, not laugh." The final effect, argues Kazin, is both strange and true.[124] Malamud's everyday Yiddishisms, his artistic rendering of space as emotional landscapes, and his shaping of characters that inhabit those places, all witness to the strange and true in Malamud's novels and short stories. Readers have debated, often against Malamud's own denials, the Jewish features of his writing.[125] Though Malamud has described himself as an American and not a Jewish writer,[126] Robert Alter notes how the controlling metaphor of imprisonment suffuses Malamud's understanding of Jewishness. The image of "claustrophobic containment" depicts the condition of the modern Jew who is "a prisoner placed in progressively restricting confinement." The Jew, like all other human beings, only more transparently so, witnesses to the "inevitable exposure to the caprice of circumstances and the insidious snarl of history."[127] Like Ozick's commitment to a heritage that binds, Malamud's works, and especially his short stories, expose his (mostly Jewish) characters to the fate of historical entanglement. He weaves his earthly language, magical atmospheres, notions of responsibility, and images of confinement into dark and bewildering moments of human desolation touched with hope. His short stories in *The Magic Barrel* (1958), *Idiots First* (1963), and *Rembrandt's Hat* (1973) offer stark portrayals of characters imprisoned in history, and the possibilities that history both reveals and forecloses.

Malamud effuses infectious sympathy for his imaginative characters, and he often does so by mooring their fate and identity to material things. One can see this already in his first novel, *The Natural* (1952), where Roy Hobbs and his "Wonderboy" bat each become magical creations fatefully tied to the other. This coupling is most expressive in Malamud's short stories, well illustrated in the opening lines of "Take Pity":

> Davidov, the census-taker, opened the door without knocking, limped into the room and sat wearily down. Out came his notebook and he was on the job. Rosen, the ex-coffee salesman, wasted, eyes despairing, sat motionless, cross-legged, on his cot. The square, clean but cold room, lit by a dim globe, was sparsely furnished: the cot, a folding chair, small table, old unpainted chests—no closets but who needed them?—and a small sink with a rough piece of green, institutional soap on its holder—you could smell it across the room. The worn black shade over the single narrow window was drawn to the ledge surprising Davidov.

"What's the matter you don't pull the shade up?" he remarked.
Rosen ultimately sighted. "Let it stay."
"Why? Outside is light."
"Who needs light?"
"What then you need?"
"Light I don't need," replied Rosen.[128]

Here we have all the elements that make Malamud's prose so expressive and stark: the American Yiddish dialogue ("What's the matter you don't pull the shade up?"), the condensed, claustrophobic feel of confinement ("no closets but who needed them?"), the oppressive weight of human suffering (the census-taker, limping, sits wearily down, matched only by the ex-coffee salesman, "wasted, eyes despairing"), and the magical ambiance saturated by physical objects (the dark room "lit by a dim globe," and the horrid smell of institutional soap). All this, as the reader discovers at the conclusion to Malamud's story, is tied to "the worn black shade." Rosen recounts to the census-taker his experience with Eva, a widow with two children, who tries to fix up the store that her dead husband Axel had left her. He councils her to run away, let the creditors take the store—for Rosen knows "a graveyard when I smell it"—but she stubbornly refuses to abandon the grocery. In his desperate attempt to help Eva, Rosen alters his will so that she and her children become his beneficiaries. He then turns on the gas stove and sticks his head inside. Malamud now returns to the black shade, and draws his bleak story to a close:

Davidov, scratching his stubbled cheek, nodded. This was the part he already knew. He got up and, before Rosen could cry no, idly raised the window shade.
It was twilight in space but a woman stood before the window.
Rosen with a bound was off his cot to see.
It was Eva, staring at him with haunted, beseeching eyes. She raised her arms to him.
Infuriated, the ex-salesman shook his fist.
"Whore, bastard, bitch," he shouted at her. "Go 'way from here. Go home to your children."
Davidov made no move to hinder him as Rosen rammed down the window shade.[129]

Like many of Malamud's stories, this one ends powerfully, yet is characteristically enigmatic and ambivalent.[130] Although the meaning of Eva's "haunted, beseeching eyes," and Rosen's violent response, still remains obscure (at least to me), the window shade, now rammed shut, absorbs the tragic sensibility that burdens Rosen's character.

Malamud often concludes his stories by returning to the material thing that embodies the tragic dimensions of his character. In "The First Seven Years," another short story in *The Magic Barrel*, he opens his tale of a shoemaker with the sound of Sobel's "fanatic pounding." Feld is irritated with his assistant Sobel, who restlessly crouches over the bench as he fixes old shoes. Hoping the young scholar Max will seek his daughter Miriam in marriage, Feld arranges their meeting, only to be disappointed at Miriam's indifference. But it is Sobel who yearns for Miriam, and he offers her books, together with his own commentary in the margins, as Miriam "read page by sanctified page, as if the word of God were inscribed on them." When Sobel admits that he has already sacrificed five years with "stingy wages" just so he can wait for Miriam to come of age, Feld reluctantly agrees to their union, but Sobel must wait another two years for marriage: "the next morning, when the shoemaker arrived, heavy-hearted, to open the store, he saw he needn't have come, for his assistant was already seated at the last, pounding leather for his love."[131] Sobel's nobel patience and fortitude is heard through that pounding, and felt in the leather of the old shoes. His character is *its* character: both are plied and molded, hoping for a better fate.

Malamud ties the leather to the character again in "The Maid's Shoes," a despondent short story in *Idiots First*. A poor widow, Rosa, seeks work from an American professor, Orlando Krantz, who is both cold and caring for the maid. She tells Krantz about her affair with a married government worker, and his desire to buy her a pair of shoes to replace her tattered old ones. She desperately requires new shoes, Rosa tells Krantz, "but you know how these things go. If I put on his shoes they may carry me to his bed." Krantz advises her to refuse Armando's gifts, and decides to buy her a pair instead in order to solve her problem. Rosa, in the end, accepts both Krantz and Armando's gifts, and her life now becomes ensnared in lies, a false pregnancy, and a final dismissal from Krantz. But the shoes remain: "Later the professor inspected the maid's room and saw that Rosa had taken all her belongings but the shoes he had given her. When his wife arrived in the apartment, shortly before Thanksgiving, she gave the shoes to the portinaia, who wore them a week, then gave them to her daughter-in-law."[132] Again here, the shoes remain as material reminders of Rosa's desperate life. They hold the promise of new beginnings (the affair with Armando), even as they return her to a wretched life with her son. Though she leaves the shoes behind for others to wear, they are carriers of her identity: their wanderings are hers as well. As the shoes remain homeless, so too Rosa.

In "Rembrandt's Hat," a story of friendship, ambition, and misunderstandings, Malamud first describes the artist Rubin and his "careless white cloth hat." Arkin, the more cerebral art historian, thought the white hat illuminated "a lonely inexpressiveness," and one day jocularly compliments Rubin on what "looks like Rembrandt's hat that he wears in one of the middle-aged self-portraits, the really profound ones, I think the one in the Rijksmuseum in Amsterdam. May it bring you the best of luck." Rubin is offended, and Arkin struggles to ascertain how such an innocent comment could provoke such a chilly reaction. As the story concludes with Arkin's gradual understanding, Malamud channels Rubin's loneliness into that white hat:

> "Excuse me, Rubin, I came in to tell you I got those hats I mentioned to you some time ago mixed up."
> "Damn right you did."
> "Also for letting things get out of hand for a while."
> "Damn right."
> Rubin, though he tried not to, then began to cry. He wept silently, his shoulders shaking, tears seeping through his coarse fingers on his face. Arkin had taken off.
> They stopped avoiding each other and spoke pleasantly when they met, which wasn't often. One day Arkin, when he went into the men's room, saw Rubin regarding himself in the mirror in his white cap, the one that seemed to resemble Rembrandt's hat. He wore it like a crown of failure and hope.[133]

For Sobel and Rosa's shoes, and Rubin's hat, the material thing absorbs the tragic hope that both expands and limits their painful lives. As readers, we visualize Malamud's characters with the things they use and wear, and come to understand their tragic dimensions in and through their material possessions. Rubin's hat is *his* hat in the very real sense that it bears his failures and hopes. Malamud accesses the tragic dimensions of his characters through material things, and in turn those things become distinguishing markers of identity. They become agents of selfhood.

It is not Armando, after all, who drags Rosa to bed, but "his shoes" that do—"if I put on his shoes *they* may carry me to his bed" (emphasis added). These material things carry something less than symbolic freight, despite the prevalent desire among Malamud readers to highlight symbolic meaning.[134] Herbert Mann has it right, I believe, in arguing that "Malamud starts with the street, the cold, the wind, the stench, the prison, and out of this he fashions an occasional triumph of the human spirit."[135] Malamud tethers that occasional triumph to the material thing itself. The human spirit, as Mann calls it, does not leave the stench and street behind, but is forever bound to it. Readers of Malamud recall Sobel and his continuous pounding of leather; they remember Rosa and the shoes that define and limit her destiny; and they recognize the failures and hopes in Rubin's mirrored vision of his white hat. Those things capture material identity, as they embody and texture the dark lives in Malamud's fiction. The magical darkness that engulfs Malamud's stories lives in the things themselves.

This is especially true for two of Malamud's well-known and, to my mind, best short stories, "The Last Mohican" and "The Magic Barrel." In "The Last Mohican," Arthur Fidelman, a failed artist but aspiring writer, arrives in Rome from America to continue his study of Giotto. He carries with him the opening chapter of his work, together with two suits to last the year. Standing before the Rome railroad station, he notices the stranger Shimon Susskind, "oddly dressed" and deathly thin. Susskind "all but licked his lips" as he approached Fidelman, and after pleasant introductions that reveal their Jewish heritage and Fidelman's business in Rome, Susskind finally asks for a suit: "would you maybe have a suit you can't use? I could use a suit."[136] As the story unfolds, Fidelman and Susskind perform a kind of dance around two physical objects: the suit and Fidelman's introductory chapter to his book. At times Susskind pursues Fidelman to once again request a suit, and so too Fidelman seeks out Susskind when he discovers his chapter missing from his hotel room. Indeed, this pattern of mutual pursuit runs through a number of Malamud's stories.[137] And like many of these other tales, Malamud focuses upon the material objects in the conclusion to "The Last Mohican." Upon learning that Susskind had indeed stolen and even burned his chapter, Fidelman still offers him his suit, and Malamud ends his story with characteristic flair: "'Susskind, come back,' he shouted, half sobbing. 'The suit is yours. All is forgiven.' He came to a dead halt but the refugee ran on. When last seen he was still running."[138] The one is at a standstill, the other racing away. We do not know if Susskind returns for his suit, nor if Fidelman recoups his lost chapter. Both things seem to be lost.

When Fidelman returns to his room unable to locate his chapter on Giotto, he attempts to rewrite it by memory. This he fails to do—though "he felt sure he knew [it] by heart," there were still "important thoughts, whole paragraphs, even pages, that went blank in the mind." Rome now becomes his prison, where "time went without work, without accomplishment." Instead of wandering the city and enjoying its beauty, he remains "glued to paper, sitting steadfastly at his desk in an attempt to re-create his initial chapter, because he was lost without a beginning." He grows anxious and disorientated, unsure "what he must do next, a feeling that was torture."[139] To relieve this claustrophobia, he searches for Susskind among the peddlers, at the synagogue, and in the ghetto. His two-week planned stay now stretches on for three months, and the loss of his chapter "was like a spell cast over him." Fidelman, like his chapter, is lost, and this because his identity is so wrapped up in the thing itself:

> There were times he scorned it [his chapter] as a man-made thing, like all such, replaceable; other times he feared it was not the chapter per se, but that his volatile curiosity had become somehow entangled with Susskind's strange personality.... Sometimes he smiled wryly at all this; ridiculous, the chapter grieved him for itself only—the precious thing he had created then lost—especially when he got to thinking of the long diligent labor, how painstakingly he had built each idea, how cleverly mastered problems of order, form, how impressive the finished product, Giotto reborn! It broke the heart. What else, if after months he was here, still seeking?[140]

Fidelman's chapter mirrors his carefully organized life and character. He writes as he lives. If Fidelman comes to Rome to find something else, he will not discover it in his own work. "The Last Mohican" is but one of several stories about Fidelman.[141] In Malamud's other portrayals, Fidelman is a rather cold painter whose sexual failures mimic his emotional immaturity.[142] And this is precisely what Susskind tells Fidelman about his chapter when he arrives with his suit: "the words were there but the spirit was missing."[143] Malamud implies, at the very end, that Fidelman comes to recognize this too. He arrives in Rome seeking a richer emotional life, and so he must abandon his opening chapter to discover a more expressive self. But to relinquish the text, Fidelman must also surrender the self that created it. He needs to run, like Susskind, from his past, but remains at "a dead halt." All might be forgiven, but the self and the text are imprisoned together. Fidelman seeks, but cannot live a more expressive life.

Susskind's appearance mirrors Fidelman's emptiness: deathly sick, wasted, a skeleton but with "a couple of pounds," he tells Fidelman that to live, "I eat air." With his flimsy shirt and "baggy knickers," Susskind follows Fidelman through Rome, requesting his "old suit" to warm his body for the cold nights. Fidelman will not relinquish his second suit, nor does he believe it practical ("it's gabardine, more like a summer suit"). Susskind's response, and the jockeying that ensues, intimate that the suit provides more than warmth:

> "On me it will be for all seasons."
> After a moment's reflection, Fidelman drew out his billfold and counted four single dollars. These he handed to Susskind.
> "Buy yourself a warm sweater."
> Susskind also counted the money. "If four," he said, "then why not five?"
> Fidelman flushed. The man's warped nerve. "Because I happen to have four available," he answered. "That's twenty-five hundred lire. You should be able to buy a warm sweater and have something left over besides."
> "I need a suit," Susskind said. "The days are warm but the nights are cold." He rubbed his arms. "What else I need I won't say."[144]

The practical Fidelman offers a sweater as far more useful to Susskind, especially for the cold Rome evenings. Why, then, does Susskind want only a suit, even one that would surely *not* keep him warm at night? When Susskind first meets Fidelman at the train station, Fidelman confesses that "I haven't had a suit for years. The one I was wearing when I ran away from Germany, fell apart." Seek relief from Jewish organizations, Fidelman responds. But to Susskind, those groups "wish to give me what they wish, not what I wish."[145] In an eerie allusion to Roth's "Eli, the Fanatic," in which the black suit is all the "greenie" possesses, the suit recalls a life before wandering and exile. The clothing, then, offers less warmth than identity—perhaps one less vacuous than Eli's. Will Susskind stop fleeing, then, and return for the suit? He was last seen still running, so Malamud tells his readers. Perhaps Susskind, like his double Fidelman, cannot find his self without the material thing. Exile for Susskind is a running away from the material things that ground identity.

Leo Finkle, the rabbinical student in Malamud's "The Magic Barrel," wants to stop running too, and hopes to settle down with a wife. But like Fidelman, he is of a practical mind, for "he might find it easier to win himself a congregation if he were married." To help him in this search, he hires the matchmaker Pinye Salzman, who appears one night at Finkle's flat "grasping a black, strapped portfolio that had been worn thin with use."[146] That portfolio contains pictures of women seeking husbands, a selection that Salzman believes suitable for the young aspiring rabbi. When he shows the Yeshiva University student six photographs, and Finkle complains of so few, Salzman explains that his "drawers are already filled to the top, so I keep them now in a barrel, but is every girl good for a new rabbi?" What comes out of the barrel are the tragic lives of women seeking a better future. We learn of Sophie P., twenty-four years of age, who is now a widow after only four months of marriage. Finkle will not consider a widow as a spouse. There is Ruth K., nineteen, an honor student with a wealthy father, but who is lame on her right foot from an automobile accident. Finkle recoils in disgust. And then there is Lily Hirschorn, a high school teacher, educated with a "well-Americanized family," who is either twenty-nine or thirty-two years of age, although when Finkle finally consents to meet her, she appears as "a woman past thirty-five and aging rapidly."[147] Each of these women, drawn forth from the magic barrel, presents a life of immense hope and sorrow:

> There were six, of varying degrees of attractiveness, but look at them long enough and they all became Lily Hirschorn: all past their prime, all starved behind bright smiles, not a true personality in the lot. Life, despite their frantic yoohooings, had passed them by; they were pictures in a brief case that stank of fish.[148]

Finkle comes to realize that he is both "unloved and loveless,"[149] and his brutal dismissal of these women underscores his failure to engage a world beyond rabbinical studies. But he finds one such picture that moves him, and he seeks out Salzman to find her. She holds a particular intensity, a strangeness that repels and attracts Finkle because she "had lived."[150]

The mesmerizing picture of Salzman's daughter Stella was unintentionally mixed in with the others from the magic barrel, or so Salzman tells Finkle. She is "a wild one," "like an animal, like a dog," Salzman complains, and no match for a rabbi. But this otherness is what attracts Finkle, for he imagines "in her, his own redemption."[151] She will lure him from his books, as other suitors draw wives from the magic barrel. Stella will redeem his own loveless life, as the women in the magic barrel seek redemption beyond a life in pictures. Finkle, though able to choose from among the women of the magic barrel, really belongs with them. Like them, life has passed him by, and they, too, remain unloved and loveless. The magic barrel is a kind of compressed prison, where persons escape only if suitors dream of them as saviors. The vivid horror of a wasted life, condensed in the pictures of Salzman's magic barrel, binds the fate of a life with material existence. Women like Sophie P. and Lily Hirschorn live full lives beyond the stench of Salzman's fish, but Finkle merely recognizes "pictures in a brief case." Only Stella lives beyond the magic barrel, perhaps because she refused to be contained there. Others had very little choice. Recall Herbert Mann's comment that Malamud begins with the street, the prison, and the stench, "and out of this he fashions an occasional triumph of the human spirit."[152] For Sophie P. and Lily H., life begins and ends with the prison and the stench. There is nothing beyond the magic barrel.

This darker Malamud, the one who chains a life to material things, is not the hopeful moralist that many of his readers take him to be. Certainly Malamud offers ethical guidance, but like Alfred Kazin, I find him far less appealing and convincing when he utters moral platitudes. This is so because much of his work undercuts the claim to a "spiritual success story."[153] His characters speak to us because they are mired in a material existence that restricts and delimits possibilities.[154] Whether it is Rosa's shoes that lead to Armando's bed, or Rubin's hat worn with dignity and despair, or the worn black shade that hides Eva's mysterious appeal, material things identify Malamud's characters. They do not live outside of those things, just as Salzman's women live only within the magic barrel. Finkle endeavors to escape, and imagines Stella as his savior. But the magic barrel delimits the possibility of that flight and the hope of a new life. The hope is that identity can be unmoored from a scarred past. Yet Malamud's prose retains a mysterious but ever vivid sensibility because he binds things to persons. Material identity is very real, as are things, but maddeningly elusive and scarred, as identity always must be.

CONCLUSION

In "The Shawl" (1980), Cynthia Ozick collapses the tragic dimensions of the Holocaust within a cloth that warms the baby Magda. As witness to a lived horror, the shawl absorbs the material needs and identity of Magda, her mother Rosa, and Rosa's niece Stella.[155] Rosa sees the baby "through a gap in the shawl," and within it Magda appears as a squirrel: "in a nest, safe, no one could reach her inside the little house of the shawl's windings." The shawl is all the protection a mother can offer her child within the confines of a concentration camp. But the shawl is also a source of comfort, even of meager sustenance, to the baby Magda. When no milk would flow from Rosa's breasts, Magda milked the shawl instead: "she sucked and sucked, flooding the threads with wetness. The shawl's good flavor, milk of linen." It was alive with her saliva and smells. When Stella "took the shawl away and made Magda die," a simple act that mirrored Stella's cold and jealous heart, Rosa in her grief takes back the shawl as her own:

> So she took Magda's shawl and filled her own mouth with it, stuffed it in and stuffed it in, until she was swallowing up the wolf's screech and tasting the cinnamon and almond depth of Magda's saliva; and Rosa drank Magda's shawl until it dried.[156]

In "Rosa," the second story in Ozick's collection, the author traces how Rosa's obsession with the shawl destroys her capacity to move beyond her past. As Rosa swallows Magda up in the shawl, she too becomes ensnared by the material. She lives her life *in* the shawl, for it captures the spit, sounds, tastes, and memories of human identity. The shawl becomes Rosa's idol because she enlivens the thing with material identity.

Ozick captures much of the narrative dimension of material identity discussed in this chapter. The stories presented here from Yezierska, Roth, Ozick, and Malamud all expose how material culture informs Jewish identity, and how a lived life is forever mired in historical things.

Yezierska shows us how we visualize the world as a material one, as her immigrant characters decode a world in and through clothing, entangled as they are within the filth and stench of sweatshop dress. Roth too reveals how persons conduct their narrative lives within material things. But the meaning that others attribute to those things, and especially to dress as a performative symbol, often obscures the fundamental mystery, even the emptiness, of material existence. Sometimes the shit is simply that: it is Roth's inheritance, but nothing more (or less). Leaping to signification and symbolic meaning too often trivializes the power of the material thing itself. Things do not require linguistic meanings to be constitutive of personal identity.

Even if Ozick invests things with symbolic power, she still reveals how linguistic selves are rooted in place, history, and memory. Her characters, like Rosa, are stuck in the past, often worship it, and witness to its power to restrict personal freedom. Edelshtein's Yiddish ties him to the ghetto—a place that governs his fate, even as he yearns for a translator to free him from that confining heritage. But he remains stuck, like his beloved Alexei, within a past that stifles and constricts. I have read Malamud along this trajectory as well, for his characters are ensnared, contained, and imprisoned in the things that define personal identity. Like Rosa and her shawl, the lives of Finkle, Fidelman, Rubin, and even Lily Hirschorn are captured by and through things: the magic barrel, an academic text, a hat and shoes. A narrative life, in which we witness the development and richness of characters through time, uncovers the material dimensions of human identity. The stories analyzed in this chapter reveal how persons are scarred by the things that identify and obligate. These materials frustrate translation, conversion, and personal transformation. Material life is a forbidding narrative.

Like other immigrants to America, Jews felt the brute force of a material life and its constraining narrative. This was certainly the case for New York City Jews at the beginning of the twentieth century. Then and there, as the first chapter in this study argues, Jews sought to become American through the consumption of products—even though, as outsiders, their consumption was rendered illegitimate. Mordecai Kaplan's obsession with journal writing remains part of this social history, for the acquisition and distribution of material things informed his search for home. The literary works reviewed in this chapter are also part of this

Jewish search and journey. Like Kaplan, the characters in the stories of Yezierska, Roth, Ozick and Malamud discover themselves in created things: a clean but materially rich apartment, a black suit or hat, shoes, even a shawl. But these things rarely, if ever, open up a new world of American possibilities. The shawl destroys Rosa's life, the shoes enslave Sobel and his Miriam to an impoverished existence, and the black suit is just a material waste, mirroring Eli's anemic Jewish heritage. These material things inhibit, confine, and suffocate. The promise of American abundance and freedom remains distant, something heard and imagined, but never viscerally felt and experienced. This is why Hannah is only a voice to Edelshtein. Her Yiddish is "the sound of a dead language on a live girl's tongue"—a "strong mouth" that, in the end, makes no impression at all. Hannah lives in a vacuum, unencumbered by the material weight of the past. Yet she is attractive for all that. For though Eli, Fidelman, Edelshtein, and the rest sink beneath the burden of material history, they all recognize Hannah as the seductive other they wish to be. She is their temptress, and as such reveals their confinement in a Jewish world made heavy by material things.

SIX

The Material Gaze: American Jewish Identity and Heritage Production

When Philip Roth published his "Imagining Jews" in *The New York Review of Books* in 1974,[1] he set out to defend his "shooting off his mouth about shooting off his semen"[2] that made *Portnoy's Complaint* (1969) such a robust, and to many, a crude book by a Jewish author. The fact that a Jew like Portnoy could be so enthralled to the passions, and sexual ones at that, appeared to overturn the accepted literary image of the rational, moral Jew who restrains himself from the more violent urges of the emotional life. The more turbulent, passionate, and sexual life of the gentile played the foil to the upright, honest, and ethical Jewish American. Recall Edelshtein's critique of Ostrover's stories in Ozick's "Envy; or, Yiddish in America," as "insanely sexual, pornographic, paranoid, freakish," and so only beloved by non-Jews.[3] Ostrover passes as a gentile because he abandons his Jewish ethical roots. But Roth wants to recover that pornographic Jew, and so celebrates this libidinous type in contrast to those conjured by Saul Bellow and Bernard Malamud. Bellow's characters are most Jewish, so Roth believes, when "they are actors in dramas of conscience where matters of principle or virtue are at issue," but are least Jewish when "appetite and quasi- or outright libidinous adventure is at the heart of a novel." When a Bellow character yells "I want!" it represents "raw, untrammeled, uncompromising, insatiable, and unsocialized desire," and "only a goy can talk like that and get away with it." So too for Malamud's novels, for his Jews are "innocent, passive, virtuous," while the gentile is "corrupt, violent, and lustful."[4] So here comes Roth's Portnoy, "a lusting Jew" and a "sexual defiler." Roth has envisioned him as the classic goy, and thereby has overturned "imagining what Jews are"[5] in American Jewish fiction. Jews no longer monopolize the righteous certitude of ethical, rational behavior, but instead are enslaved to sexual and libidinal passions. If Bellow and Malamud distinguish the Jew by his (and it usually is *his*) rational control, then Roth imagines the Jew struggling mightily with baser passions with little ability to repress them.

Roth had surely been unfair to both Bellow and Malamud, and a bit too defensive in justifying his own work.[6] But that censure would miss the larger significance of Roth's defense: the novelistic enterprise, so Roth contends, is "imagining Jews *being* imagined, by themselves and by others."[7] Novelists like Roth inscribe profiles of Jewish identity that others, Jews and non-Jews alike, imagine as fitting depictions of American Jewry. But writers also *re-imagine* those entrenched images to reveal new, or perhaps latent features of human character. Whatever one might think of Roth's sexual defilers, his works return the reader's gaze and subject it to critique. If Portnoy appears repulsive and vulgar, this reveals a good deal more about a reader's imaginings than it does about Roth's fictional character.

Literature, as Roth suggests, overflows with Jews being imagined, but so do other artistic mediums such as photography, film, and the plastic arts. This chapter focuses on graphic images to better reveal how Jews visualize themselves as American Jews. This is a vast and borderless field, and once again I will restrict my gaze to those art works that amplify the thesis of this book—to wit, that American Jews visualize materially, and do so in ways that situate identity within material things and practices. This is how Anzia Yezierska viewed her world, for her characters see materially as they engage and work with a visual culture. Yezierska exposes Jewish visual practices, and I want to transpose those modes of seeing to three other sites of visual display: the magazine covers of *Lilith* magazine, Arnold Eagle's photographic collection of Orthodox Jews in New York City (1935), and the three film versions of *The Jazz Singer* (1927, 1953, and 1980). Since the mid-1970s, *Lilith* magazine has promoted a Jewish feminist visual culture, and its covers reveal how glossy images produce new religious and ethnic sensibilities. These covers overturn received paradigms in order to establish new modes and behaviors, and so visually perform this transvaluation of value. Eagle's work from the 1930s bears witness to a world that *Lilith* has left behind.

His black-and-white photographs depict lonely, isolated, religious Jews, who with some nostalgia gaze beyond the urban landscape of New York City toward the more comforting European shtetl. These photos haunt, but together with written captions they sustain a gendered and weary image of American Jewish heritage. This nostalgic impulse, and the Jewish struggle to overcome it, are at the core of the three *Jazz Singer* films. Each movie produces compelling visions of Jewish identity, even as each transmits the aural experience of becoming American. Sound is now formative of visual experiences, and modifies the patterns of cultural heritage. The physical mediums themselves—magazine glossies, black-and-white photography, and film—shape the ways in which Jews see and hear themselves as they are and want to be.

David Morgan's work on "religious acts of seeing" locates visual practices within cultural and historical settings. Various social clues and relationships inform what Morgan calls the "sacred gaze," such that viewers are accustomed and habituated to the "social act of looking."[8] Images do not confront persons clean, as it were, without markers of cultural location and meaning. Seeing is a form of practice, as Talal Asad has used that term, in which we learn the rules to see well, and acquire visual techniques and skills sanctioned by cultural authorities.[9] Morgan has eloquently described this visual practice: "A gaze is a projection of conventions that enables certain possibilities of meaning, certain forms of experience, and certain relations among participants."[10] Elsewhere, Morgan has described religious images as a feature of social construction, in which they function to ward off chaos, and help "secure the world or sense of reality in which the self finds its existence."[11] But religious images also challenge, destroy, and replace that sense of order, as Morgan suggests.[12] They produce new gazes, as it were, and challenge and reposition others.[13] Graphic works re-imagine the world, displace the old, and help to configure new visual practices. Asad is surely right to argue that what counts as religious is a historical question, and Morgan's "religious" images might be far broader, and more complicated, than he presumes.[14] "Religious" images also challenge the very notion of religion and the sacred gaze, and seek to displace entrenched practices within other disciplines.

The images discussed in this chapter do this kind of deconstructive work by creating a visual Jewish heritage. The term *heritage* has become a term of art for such thinkers as musicologist Mark Slobin and folklorist Barbara Kirshenblatt-Gimblett, depicting "a mode of cultural production in the present that has recourse to the past."[15] Heritage is a contemporary project that marks some features of the past for survival, and others to oblivion. It also can be a racialized or ethnic practice: a mode of recovery that motivates the contemporary turn toward ethnicity and multi-culturalism.[16] As a form of cultivation, heritage works over the past to make it a usable and meaningful one for contemporary ethnic groups. Slobin calls heritage "the emerging word of choice for identification through presumed historical connection, even the most attenuated or stereotyped."[17] The covers of *Lilith* magazine (1976–present), together with the Eagle photographic collection and the three *Jazz Singer* films, redeploy Jewish seeing to produce heritage. Jewish material identity is a visual practice of heritage construction.

VISUALIZING HERITAGE:
THE COVERS OF *LILITH* MAGAZINE

Lilith magazine is one such performance of heritage production. Indeed, its very title witnesses to the cultivation of a past that displaces other forms of remembrances. Although it fosters an explicit political agenda to place Jewish women's issues at the forefront "of the Jewish community, with a view to giving women—who are more than 50% of the world's Jews—greater choices in Jewish life,"[18] *Lilith* also reappropriates the female character Lilith as a model for contemporary Jewish feminist practices. Lilith is imagined, in Jewish Midrash and the Babylonian Talmud, as a demonic first-Eve who threatens male sexual potency and kills newborn babies. But Aviva Cantor Zuckoff, who wrote the opening article of *Lilith*'s first published issue, reclaims Lilith as an independent, powerful, assertive female who rejects the role of enabler and demands "equality of woman and man based on their creation as equals by God." Even more, "it is this Lilith who is faithful to her innermost self," and she "is closer in spirit to both the original Biblical account and to Jewish women of today." Those other demonic features derive from male fears and reactions to Jewish exile, and should be discarded altogether as a relic of the past.[19] This is heritage: cultural production in the present that reconfigures a past as a meaningful one for contemporary practice.

The very appropriation of Lilith as role model does this kind of cultural work, as do the various glossy covers that have appeared throughout the magazine's published history.

Together with Zuckoff's opening article appeared the striking cover (a black-and-white sketch) of a Jewish woman balancing on a tight rope, with a chicken soup can in one hand and a raised Israeli flag in the other. With her long, flowing dress that still reveals a shapely left leg, a hat brimming with Sabbath candles and challah, and a prayer shawl (*tallit*) delicately drooped over both shoulders, this modern American Jewish woman literally juggles her appropriation of a past with her newly discovered American freedoms. With the sign of the female gender stitched on her satchel, in which we find what appears as a *yad* (a pointer) for reading Torah next to a ruler and recipe book, she can be all things to everyone, including herself. But she must walk carefully—the soup spills ever so slightly from the bowl in the left hand—balancing all her desires and responsibilities on a slim rope that leads to six block cubes that spell out, in Hebrew and English, the title *Lilith* magazine. These are children's toys, familiar to most parents, and this modern Lilith steadies herself as she enters the home brimming with kids. The caption underneath the children's blocks frames this initial cover: "Exploring the World of the Jewish Woman."[20]

This subtitle, "Exploring the World of the Jewish Woman," is important for a number of reasons. It represents a visual clue for reading the cover sketch, and the ways in which heritage is exposed visually. The Jewish woman's world is one with children and home responsibilities, but also a professional life of work and stress. She is a strong and determined leader of her synagogue, dresses modestly but elegantly, supports Israel with one hand while supervising the kitchen with the other, and manages to balance her religious, professional, and familial responsibilities with poise and grace. This portrait mirrors the world of a middle-class, baby boomer, white, and committed Jewish American woman. She is fully American, Jewish, and feminist, fulfilling all roles without sacrificing any one for the other. She is the modern Lilith that Zuckoff described in her article: capable, bold, and at ease with her complex and multiple roles. But even more, she is singular: "The Jewish Woman"—neither a suburban teenager struggling with self-esteem, nor an elderly Jewish woman coping with old age and a dignified life. *Lilith*

FIGURE 6.1. *Lilith* 1 (Fall 1976). Reprinted with permission from Lilith Publications, Inc. Copyright © 1976. To see more, and to subscribe, visit Lilith.org.

will take up these concerns, and more, in later issues; but the first issue focuses on the middle-class married woman, and the articles in this volume bear this out. One can read about Jewish women's organizations, on husbands who must learn to accept a more successful spouse, on the male fears of feminism, and, of course, about Lilith herself. All these articles are insightful and cogent, but "the world of the Jewish woman" is anything but universal and ubiquitous. She inhabits a particular world of middle-class luxury and anxiety, of social organizations and familial duties. Exploring her world reveals a particular moment of heritage construction.

Heritage is a cultural production in part because it is local—it occurs within a complex pattern of time, place, and social location. By 1976, the year this cover appeared in print, women had entered the workforce in large numbers, were innovative leaders at their synagogues, and had moved with their husbands to the American suburbs. Education and employment opportunities were just opening in equal measure for both Jewish women and men.[21] Jewish women had gained some measure of social and sexual freedom from the progressive movements of the 1960s, and they, like most American Jews, proudly supported and identified with Israel. The Jewish woman in the *Lilith* sketch appropriates a past that fits her cultural location. She accepts the home as her domain, holding the soup can and carrying the Sabbath candles. Dressed modestly, she still covers her hair, suggesting a more observant orientation. But the past sits uneasily with her modern sensibilities: her dress reveals a bare leg, even as the soup spills over. She publicly reveals her feminist loyalties on her satchel, and she wears a prayer shawl once worn by men only. This balancing act, in which "the Jewish Woman" selectively retrieves a past as her own, produces the past as heritage, for one must critique the past to authentically appropriate it. The modern Lilith has remade the past from the present, adopting those artifacts—prayer shawl, reading pointer, candles—that mark her as a modern, progressive, American, Jewish woman. She owns the past, as it were; she can pray and read Torah like other men in the synagogue, even as she too earns her income from the public sector. And she does this without abandoning her children or political commitments. The past does not weigh her down, but instead sanctions the shaping of her own future, as the editor makes clear in her opening remarks.[22] The world of the Jewish woman is a world built out of a past with an eye to the future. It is, in short, a world of Jewish heritage.

Reflecting back on this initial volume in 2003, Susan Weidman Schneider, the editor of the magazine, described the cover in this way: "From the illustration on the cover of that premier issue, it looks like we expected each Jewish woman to be all things to all people—fertile mother, chicken-soup-bearing household goddess, practicing physician, religious scholar, pious worshipper, culture icon. Talk about role diffusion!"[23] Times had indeed changed for American Jewish women in those twenty-five intervening years. In 1976, *Lilith* followed the broader trends of the American feminist movement, seeking equality in religious, political, and social domains once fervently reserved for men only, but without relinquishing the kitchen or responsibilities to children. By the year 2000, however, a second wave of feminism had challenged this focus on "male" goods, and instead sought to recover distinguishing features of female experience.[24] Weidman Schneider is very much aware of this trend: "Now we ask less about getting to be like men and more about how to value women's own experiences and methods."[25] Yet that opening sketch, and "the world of the Jewish woman," represented a different kind of heritage for Weidman Schneider in 2003. In the mid-1970s, American Jews triumphantly recalled the Israeli successes in war, and were proud of the strong, assertive Israelis who fought back their aggressors. These were not the hunched over, book-reading, fragile, and compliant "feminine" Jews of the past; these were Israeli warriors. But by 2003, American Jews carefully approached Israel as a model of that new, powerful Jew. These same Israeli warriors had become, to many in America, oppressors of another people. It is therefore significant that Weidman Schneider fails to mention the rather large Israeli flag waving majestically above the covered head of her "household goddess." This is no longer a heritage she wishes to appropriate. Weidman Schneider *sees* heritage in a new way in 2003. The covers of *Lilith* magazine visualize heritage for its readers, but heritage must still be visually read and interpreted by viewers. In this sense, heritage production is always contemporary, dynamic, and thereby evasive. *Lilith* may explore the world of the Jewish woman, but it is not the same woman that gazes at the covers of *Lilith* magazine.

FIGURE 6.2. *Lilith* 26, no. 2 (Summer 2001). Reprinted with permission from Lilith Publications, Inc. Copyright © 2001. To see more, and to subscribe, visit Lilith.org.

The production of heritage on the covers of *Lilith* succumbs to temporal displacement. Weidman Schneider really admires a different cover in 2003 than the one she published in 1976. The most prominent display of visual temporal unease appears on the cover of the Summer 2001 edition of *Lilith*. Returning to themes explored in the very first cover, this issue discusses "The Balancing Act," not of middle-class women, but of teen girls in contemporary America. And as in that first sketch, here we see a young woman balancing on a rope, but this time between two pencils. This cover recalls Philippe Petit's famous 1974 tightrope walk between the Twin Towers in New York City. Yet this *Lilith* cover evokes a more innocent childhood, together with the new fears and anxieties facing teenagers. Yet only a few months after the publication of this issue, two airplanes collided into those great symbols of American financial success, inaugurating a new fear of terrorism on American soil. In the summer of 2001, one could view a more innocent heritage of fantasy and play. But by the fall of that year, a more terrifying image had replaced that innocent one, and the visual rules had changed. As David Morgan has taught us, some visual meanings were now real possibilities, while others had been closed off entirely. The "social act of looking" is local and temporal, and so too the heritage produced by that gaze.

Subscribers to *Lilith* rarely throw away their volumes.[26] Reviewing older covers under the gaze of newer ones, readers can locate visual features within a broader frame of reference. When I canvassed these volumes during my research, some covers struck me as direct commentaries on previous ones, and when viewed together, they reveal new patterns of heritage maintenance. The cover of the Spring 1988 issue exposes silhouette images of the same woman on four playing cards, each an ace of various suits, with the caption: "What the Cards Hold for Jewish Career Women." Three of the four cards reproduce scenes that recall the sketch in the first volume: a woman lighting candles to inaugurate the Sabbath, a woman playing with her newborn child, and a woman dressed for work carrying a briefcase (this time in a well-trimmed suit without a hat). The fourth card offers something new: a woman holding a weight in her left hand, dressed in a leotard, working out at the gym. Significantly, the working woman card faces the other three, suggesting increased tension between women's professional careers and their more personal endeavors.[27] The chicken soup is gone, and so too the *tallit*

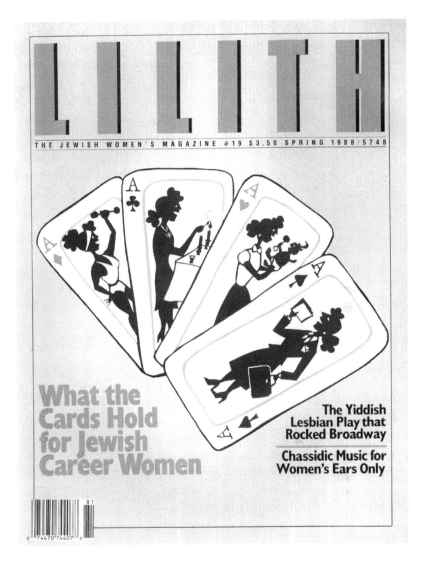

FIGURE 6.3. *Lilith* 19 (Spring 1988). Reprinted with permission from Lilith Publications, Inc. Copyright © 1988. To see more, and to subscribe, visit Lilith.org.

and feminist symbols. Apparently, this modern woman of 1988 neither prepares dinner nor reads Torah. She spends her free time, which now seems more abundant than it did in 1976, at the gym. The Israeli flag, of course, is absent, as are other visible political or social commitments. Yet despite these differences, the title of the accompanying article suggests nothing drastic has changed: "Struggling? Juggling? Trying to Integrate Our Multiple Roles." The article, based upon a four-page questionnaire in 1985 and distributed to "Jewish career women," claims that Jewish women are "different from most non-Jewish career women in combining marriage and childbearing along with their careers."[28] The juggling that Weidman Schneider observed in her 1976 cover remains in force: "role diffusion" appears the order of the day, this time in four different compartments without soup spilling over the dress.[29]

The article notes another finding that bears directly on the card depicting the mother at the gym: "Jewish day schools proved attractive to Jewish career women for their children because of the schools' long hours and the freeing up of Sunday for family time."[30] The private school system offers two primary goods for the Jewish career woman: time with family, and time for herself. These opportunities do not surface in the 1976 cover of the working, religious, and domestic Jewish woman. Staying fit at the gym and family time have now replaced the Israeli flag and *tallit*. So even as these women juggle or compartmentalize their various commitments to home and work, their roles have changed, as both the article and the cover make clear. Educated Jewish women have learned to take care of themselves and their families, but they have abandoned the social networks that once held their allegiance. They now complain about the lack of support from the Jewish community. But without the Israeli flag or religious causes, the dearth of support moves in both directions. Slobin warns of the attenuated ties to the past through heritage, as do Cohen and Eisen in their study of semi-affiliated American Jews,[31] and one can *see* this in the 1988 *Lilith* cover. With the very first cover as a visual guide to this updated version, one recognizes that only the candlesticks remain. This deck, without the religious and social ties, is much thinner than in years past.

That sense of an attenuated heritage surfaces as potent critique within the *Lilith* covers themselves. Often, these covers arrest the viewer's gaze, challenging images of heritage that appear natural and right. The painting that decorates the Summer 1998 cover is one such exposure, revealing the anxieties and opportunities of fertility treatment and adoption for Jewish families. As one such adoptive parent, I was drawn to this issue and its cover—yet another indication that heritage is local, temporal, and profoundly personal. With a quick review of the cover, I perceived a

FIGURE 6.4. *Lilith* 23, no. 2 (Summer 1998). Reprinted with permission from Lilith Publications, Inc. Copyright © 1998. To see more, and to subscribe, visit Lilith.org.

young, Asian girl held close by her mother. With the accompanying text about adoption and fertility as my visual clues, I coded the mother as Jewish and the daughter as a convert to Judaism. I visualized blond hair, in this picture, as American, and perhaps even more telling, as white. This supports Jacobson's reading that heritage production is implicitly a racial practice that visually produces and responds to cultural distinctions.[32] I quickly absorbed the evident meaning: parents and their adoptive children grow to look like one another (I noted the similar eyes and lips), such that Jews can no longer presume a racial heritage of sameness. But then I turned to the list of contents, and read with some amazement this description of the cover: "Detail from 'Mother and Child in Holland Park,' by Dora Holzhandler (b. 1928). Holzhandler, a native of Paris, lives in London."[33] I closed the magazine once again to resituate my gaze. The editors had clearly appropriated an image from outside the context of American Jewry, and by locating it underneath a heading about fertility and adoption, had provided their readers with a "detail" that Holzhandler herself could never have imagined. My initial gaze traveled from byline to painting, visualizing the mother and daughter within the context of "Pursuing Fertility/Considering Adoption." I could not have seen heritage in this way without those linguistic codes. Yet armed with these cues, the painting raises the question noted above it: "What Makes a Jew?"—or, more precisely, who looks like a Jew?

This is the production of a visual heritage, and the critical subversion of it. Adoptive practices by Jewish families reveal the visual potency of Jewish heritage—some kids just don't look Jewish, and some mothers do. But with eyes and complexion and lips that morph into strikingly similar faces, Jews can no longer mark themselves as visually different. Jews often presume heritage when the appropriation of a past is far more complex and dynamic. It once had been the Jewish nose, but now even that fails to distinguish. How do Jews produce heritage without the visual markers of identification?

One place to find those markers is in the American museum. According to Barbara Kirshenblatt-Gimblett, museums have become a critical site for heritage maintenance and production. As museums compete for viewers in the tourist market and for those seeking vivid experiences, they become a destination for discovery of heritage and authenticity.[34]

Erica Jong, Katie Roiphe & Naomi Wolf Talk Shop

the
independent
Jewish
women's
magazine

Israel
After 50:
Half a Century.
But Only Half
the Story?

How
Museums
Invent Us

Right-Wing Women
Struggle to Keep
Orthodoxy Safe
from Feminists

Volume 23, No. 4
Winter 1998-99 $4.50

Chanukah decoration
ca. 1930s
painted wood and
electric lights

FIGURE 6.5. *Lilith* 23, no. 4 (Winter 1998–99). Reprinted with permission from Lilith Publications, Inc. Copyright © 1998. To see more, and to subscribe, visit Lilith.org.

Jewish museums play within this market too, vivifying the past through immediate and personal access to material artifacts. The cover and accompanying article to the Winter edition of *Lilith*, 1998–99, associates women's experiences with material culture. The cover parades a rather glitzy image of the Jewish star of David with Christmas lights woven around the corners, together with the caption: "How Museums Invent Us." From the attached article, we learn that this "Chanukah brainstorm" belonged to Bessie Furman of Minneapolis, who in 1930 hired a carpenter and an electrician to build and sell enough of them "to pay her annual Hadassah pledge."[35] Material culture enables curators to expose Jews as more than a "People of the Book," and "to incorporate the voices of women, children and other once marginalized Jews into the 'big picture'."[36] Museums become a key material site for the production of women's heritage.

The cover story insists that women's experiences fundamentally shape Jewish practice and identity. When museums include women's lives, one sees how those lives inform Jewish character and memory. Material culture displaces textual practices (defined by that abstract, immaterial concept, "People of the Book") as the primary site of heritage production and identification. And women are now recognized as producers of that material heritage:

> "The choice whether you are going to keep kosher on the frontier, or whether, in the 1950s, you are going to let your kids sing Christmas carols in school—these aren't monumental choices. They are decisions made in the living room or kitchen, but when you add up all these choices, they shape who we have become as a people."
>
> Women frequently made those "kitchen decisions," and their choices shaped the nature of Jewish belief, practice and community.

Jewish women maintain a tight connection to objects, and museum exhibits that include Bessie Furman's wooden *Magen David* "teach us that Jewish identity isn't merely a result of rabbinic debate and institutional change, but is also a product of the home, hearth and our mothers' hands."[37] The turn to material culture, and the heritage produced therein, situates women's experiences at the center of Jewish identity. Seeing objects, especially domestic ones, can provide that "thrill of recognition"[38] that links modern Jewish identity to an enlivened past. Jewish material culture is decidedly feminine, so *Lilith* argues, and museums enable us to visually absorb that feminine heritage.

Seeing material objects in the hearth and home reveals a new visual register of recognition. Women's experiences had always been crucial and defining for Jewish identity, and museums now offer exhibitions to recognize visually those persons and objects that shape character. Tourists at museums love stories, but "when an object is reunited with its story, its charisma and persuasiveness are magnified."[39] Visual markers ingrain heritage within the body, and enliven connections to a past. The cover to the Spring 1998 volume of *Lilith* juxtaposes a photograph of two *hamantaschen* (the Jewish cookie traditionally served during the holiday of Purim) and the caption "Sex and Spirituality." The editors of *Lilith* assume their readers already associate food with sex, for otherwise the caption fails as a visual clue. But with the textual marker, the *hamantasch*, surrounded by grapes, nuts and apricots, appears as a female vagina. Susan Schnur's article on the "herstory" of the *hamantaschen* makes this point explicit: these cookies are, as she calls them, "sacred vulva cakes." The *hamantasch* is not a "Haman's pocket," but rather a "cosmic womb as a triangle with dots, or seeds, inside!" The point is that Jews must *see* these cookies within the context of female bodily experiences. If they appear as mere hats, viewers succumb to a "phony" etymology, and lose a material connection to the past. *Lilith* challenges its readers to alter their visual registers, and *find* and *taste* sex and spirituality in food:

> On the full moon of Adar [Purim], the hamantasch, God willing, should not be mistaken for a mere cookie or for Haman's tricorn hat. Hamantaschen are our, and Earth's, bodies, revered as an ultimate metaphor for the divine Creator. They were (and, given the right ritual, could once again be) sacred, representing women's capacity to birth and to nourish, from our own holy bodies.[40]

Eating, touching, and seeing food create heritage. It allows persons to absorb their sacred past and to nourish their bodies with spiritual potency. But for heritage to produce this vibrancy, it must be *seen,* and not only heard or swallowed. The hamantasch as a "mere cookie" or "tricorn hat" does not yield a *vital* heritage. But when the eyes glimpse a "cosmic womb" with seeds, the cookie performs the work of heritage production.

Lusty, Doomed Heroines from Jewish Berlin

Lilith

the
independent
Jewish
women's
magazine

Sex and Spirituality

RECLAIMING PURIM
Here for the first time, the whole Megillah!
12 pages on
* Misogyny in the Book of Esther
* Esther, Vashti and Carol Gilligan
* Rituals for Holy Body Day
* The Womantasch Itself—
from Prehistoric Art to Your Cookie Pan

Volume 23, No. 1
Spring 1998 $4.50

Shlomo Carlebach's Paradoxical Legacy to Women

FIGURE 6.6. *Lilith* 23, no. 1 (Spring 1998). Reprinted with permission from Lilith Publications, Inc. Copyright © 1998. To see more, and to subscribe, visit Lilith.org.

The covers of *Lilith* magazine challenge the visual codes in which Jews recognize, or fail to recognize, themselves as American Jews. These exhibitions of heritage graphically displace the visual clues that have become entrenched within Jewish optical practices, and replace those registers with new modes of viewing. *Lilith* reminds us that we *see* heritage, and to see is also to experience vividly connections to a past that informs identity. But *Lilith* often repositions that past to make room for a new, more expressive history. Note the cover to only its second volume in Winter 1976–77. The photo shows a bare arm disposing a white tee-shirt with the words "Princess" labeled on the front, with a star of David symbol as the dot for the letter *i* (on the inside page, the title for the cover reads, "Discarding the stereotype"). The white hand pinches the tee-shirt as if it were filth, with just two fingers clasping the shirt far away from the torso. If one turns to page forty-two of this volume, next to the *Lilith* subscription cards, we see a woman removing the same tee-shirt, only to reveal a new white one to replace the old. This one reads, "Lilith Liveth." In a later edition, *Lilith* took on the Jewish American Princess stereotype, and profoundly increased awareness of its violent and debilitating impact on American culture.[41] But this second cover focuses instead on "discarding the stereotype" and returning the female character Lilith to center stage. The expulsion of the Princess is a visual displacement, such that readers see a hand discarding one shirt on the cover, and within the magazine discover a woman replacing the Princess with Lilith.

Kirshenblatt-Gimblett writes of heritage as "the transvaluation of the obsolete, the mistaken, the outmoded, the dead, and the defunct."[42] *Lilith* magazine performs this kind of heritage production on the covers of its magazines, visually displaying what is outmoded and obsolete, and replacing it with new visual clues for encoding identity. Lilith has always lurked under the shirt of the Jewish princess—we just did not see her there until the magazine *Lilith* revealed her to us. Jewish heritage is a form of visual exposure.

THE NOSTALGIC GAZE: THE APERTURE COLLECTION OF ARNOLD EAGLE PHOTOGRAPHS

Lilith exposed the undercover Lilith in a black-and-white photograph, and so appealed to the authenticity viewers often associate with the

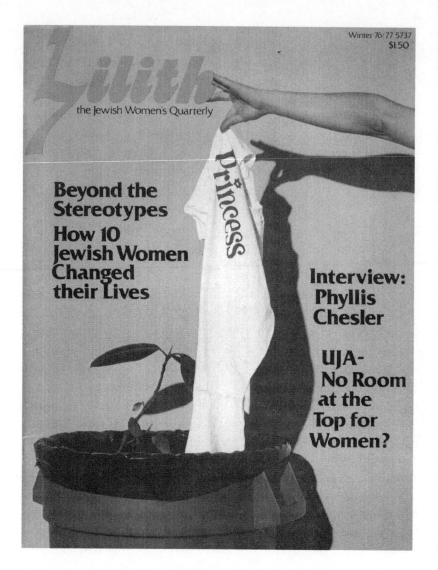

FIGURE 6.7. *Lilith* 2 (Winter 1976–77). Reprinted with permission from Lilith Publications, Inc. Copyright © 1976. To see more, and to subscribe, visit Lilith.org.

photographic image. Photography, it is often claimed, captures a real experience, and provides evidence for truth. The female adult really does exchange the Princess for Lilith—we can see her do it. The very technology suggests an autonomous, universal, and pure vision. The camera as independent machine produces facts, so it seems, "passively, transparently, with an almost pure impersonality." In short, the photo offers persuasive documentary evidence to provoke a felt experience in the viewer.[43] When social documentaries bolster progressive politics, photography (despite or even because of its transparency) appeals to the viewer's emotions in order to mold and change attitudes "toward certain public facts."[44] For *Lilith* magazine, one of those public facts is the spiritual enslavement of a strong, capable woman who demands expressive fulfillment. She throws off the false consciousness of the American princess, and reestablishes her authority as authentic Jewess. The photographic medium imparts truth to power: Lilith really does lie in waiting, and photography documents the oppression.

This kind of "decent seeing," a visual practice that evokes passionate responses to visual clues,[45] transforms photography into a powerful medium for heritage production. For as we have already witnessed, heritage constructs the past as a usable one for the present, and does so through an imaginary both nostalgic and transformative. By lending an aura of pure, unsoiled experience (photography "offers an immediate presence to the world"),[46] the photograph empowers a kind of voyeuristic escape into another world, but one drawn close by its expressive allure. Susan Sontag writes of photography as "an elegiac art" in which most subjects are, "just by virtue of being photographed, touched with pathos." Indeed, photography "has become one of the principal devices for experiencing something, for giving an appearance of participation." That art of appearance goes right to the core of the photographic mystique.[47] Experiential viewing through the camera (what Roland Barthes calls an adventure that animates the viewer)[48] can too easily "transform history into spectacle,"[49] and as Warren Sussman warns, refashion history as nostalgic memory:

> Memory is often the historian's most potent ally. But hovering as it does in that strange psychological zone between nostalgia and regret, it can often strike out on its own, producing not so much the ordered vision of the past the historian aims to develop as a picture of the The Past (even a lurid Past) in the Victorian sense.[50]

Photographs create the past as heritage, as a site of nostalgia and regret, as a eulogy to a lost world that beckons a reawakening from the contemporary viewer. This is heritage as discourse: it produces that which it purports to describe.

One such exhibit of nostalgic heritage production is the Aperture publication of Arnold Eagle's 1935 photographs of Orthodox Jews in New York City.[51] The book honored Eagle's work in the year of his death. But in 1935, Eagle had just arrived on the shores of America from Budapest, and his first photographic assignment offered something entirely foreign to this secular Jew: a religious world that, he knew even then, would "disappear in one generation." He would later become a member of the New York Film and Photo League (a precursor to the more famous left wing version—The New York Photo League),[52] becoming known more for his work in film.[53] But in this very early assignment, Eagle's photography developed from the voyeuristic impulse, seduced and fascinated by a community that, in many ways, had never made the voyage from European shtetl to urban America. The old men and women summoned in these images remain entirely Old World, apparitions within an America that belongs now to their rebellious children. In an interview only two years before his death in 1992, Eagle described his work in this way:

> My first project had nothing to do with social conditions, but I was photographing the religious Jews in New York. I spent about five or six months photographing people down on the East Side, the synagogues, the shtetl. This was 1935 and you saw very few young people following the traditions—so it was very fascinating. This group was, for me, a very important culture group, which I felt was going to disappear in one generation.[54]

Though Eagle reveals little empathy for his subjects—these are not his people, but "religious Jews" who are "a very important culture group"— the introductory text and captions that accompany his photographs certainly do, and transform his images into works of heritage production. The interplay between text and image creates powerful visual clues for locating material identity within a visual heritage. Arthur Hertzberg's introduction to Eagle's photographs functions as "an extended caption"[55] that frames the photographs as "a form of resurrection."[56] By recovering the lost past, Eagle's photos no longer document "a very important culture group." Instead, they recall an ethnic and religious heritage that requires something from the viewer, that calls the viewer to its presence and import. It is what historian Matthew Jacobson would call a "roots trip": armed with evocative captions and an introductory essay, the viewer travels beyond in order to recover origins closer to home.[57] Photographic heritage turns the nostalgic past into a source of material identity.

Hertzberg's introductory essay echoes the tenor of his own auto-biographical work, *A Jew in America*.[58] Just as Hertzberg recalled the lost heritage of immigrant parents, so too does he frame Eagle's portraits in a nostalgic return to "warm memories of their youngest years in Europe."[59] In this, Eagle's work transposes Lower East Side memories, so well documented in Hasia Diner's work,[60] to the world of the East European shtetl. This is precisely how Hertzberg visualizes Eagle's photography, for these Jews "kept the garb and the manner of the East European *shtetl;* they were 'at home only with God'."[61] The title of this collected work—*At Home Only With God*—harkens back to another world, a spiritual center in which Jews converse with God alone. America offers no such hope or comfort. Eagle's work performed a nostalgic return, as historians Steven Zipperstein and Richard Cohen have observed, that "reencountered and recreated themes" imagined as rooted in traditional Jewish society.[62] The shtetl, then, is home in a double sense: a place of religious sustenance and nostalgic memory, as well as the only place in which a Jew can live alone with God. The majority of photos in this collection (with the one exception of that most celebrated festival, the Passover seder) imagines the (male) Jew praying to his God alone, either in synagogue or by means of textual study. These Jews do not recall a shtetl bustling with communal life, but instead imagine a world devoted *only* to God. Despite the many images of male Jews praying together, these Jews are nonetheless alone. Their devotion is a singular, individual pursuit. When Hertzberg ties the "garb and manner" of shtetl life to the title of these collected photographs, he imagines the foreign Jew in America who nonetheless appropriates a distinctly modern, if not American tradition of solitary religious worship.

(A note to my readers: I was unable to obtain copyright permissions to publish the Eagle photographs that I discuss in this chapter. It surely would have been more effective to include these images alongside my analysis. But I hope readers can turn this pictorial absence into an imaginative gain, for our imaginations generate the very nostalgic heritage that Eagle's photographs seek to impose. Viewers produce *together with the photograph* an imagined heritage. They are vital accomplices to this heritage production: they create through erasures and supplant through creative memory.)

This framing of Eagle's work, in which the photographs and captions depict existentially lost Jews in a foreign land, encode the images within a narrative of solitary devotion. Many of the Jews in this book are old and beaten down from their despair in America. This too helps explain the subtitle to the work: "Believing Jews and their Children." The observant ones, the believers, must endure as their children wander in the American wasteland. The caption to one photograph reads "Remembering the *shtetl*"—a necessary reminder, for the image lacks any visual suggestion of the shtetl, or the memory of it. But with this caption as visual marker, the bearded man's glazed but hardened, intense look in this photograph now comes into focus. The caption enables the viewer to imagine, through his eyes, the *shtetl* beyond an American landscape. His wife, sitting placidly next to him, remains slightly out of focus—the background to his more sharpened view. Both, however, dress and comport to "the garb and manner" of Hertzberg's *shtetl* imaginary: simple, poor, earnest, alone.

This image of the *shtetl* Jew in America appears throughout the collection: on the cover with three Jews alone in a dark synagogue with Torah and shofar, or in the stark image of an elderly male Jew, alone, removing one of the Torah scrolls from the synagogue ark—his eyes cast down, dreary, lost in a world "only with God." In both images, worship is the serious business of gray-bearded male Jews. If no longer confined to the shtetl back home, these Jews can at least find solace, and perhaps their God, in the confines of the American synagogue. Their God dwells in the text, and they travel back home through this material medium. To believe is to study the word, but it is also to caress, honor, and keep it. The caption to one photograph underscores this material act: "Embracing God's Word." The embrace is less a passionate response than a desperate retreat in a foreign land. What else is there when one is at home *only* with God? These photographs display so little community, family, and joy. Only the text remains, and therein God dwells. Embracing the text materially signifies a return home to the East European shtetl as a religious, solitary, and male space.

The text bequeaths a lost heritage, but photography offers the possibility of return. Hertzberg believes that Eagle "sensed that their way of life was disappearing, and he committed himself to preserving images of their world on the East Side."[63] Eagle confirms this reading in his interview with the *American Society of Media Photographers* in 1990. The interviewers, Kay Reese and Mimi Leipzig, prompt Eagle to reflect upon his own personal history in response to his photography. No, he did not come from the shtetl, Eagle admits, "I came from Budapest and I wasn't exposed to this, so this was for me a new thing. Budapest is very much like New York. But then I came here and met these people and I was very taken by that thing, especially leaving Hungary with a not very friendly feeling."[64] These East Side Jews confront Eagle as the exotic other who still transport him back home. He has never seen folks like this, but they enable him to recognize New York City as an American Budapest, as a more cosmopolitan and liberated city without the "anti-Semitic official policy of a government." But what is "that thing" that grabs hold of Eagle? Sontag claims that "people robbed of their past seem to make the most fervent picture takers, at home and abroad." Experiencing life through the camera lens transforms "one person into something active, a voyeur."[65] Exiled from home, Eagle revivifies an imagined past in and through the photographic image, and actively recovers his heritage through another's "thing"—the singular devotion to a textual God. Their study becomes his adopted heritage, however new, exotic, and foreign. This is a past with roots, with substance, with Heschel's kind of "thinginess." Exposure to this "new thing" draws Budapest closer to New York. Heritage produces the imaginary past out of the present. Eagle, to be sure, did not come from the shtetl. But then, neither did these East Side Jews.

The collection of texts and photographs create an image of the shtetl that lives in a visual and reading practice, rather than a historical reality. But photography appeals to that reality, capturing material life through its mechanical lens. Though the technology "makes it possible to see, know, and feel the details of life and its styles in different places and to feel oneself part of other's [sic] experience," images never arrive clean. There remains Sontag's photographic voyeur, who like Eagle, participates in the exposed image. But there also lives Sontag's "moralist" who "always hopes that words will save the picture."[66] In *At Home Only with God,* words accompany images in order to transform them into heritage. Viewers cannot do so on their own; they must be moved, directed, informed, and shaped into a visual practice that sees heritage as a form of material embrace. To remember the shtetl, or to embrace God's word, draws the viewer into this material place, and repositions Eagle's voyeuristic practice to become the viewer's own. The viewer is now an accomplice in this form of heritage production. She embraces the shtetl as her own heritage. America not only "robbed them of the world of their youth"; it robbed the viewer's heritage as well. But linguistic captions arrive to situate heritage within the photographs. Words that save pictures can also save souls.

Hertzberg speaks to this sense of personal recovery when he describes Eagle as an "admirer" of these Orthodox Jews, impressed as he is "by the dignity . . . he encountered in New York." In his interview, Eagle recalled his fascination rather than adoration, but the documentary impulse comes through all the same. He wanted to move his viewers, expose the tragic sensibility, and as Hertzberg laments, to impart "the somber knowledge that their children would not be like them."[67] As the "believing Jews" of the collection's subtitle, the Orthodox parents nostalgically look back to the shtetl rather than dream of their children's future. They glance down, away, but never directly at the camera. They tenaciously hold onto a past, embracing and honoring it; but it is still a past imagined from the present.

Eagle photographs young girls tolerating religious observance, but they do not observe. In one striking picture of the family Passover seder, the father, mother, and older brother look adoringly at the young son as he reads, one could surmise, the four questions that elicit the retelling of the exodus. The table lies neatly decorated and clean, the children dressed beyond their years, and the ritual food for the holiday is neatly apportioned. This is an ordered, well-groomed seder. Though the boy reads carefully from the Passover Haggadah, the daughter's head hangs listlessly over her arms as she rests. She misses everything—the storytelling, the adoration, the performance—that marks this seder as a form of remembrance. These are neither her memories nor her heritage. The past invoked here is a male narrative. Boys act as girls follow along—or, in this case, simply endure. *Lilith* taught us that heritage comes in a gendered package. When Eagle arrived in New York City only to rediscover his lost Budapest, he appropriated a masculine heritage of study and order.

This male sensibility of textual dedication and structured observance continues throughout the collection. We see it in the study of texts, where men direct their focus to words, but not to each other. These men, even in the company of others, do not converse but read: they engage others through a material text. The hands that lie on a page of Talmud do not tense expectantly to turn the page; instead, they hold the page steady, heavy, with a caress that remains eternal. Time stands still in these photographs—this heritage is everlasting.

Not so, however, for the women in this collection. Like the daughter who listlessly awaits the end of the family seder, the mothers and grandmothers await their end with a withdrawn acceptance. They are resigned to their fate, rather than active makers of it. If men live in texts and ritual observance, then these Orthodox women barely survive at all. There are no memories to resurrect, a shtetl to recall, nor children to adore. This is not their life nor their heritage. They still count as "believing Jews" in this collection, but we see merely older women awaiting death. Without texts to contemplate and rituals to honor, these women look down into the abyss, and find no heritage there.

Only one of the many photographs in this collection stands by itself without caption as interpretive clue. It is the very last photograph of the Torah scroll, with the pointing *yad* directed at the very heart of the text. The viewer takes up the position of reader and responds to the call of the pointer: to read, to be at home and alone with God in and through the material text. If the previous captions have done their work as heritage production, this photograph requires little interpretive gloss: summoned to the call of the "believing Jews," the viewer appropriates a heritage in waiting. Viewers thus face a stark choice: either to appropriate or to abandon a nostalgic heritage that claims allegiance to a distant land. As Hertzberg astutely recognizes, this is a heritage more profound than the New York East Side, or even the shtetl in Eastern Europe:

> Most American Jews remember the history of their families as beginning on the East Side, but the East Side can no longer be the new beginning of American Jewish experience. Some are now looking at the faces of the these immigrants to find links to an earlier past. . . . This book is one gateway to all the centuries of the life in Europe to which

the immigrants still belonged. The pictures in this book are a form of resurrection.[68]

Heritage recovers a "new beginning" after the Holocaust, one rooted in a past that serves the needs of the present. That foundational beginning is grounded in texts: the Torah as venerated object and the collection of Eagle's photographs as "gateway" to sacred origins. The Aperture publication tethers images to texts in order to recover a visual heritage. If some look "at the faces of these immigrants," they do so by gazing at them: it is a visual practice encoded with textual markers. The links to "an earlier past" lie within the text as expectant reading. The pointer asks the viewer to take hold, read, and experience. Without captions to guide, the text speaks on its own—a form of resurrection indeed.

YOU AIN'T HEARD NOTHIN' YET:
HERITAGE IN THE JAZZ SINGER FILMS

What, exactly, has been resurrected in these Eagle photographs? Certainly not the playful, sexual, passionate Jew that Philip Roth recovers in his novels. Instead, the Eagle collection recalls the Jew whom Roth associates with Malamud and Bellow: the religious, ethical, dedicated, honorable, lonely Jew. This is a "roots trip," to be sure, but one moored to only one narrative of Jewish ethnicity. Though in the wake of renewed comfort among American minorities to publicly flaunt their ethnicity, this heritage production resurrects as much as it obscures. But that, precisely, is what heritage as discourse performs: it creates through erasures, supplants through creative memory. Photography taps into the power of heritage because it tethers experiential responses to perceived real events and images. Heritage looks, and thereby must be, exactly so.

But this is not the case for all visual mediums. Film stages a reality, and the audience knows this. It allows the viewer to leap into an imagined mode, a kind of voyeuristic escape that promises a safe return.[69] Yet film is no less indebted to heritage flights, and this especially so for urban Jews in the 1920s and 1930s. With Nickelodeans suffusing the Lower East Side in New York City, and Jewish moguls creating Hollywood productions, Jews took to the movies that held the promise of a welcoming, homogenous American landscape.[70] Films such as *Abie's Irish Rose* (1928) and *The Cohens and the Kellys* (1926) beckoned new immigrants to become Americans through romantic intermarriage, although so few of them actually did. The American melting pot would assimilate all those willing to forgo a heritage rooted in the old country:[71]

> According to these films, the easiest way to become Americanized is to marry a Catholic girl, enter into a partnership with an Irishman, or adopt a Gentile baby. These Jewish/Irish romance films reign as the assimilationist films par excellence, castigating old world ways, supporting those who turn from the traditional to the modern, and apotheosizing those who consign custom to the history books in their headlong dash to become true Americans.[72]

Heritage, it would seem, could easily become a dead past in this American race for acceptance. As Bernays, Liebman, and Fromm had counseled, the future looked bright without a darkening past to cloud it. Silent films literally muted heritage claims, and Hollywood Jewish immigrants like Carl Laemmle, William Fox, Louis Mayer, and Benjamin Warner created, in Gabler's suggestive phrase, "an empire of their own" in which "fathers were strong, families stable, people attractive, resilient, resourceful, and decent."[73] It was an America "of small towns and picket fences, of milk bottles on doorsteps, of crowing roosters and friendly neighbors."[74] When Jewish kids of immigrant parents went to the movies, they rebelled against a weighty heritage in favor of the creative lightness of new beginnings.

These cultural, religious, and generational conflicts are the stuff of silent films, as they are in the classic bridge film from silence to sound, *The Jazz Singer* (1927). Lester Friedman describes this film as "a forceful summation of the assimilationist tendencies present throughout the Silent Era,"[75] a view that holds general consensus among film critics:

> What remains most interesting about *The Jazz Singer* is the support it engenders for assimilation. Jack leaves home, changes his name, enters show business, and plans to marry a *Shiksa*. He becomes more than an acculturated Jew; he becomes completely assimilated. Although tales of generational conflict, family separations, and mixed marriages go back to the Primitive Period, few films go as far as *The Jazz Singer*.[76]

The force of this reading mirrored everyday life: Al Jolson, who married his share of gentile women, and as some claim, performed his American identity through blackface routines,[77] transformed the role of Jakie

Rabinowitz, on and off the screen, into an American Jazz performer. As Sampson Raphaelson—whose play, *The Day of Atonement* (1922), inspired *The Jazz Singer*—tells it, Jakie requires neither a wife nor a God, but "a song-number with a kick in it. The junk that Tin Pan Alley is peddling these days is rusty."[78]

But there is a good deal of heritage production in the original *Jazz Singer*, as there is in Raphaelson's play, and so too in the *Jazz Singer* remakes: the often neglected Danny Thomas version in 1953, and Neil Diamond's update in 1980. All three films offer competing visions of heritage and its impact on material Jewish identity. In discussing these three versions of Raphaelson's play, I want to locate the place of Jewish heritage within each film production. Notions of assimilation simply obscure the complex entanglements and ambiguities of the past (Jolson's 1927 film), or the utter insignificance of Jewish tradition (Thomas's 1953 rendition), and even mistake intermarriage for the immigrant narrative of the American dream (Diamond's 1980 vision). These jazz singers produce complex webs of visual heritage as modes of escape, yearning, and material identity.

The founding vision and script for all three *Jazz Singer* movies was Sampson Raphaelson's play, *The Day of Atonement*, which he wrote after watching Al Jolson perform in blackface in 1917. Though bitterly disappointed by the film version some ten years later, Raphaelson conjured the energy and charisma that Jolson projected to his adoring audiences:

> This grotesque figure in blackface, kneeling at the end of a runway which projected him into the heart of his audience, flinging out his white-gloved hands, was embracing that audience with a prayer—an evangelical moan—a tortured, imperious call that hurtled through the house like a swift electrical lariat with a twist that swept the audience right to the edge of that runway. The words didn't matter, the melody didn't matter. It was the emotion—the emotion of a cantor.[79]

Raphaelson recounts the profound ambivalence of blackface production—its grotesque beauty, the tortured moan of a performer with outstretched, white-gloved hands—that Eric Lott reveals so bracingly of blackface minstrelsy in his aptly titled work, *Love & Theft*.[80] For Raphaelson, only "the emotion of a cantor" embraces an audience with a prayer, and so his character Jakie in *Day of Atonement*, though a jazz singer, is still firmly rooted in Jewish heritage. Raised to be a cantor like his father,

Jakie moved to different rhythms and tones, even if the new jazz was but an American variant of the cantor's cry: "instead of being sinful and self-indulgent, loose and lazy, this grave-eyed boy with the ways of the street was sincerely carrying on the tradition of plaintive, religious melody of his forefathers." The stage name Jack Robin was only Jakie Rabinowitz in blackface, American style. For Raphaelson, "Jakie was simply translating the age-old music of the cantors . . . into primitive and passionate Americanese."[81] Jack falls in love with the exotic, "fairylike" Amy Prentiss, yet only befriends the earthy, perceptive, raw, and altogether Jewish Sadie Rudnick. As she tells Jack with some contempt: "She's a *Shiksa;* that's why! I've seen Jewish boys fall that way before. It ain't new to me. . . . You're the son of a poor old *Chazon,* and she's the daughter of a Boston lawyer. You're—Aw, you make me sick!"[82] Raphaelson carefully distances the "numbness" of American middle-class culture (Amy) from the real, emotional passion of ghetto life (Sadie). As Jack turns to drink, he recognizes the "chaotic, crassly unreal" life of the stage performer he has become, and yearns for the passion-infused "reality, an orderly nobility" that emanates from his father's world.[83]

Raphaelson's play is profoundly tragic: Jack's emotional roots lie in a world lost to him, for he cannot harness that energy in a culture so numb to emotional warmth. It echoes themes in Anzia Yezierska's fiction that pitted the emotional, female immigrant against the rational American male. Here, too, America yearns for immigrant passion, the emotion of a cantor turned jazz singer, to enliven its stiffness. And Jack is willing to trade in his passion for whiteness. Together he and Amy—the emotional immigrant and the prosaic *shiksa*—perform a dance of endless desire and frustration:

> Amy studied his face. She said,
> "You dance differently from any one I know."
> Jack flushed.
> "I don't suppose I dance very well. I—I wish I could dance standing straight and moving sort of—well, evenly and correctly, if you know what I mean. Like that fellow, for instance." He indicated a tall, stolid-looking youth who was soberly and skilfully [*sic*] maneuvering a sleek young creature about the polished floor.
> "That's funny," Amy remarked. "I'm crazy about the way you dance. I never quite like any one's dancing so well. You danced to-night the way you used to sing—the way you sang when I first heard you in New York."

"You *like* my dancing?" Jack leaned to her, unbelieving. His voice came huskily. "*You* don't dance that way—even on the stage. You dance more like that fellow. I don't mean stiff as him—not that. But you're his kind, if you know what I mean. I'm—I'm crazy about that quality in you. I'd give anything if I could have it—that careless, happy—Guess I'm talking like a fool," he ended lamely.[84]

Jack longs to be "white"—skillful, polished, carefree, stiff, and sober—in a world that admires, attracts, but finally rejects his "blackness."[85] Both Jews and blacks were associated with the emotions and with having the primal, animalistic urges that sweep Amy into a crazed admiration. Indeed, the character Jack dances much like Jolson performs: as a grotesque figure who kneels, flings, and twists in blackface with a tortured call and emotional depth. This is Lott's love and theft, "the dialectical flickering of racial insult and racial envy."[86] Jack knows he will never dance like Amy; but even more, he recognizes he will never be *allowed* to dance like her. He's talking like a fool. Riv-Ellen Prell vividly describes this ambivalence as a tale of fear and desire, for "America beckoned and pushed away" those imagined foreigners who were so close to home.[87] I read Raphaelson's play much like Jeffrey Melnick does, as a commentary on blackface: it evokes the conflicting registers of attraction and revulsion that surface in constructions of the other. To Melnick, Raphaelson's play explores Jewish theft of black cultural material.[88] Blackface is grotesque tragedy because it projects a world of desires that only tortures selves of all colors.

Jack understands this twisted fate, and also recognizes the claims of heritage. There is no generational struggle here, but final acceptance of a cold America and its "fancy dancing in a private school."[89] So when the Day of Atonement finally arrives, and Jack must decide whether to chant the Kol Nidre prayer in synagogue for his recently deceased father, or to perform on Broadway for an opportunity to enter mainstream America, the choice lacks all tension and conflict:

"My father's *Talis,* it is at the synagogue?"

"Yes; everything is in the *Shool,* Mr. Rabinowitz," the *Shamas* replied eagerly.

"The tunes—the *Genigen*—of the choir—are they the same my father used ten, fifteen years ago?"

"The same *Genigen,* exactly."

"All right. I'll be there at six o'clock."[90]

Jack still chants like a jazz singer, with "his dark eyes afire" and a "fluttering uncertainty, a bewildering pleading," but it comes forth as a "flood of confession." The jazz singer is at home, not only or even alone with God, but within the heritage that produced and nurtured him. The tunes are the same, with all their "majesty" and "rivulets of humility."[91] In Raphaelson's *Day of Atonement*, Jack rediscovers heritage as lost inspiration. He does not accept it, but yields only to its inescapable force. That force weighs heavily on Jack as both a source of emotional power and a marker of difference in America. Much like blackface itself, Jack's heritage repels and attracts in ways that expose disgust, reverence, roots, and longings for acceptance.

This ambivalent heritage plays its way into the 1927 film version of *The Jazz Singer*. Here, however, the tension remains in force: Jack really can make it on Broadway, and so his decision is a fateful one: he decides to return home and replace his father—who hears Jack chant the Kol Nidre prayer before his death—rather than open the Broadway production. A good many film critics argue that the movie undermines this suspense, for it adds a final scene with Jolson, in blackface, singing his "Mammy" song as his mother and Mary Dale (the movie *shiksa*) smile approvingly in the Broadway audience.[92] With this additional scene, Jack Robin appears to have it all: he appeases the claims of heritage—represented by his father—even as he finally rejects it in blackface. Read as a story of assimilation, the tension between tradition and modernity dissolves into a feel-good story of an immigrant American hero. Hollywood Jewish moguls had simply created images of America that justified their own full participation and acceptance within it.[93] Jews were legitimate newcomers, and they could balance the weight of immigrant expectations with middle-class demands of propriety. *The Jazz Singer*, in this sense, stands in for all Jews yearning for an American life, cleansed of Old-World ghosts and ghetto tenements.[94]

That balance, however, as Joel Rosenberg judiciously points out, was precarious indeed.[95] When Jack returns home to New York, finally on the brink of success, he finds only his mother there. He sits her down next to the piano, sings Irving Berlin's "Blue Skies," and then, in perhaps the most memorable scene (even Raphaelson recalls it with admiration),[96] launches into a monologue of sweet talk before he plays his more "jazzy" version. He promises his mother, Sara, a new dress (a black silk one, and a pink outfit to fit his mother's brown eyes), and a cleaner, brighter uptown apartment with green grass where (not to worry) other Jews live too. Jack draws his mother into his middle-class aspirations, and she, in turn, is swept along with Jack's revelry and vision of American life. Sara, so it seems, also wants to abandon an oppressive heritage. Only when the father enters, and the movie returns once again to silence, do viewers recall the gulf between generations. Jack's world is not theirs, and he must abandon his familial ties to become the Jack Robin of Broadway stardom.

Certainly the tension between Old-World commitments and New-World ambitions yields little suspense—we all know where Jack is going. But if Jack travels an inevitable journey, heritage claims still disturb and oppress him. He will make it, to be sure, but at a cost. The emotional price is high, and it continually reasserts its presence as tragic loss. Sara, together with the *kibbitzer* Yudelson, arrive at the Broadway rehearsals to inform Jakie of his father's ill-health, pleading for his return home to chant Kol Nidre in his father's absence. When they enter Jack's dressing room, neither recognizes him in blackface. They both stare directly at him, even past him. When Jakie calls out to his mother, Sara draws near, gazes at her son directly, and remarks, in a rhetorical mode that bites, "Jakie—this ain't you?" The original script has Yudelson remark: "It talks like Jakie, but it looks like a nigger," though in the final movie release, the line becomes, "He talks like Jakie, but he looks like his shadow."[97] Eric Lott notes how the audience of minstrel shows often confused blackface performers for black persons.[98] Here too, Jack's mother and close family friend mistake him for someone else. If Jack must perform in blackface to become American, then his change in name, from Jakie to Jack, masks a deeper transfiguring of self. As Matthew Jacobson astutely notes, "the burnt cork serves not only to change the race of the Jew, but also to eradicate race from *Judaism*."[99] The category of race belongs only to the black other. Yudelson, in the original screenplay, fails to recognize Jack as a human being. Jack Robin is only a dehumanized thing, an "it" that talks and looks, but is not a personal subject with character (a "nigger"). This, too, is a commentary on blackface, even as it exposes a toxic and violent form of racism. In both screenplay and film renditions, Jack Robin has become something monstrous—a living shadow of a former self.

And Jack is aware of this too. After he sings his "Mother of Mine, I Still Have You," Jack returns to the dressing room and removes his hairpiece. He looks wistfully ahead, ruptured and divided by the claims of heritage and his Broadway career. Indeed, without the hairpiece, Jolson appears torn between the American Jack and the Jewish Jakie. It is, to my mind, the most arresting shot in the film, for it reveals the doubleness of blackface, of seeing and being seen: the grotesque beauty of Jolson's tortured moan for acceptance. Here, Jack's blackface is full exposure: we see in and behind the blackface the full torment of a soul, fractured in the movements toward American respectability. The weight of heritage—black culture, Jewish tradition, familial ties—drags Jack into a despairing anomy. We see Jack in blackface, but no longer know who he is. And if I have understood the point of this sequence, then neither does he.

This loss of self in the struggle to become American reveals a deeper ambivalence about heritage claims. When Mary Dale, Jack's non-Jewish lover, and Harry Lee, the director of the Broadway show, hear his sorrowful chant of Kol Nidre, Mary responds: "A jazz singer—singing to his God." But in the screenplay it is Harry Lee, rather than Mary Dale, who makes this claim: "You are listening to the stage's greatest blackface comedian singing to his God." Lee thinks Jack has abandoned Broadway stardom in order to return home, and so in the original screenplay (though not the film), Lee "shrugs his shoulders in a gesture of resignation." But Mary is more hopeful: "Listen. Don't you understand? It's his last time in there. He *has* to come back to us."[100] The italicized "has" evokes a plea, a mirrored tormented moan signifying that Jack really belongs elsewhere, with "us." He is, after all, a blackface comedian and not a cantor. The film version excises this dialogue, but still evokes the ambivalent claims of heritage. Jack *has* to come back because he must return, not to middle-class respectability, but to the roots of his artistry. He is, always, a jazz singer singing to his God. In this sense, Jack belongs but cannot remain in the synagogue. Heritage is, to be sure, the source of his emotional power and greatness. Not just now and here, in the synagogue on the eve of Yom Kippur, but always and everywhere he is the jazz singer with a "cry in his voice," as Yudelson remarks, "just like his Papa." Jewish heritage as inspirational source, however distant and oppressive, is inescapable. Jack Robin cannot but be Jakie Rabinowitz singing to his God, even in blackface.

This ambiguous but ever trenchant bond to heritage is utterly lacking in the 1953 version of *The Jazz Singer*. The plot remains the same: young Jakie Rabinowitz—now the young war hero Jerry Golding—seeks a life beyond his father's expectations. Only a Rabinowitz has been cantor at this liberal, modern Philadelphia synagogue. But Jerry yearns for a broader audience in which not the reward of inheritance, but talent alone determines his future. As he struggles for earned success, he falls in love with the beautiful Judy Lane (who plays a more sophisticated, sprite, and elegant Amy Prentiss) and the plot thickens: will Jerry pursue a difficult career in show business and marry the enticing Judy, or succumb to fatherly demands and live the luxurious but staid life of a Reform cantor? His father's life is stiff but firmly middle class. This is not the tenement hovel of Jakie's parents, but the elegant, sophisticated home of a respected member of Philadelphia high society. Even Jerry's mother lacks the stigma and signs of Old-World Jewry. She is graceful, thin, charming, witty, and runs the household, together with husband and son, with a soft but steady touch. She clearly excels in bending strong wills to her lighter caress—she suggests rather than demands, supports but does not harass. She is not the overbearing Jewish mother so prominent in stereotypical images of the 1950s and 1960s. Instead, she acts as the suburban, "white" version of Molly Goldberg. In her wildly successful radio show, *The Goldbergs*, Molly dishes out homespun advice for all, though Jewish inflections texture her wise counsel. As Molly moved from radio to television, those Jewish flavors diminished, and she became much like Jerry's mother in *The Jazz Singer*: worldly, middle class, light in controversy, strong in reconciliation.[101] The mother figure in the 1953 remake sets the tone for the entire film: Jewish heritage is simply irrelevant to American Jewish identity. Heritage claims have become familial ones, and Jewish ethnicity has lost any markings of distinction.[102]

This lightness of Jewish tradition defines the father–son relationship as well. Jerry's father commands respect from his congregation, but he fears social embarrassment. Without Jerry's knowledge, his father publicly announces that Jerry will soon become the new cantor upon his retirement. Later, when Jerry renounces this heritage, his father worries about the communal reaction and the family shame. Family traditions are certainly at center: all male Goldings do this, if only because the previous generation followed along as well. Jerry owes this inheritance to his father, but not to Jews. In the final reconciling scene between father and son, Jerry's father seeks forgiveness from his son (the inversion of the 1927 film), for he now understands a son's claim to independence. Jerry must find his way, sing to his God, in the style most fitting to his American destiny. The weight of tradition vanishes, and in its place stands familial responsibilities that easily give way to social ambitions. Jerry owes less to heritage than to his father, less to Jews than to America. If the father has replaced tradition and God as the source of obligation, then he is too weak to command fidelity. The mother has taken his place—a transfer of power that a good many Jews already feared in both home and synagogue.[103] Heritage claims, once associated with the father, had morphed into a mother-knows-best form of subtle advice. This imagined feminization of Jewish culture,[104] as Prell describes so well, brings about the end of a muscular, male Jewish heritage.[105]

In the 1953 film, the loss of a viral masculinity reflects the loss of Jewish heritage itself. American Jews are now just another ethnic group in the American melting pot. They are neither different, singular, nor unusual: this is the America of Will Herberg's *Protestant, Catholic, Jew.* Note the opening scene in the film, when Jerry returns to his parents' synagogue after his tour of duty in Korea. As he steps out of the taxi, the cab driver turns to Jerry and says, in a somewhat inflected Irish accent, but in his best Yiddish, "*gut yontif.*" Jerry, unfazed by this remark, wishes the driver a Happy New Year too (it is the eve of Rosh Hashanah), to which the cabbie responds: "That's twice I'll be celebrating it this year." My question: is the cab driver Jewish? My answer: it does not matter. Ethnic Jewishness has so easily slipped into the American mainstream that heritage no longer commands attention. It seems utterly beside the point whether a gentile speaks Jewish, or a Jew drives his taxi while celebrating the new year. If Jews could enjoy two festivals, then so could gentiles. Cultural fluidity replaces ethnic insularity.

Jerry's Uncle Louie, the comic replacement to the old Jew Yudelson, depicts this effortless movement of cultural integration. He moves from business to business, following one scam upon the other, even attempting to finance one of Jerry's stage productions. But his biggest role is as matchmaker for Jerry and Judy Lane. He works, behind the scenes, to bring these two young lovers together. Judy is the elegant *shiksa* of the movie: the blonde beauty who entices Jerry from home. But the film also suggests a rather different heritage. On their way home to celebrate the Jewish Passover, Judy remarks to Jerry's mother: "I haven't been to a *seder* since I left home." Judy does not state these lines before the camera, for the lens has already turned to Jerry and his father strolling behind. It is the only line that reveals her Jewish lineage.[106] If, indeed, Judy is Jewish (and I am rather unsure of this), her Jewishness lacks all content. She, like the cab driver, can deftly move in and out of cultures and traditions. Jewishness is a label rather than a heritage, an empty modifier rather than a substantive identity. This is Roth's Eli, the fanatic on the big screen. Before the altar of romantic love, it is of little consequence whether Uncle Louie fixes up a Jew with a Jew, or a Jew with a *shiksa*. They amount to the same thing: now firmly entrenched in middle-class American suburbia, Jews are like every other white American. Blackface is gone, and so too Jewish heritage.

If Danny Thomas's 1953 *Jazz Singer* replaced heritage with cultural assimilation, then Neil Diamond's 1980 version recovered the Jewish past, but one quite different from the original film.[107] The Jew now stands in as the archetypical American: Jesse Rabinowitch's Jewish heritage is an American story of immigration.[108] Matthew Jacobson argues that this ethnic revival emerges together with appeals to heritage "as an idiom of American nationalism,"[109] and the opening scene of Diamond's *Jazz Singer* makes his point explicit. Entitled "Immigrants" in the chapter menu, the scene opens with a pictorial of Neil Diamond, with right hand stretched skyward, singing into the microphone held in his left hand. This silhouette foreshadows the climatic final scene, in which Diamond sings before his father and adoring young fans. On stage, as Diamond concludes his paean to America, the shot morphs into a silhouette of Diamond, with right hand outstretched toward the crowd, head bowed, and microphone slightly lowered from his head. The change in angle and address from this first to last scene is necessary. As Diamond concludes his film, he acknowledges his worshiping audience, and this image becomes the marketing photo on the DVD cover and the countless merchandise that accompanied its release. But it will not do for the opening scene, because here Diamond's image segues into a sweeping panoramic shot of the Statue of Liberty. Diamond's posture mirrors the form and position of the statue within the visual boundaries of the film, so the transition is both seamless and symbolic: the Statue of

Liberty visually replaces Diamond's silhouette. And this is precisely the point: Diamond's *Jazz Singer* is a "roots trip"—a recovery of the sacred sites (the Statue of Liberty, together with Ellis Island) that ground the immigrant narrative. Jesse Rabinowitch is an American like all other immigrants.

As Jacobson astutely points out, the "continuing tradition of immigration" masks a more sinister history of "conflict, inequality, and violence." This more unifying vision was not lost on Michael Dukakis, who appropriated Diamond's "America" as his theme song for his 1988 presidential candidacy. Dukakis called attention to his immigrant past as a "common denominator among all Americans."[110] Diamond, too, articulates this vision of inclusion, even as he silences other, more oppressive narratives. The opening scene moves from the Statue of Liberty to the crowded, teeming, and immigrant streets of New York City. We see swarms of immigrant newcomers—Chinese, Indian, Hispanic, African, Polish, Greek, Russian and yes, Jews—all "coming to America," as the background anthem suggests. The lyrics shape the vibrant, multiethnic populace into a sweeping immigrant narrative of liberation:

Far
We've been traveling far
Without a home
But not without a star

Free
Only want to be free
We huddle close
Hang on to a dream

On the boats and on the planes
They're coming to America
Never looking back again
They're coming to America.[111]

The song concludes with "My country 'tis of thee" shaped to Diamond's tune, so that coming to America transforms into a patriotic act of citizenship. America is an immigrant nation, with Jews as typical immigrants. Their heritage maps onto an American story that displaces Plymouth Rock for Ellis Island as "our national myth of origins."[112]

That transformation underlies the musical score of Diamond's "America." As it concludes with "sweet land of liberty," the chorus shouts

"Today"—the immigrant narrative is a contemporary American story and dream. But the song opens in this final scene with the haunting melody of Kol Nidre, and then, with syncopated orchestral rhythms, transforms into the upbeat tune of "America." Like Thomas's 1953 *Jazz Singer*, Diamond's remake displaces the past with softer images and tones. Kol Nidre evokes a more somber mood, but immigrant Jews "want to be free," and they are "never looking back again." That smooth orchestral transition brilliantly dislodges one set of roots for another. The immigrant narrative is the only one that counts today. And so Diamond's "America," his national anthem, frames the movie in both content and form: as opening and closing sequence, his "America" is *the* America of immigrant opportunity. In between those clips we witness scenes like Jesse traveling to Los Angeles to meet Molly Bell, his agent and love interest—the modern, hip, and funny Judy Lane and Mary Dale. As they descend on the airport escalator, she introduces herself, noting that her last name used to be much longer (Bellengokavella). Not to be outdone, Diamond admits that he, too, once traveled under a different name (he is now Jess Robin). Molly is impressed ("that's not bad," she admits), but the message is even stronger: these two young lovers are immigrants, both striving to make it in America. They are on even footing, and the Jew takes his place among other immigrants. The *shiksa* is really just another searcher, traveling far, with a dream to share. Immigrants, even Jewish ones, are coming to America, today.

It is tempting to interpret the three *Jazz Singer* films as period pieces. Surely they reflect the altered landscape of American Jewish culture. In the 1920s, a generation of American-born Jews were now rebelling against their East European immigrant parents, and the conflicts surrounding language, dress, culture, and religion infused urban Jewish life. This is the Al Jolson story, the cantor prodigy who becomes the great American jazz singer. But the 1920s were also a time of intense antisemitism, and American Jews defensively withdrew to the family and its secure protection. These movements of embrace and rejection certainly informed the ambivalent heritage of the original *Jazz Singer* film. By the 1950s, many Jews had established themselves within a white, middle-class suburban culture. They had made it in America. But even here their success was both limited and uncertain, and the "five o'clock shadow" often set in.

As one Jewish suburbanite recalled: "It's kind of '9 to 5' arrangement. The ghetto gates, real or imagined, close at 5:00 PM. . . . After five o'clock there is no social contact, no parties, no home visits, no golf clubs—no nothing."[113] Appeals to heritage disappear so that Jews can meld in quietly, without appearing "too Jewish." This is Roth's Woodenton of "Eli, the Fanatic," where Art and Ted desire a bland acceptance among their Christian neighbors. Yet with the flaunting of cultural difference in the next decade and beyond, Jews could unabashedly return to their roots, together with other ethnic groups, and be counted within multicultural America. Their story was *the* American story, where a Rabinowitch becomes Robin, much like a Bellengokavella morphs into the more pleasant sounding Bell. These *Jazz Singers* do indeed reflect an American cultural history, but they also produce it as well. They feed back into the American self-image and reaffirm cultural transitions. As visual productions, the *Jazz Singer* pictures enact Jewish identity in America.

These films also move beyond their cultural boundaries to reveal the aural dimensions of heritage production. The American historian Leigh Schmidt has taught us how sounds access other worlds, and the ear materially serves as the conduit to revelatory experiences.[114] We see heritage, to be sure; but we also hear it. Music plays a central role in all three *Jazz Singer* films, and becomes a mode of heritage communication. Jolson's "Blue Skies" rendition magically transforms silence into sound. In that scene alone, with the straight and "jazzy" versions, together with Jolson's classic small talk, we hear the dynamics and conflicts of Jewish heritage. That ambivalence can no longer be heard in Danny Thomas's remake, where his jazz, much like his heritage, effortlessly seeps into the American mainstream. It is a kind of silence that mutes dissonant heritage voices. But those cacophonous voices return in Neil Diamond's *Jazz Singer*. We see the Statue of Liberty, but hear "Coming to America" with all its immigrant force. Film, like radio and even photography, speaks and sings heritage in discordant sounds and upbeat rhythms. Diamond's "America" tune got it right: as the somber Kol Nidre melody segues into the lively beat of "Coming to America," we see as much as hear the transition. This is both how Jolson performed in the original classic, and what Thomas altogether lacked in his remake. With one hand stretched high to mirror the Statue of Liberty, and the other drawing the microphone to his lips, Diamond blends sights and sounds to produce a compelling heritage: it is seen, and heard, in no other way.

CONCLUSION

Heritage production is serious business, especially so as entertainment and camp chic. When Jen Taylor Friedman created her Barbie dressed up in *tefillin* and *tallit,* she had playful spectacle in mind. Adorned with "a lovely frum denim skirt," this 2006 hip Barbie transforms into a "nice Modern Orthodox girl."[115] With *tallit* (the Jewish prayer shawl) and *tefillin* (phylacteries) worn over her blonde hair and slim, elegant left arm, Barbie also comes with a Jewish prayer book and one volume of Talmud. This Barbie can do it all, at least as well, if not better than her partner Ken: she reads and teaches Torah, studies Talmud, and radiates grace and ease. She *davens* and looks good doing it too. Though Barbie has weathered more than eighty careers since her first appearance in 1959, her Jewish inventor, Ruth Handler, might well be surprised to discover that this American *shiksa* has returned to her Jewish roots. Though named after Handler's daughter Barbara, the Barbie doll translates familial into national images, clothing herself in American dress, as an American idol. Yet with *tefillin* and *tallit,* and the material possessions that confer learning and wisdom (*siddur* and Talmud), Taylor Friedman's Barbie is just as American as those other Barbie creations. This is even more true in the short film *The Tribe* (2006), directed by Tiffany Shlain, in which Barbie takes center stage in negotiating Jewish identity in America. Judaism has finally become hip.

This Barbie in *tefillin* is not your Bible Doll of the 1940s and 1950s— Diana Forman's "doll with a purpose" that created "happy experiences and memories which are associated with the Bible."[116] Taylor Friedman's Barbie send-up transposes Jewish experiences into American garb. Barbie not only wears traditional male religious signs; she does so as an American woman. She wears them well because they are hers, and she can still look sexy in the long, denim skirt without sacrificing her Orthodox Jewish modesty. This is the Jewish fantasy in reverse: Jews need not become Americans to make it, but Americans must be Jewish to have style. Heritage production comes in many forms, and this one is "fashionable, cool, even sexy."[117] Barbie in *tefillin* appropriates male

FIGURE 6.8. Barbie reads Torah somewhere else. Courtesy of Jen Taylor Friedman.

religious objects for female use and care, and converts those religious commodities into fashionable American wear. Signs of male, Jewish, religious power are now trendy ornaments when appropriated by an American *shiksa*. This Barbie could easily slip into something more comfortable, but she need not do so. Her get-up might even work for a relaxed, evening date with friends. In any case, Barbie is at home, with or without *tefillin*. Jewish heritage is just one of the fashionable modes of being American.

Taylor Friedman's Barbie in *tefillin* and *tallit* is only one such model of the Jewish imaginary, but the doll helps to frame the issues so pronounced in modern Jewish heritage. The heritage productions discussed in this chapter—*Lilith* covers, Eagle's black-and-white photography, the *Jazz Singer* movies—all play with notions of style, authenticity, and American Jewish identity, as do other well-known cultural products, such as the three volumes of *The Jewish Catalog*.[118] *Lilith* magazine has reimagined a feminist Jewish heritage with style and dignity, from its very first cover, through the spring 1988 silhouette image of women on playing cards, and certainly in the volume on material culture and Jewish museums. Perhaps the woman who adorns the original cover with soup in one hand, Israeli flag in the other, appears less nimble and elegant than Barbie in denim skirt and soft lighting. Yet she gracefully balances social expectations with her own desires, and walks a fine line, literally, toward American and Jewish respectability. She is not the *shlumpy* housewife, but the tall, upright, assertive career woman who adopts Lilith as her female idol. This is her authentic self—like the imagined Lilith character, she embodies independence, boldness, and sexual energy. She is, as Susan Weidman Schneider asserts, a "chicken-soup-bearing household goddess." This cultural icon, like the more recent Barbie in *tefillin*, fashions modern Jewish identity through a revision of Jewish heritage. We see this goddess, much like Barbie, by reimagining a past in the cultural terms of the present. Authenticity recovered is a fashionable heritage regained.

Eagle's arresting portraits of 1930s Orthodoxy in New York City recover a very different heritage. These photographs—in part because they are black-and-white, without the color and vibrancy of an enticing, trendy American image—actively reject style in favor of a more earthy, grounded experience in Jewish texts and study. Eagle's Jews will adopt neither American cultural patterns nor American dress to thrive in the urban landscape. Instead they will die here, with the male gaze directed at God and Torah, and the female blank stare of despair and resignation addressed to no one and no thing in particular. Black-and-white photography solidifies this sense of lost past and heritage, but in so doing also actively creates it. Authenticity lives beyond the ocean frontiers in the shtetl, never making the journey to the American promised land. Eagle's photos, together with the captions that frame them, record this authentic absence as a wounded presence—a specter that lives in individual communions with God and text, together with tragic recognitions of loss. With all the real social and material gains made by modern Liliths and hip Barbies, Eagle's photographs remind us that heritage production is a form of violence that effaces other exposures of authenticity. Those others are displaced as foreigners, alone and lonely with their God. Eagle sought to recover their heritage through photographic image. The medium, in this sense, confers the message: photography functions as witness to a lost world. Without an authentic Jewish identity in America, there is no style and color.

The *Jazz Singer* movies returned style and sound to American Jews in ways that mimicked Jewish cultural experiences in the 1920s, 1950s, and 1980s. The ambivalent heritage that Jolson embodied and performed gave way to the easy acculturation and middle-class sensibility of Danny Thomas's ambitions. Neil Diamond transformed these social patterns into an immigrant narrative of new beginnings, in which Jews become American by reclaiming their immigrant roots. When the Kol Nidre melody segues into Diamond's "America," Jewish style and sound create an authentic American identity. The tragic ambivalence so pronounced in Jolson's blackface, or the comforting solidarity of Thomas's 1953 remake, recede before Diamond's audacious claim to American icon. Taylor Friedman's Barbie in *tefillin,* though not following the pattern of immigrant chic in Diamond's movie, nonetheless captures his sense of belonging.

Perhaps this explains why heritage inspires through visual mediums. The violence of displacement expels treasured images for new, more heroic visions. To see these movements of dislocation is to perform them, creating new cultural and religious patterns that subdue a past. We see this in the trashing of the American Jewish Princess for the Lilith within; or in the taking up of the *yad,* in that final Eagle photograph, to become reader and bearer of authentic tradition; in identifying with Diamond's outstretched hand as it morphs into the raised arm of the Statue of Liberty; and certainly in the playing of Orthodox chic, American style. The viewer is an accomplice, and not merely a witness to these acts of heritage production. Viewing heritage is an active gaze of destruction, recovery, and creation.

American or Jewish
Material Identity?

A nagging question has continued to haunt these chapters, one that I have refused to engage until now: in what sense is material Jewish identity in America a specifically Jewish or American expression? More than one colleague has put this challenge to my work, and I have deflected the issue ever so cautiously. There are indeed many ways to think of Jewish material identity in its American form. One can locate cultural, religious, and economic currents that Jews appropriate, revise, or swallow whole. And there may be Jewish traits that principally inform identity in America, in both material and other ways. How should we distill the Jewish from American features? This is, to be sure, a good question. But it is also a misleading one when confronting material identity, and I want to explain why that is in this conclusion. It is an awkward question, in one sense, because Jews, like most other Americans, do not hold fixed identities, as David Biale and Jonathan Freedman, among others, have convincingly argued.[1] Even if they did, one would have to reify those identities—Jewish and American—to such a base level that the comparison would yield only unproductive platitudes and imprecise formulations. It is, moreover, an unproductive question because so much of material identity undercuts the false dualism between American culture and Jewish ethnicity. American Jews or Jewish Americans (with or without the hyphen) think and work with things in ways that bridge and complicate identity. To label the one Jewish, the other American, is to miss how material possessions, and the way persons identify with them, absorb multiple narratives, conflicting histories, tragic and hopeful visions, and diverse constructions of heritage. We would do well to heed Jonathan Freedman's critique that traditional Jewish identity politics,

> stresses the need for purity, consistency, essence, limits, boundaries in defining what is and is not Jewish. This is of course one impulse in Judaism as a religious practice itself, one in which the delineation of the clean and the unclean, the pure and the corrupt, is central, definitional. But it's more powerfully, and more problematically, a repeated impulse in the critical response of American Jews in a multiracial, multicultural America—an impulse to (as it were) circle the wagons, to define Jewishness as well as Judaism (itself a notoriously multiple religious practice and identity) in monolithic, essentializing terms.[2]

One certainly could disentangle this material mess, circle the wagons, and seek a clearer vision of a reified identity. But the price would be high, and the gain far too little.

Mordecai Kaplan's journal is certainly an American product. It captures the modernist preoccupations of America in the 1920s and 1930s, together with Kaplan's desire to create a lasting presence in the American landscape. Kaplan yearns for home, and the journal becomes his artistic mode to fashion it for American Jews like himself—searching but forever tied to Judaism in America. His compulsive writing evoked an archive fever that manifested a particularly virulent American strain: a fear that commodities, like Kaplan's journal, would disappear, and so too the self personified in things. Those objects were both prized for their stubborn allure and feared for their eventual loss, counted as waste in the economic cycle of consumption and ever more production. Kaplan's nightmare of libraries overrun with journals exposed this frenzy, even as it induced it to a fever pitch. These are American anxieties, located within the burgeoning market economy and the modernist focus on self-creation.

Are there Jewish concerns as well lurking in Kaplan's fever? Do Kaplan's obsessive journal writing and fear of loss suggest Jewish unease too? We recognize some of this in Kaplan's desire to impress on his children a Jewish home, full of Hebrew, dance, song, and learning. Or perhaps we find it in Kaplan's reflections on memory, and the claims to Jewish responsibility and heritage. Certainly Kaplan's vision of a civilization nourishes a Jewish sensibility that moves beyond faith, belief, and spiritual experience, even as it includes them all. Religion is so much more than prayer and learning, so Kaplan argued, in both conception and practice. Kaplan's legacy in America is a Jewish one, for it reflects abiding Jewish musings on place, performance, and commitment.

Yet Kaplan's Jewish and American identities soon become muddled when we look at how he works with things. Recall his train ride to Schenectady as Kaplan scrambles to find additional scraps to use, inscribe, and enact his identity:

> But I must keep up this diary. It is the only evidence I have that I have ever existed. I need it to counteract the feeling of blankness with which I am often seized. My past is as though it was not so that I feel forced to turn the pages of the diary to convince myself that I have lived.[3]

Or note his serious play with clay, and the bust he molds of his father: "I was up till 3:30 in the morning. I simply could not tear myself away from it until I managed to retrieve the resemblance to father, and in this I succeeded only by restoring the very face lines that Tepper criticized most severely as not being human."[4] In both accounts, Kaplan evinces an American fear of loss, the Jewish passion for memory, a trace of a past and a father, and a desire to return through material performances. But in what sense do these material acts enforce this dualism, such that we must disentangle the American from the Jewish Kaplan to better understand him? Deciphering some Jewish essence here, I believe, only weeds out the material power of the things themselves. We gloss over the ways in which the physical diary and the very turning of its pages establish and justify a life. We miss how physical things revivify a past, control and inform our passions, and turn budding writers into passionate artists. These are neither Jewish nor American movements. They are material performances that cultivate, even as they challenge, Jewish identity in America. Instead of gazing beyond the things to the American and Jewish substance, it is better to situate that gaze directly on the things themselves, much like Kaplan does on the train and in the early hours of morning. What we need to appreciate is Kaplan's fixation, his thrill and despair, and his passion for physical objects. He is both a creature and a builder of material culture, not as a Jew or an American, but as a tormented soul yearning for place, presence, and acceptance. His is the struggle for a material identity in America.

Kaplan's diaries produce a Jew staking a claim in America. Struggling for a Jewish material presence evoked the anxieties of homelessness, both within Judaism and beyond it. I do not wish to claim that as a Jew in America, Kaplan explores fundamental Jewish sensibilities in a particular place. Instead, I suggest that material identity in America weaves together too many narratives, concerns, traditions, and desires to fully disentangle and to make sense of a pristine Jewish or American identity. Kaplan is a Jew in America, but the performance of that identity undercuts the very distinction captured by that phrase. Label them American Jews, or Jewish Americans. Either way, their cultural enactments reveal more complex interweavings of identity. Performance is not a descriptive label that language reifies, but instead is a complex and ambiguous act of identity. It evokes and conjures up identity, but does not solidify or express it.

We witness this kind of haunting, performative exposure in Edward Bernays, Joshua Loth Liebman, and Eric Fromm. Each Jewish thinker appropriated a past to justify a humanistic, psychological mode of human flourishing, even as they rejected their past to see more clearly to an unencumbered future. As David Lowenthal astutely notes, "those who felt the pull of the past had the more strongly to resist it."[5] Bernays's public relations counsel liberated the self from traditional constraints, only to enslave it to new passions that better align with progressive politics. He pioneered a psychology of exposure, in which persons uncover and freely engage inner drives and yearnings.[6] Emancipated from the herd mentality, Americans could now buy the very products that satiate their fully disclosed wishes. These exposures are exposures of a liberated self yearning for material fulfillment. This mode of human flourishing overcomes restrictive burdens of the past. Liebman, too, would overcome oppressive fathers so that their sons and daughters could move beyond the horrors of the Second World War. Though the biblical prophets offered constructive psychological advice, Liebman's own form of self-help was far more personal, subjective, and reassuring. Americans really could aspire to "spiritual stability," for we could now "draw the picture of our own soul."[7] That soul would no longer be darkened by past horrors, but would be liberated by a torrent of self-exposure: "Seal up even a small teakettle, place it over a flame, and it will wreck a house. But let the powerful vapors escape, and the kettle *sings*."[8] This musical performance enables selves to grow up, and decouples them from infantile fears and tyrannical forbears. We could undo the past, so Liebman promises, through outpourings of mature emotions.

Yet even as Bernays and Liebman attempted to silence the haunted past, Fromm's work exposed the scars and unbreakable ties to it. More radical than Liebman, Fromm divorced the self from "primary ties" that constrict and weigh down human flourishing: "the primary ties block his full human development; they stand in the way of the development of his reason and his critical capacities."[9] But even Fromm could not entirely let go of his heritage, and certainly not his Jewish one. His account of love exposed the schizophrenic wrestling with demands to "love everybody," and the erotic passions that reveal more intimate commitments. Fromm, too, would appeal to primary ties of love, and to the texts and teachers that nourished his development.[10] Much like Bernays and Liebman before him, Fromm craves past authorities, even as he rebels against them. The self yearns for unrestrained freedom, but forever returns to more humble, constrictive origins—precisely the movement that Fromm so powerfully outlines in his *Escape from Freedom*. This tense movement, articulated in the works of Bernays, Liebman, and Fromm, reveals the burdens of inheritance and the emotive power of escape. According to Lowenthal, this ambivalence to the past has deep American roots.[11] I, for one, do not know whether these roots are Jewish, American, or both. But at least one of my forbears was right in this: escape from freedom is a tragic *human* performance for all those who recognize the burdens and blessings of inheritance.

The blessings of the Jewish past, and the halakhic mind that constructs them, are most pronounced in the works of Joseph Soloveitchik. His readers and disciples often distinguish his "Jewish" works, intended for a more intimate audience, from his more philosophical texts that spoke to the broader public.[12] Soloveitchik could write philosophically about particular legal, halakhic matters, thereby blending but always distinguishing his Jewish commitments from more general concerns. His writing on Jewish law appropriated the very American language of the urban holy, where the inner streets of the city transform into sites of redemptive possibility. One could sink low, spiritually and physically, within urban chaos, only to rise up exalted and redeemed through a re-ordering of chaos into articulated byways of holiness. Soloveitchik channeled Liebman's mapping of the soul into a Jewish urban performance. This dynamic but ordered separation, in which Soloveitchik's halakhic man acts in the image of his God in Genesis, weaves together narratives of the American city with the creative legal structures of Jewish law. It seems clear, then, what should count as American, and so too Jewish, in Soloveitchik's legal and philosophical works. Of all the Jewish thinkers studied in this book, Soloveitchik appears most at ease with this bifurcation, and like his halakhic man, most adept at separation and division.

Yet material places are not merely the site of Jewish thought, but the very substance of it. Soloveitchik's halakhic discourse is so thoroughly indebted to images of the urban holy, so suffused and informed by them, that he in turn helps to establish that very discourse. He *creates* the urban holy. To disentangle the American urban holy from the Jewish law would cause a loss of this productive voice in *Halakhic Man* and *Lonely Man of Faith*. I take this to be Soloveitchik's peculiar genius: his capacity to unapologetically capture American visions of the city within a Jewish legal framework. But once he ensnares the one within the other, it is both fruitless and damaging to dissolve this holy urban alliance. The power and allure of Soloveitchik's thought lies precisely in this creative mix. Questions about an American or Jewish audience, or commitments to existential philosophy or Jewish legal practices, obscure what Soloveitchik actually *does* in his texts. His works are productive: they expose constructions of material Jewish identity in America that frustrate binary oppositions like American and Jewish. This, only in part, accounts for Soloveitchik's widespread influence upon modern Orthodoxy in America. His works *perform* the American urban holy: they fuse, into a more perfect union, the desolate alienation of the lonely man of faith with the salvific and spiritual renewal of halakhic man.

That union had grown too close, so Abraham Joshua Heschel believed, to the material practices of consumption. Things of space had invaded holiness in time—so much so that American Jews could no longer develop spiritual sensibilities. The fetishized object, and the idol worship evoked by it, transformed holy selves into enslaved things that traffic in capitalist markets of supply and demand. Heschel sought to curb this material excess and waste by appealing to moments of transcendence. This taste of eternity would nourish sabbatical time, when we "displace the coveting of things in space for *coveting the things in time.*"[13] The displacement of spacial things became Heschel's religious obsession, and I argued in chapter 4 that he failed to weed out all signs of materiality from his eternal Sabbath. But it was a productive failure, for he exposed the inescapable features of material identity in America. Things were everywhere, in time and space, and this because Heschel could not categorically distinguish Jewish time from American space. Much like Soloveitchik's works, Heschel's texts perform the very point I want to make: sharp divisions between American and Jewish identity rupture in the demonstrative acts of material culture. Heschel labors to make this divide stick, and to protect the holiness of Jewish time and tradition. But in that labor he evokes the messy entanglements that inform material practices. A thing often fails "to identify itself as a thing, as a matter of fact."[14] But it does not have to, because Heschel cannot but do so himself. There are tablets of the heart and bricks of the soul[15] because the material self goes all the way down, for the American and the Jew.

Though Heschel elegantly split the American from the Jew, space from time, and justice from holiness, he nonetheless was captured by both. Coveting things in time bridges American and Jewish identities. We see this most emphatically in the American Jewish literature of Anzia Yezierska, Philip Roth, Cynthia Ozick, and Bernard Malamud. They each write about things and the tragic, hopeful dimensions of human finitude. For Yezierska's young, female immigrant characters, visuality marks entry into the American landscape. They see the world in and through clothes, dirt, and apartment furniture. These objects are more than symbols of working-class desires for acceptance within "clean" society; they are primary things of engagement. Yezierska's characters work with and are surrounded by things. These material enactments capture their American and Jewish existence: nothing more, but certainly not less. For Eli Peck, Roth's suburban Jewish fanatic, clothes weigh heavily upon him, but without the symbolic freight. The black coat is just the stuff of Jewish heritage, but the meaning of that past remains obscure and hidden. Sometimes, as Roth tells us in *Patrimony,* the shit is just that.[16] And so too with blackness: *that* it is meaningful, to be sure, but Eli does not know *what* it means. It is an empty signifier, hollowed out by an attenuated Jewish suburban life. The things remain, even Eli's things, and "that's all he's got."[17]

Cynthia Ozick's characters have so much more. They personify ideas and conflicts, much like Dostoevsky's tragic heroes. But with Ozick, the material stuff of language is the central actor in a play about loyalty, betrayal, heritage, and place. Yiddish is more than a linguistic medium; it is an active force that constitutes human characters and their commitments to Jewish tradition. Though Edelshtein and Hannah maintain clear notions of what belongs to American and Jewish worlds, Yiddish in America fuses these traditions to reveal more complex webs of associations. Translation is an ambiguous act of resurrection, for it enlivens the dead even as it digs the grave once again. It is death either way, as Edelshtein succinctly laments.[18] To worship a language, as Edelshtein surely does, is both a form of loyalty and idolatry. It is, at once, a recovery of heritage, and a failure to live fully. Distinguishing the American Hannah from the Jewish Edelshtein glosses over these subtle movements of acceptance and rejection, and the tragic desire to return home.

Malamud's short stories, no doubt, also trade in these expressive modes, and do so in ways that identify material things with human character. A lost thing is a lost soul in Malamud's narratives. Materials are burdens to embody rather than objects to unload. And Malamud's characters are truly burdened by things: the weight of hats, shoes, texts, and barrels. These are neither Jewish nor American things, but existential weights of material existence. Jews, to be sure, feel the force of weighty objects. But they do so not as Americans or only as Jews, but as tragic characters stuck in materiality. To live beyond such material things is an unreal life. Perhaps this is the meaning, in the end, of Eva's "haunted, beseeching eyes" as she stands behind the black shade.[19] She beckons toward a lighter world, much like Ozick's Hannah, beguiling and tempting those grounded in material identity.

And so the inevitable question: is Barbie in *tefillin* a Jewish send-up of American chic, or an American acceptance of Jewish cool? It is certainly both. And yet to leave the answer at that would obscure the material dimensions of Jewish identity I have traced in this book. We gaze at the world materially, as Yezierska reveals, with the things at hand, and create heritage by producing material images. We construct identity by working with things and images, Jews no less than other Americans. If the *Jazz Singer* films projected a torn or emasculated heritage, or even an American immigrant story, they did so through visual mediums that create, embody, and fashion the ways in which Jews imagine themselves, and how others see Jews. This visual exposure captures the expressive gaze of Eagle's black-and-white photography in the Aperture collection, as well as the *Lilith* covers that span decades of Jewish feminism in America. Material identity unwinds clear patterns of national affiliation (American) and ethnic–religious ones (Jewish). The American Jews discussed in this book are grounded in more discontinuous roots, in spaces less secure and defined, in homes far more fragmented and worn.

But this is not bad news. Material culture and Jewish thought in America offer a vibrant physicality: in the personified journal and creative arts; in the psychological and social inheritance that enables, even as it limits human flourishing; in the urban streets of creative engagement and faithful mappings; in a time when things have their place, and their allure; in the narrative dimensions of material existence; and in the visual modes of heritage. Material identity is all this and more. But it is not less, as a false boundary between American and Jewish would make it. The richness of things elicits imaginative acts of identity formation and mutations. And this is good news indeed.

NOTES

Introduction

1. Mel Scult, ed., *Communings of the Spirit: The Journals of Mordecai M. Kaplan 1913–1934*, vol. I (Detroit, Mich.: Wayne State University Press and The Reconstructionist Press, 2001), 288–89.

2. Some of the best work in these fields have been published recently by Leora Batnitzky, Zachary Braiterman, and Martin Kavka. See Leora Batnitzky, *Leo Strauss and Emmanuel Levinas: Philosophy and the Politics of Revelation* (Cambridge: Cambridge University Press, 2006); Zachary Braiterman, *The Shape of Revelation: Aesthetics and Modern Jewish Thought* (Stanford, Calif.: Stanford University Press, 2007); and Martin Kavka, *Jewish Messianism and the History of Philosophy* (Cambridge: Cambridge University Press, 2004).

3. See Jonathan Freedman, *Klezmer America: Jewishness, Ethnicity, Modernity* (New York: Columbia University Press, 2008). Freedman's study is both fresh and persuasive in its account of Jewish cultural possibilities. He typically highlights the creative energies of ethnic discourse, explaining his provocative title in this way: "It is this latter aspect of the klezmer and postklezmer phenomenon that I'm invoking here as an organizing trope: a tradition of dynamic innovation wrought in the encounter between Jewish and gentile cultures that has the property of reanimating both, creating in this interplay new configurations of ethnic belonging, new aesthetic forms in which to express them, and ultimately new vessels for delineating and interrogating the experience of a multiracial, multiethnic modernity at large" (22).

4. Barbara Kirshenblatt-Gimblett, *Destination Culture: Tourism, Museums, and Heritage* (Berkeley: University of California Press, 1998), 81 and 128.

5. Ibid., 128.

6. Matthew Frye Jacobson, *Roots Too: White Ethnic Revival in Post-Civil Rights America* (Cambridge, Mass.: Harvard University Press, 2006), especially pp. 8–9, 58, and 244.

7. Robert Orsi, "Introduction: Crossing the Line," in *Gods of the City: Religion and the American Urban Landscape*, ed. Robert Orsi (Bloomington: Indiana University Press, 1999), 1–78, especially p. 12.

8. Robert Orsi, "Everyday Miracles: The Study of Lived Religion," in *Lived Religion in America*, ed. David Hall (Princeton, N.J.: Princeton University Press, 1997), 3–21, especially p. 5.

9. See Abraham Joshua Heschel, *The Earth Is the Lord's: The Inner World of the Jew in Eastern Europe* (Woodstock, Vt.: Jewish Lights, 1995), 14; and Heschel, *The Sabbath: Its Meaning for Modern Man* (New York: Farrar, Straus and Giroux, 1951), 91.

10. For an example of this kind of analysis of religion, see Elisabeth Arweck and William Keenen, "Introduction: Material Varieties of Religious Expression," in *Materializing Religion: Expression, Performance and Ritual*, ed. Elisabeth Arweck and William Keenan (Hampshire, England: Ashgate, 2006), 1–20, especially pp. 3–6.

11. David Morgan and Sally Promey, eds., *The Visual Culture of American Religions* (Berkeley: University of California Press, 2001), 16. Also see Colleen McDannell, *Material Christianity: Religion and Popular Culture in America* (New Haven, Conn.: Yale University Press, 1995), 1–16.

12. David Morgan, *The Sacred Gaze: Religious Visual Culture in Theory and Practice* (Berkeley: University of California Press, 2005), 5, 29, and 46. Notions of the gaze have produced a cottage industry of texts in response to Foucault and Lacan's seminal works in this area. Indeed, the term *gaze* has become a fashionable, loaded term that covers a wide variety of practices, methods, and visions. See, for example, Michel Foucault, *This Is Not a Pipe* (Berkeley: University of California Press, 1983); Foucault, *The Order of Things* (New York: Vintage Books, 1994), especially pp. 3–16 for his trenchant and famous analysis of "Las Meninas"; Jacques Lacan, *The Four Fundamental Concepts of Psychoanalysis* (New York: W.W. Norton & Co., 1981), especially "Of the Gaze as *Object Petit a*"; James Elkins, *Visual Studies: A Skeptical Introduction* (New York: Routledge, 2003); Martin Jay, *Downcast Eyes: The Denigration of Vision in Twentieth-Century French Thought* (Berkeley: University of California Press, 1993); and Marita Sturken and Lisa Cartwright, *Practices of Looking: An Introduction to Visual Culture* (Oxford: Oxford University Press, 2001).

13. See W. T. J. Mitchell, *What Do Pictures Want? The Lives and Loves of Images* (Chicago: University of Chicago Press, 2005), 33, and his move away from "what pictures *do* to what they *want*, from power to desire." The Jewish look that I discuss in chapter 6 attempts to blend power (what pictures do) with Jewish desires of representation.

14. David Morgan, *Visual Piety: A History and Theory of Popular Religious Images* (Berkeley: University of California Press, 1998), 3.

15. For a sampling of significant works in the field that have informed this study, see Kenneth Ames, "Material Culture as Non Verbal Communication: A Historical Case Study," *Journal of American Culture* 3 (1980): 619–41; McDannell, *Material Christianity*; Morgan, *The Sacred Gaze*; Jenna Weissman Joselit, *The Wonders of America: Reinventing Jewish Culture, 1880–1950* (New York: Henry Holt and Co., 1994); and Kirshenblatt-Gimblett, *Destination Culture*.

16. Morgan and Promey, eds., *The Visual Culture of American Religions*, 16.

17. Ibid., 17.

18. Freedman, *Klezmer America*, 15. "It's the central thesis of my project that dealing with the collective fictions that accrete around the example of Jews, Jewishness, and Judaism can unsettle even the most seemingly secure of the seemingly calcified categories by which our culture parses otherness" (15).

1. The Material Self

1. I will employ the terms *diary* and *journal* interchangeably, although I recognize that some regard them as two distinct forms of writing.

2. Mel Scult, *Judaism Faces the Twentieth Century: A Biography of Mordecai M. Kaplan* (Detroit, Mich.: Wayne State University Press, 1993), 237–38; and Scult, ed., *Communings of the Spirit*, 31.

3. At this time, only one volume of his journals has been published, with two more volumes intended for publication in the near future.

4. Jacques Derrida, *Archive Fever: A Freudian Impression* (Chicago: University of Chicago Press, 1995).

5. Scult, *Judaism Faces the Twentieth Century*, 19–27.

6. Andrew R. Heinze, *Adapting to Abundance: Jewish Immigrants, Mass Consumption, and the Search for American Identity* (New York: Columbia University Press, 1990); Joselit, *The Wonders of America*; and Riv-Ellen Prell, *Fighting to Become Americans: Assimilation and the Trouble between Jewish Women and Jewish Men* (Boston: Beacon Press, 1999).

7. *Cultural studies* is a broad term that has taken on numerous meanings. In this book, I use this term to designate fields of inquiry that focus on human acts of cultural significance and material culture—home building, economic and material practices, literature, identity formation, and art. For some representative works in these fields, see Ames, "Material Culture as Non Verbal Communication," 619–41; Marc Manganaro, *Culture, 1922: The Emergence of a Concept* (Princeton, N.J.: Princeton University Press, 2002); and Michael North, *Reading 1922: A Return to the Scene of the Modern* (New York: Oxford University Press, 1999).

8. William Spengemann and L. R. Lundquist, "Autobiography and the American Myth," *American Quarterly* 17, no. 3 (1965): 502.

9. See Elizabeth Podnieks, *Daily Modernism: The Literary Diaries of Virginia Woolf, Antonia White, Elizabeth Smart, and Anaïs Nin* (Montreal: McGill-Queen's University Press, 2000).

10. Ibid., 43, 7.

11. See the Kaplan Diaries at *The Eisenstein Reconstructionist Archives of the Reconstructionist Rabbinical College*, Wyncote, Pa. For an example of Kaplan's editing of the typed copies, see the June 19, 1930, entry (Vol. 6). In the handwritten diaries, Kaplan writes "known as the double stand of truth," but the typed version reads, "known as the double standard of truth." Many thanks to the archivist of this collection, Kim Tieger, for her explanation and understanding of Kaplan's diaries.

12. Podnieks, *Daily Modernism*, 7 and 15.

13. Scult, *Communings of the Spirit*, 73–74, 127.

14. For the most telling examples of these views, see Clement Greenberg, "Avant-Garde and Kitsch," in *Art and Culture: Critical Essays* (Boston: Beacon Press, 1961), 3–21; and Oswald Spengler, *The Decline of the West* (New York: Oxford University Press, 1991), 24–25, 245–54.

15. See Warren Susman, *Culture as History: The Transformation of American Society in the Twentieth Century* (Washington, D.C.: Smithsonian Institution Press, 2003), 71, 93–95, 107, especially p. 93.

16. Scult, *Communings of the Spirit*, 104.

17. Ibid., 237–51. Note, however, Jon Butler's comment that in his masterwork, *Judaism as a Civilization* (1934), Kaplan has very little to say about "lived religion" in New York City. See Jon Butler, "Three Minds, Three Books, Three Years: Reinhold Niebuhr, Perry Miller, and Mordecai Kaplan on Religion," *Jewish Social Studies* 12, no. 2 (2006): 17–29, especially p. 25.

18. Scult, *Communings of the Spirit*, 104.

19. Ibid., 35 and 341.

20. Melissa Klapper, *Jewish Girls Coming of Age in America, 1860–1920* (New York: New York University Press, 2005), 13.

21. See Joan Jacobs Brumberg, "The 'Me' of Me: Voices of Jewish Girls in Adolescent Diaries of the 1920s and 1950s," in *Talking Back: Images of Jewish Women in American Popular Culture*, ed. Joyce Antler (Hanover, N.H.: University Press of New England, 1998), 53.

22. Scult, *Communings of the Spirit*, 336.

23. Ibid., 282.

24. See Ann Douglas, *Terrible Honesty: Mongrel Manhattan in the 1920s* (New York: Farrar, Straus and Giroux, 1995), 44–47, 122–29. I will have more to say about Freud and modernism later in this chapter, as well as in chapter 2.

25. North, *Reading 1922*, 66–67, 76–80.

26. Scult, *Communings of the Spirit*, 282.

27. See Joshua Loth Liebman, *Peace of Mind: Insights on Human Nature that Can Change Your Life* (New York: Carol Publishing Group, 1994). I treat Liebman's views at length in the next chapter.

28. Scult, *Communings of the Spirit*, 279.

29. Ibid., 244.

30. Ibid., 401.

31. Klapper, *Jewish Girls Coming of Age*, 13.

32. See Walter Benjamin, "The Work of Art in the Age of Mechanical Reproduction," in *Illuminations*, ed. Hannah Arendt (New York: Schocken Books, 1968), 217–51, especially p. 221.

33. Scult, *Communings of the Spirit*, 233.

34. Ibid., 244.

35. Ibid., 252–53.

36. Ibid., 225.

37. Ibid., 103.

38. Ibid., 423 and 140.

39. Julian Huxley (1887–1975) published *Religion without Revelation* (1927), a book that Kaplan admired for its clarity and vision.

40. Scult, *Communings of the Spirit*, 366.

41. Ibid., 230.

42. Ibid., 314.

43. Ibid.

44. See R. Bachya ben Joseph ibn Paquda, *Duties of the Heart*, Vol. I, trans. Daniel Haberman (Jerusalem and New York: Feldheim Publishers, 1996), 166–69; and Scult, *Communings of the Spirit*, 334.

45. Scult, *Communings of the Spirit*, 357.

46. Ibid.

47. Ibid., 370.

48. Ibid.

49. Ibid., 257. According to Walter Benn Michaels, modernist literature can indicate many things, but one of them is the passionate interest in "the materiality of the signifier, in the relation of signifier to signified, in the relation of sign to referent." Kaplan is deeply embedded in this discourse. See Walter Benn Michaels, *Our America: Nativism, Modernism, and Pluralism* (Durham, N.C.: Duke University Press, 1995), 2.

50. For a discussion of the term *self-fashioning* in Renaissance literature, but in tones that echo even today, see Stephen Greenblatt, *Renaissance Self-Fashioning* (Chicago: University of Chicago Press, 1980).

51. Mordecai Kaplan, *Art and Ethics* (Hebrew) (Jerusalem: Rubin Mass, 1954), especially p. 58.

52. Mordecai Kaplan, *Questions Jews Ask: Reconstructionist Answers* (New York: Reconstructionist Press, 1956).

53. Ibid., 373.

54. Ibid.

55. See as well Kaplan's discussion of art and culture in Mordecai Kaplan, *The Future of the American Jew* (New York: Reconstructionist Press, 1967), 350–58.

56. Kaplan, *Questions Jews Ask*, 371.

57. Ibid., 373.

58. Ibid., 369.

59. See Kalman Bland, *The Artless Jew: Medieval and Modern Affirmations and Denials of the Visual* (Princeton, N.J.: Princeton University Press, 2000), 48.

60. Jenna Weissman Joselit, "Bezalel Comes to Town: American Jews and Art," *Jewish Studies Quarterly* II (2004): 355.

61. Kaplan, *Questions Jews Ask*, 369.

62. Ibid., 370.

63. Mordecai Kaplan, *Judaism as a Civilization: Toward a Reconstruction of American-Jewish Life* (New York: Macmillan, 1934), 389.

64. Scult, *Communings of the Spirit,* 419.

65. Kaplan, *The Future of the American Jew,* 357–58.

66. The sentence in the original reads: "The Jew will have to save Judaism before Judaism will be in a position to save the Jew." See Kaplan, *Judaism as a Civilization,* 521–22.

67. Scult, *Communings of the Spirit,* 439.

68. Ibid.

69. Ibid., 375.

70. Ibid., 439.

71. Ibid., 439–40.

72. Ibid., 289.

73. See Ann Douglas, *The Feminization of American Culture* (New York: Alfred A. Knopf, 1977); and Ann Taves, *Fits, Trances and Visions* (Princeton, N.J.: Princeton University Press, 1999).

74. Quotation taken from David Morgan, *Protestants and Pictures: Religion, Visual Culture, and the Age of American Mass Production* (New York: Oxford University Press, 1999), 25.

75. Scult, *Communings of the Spirit*, 256.

76. Yosef Hayim Yerushalmi, *Freud's Moses: Judaism Terminable and Interminable* (New Haven, Conn.: Yale University Press, 1991).

77. Derrida, *Archive Fever*, 2.

78. Ibid., 19.

79. Jacques Derrida, *Of Grammatology* (Baltimore, Md.: Johns Hopkins University Press, 1974), 47 and 70.

80. Derrida, *Archive Fever*, 64–65.

81. Scult, *Communings of the Spirit*, 485.

82. Ibid., 339–40.

83. Janice Radway, *A Feeling for Books: The Book-of-the-Month Club, Literary Taste, and Middle-Class Desire* (Chapel Hill: University of North Carolina Press, 1997), 138.

84. Ibid., 137–38.

85. Scult, *Communings of the Spirit*, 340.

86. Sigmund Freud, "A Note upon the 'Mystic Writing-Pad'," in *The Standard Edition of the Complete Psychological Works of Sigmund Freud*, ed. James Strachey (London: Hogarth Press, 1961), 227–28; Sigmund Freud, "Notiz Über den 'Wunderblock'," in *Gesammelte Werke* (Frankfurt am Main: S. Fischer, 1948), 3 and 5.

87. Jacques Derrida, *Writing and Difference* (Chicago: University of Chicago Press, 1978), 226 and 228.

88. Scult, *Communings of the Spirit*, 340.

89. See most recently Noam Pianko, "Reconstructing Judaism, Reconstructing America: The Sources and Functions of Mordecai Kaplan's 'Civilization'," *Jewish Social Studies* 12, no. 2 (2006): 39–55; and Deborah Dash Moore, "Judaism as a Gendered Civilization: The Legacy of Mordecai Kaplan's Magnum Opus," *Jewish Social Studies* 12, no. 2 (2006): 172–86.

90. Gail Bederman, *Manliness & Civilization: A Cultural History of Gender and Race in the United States, 1880–1917* (Chicago: University of Chicago Press, 1995), 38–39.

91. See Pianko's article on the sources of Kaplan's term *civilization*, and Kaplan's claim to reconstruct America and not only Judaism. Pianko, "Reconstructing Judaism, Reconstructing America," 39–55.

92. See Eric Goldstein, *The Price of Whiteness: Jews, Race, and American Identity* (Princeton, N.J.: Princeton University Press, 2006), 41.

93. Susman, *Culture as History*, 114–18.

94. See Douglas, *Terrible Honesty*, 179–216; and Susman, *Culture as History*, 156, 184–210.

95. See Manganaro, *Culture, 1922*.

96. Goldstein, *The Price of Whiteness*, 182–83.

97. Susman, *Culture as History*, 66–72.

98. Scult, *Communings of the Spirit*, 315.

99. Ibid., 316.

100. Ibid., 277.

101. For a helpful article, see Cara Kaplan, "On Modernism and Race," *Modernism/Modernity* 4, no. 1 (1997): 157–69, in which she reviews Walter Benn Michaels, *Our America: Nativism, Modernism, and Pluralism* and Ann Douglas, *Terrible Honesty: Mongrel Manhattan in the 1920s*.

102. Susman, *Culture as History*, xxii–xxiii.

103. Kaplan, *Judaism as a Civilization*, 202.

104. Ibid., 203.

105. Ibid.

106. Ibid., 203–204.

107. Scult, *Communings of the Spirit*, 121–22.

108. Spengler, *The Decline of the West*, 24–25, 245–48, especially p. 246.

109. Scult, *Communings of the Spirit*, 122.

110. For notions of the city, see Andrew R. Heinze, *Jews and the American Soul: Human Nature in the Twentieth Century* (Princeton, N.J.: Princeton University Press, 2004), 91; and Orsi, "Introduction: Crossing the Line," in *Gods of the City*, 1–78.

111. Scult, *Communings of the Spirit*, 121–22.

112. Ibid., 271.

113. Heinze, *Adapting to Abundance*, 69.

114. Ibid., 70.

115. Ibid.

116. Scult, *Communings of the Spirit*, 392.

117. Beth Wenger, *New York Jews and the Great Depression* (New Haven, Conn.: Yale University Press, 1996), 10–11.

118. Scult, *Communings of the Spirit*, 437.

119. Wenger, *New York Jews and the Great Depression*, 158–59.

120. Here is where I see the work of immigrant literature expanding our views of American modernism, opening currents to Paul Gilroy's transatlantic productions or Michael North's analysis of "global mobility." We should explore how immigrant groups confront modernist dilemmas, and so recognize how Kaplan's works, as modernist and immigrant struggles for place, fashion the self within the American landscape. See Paul Gilroy, *The Black Atlantic: Modernity and Double Consciousness* (Cambridge, Mass.: Harvard University Press, 1993); and North, *Reading 1922*, 11–15.

121. Heinze, *Adapting to Abundance*, 7–8.

122. Ibid., 30.

123. See the very important work by Walter Benn Michaels, *Our America: Nativism, Modernism, and Pluralism*. Michaels maps the trajectory from the commitment to Americanization through "the transformation of immigrants" to "the revision of American national identity as a form of racial identity" (136).

124. Heinze, *Adapting to Abundance*, 47.

125. Ibid., 83–84.

126. See Colleen McDannell, *The Christian Home in Victorian America, 1840–1900* (Bloomington: Indiana University Press, 1986), 42–45.

127. Heinze, *Adapting to Abundance*, 143.

128. Douglas, *Terrible Honesty*, 365–66.

129. See Klapper, *Jewish Girls Coming of Age*, 197–98.

130. See Jenna Weissman Joselit, "'A Set Table': Jewish Domestic Culture in the New World, 1880–1950," in *Getting Comfortable in New York: The American Jewish Home, 1880–1950*, ed. Susan Braunstein and Jenna Weissman Joselit (New York: The Jewish Museum, 1990), 21–76, especially pp. 34–37.

131. Prell, *Fighting to Become Americans*, 10, 12.

132. Ibid., 43–44.

133. Ibid., 23.

134. Ibid., 26.

135. See Michaels, *Our America.*

136. Prell, *Fighting to Become Americans*, 36.

137. Ibid., 53.

138. Ibid., 56.

139. Ibid., 94.

140. Bill Brown, "The Tyranny of Things (Trivia in Karl Marx and Mark Twain)," *Critical Inquiry* 28, no. 2 (2002): 442–69.

141. Ibid., 446, 465, 468.

142. See diary entry May 27, 1929 (Vol. 5, 1929–30), *The Eisenstein Reconstructionist Archives of the Reconstructionist Rabbinical College*, Wyncote, Pa.

143. Scult, *Communings of the Spirit*, 334.

144. Ibid., 381.

145. See Douglas, *Terrible Honesty.*

2. The Material Past

1. See Nathan Hale, Jr., *The Rise and Crisis of Psychoanalysis in the United States: Freud and the Americans, 1917–1985* (New York: Oxford University Press, 1995), 5–6, 75–76, 276–99; and North, *Reading 1922*, 65–67.

2. Hale quotes Freud to reveal this very distance: "They [Americans] create for themselves a kind of hodge podge of psychoanalysis and other elements and boast of their doings as a sign of broadmindedness while they actually reveal thereby a lack of judgment." See Hale, *The Rise and Crisis of Psychoanalysis*, 7. Also, see Freud, "An Autobiographical Study," *Standard Edition of the Complete Psychological Works of Sigmund Freud* 20 (London: Hogarth Press, 1953–66), 52, where Freud complains that psychoanalysis in America is "watered down" and "many abuses which have no relation to it find a cover under its name."

3. See F. H. Matthews, "The Americanization of Sigmund Freud: Adaptations of Psychoanalysis before 1917," *Journal of American Studies* 1 (1967): 39–62.

4. See David Lowenthal, *The Past Is a Foreign Country* (Cambridge: Cambridge University Press, 1985), especially pp. 63–73 and 105–24, for his astute discussion of the "benefits and burdens of the past."

5. Heinze, *Jews and the American Soul*, 217–39.

6. See Mark Crispin Miller, "Introduction," in Edward Bernays, *Propaganda* (New York: Ig Publishing, 1928), 10–33; and Larry Tye, *The Father of Spin: Edward L. Bernays and the Birth of Public Relations* (New York: Henry Holt and Co., 1998).

7. Edward Bernays, *Propaganda* (New York: Ig Publishing, 1928), 78–79.

8. North, *Reading 1922*, 65–67; Hale, *The Rise and Crisis of Psychoanalysis*, 75–76.

9. Robert Fuller, *Americans and the Unconscious* (New York: Oxford University Press, 1986), 112.

10. Hale, *The Rise and Crisis of Psychoanalysis*, 7.

11. See Fuller, *Americans and the Unconscious*, 100–101.

12. Tye, *The Father of Spin*, 107.

13. See Edward Bernays, *Biography of an Idea: Memoirs of Public Relations Counsel* (New York: Simon and Schuster, 1965), 288, where Bernays tells us that he and his wife Doris adopted the name "Public Relations Council" in 1920, "hoping its professional implications would carry over to the new field."

14. Ibid., 270.

15. See the opening pages of *Biography of an Idea,* where Bernays notes his relations to Freud quite frequently.

16. Gustave Le Bon, *The Crowd: A Study of the Popular Mind* (Mineola, N.Y.: Dover, 2002).

17. Ibid., 4–8.

18. Ibid., 10, 22.

19. Ibid., 8, 133.

20. Wilfred Trotter, *Instincts of the Herd in Peace and War* (New York: Cosmo Classics, 2005), 23. For Trotter's view of Le Bon, see pp. 26 and 42. Trotter wrote the first two essays, which lay out his theory of the herd, in 1908 and 1909.

21. Ibid., 20. Also see Fuller, *Americans and the Unconscious,* 130.

22. Trotter, *Instincts of the Herd,* 30.

23. Ibid., 42.

24. Walter Lippmann, *Public Opinion* (New York: Free Press Paperbacks, 1922), 17–19.

25. See North, *Reading 1922,* 74: "What is most consistently remarkable about Bernays' book, however, is the relative artlessness with which he reveals the more sinister side of public relations and the unself-consciousness with which he calls on Lippmann to support conclusions that should have made Lippmann writhe."

26. Edward Bernays, *Crystallizing Public Opinion* (New York: Boni and Liveright, 1923), 116, 75, 98–99.

27. North, *Reading 1922,* 75.

28. Bernays, *Crystallizing Public Opinion,* 19.

29. Ibid., 26.

30. North, *Reading 1922,* 80.

31. Bernays, *Crystallizing Public Opinion,* 61.

32. Bernays, *Biography of an Idea,* 785.

33. Bernays, *Crystallizing Public Opinion,* 122.

34. Ibid., 214.

35. Ibid., 215.

36. Ibid., 216–17.

37. Ibid., 218.

38. Ibid., 68.

39. Bernays, *Propaganda,* 74.

40. Miller, "Introduction," in Edward Bernays, *Propaganda,* 17.

41. Bernays, *Propaganda,* 37.

42. Ibid., 39.

43. Ibid., 44–45.

44. Ibid., 70, 64.

45. Ibid., 64.

46. Ibid., 57.

47. Ibid., 71.

48. Edward Bernays, *Public Relations* (Norman: University of Oklahoma Press, 1952), 95–96.

49. Bernays, *Propaganda,* 48.

50. Ibid., 148.

51. See Bernays, *Biography of an Idea,* 386. It was A. A. Brill who originally suggested the phrase "Torches of Freedom" to Bernays; also see Tye, *The Father of Spin,* 23–50.

52. Heinze, *Jews and the American Soul,* 200–201.

53. Hale, *The Rise and Crisis of Psychoanalysis,* 276, 285, 359.

54. Philip Rieff, *The Triumph of the Therapeutic: Uses of Faith after Freud* (Chicago: University of Chicago Press, 1966), 31 and 37.

55. See Matthews, "The Americanization of Sigmund Freud," 55–60.

56. Hale, *The Rise and Crisis of Psychoanalysis,* 278.

57. Ibid., 299.

58. Liebman, *Peace of Mind,* 10.

59. Heinze, *Jews and the American Soul,* 202–204.

60. See Louis Schneider, and Stanford Dornbusch, *Popular Religion: Inspirational Books in America* (Chicago: University of Chicago Press, 1958), 162; and Heinze, *Jews and the American Soul,* 391 fn. 2.

61. See Morris Lichtenstein, *Peace of Mind: Jewish Science Essays* (New York: Jewish Science Publishing, 1927), especially pp. 72–77: "It avails one naught to brood over the difficulties of the past; the memory and mental repetition of past hardships serve but to mar the joy that might be found in new experiences. The miseries of the past are gone; they have been carried away by the current of time; they have made room for new experiences, for new events to take their place. Why brood over them and bend under their weight forever?" (72). Also see Ellen Umansky, *From Christian Science to Jewish Science: Spiritual Healing and American Jews* (New York: Oxford University Press, 2005), especially pp. 87–113.

62. See Donald Meyer, *The Positive Thinkers: A Study of the American Quest for Health, Wealth and Personal Power from Mary Baker Eddy to Norman Vincent Peale* (New York: Doubleday, 1965), 306. Umansky tends to highlight the differences between Lichtenstein and Liebman, despite their common book titles. See Umansky, *From Christian Science to Jewish Science,* 182–85.

63. Heinze, *Jews and the American Soul,* 205.

64. Ibid., 212.

65. See the important and eloquently argued doctoral dissertation on the "middle-brow" reading American public at this time by Matthew S. Hedstrom, "Seeking a Spiritual Center: Mass Market Books and Liberal Religion in America, 1921–1948" (University of Texas at Austin, 2006).

66. See, for example, Will Herberg, *Protestant–Catholic–Jew: An Essay in American Religious Sociology* (Chicago: University of Chicago Press, 1955).

67. Richard Weiss, *The American Myth of Success: From Horatio Alger to Norman Vincent Peale* (Urbana: University of Illinois Press, 1969), 230, 133.

68. Ibid., 168–69; see also Meyer, *The Positive Thinkers,* 16.

69. Schneider, and Dornbusch, *Popular Religion,* 31–41.

70. See Weiss, *The American Myth of Success*, 227–29; Meyer, *The Positive Thinkers*, 245–46; and Robert Fuller, *Americans and the Unconscious*, 183–84.

71. Norman Vincent Peale, *The Power of Positive Thinking: A Practical Guide to Mastering the Problems of Everyday Living* (Philadelphia: Running Press, 1952), 125, 52.

72. Ibid., 9–10.

73. Ralph Waldo Trine, *In Tune with the Infinite* (New York: Dodge Publishing Co., 1910), 91, 105, 222. See also Fuller, *Americans and the Unconscious*, 181, where he claims that for Trine, "mental healing was proof that 'thoughts are forces'. . . . 'As a man thinketh, so he is' was no mere aphorism for the New Thoughters. It was metaphysical law."

74. Mary Pickford, *Why Not Try God?* (New York: H.C. Kinsey & Co., 1934), 8, 23, 21.

75. Ibid., 12.

76. Emmet Fox, *Power through Constructive Thinking* (New York: HarperCollins, 1989), vii.

77. Joshua Liebman, *Psychiatry and Religion* (Boston: Beacon Press, 1948), ix.

78. Ibid., xi, 27, 33–34.

79. Ibid., 27.

80. Ibid., 33.

81. Ibid., x–xi, 31; also see Lowenthal, *The Past Is a Foreign Country*, 106–107.

82. Liebman, *Peace of Mind*, 6.

83. Ibid., 11–12.

84. Ibid., 27–28, 37.

85. Ibid., 179.

86. Ibid., 10.

87. Ibid., 12, 177.

88. Ibid., 179, 20.

89. Ibid., 15.

90. Ibid., 14.

91. Ibid., 201.

92. Ibid., 14.

93. See Heinze, *Jews and the American Soul*, 217, where he claims that Liebman's *Peace of Mind* is "an emphatically *Jewish* text," and a book that "transmitted a modern Jewish theology."

94. Liebman, *Peace of Mind*, 122.

95. Ibid., 24. See also Heinze, *Jews and the American Soul*, 222–23.

96. Liebman, *Peace of Mind*, 162.

97. Ibid., 143. This appeal to "healthy-mindedness" appropriates the language of William James and his influential work, *The Varieties of Religious Experience* (New York: Modern Library, 1902). Liebman was greatly influenced by James and his account of religion. See Heinze, *Jews and the American Soul*, 224, 397 fn. 15. An even stronger argument for James's influence on Liebman can be found in Hedstrom, *Seeking a Spiritual Center*, 327–32.

98. Liebman, *Peace of Mind*, 200.

99. Ibid., 155, 200.

100. Ibid., 21, 26.

101. Ibid., 43.

102. Ibid., 97.

103. Ibid., 91.

104. Ibid., 146–47, 149.

105. Ibid., 151.

106. Ibid., 154–55.

107. Heinze, *Jews and the American Soul,* 230.

108. Liebman, *Peace of Mind,* 168.

109. Heinze, *Jews and the American Soul,* 230; see also Liebman, *Peace of Mind,* 171.

110. Liebman, *Peace of Mind,* 161.

111. Ibid., 173.

112. Heinze, *Jews and the American Soul,* 205.

113. Liebman, *Peace of Mind,* 156. Marc Connelly, the author of the Pulitzer Prize-winning play *Green Pastures* (1930), originally staged his play (based on Roark Bradford's book, *Ol' Man Adam an' His Chillun*) at the Mansfield Theatre in New York City. Connelly transplanted the characters and stories of the Hebrew Bible to the rural, black American South. See *The Green Pastures,* ed. Thomas Cripps (Madison: University of Wisconsin Press, 1979).

114. Liebman, *Peace of Mind,* 193.

115. Ibid., 203.

116. Ibid., 78.

117. Ibid., 29.

118. Ibid., 31–32.

119. Ibid., 33–34.

120. Ibid., 37, 27.

121. See Andrew R. Heinze, "Peace of Mind (1946): Judaism and the Therapeutic Polemics of Postwar America," *Religion and American Culture* 12, no. 1 (2002): 31–58, especially pp. 48–49; and Umansky, *From Christian Science to Jewish Science,* 185.

122. Fulton Sheen, *Peace of Soul* (New York: McGraw-Hill, 1949).

123. Ibid., 1–2.

124. Heinze argues that both Sheen and Billy Graham "implicitly challenged Liebman," but also states that Sheen "took on Liebman's thesis more completely." If Heinze claims here that Sheen directly critiques Liebman, as I argue, then we agree on this point. See Heinze, "Peace of Mind (1946)," 49.

125. Sheen, *Peace of Soul,* 83–84. See too Heinze, "Peace of Mind (1946)," 49.

126. Sheen, *Peace of Soul,* 190.

127. Ibid., 192.

128. Ibid., 193.

129. Ibid., 213.

130. Ibid., 67.

131. Ibid., 10.

132. See Matthews, "The Americanization of Sigmund Freud," 43–44.

133. Sheen, *Peace of Soul,* 37.

134. Ibid., 61.

135. Ibid., 72.

136. Ibid., 66, 69.

137. Ibid., 93.

138. Ibid., 95–96.

139. Ibid., 98, 106.

140. Also see Heinze, "Peace of Mind (1946)," 49: "Whereas Liebman convicted traditional religion of overburdening modern men and women with guilt, Sheen argued the opposite: a sense of sin and acts of confession were the only source of salvation and inner peace."

141. Heinze, *Jews and the American Soul,* 242–46. In an earlier article, Heinze makes this claim: "The reactions of Graham and Sheen to *Peace of Mind* were motivated not by anti-Semitism (although the rhetoric in *Peace of Soul* leaves one wondering) but by a revolutionary change that was happening before their eyes." It remains unclear, in my reading of Heinze, whether he is willing to go as far as I do in describing Sheen's polemic as a form of anti-Judaism. He certainly suggests this, but allows his readers to form their own conclusions. See Heinze, "Peace of Mind (1946)," 49.

142. Sheen, *Peace of Soul,* 31.

143. See Heinze, *Jews and the American Soul,* 244. The quotation is taken from Fulton Sheen, *Life Is Worth Living* (New York: McGraw-Hill, 1954).

144. For Sheen, psychoanalysis is a secular, modern form of ancient Judaism: they both turn "nasty people" into nice ones. He reimagines a scene in the Gospel of Luke in which a Pharisee—who, Sheen observes, "was a very nice man"—prays at the steps of the Temple. One can sense, even through his disdainful tone, how Sheen conflates Jewish views with psychoanalysis in his version of the Pharisee's prayer: "I thank thee, O Lord, that my Freudian adviser has told me that there is no such thing as guilt, that sin is a myth, and that Thou, O Father, art only a projection of my father complex. There may be something wrong with my repressed instincts, but there is nothing wrong with my soul. I contribute 10 per cent of my income to the Society for the Elimination of Religious Superstitions, and I diet for my figure three times a week. Oh, I thank Thee that I am not like the rest of men, those nasty people, such as the Christian there in the back of the temple who thinks that he is a sinner, that his soul stands in need of grace, that his conscience is burdened with extortion, and that his heart is weighted down with a crime of injustice. I may have an Oedipus complex, but I have no sin." This is pernicious, vengeful prose, in part because it mocks Jewish practice, but also because it advances contemporary stereotypes that feminize the Jewish male. For Sheen, Americans are "nasty people" burdened with sin. But not Jews: like other nice people, they "do not come to God, because they think they are good through their own merits or bad through inherited instincts." Even more, "Like the Pharisee in the front of the temple, they believe themselves to be very respectable citizens. Elegance is their test of virtue." Jesus preferred nasty people, so Sheen tells us, and Americans should too. See Sheen, *Peace of Soul,* 53 and 56. Also see Heinze, "Peace of Mind (1946)," 49, where Heinze cites the same quotation, which he claims "barely disguised the Jewish–Christian polemic he [Sheen] saw in the psychological evangelism of . . . Liebman."

145. Heinze disagrees with this claim: "It is significant that Rabbi Joshua Liebman's *Peace of Mind* (1946), the most popular inspirational book in America between Trine's *In Tune with the Infinite* (1897) and Norman Vincent Peale's *The Power of Positive Thinking* (1952), did not accept the powerful mind-over-matter metaphysics of Trine and Peale. Following Freud, Liebman depicted the subconscious as a site

of deep conflict." See Andrew R. Heinze, "Jews and American Popular Psychology: Reconsidering the Protestant Paradigm of Popular Thought," *The Journal of American History* 88, no. 3 (2001): 950–78, especially pp. 971–73.

146. Liebman, *Peace of Mind*, 47, 50.

147. Ibid., 49.

148. Ibid., 89, 87.

149. Heinze, *Jews and the American Soul*, 210–13 (quotation taken from pp. 211–12). On his general agreement with Heinze on this point, see Hedstrom, *Seeking a Spiritual Center*, 349–55.

150. Prell, *Fighting to Become Americans*, 43–44.

151. Liebman, *Peace of Mind*, 5, 101.

152. Ibid., 56.

153. See Umansky, *From Christian Science to Jewish Science*, 89, where she claims that for Lichtenstein, men were "the builders of life while women the preservers," and that "happy women needed to be loved." As wives and mothers, "women were able to find personal fulfillment and to make their greatest contribution to Jewish life." Umansky cites Lichtenstein's essay "Men, Women and their Differences" in *Jewish Science Interpreter* 8, II (December 1930).

154. Erich Fromm, "Sex and Character," in *The Dogma of Christ*, ed. Erich Fromm (New York: Holt, Rinehart and Winston, 1955), 107–127. Fromm's essay "Sex and Character" was first published in 1949.

155. Ibid., 113–18.

156. Erich Fromm, *The Art of Loving* (New York: Harper & Row, 1956), 31.

157. Liebman, *Peace of Mind*, 171–73; also see Lowenthal, *The Past Is a Foreign Country*, 108–109.

158. Liebman, *Peace of Mind*, 174.

159. For a notion of counterhistory as "a form of polemic in which the sources of the adversary are exploited and turned 'gegen den Strich,'" see Susannah Heschel, *Abraham Geiger and the Jewish Jesus* (Chicago: University of Chicago Press, 1998), 14; also see Amos Funkenstein, *Perceptions of Jewish History* (Berkeley: University of California Press, 1993), 36–40; and David Biale, *Gershom Scholem: Kabbalah and Counter-History* (Cambridge, Mass.: Harvard University Press, 1979).

160. Fuller, *Americans and the Unconscious*, 126.

161. Rainer Funk, *Erich Fromm: His Life and Ideas* (New York: Continuum, 2000), 142.

162. Erich Fromm, *Escape from Freedom* (New York: Henry Holt and Co., 1941), x.

163. Ibid., 24, 34; also see Lowenthal, *The Past Is a Foreign Country*, 110: "As the nation shook off the historical past, so its citizens divested themselves of family heritage."

164. Fromm, *Escape from Freedom*, 256.

165. Erich Fromm, *Psychoanalysis and Religion* (New Haven, Conn.: Yale University Press, 1950), 89–90.

166. Ibid., 91.

167. Erich Fromm, *Man for Himself: An Inquiry into the Psychology of Ethics* (New York: Fawcett Premier, 1947), vii.

168. Erich Fromm, *The Art of Loving* (New York: Harper & Row, 1956), 89.

169. Fromm, *Psychoanalysis and Religion,* 79.

170. Ibid., 81.

171. Ibid., 82–83.

172. Ibid., 79.

173. Ibid., 114.

174. Ibid., 52.

175. Ibid., 57–58, 63.

176. Ibid., 48.

177. Ibid., 112.

178. Ibid., 113.

179. Ibid., 37.

180. Ibid., 47. See note 144 above for the reference to Sheen.

181. Erich Fromm, *The Sane Society* (New York: Henry Holt and Co., 1955), 41, 52, 353.

182. Fromm, *The Art of Loving,* 53.

183. Erich Fromm, *The Heart of Man: Its Genius for Good and Evil* (New York: Harper & Row, 1964), 107.

184. Erich Fromm, *You Shall Be as Gods: A Radical Interpretation of the Old Testament and Its Tradition* (New York: Fawcett World Library, 1966), 57, 71–72.

185. See, for example, Avishai Margalit's discussion of ethical and moral duties in his *The Ethics of Memory* (Cambridge, Mass.: Harvard University Press, 2002).

186. Funk, *Erich Fromm,* 136–38.

187. Fromm, *The Art of Loving,* 90.

188. Ibid., 39, 44, 108.

189. Ibid., 44, 39.

190. Ibid., 46.

191. Ibid., 47.

192. Ibid., 101–102.

193. Fromm, *You Shall Be as Gods,* 14.

194. Ibid., 15.

195. See Harold Bloom, *The Anxiety of Influence: A Theory of Poetry* (New York: Oxford University Press, 1973).

3. Material Place

1. McDannell, *The Christian Home in Victorian America, 1840–1900,* 25–26.

2. Kenneth Ames, "Meaning in Artifacts: Hall Furnishings in Victorian America," *Journal of Interdisciplinary History* 9, no. 1 (1978): 19–46, especially pp. 37–39.

3. McDannell, *The Christian Home in Victorian America,* 26.

4. Ibid., 28. Also see Kirk Jeffrey, "The Family as Utopian Retreat from the City: The Nineteenth-Century Contribution," *Soundings* 55, no. 1 (1972): 21–41; and Maxine van de Wetering, "The Popular Concept of 'Home' in Nineteenth-Century America," *Journal of American Studies* 18, no. 1 (1984): 5–28.

5. Orsi, "Introduction: Crossing the Line," in *Gods of the City,* 12.

6. Ibid., 4.

7. Barbara Kirshenblatt-Gimblett, "The Future of Folklore Studies in America: The Urban Frontier," *Folklore Forum* 16, no. 2 (1983): 175–234, especially pp. 179, 183, and 185.

8. See John Higham, *Send These to Me: Jews and Other Immigrants in Urban America* (New York: Atheneum, 1975), 22; and Orsi, "Introduction: Crossing the Line," 19–20.

9. Orsi, "Introduction: Crossing the Line," 19–20, 33.

10. See Robert Orsi, "The Religious Boundaries of an In-between People: Street *Feste* and the Problem of the Dark-Skinned Other in Italian Harlem, 1920–1990," *American Quarterly* 44, no. 3 (1992): 313–47.

11. See Susman, *Culture as History*, 238–39.

12. Orsi, "Introduction: Crossing the Line," 5.

13. Ibid., 2–3.

14. Ibid., 2.

15. Ibid., 38.

16. It is both ironic and sad that the site of the World's Columbian Exposition, according to one observer, stands now as "an urban no-man's land" that "resembles a war zone." See Stephen Marini, *Sacred Song in America: Religion, Music, and Public Culture* (Urbana: University of Illinois Press, 2003), 101.

17. The felicitous phrase comes from Orsi, "Introduction: Crossing the Line," 54.

18. See Aharon Lichtenstein, "R. Joseph Soloveitchik," in *Great Jewish Thinkers of the Twentieth Century*, ed. Simon Noveck (Washington, D.C.: B'nai B'rith Books, 1985), 281–98.

19. Joseph Soloveitchik, *Halakhic Man*, trans. Lawrence Kaplan (Philadelphia: The Jewish Publication Society, 1983), 3–4. For the original Hebrew, see *Ish ha-Halakha— Galui ve-Nistar* (Jerusalem: World Zionist Organization, 1979), 9–113. Kaplan's translation is accurate and beautifully rendered. I include the Hebrew transliteration only when it figures crucially in my argument.

20. Soloveitchik, *Halakhic Man*, 4.

21. Orsi, "Introduction: Crossing the Line," 2–4.

22. Joseph Soloveitchik, "Kol Dodi Dofek: It Is the Voice of My Beloved That Knocketh," in *Theological and Halakhic Reflections on the Holocaust*, ed. Bernhard H. Rosenberg and Fred Heuman (Hoboken: Ktav Publishing House, 1992), 51–117. Quotation taken from p. 56.

23. Soloveitchik, *Halakhic Man*, 4.

24. David Singer and Moshe Sokol, "Joseph Soloveitchik: Lonely Man of Faith," *Modern Judaism* 2, no. 3 (1982): 227–72.

25. Ibid., 239.

26. Ibid., 240 and 258–60.

27. Soloveitchik, *Halakhic Man*, 40.

28. For similar imagery, see Soloveitchik, "U-Vikashtem mi-Sham," in *Ish ha-Halakha—Galui ve-Nistar*, where he reiterates the transcendent movements of *homo religiosus;* also see Allan Nadler, "Soloveitchik's Halakhic Man: Not a 'Mithnagged'," *Modern Judaism* 13, no. 2 (1993): 124.

29. Soloveitchik, *Halakhic Man*, 19.

30. Ibid., 72.

31. Soloveitchik, "U-Vikashtem mi-Sham," 205–206. Also see Lawrence Kaplan, "Rabbi Joseph B. Soloveitchik's Philosophy of Halakhah," *The Jewish Law Annual* 7 (1988): 176–78. Though published in 1979, "U-Vikashtem mi-Sham" began as an essay with the title *Ish ha-Elohim* (The Man of God) only a few years after *Halakhic Man*. See Aviezer Ravitzky, "Rabbi J. B. Soloveitchik on Human Knowledge: Between Maimonidean and Neo-Kantian Philosophy," *Modern Judaism* 6, no. 2 (1986): 157–88, especially p. 182 fn. 17.

32. Ravitzky, "Rabbi J. B. Soloveitchik on Human Knowledge," 157–88, especially p. 179.

33. See Kaplan, "Rabbi Joseph B. Soloveitchik's Philosophy of Halakhah," 139–97.

34. David Hartman, *Love and Terror in the God Encounter* (Woodstock, Vt.: Jewish Lights Publishing, 2001), 48.

35. Soloveitchik, *Halakhic Man*, 20–21.

36. Kaplan, "Rabbi Joseph B. Soloveitchik's Philosophy of Halakhah," 149, 152–54.

37. Hartman, *Love and Terror*, 49.

38. Kaplan, "Rabbi Joseph B. Soloveitchik's Philosophy of Halakhah," 148 and 161.

39. Soloveitchik, *Halakhic Man*, 26.

40. Elliot Dorff, "Halakhic Man: A Review Essay," *Modern Judaism* 6, no. 1 (1986): 91–98, especially pp. 93–94.

41. Hartman, *Love and Terror*, 23–28.

42. Soloveitchik, *Halakhic Man*, 28.

43. Ibid., 29.

44. See Jon Levenson, *Creation and the Persistence of Evil: The Jewish Drama of Divine Omnipotence* (San Francisco: Harper & Row, 1988), 17 and 47; and Soloveitchik, *Halakhic Man*, 72.

45. Soloveitchik, *Halakhic Man*, 102.

46. Ibid., 103.

47. Ibid.

48. Levenson, *Creation and the Persistence of Evil*, 17.

49. Soloveitchik, *Halakhic Man*, 28.

50. Ibid., 57.

51. Ibid., 59.

52. Ibid.

53. Joseph Soloveitchik, *The Halakhic Mind: An Essay on Jewish Tradition and Modern Thought* (New York: Seth Press, 1986).

54. See Kaplan, "Rabbi Joseph B. Soloveitchik's Philosophy of Halakhah," 143–44.

55. Soloveitchik, *The Halakhic Mind*, 74.

56. Ibid., 74–75.

57. Ibid., 69.

58. Ibid., 86.

59. Ibid., 68 and 86.

60. Ibid., 85.

61. See Soloveitchik, "U-Vikashtem mi-Sham," 215 and 136, and Nadler's discussion and translation in his "Soloveitchik's Halakhic Man," 135–36.

62. Soloveitchik, *Halakhic Man*, 65.

63. Dorff, "Halakhic Man," 95.

64. Soloveitchik, *Halakhic Man*, 65–66.

65. Ibid., 67.

66. Ibid., 94.

67. See Kevin Lynch, *Good City Form* (Cambridge, Mass.: MIT Press, 1981), 73–98.

68. Ibid., 81.

69. Witold Rybczynski, *City Life: Urban Expectations in a New World* (New York: Scribner, 1995), 42–46.

70. Lynch, *Good City Form*, 83–86.

71. Rybczynski, *City Life*, 46.

72. Lynch, *Good City Form*, 88.

73. Rybczynski, *City Life*, 64–66.

74. Heinze, *Adapting to Abundance*, 42.

75. Joseph Soloveitchik, *The Lonely Man of Faith* (New York: Doubleday, 1965), 3–5.

76. Ibid., 23.

77. See Hartman, *Love and Terror*, 97–101; and Lawrence Kaplan, "Models of the Ideal Religious Man in Rabbi Soloveitchik's Thought" (Hebrew), *Jerusalem Studies in Jewish Thought* 4, nos. 3–4 (1984–85): 337–39.

78. Soloveitchik, *The Lonely Man of Faith*, 37.

79. Ibid., 41–42.

80. Hartman, *Love and Terror*, 109.

81. See Eugene Borowitz, "The Typological Theology of Rabbi Joseph B. Soloveitchik," *Judaism* 15, no. 2 (1966): 203–210.

82. Soloveitchik, *The Lonely Man of Faith*, 26–27.

83. Ibid., 29.

84. Hartman, *Love and Terror*, 110.

85. Soloveitchik, *The Lonely Man of Faith*, 45.

86. Ibid., 24.

87. Ibid., 47.

88. Ibid., 53.

89. Ibid., 22.

90. Ibid., 53.

91. Ibid., 71.

92. Ibid., 79–80.

93. Ibid., 84.

94. Ibid., 57.

95. Ibid., 58.

96. Ibid., 59.

97. Ibid., 60.

98. Ibid., 58.

99. Quoted from Nadler, "Soloveitchik's Halakhic Man," 139.

100. Joseph Soloveitchik, "Confrontation," *Tradition* 6, no. 2 (1964): 5–29; and Hartman, *Love and Terror*, 132.

101. Soloveitchik, "Confrontation," 5–7.

102. Ibid., 8.

103. Zachary Braiterman, "Joseph Soloveitchik and Immanuel Kant's Mitzvah-Aesthetic," *AJS Review* 25, no. 1 (2000–2001): 1–24, especially p. 4.

104. Soloveitchik, "Confrontation," 9.

105. Ibid., 27.

106. Soloveitchik, "Kol Dodi Dofek," 56.

107. Ibid., 52.

108. Ibid., 54.

109. Ibid., 92–94.

110. Ibid., 92–93.

111. Ibid., 94.

112. Soloveitchik, *Lonely Man of Faith*, 109–10.

113. Ibid., 110–12.

114. Ibid., 110.

115. Ibid., 111–12.

116. Etan Diamond, *And I Will Dwell in Their Midst: Orthodox Jews in Suburbia* (Chapel Hill: University of North Carolina Press, 2000).

4. Material Presence

1. See Donald Moore, *The Human and the Holy: The Spirituality of Abraham Joshua Heschel* (New York: Fordham University Press, 1989), 151–56.

2. Abraham Joshua Heschel, *Torah min Hashamayim ba-Aspaklaria shel Hadorot* (New York: Shontsin, 1962); and Abraham Joshua Heschel, *Heavenly Torah as Refracted through the Generations,* trans. Gordon Tucker (New York: Continuum, 2005).

3. See Edward Kaplan, *Holiness in Words: Abraham Joshua Heschel's Poetics of Piety* (Albany: State University of New York Press, 1996), especially pp. 115–31; Morris Faierstein, "Abraham Joshua Heschel and the Holocaust," *Modern Judaism* 19, no. 3 (1999): 255–75; Robert Eisen, "A. J. Heschel's Rabbinic Theology as a Response to the Holocaust," *Modern Judaism* 23, no. 3 (2003): 211–25; Reuven Kimelman, "Rabbis Joseph B. Soloveitchik and Abraham Joshua Heschel on Jewish–Christian Relations," *Modern Judaism* 24, no. 3 (2004): 251–71; and see as well Abraham Joshua Heschel, "From Mission to Dialogue?" *Conservative Judaism* 21, no. 3 (1967): 1–11.

4. See Emil Fackenheim's review of *God in Search of Man, Conservative Judaism* 15 (1960): 50–53; Eliezer Berkovits, *Major Themes in Modern Philosophies of Judaism* (New York: Ktav Publishing House, 1974), 192–224, and Arnold Eisen, "Re-Reading Heschel on the Commandments," *Modern Judaism* 9, no. 1 (1989): 1–33, especially pp. 1–2 for his review of this type of literature.

5. See Abraham Joshua Heschel, *The Earth Is the Lord's; and the Sabbath* (Cleveland: World Publishing Co., 1963). See Edward Kaplan, *Spiritual Radical: Abraham Joshua Heschel in America, 1940–1972* (New Haven, Conn.: Yale University Press, 2007), 102–104.

6. Heschel, *The Earth Is the Lord's*, 13.

7. Ibid., 14.

8. Kaplan, *Holiness in Words*, 49.

9. Ibid., 85.

10. See Eisen, "Re-Reading Heschel."

11. See Heschel, *The Sabbath*, 91.

12. Ibid., 9.

13. Ibid., 5.

14. Ibid., 9.

15. Ibid., 6.

16. See Kaplan, *Holiness in Words*, 45–59; and Eisen, "Re-Reading Heschel," 4–5.

17. Heschel, *The Sabbath*, 9–10.

18. Ibid., 10.

19. Ibid., 9–10.

20. Ibid., 80.

21. Ibid., 5.

22. See Bruce Graeber, "Heschel and the Philosophy of Time," *Conservative Judaism* 33 (Spring 1980): 44–56, especially p. 55.

23. Heschel, *The Sabbath*, 90–91.

24. Ibid., 75–76.

25. Ibid., 79.

26. Heschel, *Torah min Hashamayim ba-Aspaklaria shel Hadorot*, 54–55; Heschel, *Heavenly Torah as Refracted through the Generations*, trans. Gordon Tucker, 94–95.

27. Heschel, *The Sabbath*, 95.

28. Heschel, *The Earth Is the Lord's*, 14.

29. Heschel, *The Sabbath*, 95–96.

30. Abraham Joshua Heschel, *Man Is Not Alone: A Philosophy of Religion* (New York: Noonday Press, 1951), 8.

31. Ibid., 8–9.

32. Heschel, *The Sabbath*, 98–99.

33. Ibid., 97.

34. Ibid., 100.

35. Heschel, *The Earth Is the Lord's*, 13–14.

36. Kaplan, *Holiness in Words*, 78.

37. Ibid., 49.

38. Abraham Holtz, "Religion and the Arts in the Theology of Abraham Joshua Heschel," *Conservative Judaism* 28, no. 1 (1973): 27–39. The quotation is taken from p. 38.

39. See the arduous but provocative account of metaphor in Josef Stern, *Metaphor in Context* (Cambridge, Mass.: MIT Press, 2000).

40. Barbara Kirshenblatt-Gimblett, "Imagining Europe: The Popular Arts of American Jewish Ethnography," in *Divergent Jewish Cultures: Israel and America*, ed. Deborah Dash Moore and S. Ilan Troen (New Haven, Conn.: Yale University Press, 2001), 155–91, especially pp. 173–74.

41. Heschel, *The Earth Is the Lord's*, 15.

42. See Ismar Schorsch, "The Myth of Sephardic Supremacy," *Leo Baeck Institute Year Book* 34 (1989): 47–66.

43. Heschel, *The Earth Is the Lord's*, 31.

44. Ibid.

45. Heschel, *The Sabbath*, 99.

46. Janice Radway, in her discussion of books as commodities in the 1920s, notes how "middle-brow" culture often described books in much the same way. Books are

"full of suggestion" and allure, shimmering with aura and emotional experience. They were "not mere objects only," but conduits of personal meaning and affection. See Radway, *A Feeling for Books*, 147–48.

47. Heschel, *The Earth Is the Lord's*, 42.

48. Ibid., 50.

49. Ibid., 33.

50. See Kaplan, *Holiness in Words*, 56.

51. Heschel, *The Sabbath*, 8.

52. Kaplan, *Holiness in Words*, 85.

53. Heschel, *The Earth Is the Lord's*, 45.

54. Jeffrey Shandler, "Heschel and Yiddish: A Struggle with Signification," *The Journal of Jewish Thought and Philosophy* 2 (1993): 245–99, especially pp. 271–72 and 275.

55. Abraham Joshua Heschel, *God in Search of Man: A Philosophy of Judaism* (New York: Noonday Press, 1955), 213.

56. Heschel, *The Earth Is the Lord's*, 79–80.

57. Heschel discusses a good deal of Sephardi and Ashkenaz culture in chapter 3, "The Two Great Traditions," though he appended this chapter to the original Yiddish version of *The Earth Is the Lord's*. On January 7, 1945, Heschel delivered a talk in Yiddish to the YIVO Conference in New York entitled "The Eastern European Era in Jewish History." In 1946 an English translation appeared in print, and versions of this essay have since been published in other volumes on East European history. Heschel edited and expanded this translation into the book he called *The Earth Is the Lord's* in 1950. Much of chapter 3 draws from an earlier essay he published in *Commentary* in 1948. In that article, Heschel contrasted Ashkenaz and Sephardi societies to highlight features of postwar American Jewish culture. Clearly, much had been lost in coming to America. See Shandler, "Heschel and Yiddish," 268–69, 276, 280. Also see Kaplan, *Spiritual Radical*, 100.

58. Heschel, *The Earth Is the Lord's*, 31.

59. Ibid., 35.

60. On Heschel's romantic view of Ashkenaz culture, and his easy dismissal of Sephardi art, see Milton Hindus, "Review of *The Earth Is the Lord's* and *The Sabbath*," *Conservative Judaism* 20, no. 1 (1965): 69–74, especially p. 70.

61. Heschel, *The Earth Is the Lord's*, 26.

62. Ibid., 41.

63. Ibid., 49.

64. Ibid., 62.

65. Ibid., 93.

66. See Radway, *A Feeling for Books*, 5–6, 127–53; and Joan Shelley Rubin, *The Making of Middle-Brow Culture* (Chapel Hill: University of North Carolina Press, 1992), especially pp. xii–xvi.

67. Radway, *A Feeling for Books*, 284–85.

68. See, for example, Faierstein, "Abraham Joshua Heschel and the Holocaust," 258–59; and Hindus, "Review of *The Earth Is the Lord's* and *The Sabbath*," 69–70.

69. Heschel, *The Earth Is the Lord's*, 26.

70. Ibid., 55.

71. Ibid., 105.

72. See Joselit, *The Wonders of America*, 259–60.

73. Heschel, *The Sabbath*, 19.

74. Ibid.

75. Ibid., 8.

76. Joselit, *The Wonders of America*, 254; and Leigh Eric Schmidt, *Consumer Rites: The Buying and Selling of American Holidays* (Princeton, N.J.: Princeton University Press, 1995), 159–69.

77. Heschel, *The Sabbath*, 15.

78. Kaplan, *Holiness in Words*, 56.

79. Stern, *Metaphor in Context*, 59.

80. Kaplan, *Holiness in Words*, 56.

81. Heschel, *Man is Not Alone*, 71.

82. Heschel, *The Sabbath*, 15.

83. Kaplan, *Holiness in Words*, 85.

84. Heschel, *God in Search of Man*, 244; also see Kaplan, *Holiness in Words*, 55.

85. Heschel, *The Earth Is the Lord's*, 98.

86. Heschel, *The Sabbath*, 16.

87. Ibid., 16–17.

88. Ibid., 91.

89. Moshe Halbertal and Avishai Margalit, *Idolatry* (Cambridge, Mass.: Harvard University Press, 1992), 237–40. For a helpful discussion of the interplay between idolatry and iconoclasm, or the "violence of seeing," see Morgan, *The Sacred Gaze*, 115–46.

90. Halbertal and Margalit, *Idolatry*, 239.

91. Ibid., 64.

92. Ibid., 31.

93. Heschel, *The Sabbath*, 28.

94. Ibid., 99.

95. Heschel, *The Earth Is the Lord's*, 106.

96. Ibid., 107.

97. Halbertal and Margalit, *Idolatry*, 25–31.

98. Heschel, *The Earth Is the Lord's*, 107.

99. Heschel, *The Sabbath*, 24.

100. Heschel, *The Earth Is the Lord's*, 109.

101. Heschel, *The Sabbath*, 29.

102. Ibid.

103. Eisen, "Re-Reading Heschel," 17.

104. Ibid., 25.

105. Heschel, *The Sabbath*, 6.

106. Ibid., 3.

107. Heschel, *The Earth Is the Lord's*, 14.

108. Holtz, "Religion and the Arts in the Theology of Abraham Joshua Heschel," 34.

109. Ibid., 31.

110. See Heschel, *The Sabbath*, 35–41, 47–48. Heschel takes this story from Shabbat 33b in the Talmud, or so he tells us in the footnotes to this story.

111. Ibid., 35.

112. Ibid., 36.

113. Ibid., 37.

114. Ibid., 38.

115. Ibid., 36, 39.

116. Ibid., 41.

117. Ibid., 40.

118. See Heschel, "From Mission to Dialogue?" 1–11. Also see the essays in *No Religion Is an Island: Abraham Joshua Heschel and Interreligious Dialogue,* ed. Harold Kasimow and Byron Sherwin (Maryknoll, N.Y.: Orbis Books, 1991).

119. Heschel, "From Mission to Dialogue?" 3.

120. Ibid., 1.

121. Heschel, *The Sabbath,* 47.

122. Ibid., 48.

123. Ibid.

124. Eisen, "Re-Reading Heschel," 26.

125. Heschel, *The Sabbath,* 52–54.

126. Ibid., 29.

127. Ibid., 90–91.

128. Joselit, *The Wonders of America,* 252–60.

129. Ibid., 256–58; and see Elliot Dorff, *The Unfolding Tradition: Jewish Law after Sinai* (New York: Aviv Press, 2005), 482–87; and Marshall Sklare, *Conservative Judaism: An American Religious Movement* (New York: Schocken Books, 1955), 100–101, 121–22.

130. See Morris Adler, Jacob Agus, and Theodore Friedman, "Responsum on the Sabbath," *Proceedings of the Rabbinical Assembly of America* 14 (1950): 112–37.

131. Joselit, *The Wonders of America,* 258–59.

132. Betty Greenberg and Althea Silverman, *The Jewish Home Beautiful* (New York: National Women's League of the United Synagogue of America, 1941).

133. Jenna Weissman Joselit, "The Jewish Home Beautiful," ed. Jonathan Sarna, *The American Jewish Experience,* 2nd ed. (New York: Holmes & Meier, 1997), 236–42, especially pp. 239–40.

134. Greenberg and Silverman, *The Jewish Home Beautiful,* 13–14; and Kirshenblatt-Gimblett, *Destination Culture,* 126.

135. Heschel, *The Sabbath,* 16.

136. See Kirshenblatt-Gimblett, "Kitchen Judaism," in *Getting Comfortable in New York,* 77–105, especially pp. 101–102.

137. See Joselit, "A Set Table," 21–76, especially pp. 51–53.

138. Greenberg and Silverman, *The Jewish Home Beautiful,* 38.

139. Ibid., 65–67.

140. Joselit, "The Jewish Home Beautiful," 241.

141. Heschel, *The Sabbath,* 66.

142. Greenberg and Silverman, *The Jewish Home Beautiful,* 14.

143. Heschel, *The Sabbath,* 67.

144. Joselit, *The Wonders of America,* 259.

145. For background on Schor's friendship with Heschel as well as their work together, see Kaplan, *Spiritual Radical,* 125–28, 204.

146. Shandler, "Heschel and Yiddish: A Struggle with Signification," 283–84. See also Kirshenblatt-Gimblett, "Imagining Europe: The Popular Arts of American Jewish Ethnography," 175.

147. Nahum Glatzer, "Review of *The Sabbath*," *Judaism* 1, no. 3 (1952): 283–86, especially pp. 285–86; also see Kaplan, *Spiritual Radical*, 128 and 412 fn. 37.

148. For the notion of revivification, see Margalit, *The Ethics of Memory*.

5. The Material Narrative

1. See Michael Kramer and Hana Wirth-Nesher, "Introduction," in *The Cambridge Companion to Jewish American Literature*, ed. Michael Kramer and Hana Wirth-Nesher (Cambridge: Cambridge University Press, 2003), 1–11.

2. Indeed, cultural literary theorists such as Jonathan Freedman celebrate the diversity and decentering of American Jewish identity. See Freedman, *Klezmer America*.

3. Prell, *Fighting to Become Americans*, 56–57.

4. Anzia Yezierska, *Red Ribbon on a White Horse* (New York: Scribner, 1950).

5. Anzia Yezierska, *Hungry Hearts* (Boston: Houghton Mifflin, 1920).

6. Anzia Yezierska, *Salome of the Tenements* (New York: Grosset and Dunlap, 1923).

7. Anzia Yezierska, *Bread Givers* (Garden City, N.Y.: Doubleday, 1925).

8. See Alice Kessler Harris, "Introduction," in *Bread Givers* (New York: Persea Books, 1975); Katherine Stubbs, "Reading Material: Contextualizing Clothing in the Work of Anzia Yezierska," *MELUS* 23, no. 2 (1998): 157–72; and Magdalena Zaborowska, *How We Found America: Reading Gender Through East European Immigrant Narratives* (Chapel Hill: University of North Carolina Press, 1995).

9. See Jacobson, *Roots Too*, 271.

10. Louise Levitas Henriksen, *Anzia Yezierska: A Writer's Life* (New Brunswick, N.J.: Rutgers University Press, 1988).

11. Mary Dearborn, *Love in the Promised Land: The Story of Anzia Yezierska and John Dewey* (New York: Free Press, 1988). Donald Weber, in his discussion of Dearborn's text, calls the Dewey affair a "foundational scene" as it became "the primal episode she [Yezierska] reworked over and again in her fiction." See Donald Weber, *Haunted in the New World: Jewish American Culture From Cahan to the Goldbergs* (Bloomington: Indiana University Press, 2005), 25–26.

12. See Ruth Wisse, *The Modern Jewish Canon: A Journey Through Language and Culture* (New York: Free Press, 2000), 273.

13. Weber, *Haunted in the New World*, 25.

14. Ibid.

15. See Bruno Latour, *We Have Never Been Modern* (Cambridge, Mass.: Harvard University Press, 1993), especially pp. 79–82 for his account of objects as mediators that do more than signify as they "redeploy" and "betray" meaning.

16. Stubbs, "Reading Material," 160–61. Also see Sandra Ley, *Fashion for Everyone: The Story of Ready-to-Wear 1870's–1970's* (New York: Charles Scribner's Sons, 1975).

17. On this notion of reading images as a text, I have found Roland Barthes's work the most engaging and lucid. See his essays "The Photographic Message," "Rhetoric

of the Image," and "The Third Meaning" in Roland Barthes, *Image, Music, Text* (New York: Hill and Wang, 1977), 15–68.

18. Stubbs, "Reading Material," 157.

19. See, for example, Christopher Okonkwo, "Of Repression, Assertion, and the Speakerly Dress: Anzia Yezierska's *Salome of the Tenements*," *MELUS* 25, no. 1 (2000): 129–45.

20. Stubbs, "Reading Material," 159.

21. For helpful reflections on the differences between reading and seeing things, see Foucault, *This Is Not a Pipe*.

22. Anzia Yezierska, "Wings," in *How I Found America: Collected Stories of Anzia Yezierska* (New York: Persia Books, 1991), 3–16.

23. Ibid., 4.

24. See Jenna Weissman Joselit, "Mirror, Mirror on the Wall: Clothing, Identity, and the Modern Jewish Experience," 107–22, especially pp. 108–14 on her discussion of reading clothing as a sign of Emancipation and "the viability of modernization itself."

25. Anzia Yezierska, "Soap and Water," in *How I Found America*, 71.

26. On the social and cultural meanings of cleanliness during this period, see Joselit, "A Set Table," 21–76, especially pp. 25–27.

27. Yezierska, "Soap and Water," 72–73.

28. Ibid., 74.

29. Ibid., 75.

30. Ibid., 72.

31. Yezierska, *Bread Givers*, 241. Note the very similar description that Yezierska offers of her new apartment after she returned from Hollywood in her semi-autobiographical *Red Ribbon on a White Horse*: "I looked about my living room flooded with sunshine. For once I had treated myself to the fine expensive things I had always wanted. I had spent a lot of time and money choosing the furnishings that had transformed the over-stuffed hotel apartment into its present austerity. The bare, unpainted floor, scrubbed to show the grain of the wood, pale-gray walls, plain unpainted furniture: a desk, a chair, an open bookshelf, a low couch covered with monk's cloth. There was an air of coolness and aloneness about the room. Except for the flowers, it might have been a nun's cell." See Yezierska, *Red Ribbon on a White Horse*, 120.

32. See Joselit, "A Set Table," 27–28, on the "gospel of simplicity" of a sparse, well-decorated home.

33. Stubbs, "Reading Material," 158.

34. As Irving Howe once quipped, Eli "undergoes a kind of moral conversion in which he identifies or hallucinates himself as a victim in kaftan." See Irving Howe, "Philip Roth Reconsidered," *Commentary* 54, no. 6 (1972): 69–77, especially p. 71.

35. Philip Roth, "Eli, the Fanatic," *Commentary* 27, no. 4 (1959): 292–309; and Philip Roth, *Goodbye, Columbus* (New York: Vintage Books, 1959), 249–98. All citations of "Eli, the Fanatic" will be from the *Goodbye, Columbus* collection. For a glance at the initial critical reception of Roth's book, together with Roth's own response, see "Letters from Readers," *Commentary* 37, no. 4: 6–16, and Roth's reply, 16–19; and Philip Roth, "Writing about Jews," *Commentary* 36, no. 6: 446–52 (reprinted in Philip Roth, *Reading Myself and Others* [New York: Vintage Books, 2001], 193–211).

36. Roth, "Eli, the Fanatic," 276–77.

37. Ibid., 298.

38. Hana Wirth-Nesher, "Resisting Allegory, or Reading 'Eli, the Fanatic' in Tel Aviv," *Prooftexts* 21, no. 1 (2001): 103–112, especially p. 105.

39. As a professor at Lafayette College, Wirth-Nesher located the symbolic import of Eli's act in the "crossing over to the side of collective memory and responsibility," and as "an allegory about the perils of assimilation, about the moral price paid for turning one's back on one's heritage." But as a professor at Tel Aviv University, and a liberal Jew in the midst of a far less pluralistic society, she discovers something else: together with her students, she is disturbed by Eli's identification with an Orthodox Holocaust survivor as the ideal representative of Jewish tradition. See Wirth-Nesher, "Resisting Allegory, or Reading 'Eli, the Fanatic' in Tel Aviv," 106–107.

40. Ibid., 112.

41. Sol Gittleman, "The Pecks of Woodenton, Long Island, Thirty Years Later: Another Look at 'Eli, the Fanatic'," *Studies in American Jewish Literature* 8, no. 1 (1989): 138–42.

42. Roth, "Eli, the Fanatic," 295.

43. Ibid., 249–53.

44. Ibid., 253.

45. Ibid., 258.

46. Ibid., 254, 259–61.

47. Ibid., 262–64.

48. Ibid., 265.

49. Ibid., 259–61, 271.

50. Ibid., 271.

51. Ibid., 272–73.

52. Ibid., 282–83.

53. See Wirth-Nesher, "Resisting Allegory," 105.

54. Roth, "Eli, the Fanatic," 285.

55. Ibid., 285.

56. Ibid., 285–86.

57. Ibid., 290.

58. Ibid., 292–93.

59. Ibid., 297–98.

60. Philip Roth, *Patrimony* (New York: Simon and Schuster, 1991).

61. Ibid., 172.

62. Ibid., 176.

63. See Elisa New, "Cynthia Ozick's Timing," *Prooftexts* 9, no. 3 (1989): 288–94, where she states that "for the believer in the idea of a Jewish-American literature, Ozick comes as if to lead us out of Philip Roth's suburban Egypt" (288). Also see Ruth Wisse, "American Jewish Writing, Act II," *Commentary* 61, no. 6 (1976): 40–45, reprinted as Ruth Wisse, "Ozick as American Jewish Writer," in *Cynthia Ozick,* ed. Harold Bloom (New York: Chelsea House Publishers, 1986), 35–45.

64. Wisse, "American Jewish Writing," 43.

65. New, "Cynthia Ozick's Timing," 293.

66. See Cynthia Ozick, "America: Toward Yavneh," *Judaism* 19, no. 3 (1970): 264–82, especially p. 279. Ozick originally delivered this essay as a lecture at the Weizmann

Institute in Israel at the 8th Annual American-Israeli Dialogue on Culture in the Arts in 1970.

67. Cynthia Ozick, "Judaism & Harold Bloom," *Commentary* 67, no. 1 (1979): 43–51, especially pp. 46 and 50. For Bloom's mild response, see his "Introduction" in *Cynthia Ozick*, 1–7, where he believes Ozick is "all the stronger writer for being so self-deceived a reader, including a misreader of the fictions of Cynthia Ozick" (5). Also see Erella Brown, "The Ozick–Bloom Controversy: Anxiety of Influence, Usurpation as Idolatry, and the Identity of Jewish American Literature," *Studies in American Jewish Literature* 11, no. 1 (1992): 62–82; and Timothy Parrish, "Creation's Covenant: The Art of Cynthia Ozick," *Texas Studies in Literature and Language* 43, no. 4 (2001): 440–64.

68. Ozick, "Judaism & Harold Bloom," 51.

69. New, "Cynthia Ozick's Timing," 289.

70. Cynthia Ozick, "Envy; Or, Yiddish in America: A Novella," *Commentary* 48, no. 5 (1969): 33–53.

71. Cynthia Ozick, "Envy; or, Yiddish in America," in *The Pagan Rabbi and Other Stories* (Syracuse, N.Y.: Syracuse University Press, 1971), 39–100. All future citations from "Envy; or, Yiddish in America" will be cited from this volume.

72. According to Sarah Cohen, Ozick originally entitled her story "Yiddish in America," but Norman Podhoretz, editor of *Commentary*, later gave it the title "Envy." See Sarah Blacher Cohen, *Cynthia Ozick's Comic Art: From Levity to Liturgy* (Bloomington: Indiana University Press, 1994), 62. For a helpful summary of Ozick's story, see Elaine Kauvar, *Cynthia Ozick's Fiction: Tradition and Invention* (Bloomington: Indiana University Press, 1993), 53–58.

73. Ozick, "Envy," 47.

74. Cynthia Ozick, "A Bintel Brief for Jacob Glatstein," *Jewish Heritage* 14, no. 1 (1972): 58–60, especially p. 60. For the view that, despite Ozick's insistence, *Envy* portrays a Yiddish that is "parochial, simplistic and sentimental," see Leah Garrett, "Cynthia Ozick's *Envy*: A Reconsideration," *Studies in American Jewish Literature* 24 (2005): 60–81.

75. Ozick, "A Bintel Brief for Jacob Glatstein," 60.

76. Kauvar, *Cynthia Ozick's Fiction*, 58–62, especially p. 60.

77. See Joseph Lowin, *Cynthia Ozick* (Boston: Twayne Publishers, 1988), 22–24; and Cohen, *Cynthia Ozick's Comic Art*, 54.

78. Ozick, "Envy," 47 and 69.

79. Cynthia Ozick, "Four Questions of the Rabbis," *Reconstructionist* 38, no. 1 (1972): 20–23, especially p. 23. Also see Deborah Heiligman Weiner, "Cynthia Ozick, Pagan vs. Jew (1966–1976)," in *Studies in American Jewish Literature: Number 3*, ed. Daniel Walden (Albany: State University of New York Press, 1983), 179–93.

80. Ozick, "America: Toward Yavneh," 282.

81. Jeffrey Shandler, *Adventures in Yiddishland: Postvernacular Language and Culture* (Berkeley: University of California Press, 2006), 4, 22, 114–16.

82. See Sanford Pinsker, "Jewish Tradition and the Individual Talent," in *Cynthia Ozick*, ed. Harold Bloom, 121–25, especially p. 124.

83. Ozick, "Envy," 74.

84. Ibid., 42.

85. See Cohen, *Cynthia Ozick's Comic Art,* 56: "Kissing him [the boy Alexei] and dreaming about him through the years were not signs of Edelshtein's latent pederasty, but of his attempt to embrace the Western Civilization chosen for Alexei."

86. Ozick, "Envy," 81.

87. Ibid., 42.

88. Ibid., 68–69.

89. Ibid., 93.

90. Ibid., 73–75.

91. Ibid., 79–80.

92. Ibid., 65.

93. Ibid., 81.

94. See Cohen, *Cynthia Ozick's Comic Art,* 58: "We are not to side with Hannah, however. Her devotion to the worldly Ostrover, who speaks for humanity, and her scorn of the ghetto poet, who speaks for Jews, shows the limitations of American-born Jewish youth who would readily sacrifice the parochial for the universal and in so doing lose their distinctiveness." Also see Janet Cooper, "Triangles of History and the Slippery Slope of Jewish American Identity in Two Stories by Cynthia Ozick," *MELUS* 25, no. 1 (2000): 181–95, especially pp. 192–93.

95. See Kauvar, *Cynthia Ozick's Fiction,* 40 and 62, where Kauvar explains her interest in the "dialectical structure" of Ozick's work, especially as it relates to the themes of her first novel, *Trust.*

96. Ozick, "Envy," 94.

97. Ibid.

98. Ibid., 95.

99. Ibid., 96.

100. Ibid., 100.

101. Ibid., 48–55: "Who makes the language Ostrover is famous for? You ask: what has persuaded *them* that he's a 'so-called modern'? . . . When I fight for five hours to make Ostrover say 'big' instead of 'gargantuan,' when I take out all the nice homey commas he sprinkles like a fool, when I drink his wife's stupid tea and then go home with a watery belly—*then* he's being turned into a 'modern,' you see? I'm the one" (55).

102. Ibid., 83.

103. Ibid., 56.

104. Ibid., 42–43.

105. Cohen, *Cynthia Ozick's Comic Art,* 50.

106. Ozick, "Envy," 55.

107. See, among the many works on Ozick and the Holocaust, Hana Wirth-Nesher, "The Languages of Memory: Cynthia Ozick's *The Shawl,*" in *Multilingual America,* ed. Werner Sollors (New York: New York University Press, 1998), 313–26; Joseph Al-kana, "'Do We Know the Meaning of Aesthetic Gratification?': Cynthia Ozick's *the Shawl,* the Akedah, and the Ethics of Holocaust Literary Aesthetics," *Modern Fiction Studies* 43, no. 4 (1997): 963–90; and Cynthia Ozick, *The Shawl* (New York: Vintage Books, 1980).

108. Ozick, "Envy," 68–69.

109. Ozick has written extensively on the notion of idols and aesthetics. See Ozick, "America: Toward Yavneh," 264–82; Ozick, "Response to Alan Mintz's 'Is Our Schizo-

phrenia Historically Important?,'" *Response* 6, no. 3 (1972): 87–93; Ozick, "The Riddle of the Ordinary," *Moment* 1, no. 2 (1975): 55–59; Ozick, "Judaism & Harold Bloom," 43–51, especially pp. 47–48 for her four-part definition of an idol; Weiner, "Cynthia Ozick, Pagan vs. Jew," 179–193; New, "Cynthia Ozick's Timing," 288–94; Brown, "The Ozick-Bloom Controversy," 62–82; Parrish, "Creation's Covenant," 440–64; Elaine Kauvar, "Courier for the Past: Cynthia Ozick and Photography," *Studies in American Jewish Literature* 6 (1987): 129–46; and Kauvar, "The Dread of Moloch: Idolatry as Metaphor in Cynthia Ozick's Fiction," *Studies in American Jewish Literature* 6 (1987): 111–28.

110. Ozick, "Envy," 47 and 95.

111. Ozick, "Response to Alan Mintz's 'Is Our Schizophrenia Historically Important,'" 91; also see Weiner, "Cynthia Ozick, Pagan vs. Jew," 183–84.

112. Ozick, "Envy," 43, 91, 95.

113. Ibid., 92–93.

114. Ibid., 94–96. Hannah: "I didn't go looking for it"; Edelshtein: "I didn't ask to be born into Yiddish. It came to me."

115. Ibid., 97.

116. Ibid., 97–98.

117. Ibid., 98–99.

118. Ibid., 79.

119. Ibid., 82.

120. Ibid., 86.

121. Ibid., 51.

122. Ibid., 94.

123. See Alfred Kazin, "Review of Bernard Malamud, *The Assistant*," *Commentary* 24, no. 1 (1957): 89–92, especially p. 90.

124. Ibid., 90.

125. See, for example, Evelyn Avery, "Pictures of Malamud," *Studies in American Jewish Literature* 7, no. 2 (1988): 224–32; Marcia Gealy, "Malamud's Short Stories: A Reshaping of Hasidic Tradition," *Judaism* 28, no. 1 (1979): 51–61; David Hirsch, "Jewish Identity and Jewish Suffering in Bellow, Malamud and Philip Roth," *Jewish Book Annual* 29 (1971): 12–22; and David Mesher, "Malamud's Jewish Metaphors," *Judaism* 26, no. 101 (1977): 18–26.

126. See Yolanda Ohana, "An Interview with Bernard Malamud: A Remembrance," *Studies in American Jewish Literature* 14 (1995): 64–71, especially p. 64.

127. Robert Alter, "Malamud as Jewish Writer," *Commentary* 42, no. 3 (1966): 71–76. For notions of confinement and "compression," see Sanford Pinsker, "Cityscape as Moral Fable: The Place of Jewish History and American Social Realism in Bernard Malamud's Imagination," *Studies in American Jewish Literature* 14 (1995): 28–38.

128. Bernard Malamud, "Take Pity," in *The Magic Barrel* (New York: Pocket Books, 1972), 82.

129. Ibid., 90.

130. See Pinsker, "Cityscape as Moral Fable," 32–33.

131. Bernard Malamud, "The First Seven Years," in *The Magic Barrel*, 13–24, especially pp. 13, 17, and 24.

132. Bernard Malamud, "The Maid's Shoes," in *Idiots First* (New York: Dell Publishing Co., 1966), 139–54, especially pp. 146 and 154.

133. Bernard Malamud, "Rembrandt's Hat," in *Rembrandt's Hat* (New York: Farrar, Straus and Giroux, 1973), 127–41, especially pp. 127–29 and 140–41.

134. See, for example, Victoria Aarons, "Malamud's Gatekeepers: The 'Law' and Moral Reckoning," *Studies in American Jewish Literature* 18 (1999): 5–10; and Josephine Knopp, "The Ways of Mentshlekhayt: A Study of Morality in Some Fiction of Bernard Malamud and Philip Roth," *Tradition* 13, no. 3 (1973): 67–84; Bonnie Lyons, "The Female Characters in Bernard Malamud's Stories," *Studies in American Jewish Literature* 17 (1998): 129–36.

135. Herbert Mann, "The Malamudian World: Method and Meaning," *Studies in American Jewish Literature* 4, no. 1 (1978): 2–12, especially p. 11.

136. Bernard Malamud, "The Last Mohican," in *The Magic Barrel*, 145.

137. See Lyons, "The Female Characters in Bernard Malamud's Stories," 129: "Many of the stories are about the interplay between two central characters and how often the pattern is a quest. Character A literally or figuratively pursues Character B, Character B subsequently pursues Character A—Fidelman and Susskind in 'The Last Mohican,' Ginzburg and Mendel in 'Idiots First,' Leo and Salzman in 'The Magic Barrel.'"

138. Malamud, "The Last Mohican," 165.

139. Ibid., 155–56.

140. Ibid., 160.

141. See "Still Life" and "Naked Nude" in *Idiots First,* as well as Bernard Malamud, *Pictures of Fidelman* (New York: Farrar, Straus and Giroux, 1969).

142. See, for example, "Still Life" in *Idiots First* and Steven Rubin, "Malamud and the Theme of Love and Sex," *Studies in American Jewish Literature* 4, no. 1 (1978): 19–23.

143. Malamud, "The Last Mohican," 164.

144. Ibid., 148.

145. Ibid., 145.

146. Malamud, "The Magic Barrel," in *The Magic Barrel*, 174.

147. Ibid., 176–79, 183. Also see Timothy Parrish, "Women in the Fiction of Bernard Malamud: Springboards for Male Self-Transformation?" *Studies in American Jewish Literature* 16 (1997): 103–114, especially pp. 107–110 for Parish's discussion of "The Magic Barrel." For a more critical appraisal of Malamud's depiction of female characters, see Chiara Briganti, "Mirrors, Windows and Peeping Toms: Women as the Object of Voyeuristic Scrutiny in Bernard Malamud's *A New Life* and *Dubin's Lives,*" *Studies in American Jewish Literature* 3 (1983): 151–65.

148. Malamud, "The Magic Barrel," 187.

149. Ibid., 184.

150. Ibid., 188.

151. Ibid., 192. Also see Pinsker, "Cityscape as Moral Fable," 33, for his reading of the final scene in "The Magic Barrel."

152. Mann, "The Malamudian World: Method and Meaning," 11.

153. See Lyons, "The Female Characters in Bernard Malamud's Stories," 129.

154. Ruth Wisse offers a very different reading of Malamud. She believes his characters "now seem to function as symbolic apparitions in the real America," and they

"dissolve into a fiction of enchantment or anonymity." See Wisse, *The Modern Jewish Canon*, 292.

155. For a sophisticated reading of *The Shawl*, together with its companion piece, *Rosa*, see Wirth-Nesher, "The Languages of Memory: Cynthia Ozick's *The Shawl*."

156. Ozick, *The Shawl*, 4–6, 10.

6. The Material Gaze

1. Philip Roth, "Imagining Jews," *The New York Review of Books*, September 29, 1974. All citations are taken from Philip Roth, "Imagining Jews," in *Reading Myself and Others* (New York: Vintage Books, 2001), 251–80.

2. Roth, "Imagining Jews," in *Reading Myself and Others*, 258.

3. Ozick, "Envy," 47.

4. Roth, "Imagining Jews," 260–66.

5. Ibid., 277–79.

6. See Andrew Furman, "Imagining Jews, Imagining Gentiles: A New Look at Saul Bellow's *The Victim* and Bernard Malamud's *The Assistant*," *Studies in American Jewish Literature* 16 (1997): 93–102, especially p. 93.

7. Roth, "Imagining Jews," 279.

8. Morgan, *The Sacred Gaze*, 3.

9. Talal Asad, *Genealogies of Religion: Discipline and Reasons of Power in Christianity and Islam* (Baltimore, Md.: Johns Hopkins University Press, 1993), 62.

10. Morgan, *The Sacred Gaze*, 4.

11. Morgan, *Visual Piety*, 205.

12. Morgan, *The Sacred Gaze*, 29.

13. W. J. T. Mitchell's work in this area is important, for he insightfully reveals the insecure and open-ended process of looking. See W. J. T. Mitchell, *Iconology: Image, Text, Ideology* (Chicago: University of Chicago Press, 1986); and Mitchell, *Picture Theory* (Chicago: University of Chicago Press, 1994), especially the opening methodological section. For influential notions of the gaze, see the introduction to this book, n. 12.

14. See Asad, *Genealogies of Religion*, especially the first chapter, "The Construction of Religion as an Anthropological Category," pp. 27–54.

15. Barbara Kirshenblatt-Gimblett, "Theorizing Heritage," *Ethnomusicology: Journal of the Society for Ethnomusicology* 39, no. 3 (1995): 367–80, especially p. 370.

16. See Jacobson, *Roots Too*, 317. Jacobson's fascinating study of white ethnic revival focuses on how the twentieth-century "white" person claimed an immigrant heritage with roots from Ellis Island rather than Plymouth Rock. This "ethnic disavowal of whiteness" denoted "relatively recent arrival, underdog credentials, and innocence in white supremacy's history of conquest and enslavement" (317).

17. Mark Slobin, *Fiddler on the Move: Exploring the Klezmer World* (Oxford: Oxford University Press, 2000), 13.

18. Susan Weidman Schneider, "From the Editors," *Lilith* 1, no. 1 (Fall 1976): 3.

19. Aviva Cantor Zuckoff, "The Lilith Question," *Lilith* 1, no. 1 (Fall 1976): 5–10, 38.

20. *Lilith* 1, no. 1 (Fall 1976).

21. Prell, *Fighting to Become Americans*, 201–203.

22. Weidman Schneider, "From the Editors," 3.

23. Weidman Schneider, "From the Editor," *Lilith* 28, no. 1 (Spring 2003): 2.

24. See Ellen Umansky, "Jewish Women in the Twentieth-Century U.S.," in *Jewish Women in Historical Perspective,* ed. Judith Baskin (Detroit, Mich.: Wayne State University Press, 1991), 265–88.

25. Susan Weidman Schneider, "Lilith Looks Back," *Lilith* 19, no. 3 (Fall 1994): 16.

26. Susan Weidman Schneider emphasized this point to me in our telephone conversation in May 2007. Anecdotally, I told Susan that both my wife and mother have saved every cover since the beginning of their subscriptions.

27. I want to thank Mara Benjamin for noting this at my talk, "Visualizing Heritage: The Pictorial Covers of *Lilith* Magazine," *Association for Jewish Studies,* Toronto, Canada: December 16, 2007.

28. Amy Stone, "Struggling? Juggling? Trying to Integrate our Multiple Roles," *Lilith* 19 (Spring 1988): 6.

29. I want to thank Ellen Umansky for this suggestion at my talk, "Visualizing Heritage."

30. Stone, "Struggling? Juggling? Trying to Integrate our Multiple Roles," 7.

31. Steven Cohen and Arnold Eisen, *The Jew Within: Self, Family, and Community in America* (Bloomington: Indiana University Press, 2000).

32. See Jacobson, *Roots Too,* 11–71.

33. *Lilith* 23, no. 2 (Summer 1998).

34. See Kirshenblatt-Gimblett, *Destination Culture.*

35. Carolyn Feibel, "How Museums Invent Us," *Lilith* 23, no. 4 (Winter 1998–99): 26. For background into the increased popularity of Chanukah celebrations, see Joselit, "A Set Table," 21–76, especially pp. 61–63.

36. Feibel, "How Museums Invent Us," 26–27.

37. Ibid., 27–28.

38. Ibid., 29.

39. Ibid., 28.

40. Susan Schnur, "From Prehistoric Cave Art to Your Cookie Pan: Tracing the Hamantasch Herstory," *Lilith* 23, no. 1 (Spring 1998): 22–24.

41. See *Lilith* 17 (Fall 1987); and Prell, *Fighting to Become Americans,* 179.

42. Kirshenblatt-Gimblett, "Theorizing Heritage," 369.

43. William Stott, *Documentary Expression and Thirties America* (New York: Oxford University Press, 1973), 8–12, 31.

44. Ibid., 21.

45. Ibid., 12.

46. Roland Barthes, *Camera Lucida: Reflections on Photography* (New York: Hill and Wang, 1981), 84.

47. See Jay, *Downcast Eyes,* 124–47.

48. Barthes, *Camera Lucida,* 20.

49. Susan Sontag, *On Photography* (New York: Farrar, Straus and Giroux, 1973), 110.

50. Warren Susman, "The Thirties," in *The Development of an American Culture,* ed. Stanley Coben and Lorman Ratner (New York: St. Martin's Press, 1983), 215–60, especially pp. 216–17.

51. Arnold Eagle, *At Home Only with God: Believing Jews and Their Children* (New York: Aperture Foundation, 1992).

52. I appreciate the help in tracking down this information from Lauren Strauss and Deborah Dash Moore.

53. See MacDonald Moore and Deborah Dash Moore, "Observant Jews and the Photographic Arena of Looks," in *You Should See Yourself: Jewish Identity in Postmodern American Culture,* ed. Vincent Brook (New Brunswick, N.J.: Rutgers University Press, 2006), 176–204.

54. Interview by Kay Reese and Mimi Leipzig in 1990 for the *American Society of Media Photographers.* See http://web.archive.org/web/20060923050059/www.asmp .org/60th/interview_arnold_eagle.php.

55. Sontag, *On Photography,* 108.

56. Arthur Hertzberg, "Introductory Essay," in *At Home Only with God,* 8.

57. Jacobson, *Roots Too,* 58.

58. Arthur Hertzberg, *A Jew in America: My Life and a People's Struggle for Identity* (New York: HarperCollins, 2002).

59. Hertzberg, "Introductory Essay," 1.

60. Hasia R. Diner, *Lower East Side Memories* (Princeton, N.J.: Princeton University Press, 2000).

61. Hertzberg, "Introductory Essay," 1.

62. Richard Cohen, *Jewish Icons: Art and Society in Modern Europe* (Berkeley: University of California Press, 1998), 157; Steven Zipperstein, *Imagining Russian Jewry: Memory, History, Identity* (Seattle: University of Washington Press, 1999), 16–39, especially pp. 23–24 for Zipperstein's reading of Hutchins Hapgood's *The Spirit of the Ghetto* (1902).

63. Hertzberg, "Introductory Essay," 1.

64. Interview by Kay Reese and Mimi Leipzig in 1990 for the *American Society of Media Photographers.* See http://web.archive.org/web/20060923050059/www.asmp .org/60th/interview_arnold_eagle.php.

65. Sontag, *On Photography,* 10.

66. Ibid., 107.

67. Hertzberg, "Introductory Essay," 3.

68. Ibid., 8.

69. See Jay, *Downcast Eyes,* 456–91.

70. See J. Hoberman and Jeffrey Shandler, eds., *Entertaining America: Jews, Movies, and Broadcasting* (Princeton, N.J.: Princeton University Press, 2003), 15–24; and Neal Gabler, *An Empire of Their Own: How the Jews Invented Hollywood* (New York: Crown, 1988).

71. See Patricia Erens, *The Jew in American Cinema* (Bloomington: Indiana University Press, 1984), 91, 106–107. Erens calls *Abie's Irish Rose* "the definitive statement on intermarriage and assimilation" (106). Also see Prell, *Fighting to Become Americans,* 71–77.

72. Lester Friedman, *The Jewish Image in American Film* (Secaucus, N.J.: Citadel Press, 1987), 109–110.

73. Gabler, *An Empire of Their Own,* 5–6.

74. Joel Rosenberg, "Jewish Experience on Film—An American Overview," *American Jewish Year Book* 96 (1996), 3–50, especially p. 13.

75. Friedman, *The Jewish Image in American Film*, 111.

76. Erens, *The Jew in American Cinema*, 104; and also see David Desser, "The Cinematic Melting Pot: Ethnicity, Jews, and Psychoanalysis," in *Unspeakable Images: Ethnicity and the American Cinema*, ed. Lester Friedman (Urbana: University of Illinois Press, 1991), 379–403, especially p. 399 where he takes this stand on *The Jazz Singer*: "Intermarriage becomes secondary to assimilation. The Jewish man is de-Semiticized—Jakie Rabinowitz becomes Jack Robin, after all."

77. See Michael Rogin, *Blackface, White Noise: Jewish Immigrants in the Hollywood Melting Pot* (Berkeley: University of California Press, 1996); and Jeffrey Melnick, *A Right to Sing the Blues: African Americans, Jews, and American Popular Song* (Cambridge, Mass.: Harvard University Press, 1999), especially pp. 60–80.

78. Sampson Raphaelson, "The Day of Atonement," in *The Jazz Singer*, ed. Robert Carringer (Madison: University of Wisconsin Press, 1979), 147–67 (quotation from p. 147).

79. Quotation taken from Robert Carringer, *The Jazz Singer* (Madison: University of Wisconsin Press, 1979), 11.

80. Eric Lott, *Love & Theft: Blackface Minstrelsy and the American Working Class* (New York: Oxford University Press, 1993).

81. Raphaelson, "The Day of Atonement," 151.

82. Ibid., 153.

83. Ibid., 155.

84. Ibid., 157–58.

85. See Rogin, *Blackface, White Noise*, 101.

86. Lott, *Love & Theft*, 18.

87. Prell, *Fighting to Become Americans*, 56–57.

88. Melnick, *A Right to Sing the Blues*, 104–107.

89. Raphaelson, "The Day of Atonement," 153.

90. Ibid., 164.

91. Ibid., 166–67.

92. This last scene is missing in the screenplay. It ends with Jack's father fading in the background "as he slowly raises his hand in a blessing." See Carringer, *The Jazz Singer*, 133.

93. Gabler, *An Empire of Their Own*, 5–7.

94. See W. T. Lhamon Jr., *Raising Cain: Blackface Performance from Jim Crow to Hip Hop* (Cambridge, Mass.: Harvard University Press, 1998), 102–115, and his discussion of strategic readings of assimilation of *The Jazz Singer*. Although Lhamon criticizes interpretations that replace "ethnicity or Jewishness with whiteness," he still defends a reading of "continual transactions of assimilation" (107).

95. Joel Rosenberg, "What You Ain't Heard Yet: The Languages of *The Jazz Singer*," *Prooftexts* 22 (2002): 11–54, especially p. 45, where Rosenberg describes the "core strategy of the film's form" as a "polyphony of opaque Jewish languages and mutually incomprehensible life choices," and notes how the film "captures the irreconcilabilities of American Jewish life and a particular dialectic of tradition and modernity." Note, too, Rosenberg's counter-reading to the "Mammy" scene, in which Jack "seems trapped" rather than fully assimilated (p. 43). Also see Joel Rosenberg, "Jewish Experience on Film," 21.

96. Carringer, *The Jazz Singer*, 20–21.

97. Ibid., 120. Also see Rosenberg, "What You Ain't Heard Yet," 42.

98. Lott, *Love & Theft*, 20.

99. Matthew Frye Jacobson, *Whiteness of a Different Color: European Immigrants and the Alchemy of Race* (Cambridge, Mass.: Harvard University Press, 1998), 121.

100. Carringer, *The Jazz Singer*, 133.

101. See Prell, *Fighting to Become Americans*, 169–72; and Hoberman and Shandler, eds., *Entertaining America*, 113–22.

102. See Jeffrey Shandler, *Jews, God, and Videotape: Religion and Media in America* (New York: New York University Press, 2009), 43.

103. Prell, *Fighting to Become Americans*, 142–76.

104. For background to the perceived feminization of culture, and the fears associated with it, see Ann Douglas, *The Feminization of American Culture*.

105. Prell, *Fighting to Become Americans*, 151–57, 171–74.

106. See Krin Gabbard, *Jammin' at the Margins: Jazz and the American Cinema* (Chicago: University of Chicago Press, 1996), 48, where she claims that "even the problem of intermarriage is solved by having Peggy Lee, Danny Thomas's love interest, drop a line about attending a seder to hint that she too may be Jewish." Stephen Whitfield has uncovered the background to this "drop." He argues that "studio executives were persuaded by a resourceful rabbi that the subject of intermarriage did not belong in so uplifting a film. Peggy Lee's character therefore was made into a Jew by inserting a line about not having attended a seder since she left home." See Stephen Whitfield, *Voices of Jacob, Hands of Esau: Jews in American Life and Thought* (Hamden, Conn.: Archon Books, 1984), 162–63.

107. See Whitfield, *Voices of Jacob, Hands of Esau*, 159–79.

108. See J. Hoberman, "Is 'The Jazz Singer' Good for the Jews?" *The Village Voice* 26, no. 2 (1981): 1–33; also Joel Rosenberg, "Jewish Experience on Film," 34–35.

109. Jacobson, *Roots Too*, 56.

110. Ibid., 56–57, 325. Also see Freedman, *Klezmer America*, 13–15.

111. See www.sing365.com/music/lyric.nsf/America-lyrics-Neil-Diamond/1FDC2C80119D090A4825696900168500.

112. Jacobson, *Roots Too*, 9.

113. Quotation from Prell, *Fighting to Become Americans*, 159. See Albert Gordon, *Jews in Suburbia* (Boston: Beacon Press, 1959), 170.

114. Leigh Eric Schmidt, *Hearing Things: Religion, Illusion, and the American Enlightenment* (Cambridge, Mass.: Harvard University Press, 2000).

115. See www.HaSoferet.com.

116. Joselit, *The Wonders of America*, 83–84.

117. Freedman, *Klezmer America*, 138.

118. Richard Siegel, Michael Strassfeld, and Sharon Strassfeld, eds., *The First Jewish Catalog: A Do-It-Yourself Kit* (Philadelphia: The Jewish Publication Society of America, 1973).

Conclusion

1. See the collection of essays in *Insider/Outsider: American Jews and Multiculturalism*, ed. David Biale, Michael Galchinsky, and Susannah Heschel (Berkeley: University of California Press, 1998), and especially David Biale, "The Melting Pot and

Beyond: Jews and the Politics of American Identity," 17–33; also Freedman, *Klezmer America,* 22, where Freedman has this to say: "It is this latter aspect of the klezmer and postklezmer phenomenon that I'm invoking here as an organizing trope: a tradition of dynamic innovation wrought in the encounter between Jewish and gentile cultures that has the property of reanimating both, creating in this interplay new configurations of ethnic belonging, new aesthetic forms in which to express them, and ultimately new vessels for delineating and interrogating the experience of a multiracial, multiethnic modernity at large."

2. Freedman, *Klezmer America,* 35.

3. Scult, *Communings of the Spirit,* 256.

4. Ibid., 370.

5. Lowenthal, *The Past Is a Foreign Country,* 114.

6. Bernays, *Crystallizing Public Opinion,* 122.

7. Liebman, *Peace of Mind,* 6, 11.

8. Ibid., 37.

9. Erich Fromm, *Escape from Freedom,* 34.

10. Fromm, *The Art of Loving,* 47; Fromm, *You Shall Be as Gods,* 14.

11. Lowenthal, *The Past Is a Foreign Country,* 105–124.

12. See, for example, Lawrence Kaplan, "Models of the Ideal Religious Man in Rabbi Soloveitchik's Thought," 337–39.

13. Heschel, *The Sabbath,* 91.

14. Ibid., 5.

15. See Heschel, *The Earth Is the Lord's,* 14.

16. Roth, *Patrimony,* 176.

17. Roth, "Eli, the Fanatic," 264.

18. "Yiddish! Choose death or death. Which is to say death through forgetting or death through translation." See Ozick, "Envy," 74.

19. Malamud, "Take Pity," 90.

BIBLIOGRAPHY

Aaron, Victoria. "Malamud's Gatekeepers: The 'Law' and Moral Reckoning." *Studies in American Jewish Literature* 18 (1999): 5–10.

Adler, Morris, et al. "Responsum on the Sabbath." *Proceedings of the Rabbinical Assembly of America* 14 (1950): 112–37.

Alkana, Joseph. "'Do We Know the Meaning of Aesthetic Gratification?': Cynthia Ozick's *The Shawl*, the Akedah, and the Ethics of Holocaust Literary Aesthetics." *Modern Fiction Studies* 43, no. 4 (1997): 963–90.

Alter, Robert. "Malamud as Jewish Writer." *Commentary* 42, no. 3 (1966): 71–76.

Ames, Kenneth. "Material Culture as Non Verbal Communication: A Historical Case Study." *Journal of American Culture* 3 (1980): 619–41.

———. "Meaning in Artifacts: Hall Furnishings in Victorian America." *Journal of Interdisciplinary History* 9, no. 1 (1978): 19–46.

Arweck, Elisabeth, and William Keenen, eds. *Materializing Religion: Expression, Performance and Ritual.* Hampshire, England: Ashgate, 2006.

Asad, Talal. *Genealogies of Religion: Discipline and Reasons of Power in Christianity and Islam.* Baltimore, Md.: Johns Hopkins University Press, 1993.

Avery, Evelyn. "Pictures of Malamud." *Studies in American Jewish Literature* 7, no. 2 (1988): 224–32.

Barthes, Roland. *Camera Lucinda: Reflections on Photography.* New York: Hill and Wang, 1981.

———. *Image, Music, Text.* New York: Hill and Wang, 1977.

Batnitzky, Leora. *Leo Strauss and Emmanuel Levinas: Philosophy and the Politics of Revelation.* Cambridge: Cambridge University Press, 2006.

Bederman, Gail. *Manliness & Civilization: A Cultural History of Gender and Race in the United States, 1880–1917.* Chicago: University of Chicago Press, 1995.

Benjamin, Walter. "The Work of Art in the Age of Mechanical Reproduction." In *Illuminations*, ed. Hannah Arendt. New York: Schocken Books, 1968.

Berkovits, Eliezer. *Major Themes in Modern Philosophies of Judaism.* New York: Ktav Publishing House, 1974.

Bernays, Edward. *Biography of an Idea: Memoirs of Public Relations Counsel.* New York: Simon and Schuster, 1965.

———. *Crystallizing Public Opinion*. New York: Boni and Liveright, 1923.

———. *Propaganda*. New York: Ig Publishing, 1928.

———. *Public Relations*. Norman: University of Oklahoma Press, 1952.

Biale, David. *Gershom Scholem: Kabbalah and Counter-History*. Cambridge, Mass.: Harvard University Press, 1979.

———, Michael Galchinsky, and Susannah Heschel, eds. *Insider/Outsider: American Jews and Multiculturalism*. Berkeley: University of California Press, 1998.

Bland, Kalman. *The Artless Jew: Medieval and Modern Affirmations and Denials of the Visual*. Princeton, N.J.: Princeton University Press, 2000.

Bloom, Harold. *The Anxiety of Influence: A Theory of Poetry*. New York: Oxford University Press, 1973.

———. *Cynthia Ozick*. New York: Chelsea House Publishers, 1986.

Borowitz, Eugene. "The Typological Theology of Rabbi Joseph B. Soloveitchik." *Judaism* 15, no. 2 (1966): 203–210.

Braiterman, Zachary. "Joseph Soloveitchik and Immanuel Kant's Mitzvah-Aesthetic." *AJS Review* 25, no. 1 (2000–2001): 1–24.

———. *The Shape of Revelation: Aesthetics and Modern Jewish Thought*. Stanford, Calif.: Stanford University Press, 2007.

Briganti, Chiara. "Mirrors, Windows and Peeping Toms: Women as the Object of Voyeuristic Scrutiny in Bernard Malamud's *A New Life* and *Dubin's Lives*." *Studies in American Jewish Literature* 3 (1983): 151–65.

Brown, Bill. "The Tyranny of Things (Trivia in Karl Marx and Mark Twain)." *Critical Inquiry* 28, no. 2 (2002): 442–69.

Brown, Erella. "The Ozick–Bloom Controversy: Anxiety of Influence, Usurpation as Idolatry, and the Identity of Jewish American Literature." *Studies in American Jewish Literature* 11, no. 1 (1992): 62–82.

Brumberg, Joan Jacobs. "The 'Me' of Me: Voices of Jewish Girls in Adolescent Diaries of the 1920s and 1950s." In *Talking Back: Images of Jewish Women in American Popular Culture*, ed. Joyce Antler. Hanover, N.H.: University Press of New England, 1998, 53–67.

Butler, Jon. "Three Minds, Three Books, Three Years: Reinhold Niebuhr, Perry Miller, and Mordecai Kaplan on Religion." *Jewish Social Studies* 12, no. 2 (2006): 17–29.

Carringer, Robert. *The Jazz Singer*. Madison: University of Wisconsin Press, 1979.

Cohen, Richard. *Jewish Icons: Art and Society in Modern Europe*. Berkeley: University of California Press, 1998.

Cohen, Sarah Blacher. *Cynthia Ozick's Comic Art: From Levity to Liturgy*. Bloomington: Indiana University Press, 1994.

Cohen, Steven, and Arnold Eisen. *The Jew Within: Self, Family and Community in America*. Bloomington: Indiana University Press, 2000.

Cooper, Janet. "Triangles of History and the Slippery Slope of Jewish American Identity in Two Stories by Cynthia Ozick." *MELUS* 25, no. 1 (2000): 181–95.

Cripps, Thomas, ed. *The Green Pastures*. Madison: University of Wisconsin Press, 1979.

Dearborn, Mary. *Love in the Promised Land: The Story of Anzia Yezierska and John Dewey*. New York: Free Press, 1988.

Derrida, Jacques. *Archive Fever*. Chicago: University of Chicago Press, 1995.

———. *Of Grammatology*. Baltimore, Md.: Johns Hopkins University Press, 1974.

———. *Writing and Difference*. Chicago: University of Chicago Press, 1978.

Desser, David. "The Cinematic Melting Pot: Ethnicity, Jews, and Psychoanalysis." In *Unspeakable Images: Ethnicity and the American Cinema*, ed. Lester Friedman. Urbana: University of Illinois Press, 1991, 379–403.

Diamond, Etan. *And I Will Dwell in Their Midst: Orthodox Jews in Suburbia*. Chapel Hill: University of North Carolina Press, 2000.

Diamond, Neil. www.sing365.com/music/lyric.nsf/America-lyrics-Neil-Diamond/1FDC 2C80119D090A4825696900168500 (accessed July, 2009).

Diner, Hasia R. *Lower East Side Memories*. Princeton, N.J.: Princeton University Press, 2000.

Dorff, Elliot. "Halakhic Man: A Review Essay." *Modern Judaism* 6, no. 1 (1986): 91–98.

———. *The Unfolding Tradition: Jewish Law after Sinai*. New York: Aviv Press, 2005.

Douglas, Ann. *The Feminization of American Culture*. New York: Alfred A. Knopf, 1977.

———. *Terrible Honesty: Mongrel Manhattan in the 1920s*. New York: Farrar, Straus and Giroux, 1995.

Eagle, Arnold. *At Home Only with God: Believing Jews and Their Children*. New York: Aperture Foundation, 1992.

Eisen, Arnold. "Re-Reading Heschel on the Commandments." *Modern Judaism* 9, no. 1 (1989): 1–33.

Eisen, Robert. "A. J. Heschel's Rabbinic Theology as a Response to the Holocaust." *Modern Judaism* 23, no. 3 (2003): 211–25.

Elkins, James. *Visual Studies: A Skeptical Introduction*. New York: Routledge, 2003.

Erens, Patricia. *The Jew in American Cinema*. Bloomington: Indiana University Press, 1984.

Fackenheim, Emil. "Review of *God in Search of Man*." *Conservative Judaism* 15 (1960): 50–53.

Faierstein, Morris. "Abraham Joshua Heschel and the Holocaust." *Modern Judaism* 19, no. 3 (1999): 255–75.

Feibel, Carolyn. "How Museums Invent Us." *Lilith* 23, no. 4 (Winter 1988–99): 26–30.

Foucault, Michel. *The Order of Things*. New York: Vintage Books, 1994.

———. *This Is Not a Pipe*. Berkeley: University of California Press, 1983.

Fox, Emmet. *Power through Constructive Thinking*. New York: HarperCollins, 1989.

Freedman, Jonathan. *Klezmer America: Jewishness, Ethnicity, Modernity*. New York: Columbia University Press, 2008.

Freud, Sigmund. "A Note upon the 'Mystic Writing-Pad'." In *The Standard Edition of the Complete Psychological Works of Sigmund Freud*, ed. James Strachey. London: Hogarth Press, 1961, 227–32.

———. "Notiz Über den 'Wunderblock'." In *Gesammelte Werke*. Frankfurt am Main: S. Fischer, 1948, 3–8.

Friedman, Jen Taylor. http://HaSoferet.com (accessed July 2009).

Friedman, Lester. *The Jewish Image in American Film*. Secaucus, N.J.: Citadel Press, 1987.

Fromm, Erich. *The Art of Loving*. New York: Harper & Row, 1956.

———. *The Dogma of Christ*. New York: Holt, Rinehart and Winston, 1955.

———. *Escape from Freedom*. New York: Henry Holt and Co., 1941.

———. *The Heart of Man: Its Genius for Good and Evil.* New York: Harper & Row, 1964.

———. *Man for Himself: An Inquiry into the Psychology of Ethics.* New York: Fawcett Premier, 1947.

———. *Psychoanalysis and Religion.* New Haven, Conn.: Yale University Press, 1950.

———. *The Sane Society.* New York: Henry Holt and Co., 1955.

———. *You Shall Be as Gods: A Radical Interpretation of the Old Testament and Its Tradition.* New York: Fawcett World Library, 1966.

Fuller, Robert. *Americans and the Unconscious.* New York: Oxford University Press, 1986.

Funk, Rainer. *Erich Fromm: His Life and Ideas.* New York: Continuum, 2000.

Funkenstein, Amos. *Perceptions of Jewish History.* Berkeley: University of California Press, 1993.

Furman, Andrew. "Imagining Jews, Imagining Gentiles: A New Look At Saul Bellow's *The Victim* and Bernard Malamud's *The Assistant.*" *Studies in American Jewish Literature* 16 (1997): 93–102.

Gabbard, Krin. *Jammin' at the Margins: Jazz and the American Cinema.* Chicago: University of Chicago Press, 1996.

Gabler, Neal. *An Empire of Their Own: How the Jews Invented Hollywood.* New York: Crown, 1988.

Garrett, Leah. "Cynthia Ozick's *Envy:* A Reconsideration." *Studies in American Jewish Literature* 24 (2005): 60–81.

Gealy, Marcia. "Malamud's Short Stories: A Reshaping of Hasidic Tradition." *Judaism* 28, no. 1 (1979): 51–61.

Gilroy, Paul. *The Black Atlantic: Modernity and Double Consciousness.* Cambridge, Mass.: Harvard University Press, 1993.

Gittleman, Sol. "The Pecks of Woodenton, Long Island, Thirty Years Later: Another Look at 'Eli, the Fanatic'." *Studies in American Jewish Literature* 8, no. 1 (1989): 138–42.

Glatzer, Nahum. "Review of *the Sabbath.*" *Judaism* 1, no. 3 (1952): 283–86.

Goldstein, Eric. *The Price of Whiteness: Jews, Race, and American Identity.* Princeton, N.J.: Princeton University Press, 2006.

Gordon, Albert. *Jews in Suburbia.* Boston: Beacon Press, 1959.

Graeber, Bruce. "Heschel and the Philosophy of Time." *Conservative Judaism* 33 (Spring 1980): 44–56.

Greenberg, Betty, and Althea Silverman. *The Jewish Home Beautiful.* New York: National Women's League of the United Synagogue of America, 1941.

Greenberg, Clement. "Avant-Garde and Kitsch." In *Art and Culture: Critical Essays.* Boston: Beacon Press, 1961, 3–21.

Greenblatt, Stephen. *Renaissance Self-Fashioning.* Chicago: University of Chicago Press, 1980.

Halbertal, Moshe, and Avishai Margalit. *Idolatry.* Cambridge, Mass.: Harvard University Press, 1992.

Hale, Nathan, Jr. *The Rise and Crisis of Psychoanalysis in the United States: Freud and the Americans, 1917–1985.* New York: Oxford University Press, 1995.

Harris, Alice Kessler. "Introduction." In *Bread Givers.* New York: Persea Books, 1975.

Hartman, David. *Love and Terror in the God Encounter*. Woodstock, Vt.: Jewish Lights Publishing, 2001.

Hedstrom, Matthew S. "Seeking a Spiritual Center: Mass Market Books and Liberal Religion in America, 1921–1948." Austin: University of Texas, 2006.

Heinze, Andrew R. *Adapting to Abundance: Jewish Immigrants, Mass Consumption, and the Search for American Identity*. New York: Columbia University Press, 1990.

———. "Jews and American Popular Psychology: Reconsidering the Protestant Paradigm of Popular Thought." *Journal of American History* 88, no. 3 (2001): 950–78.

———. *Jews and the American Soul: Human Nature in the Twentieth Century*. Princeton, N.J.: Princeton University Press, 2004.

———. "Peace of Mind (1946): Judaism and the Therapeutic Polemics of Postwar America." *Religion and American Culture* 12, no. 1 (2002): 31–58.

Henriksen, Louise Levitas. *Anzia Yezierska: A Writer's Life*. New Brunswick, N.J.: Rutgers University Press, 1988.

Herberg, Will. *Protestant–Catholic–Jew: An Essay in American Religious Sociology*. Chicago: University of Chicago Press, 1955.

Hertzberg, Arthur. *A Jew in America: My Life and a People's Struggle for Identity*. New York: HarperCollins, 2002.

Heschel, Abraham Joshua. *The Earth Is the Lord's: The Inner World of the Jew in Eastern Europe*. Woodstock: Jewish Lights, 1995.

———. "From Mission to Dialogue?" *Conservative Judaism* 21, no. 3 (1967): 1–11.

———. *Heavenly Torah as Refracted through the Generations*. Trans. Gordon Tucker. New York: Continuum, 2005.

———. *Man Is Not Alone: A Philosophy of Religion*. New York: Noonday Press, 1951.

———. *The Sabbath: Its Meaning for Modern Man*. New York: Farrar, Straus and Giroux, 1951.

———. *Torah min Hashamayim ba-Aspaklaria shel Hadorot*. New York: Shontsin, 1962.

Heschel, Susannah. *Abraham Geiger and the Jewish Jesus*. Chicago: University of Chicago Press, 1998.

Higham, John. *Send These to Me: Jews and Other Immigrants in Urban America*. New York: Atheneum, 1975.

Hindus, Milton. "Review of *The Earth Is the Lord's* and *The Sabbath*." *Conservative Judaism* 20, no. 1 (1965): 69–74.

Hirsch, David. "Jewish Identity and Jewish Suffering in Bellow, Malamud and Philip Roth." *Jewish Book Annual* 29 (1971): 12–22.

Hoberman, J. "Is 'The Jazz Singer' Good for the Jews?" *Village Voice* 26, no. 2 (1981): 1–33.

Hoberman, J., and Jeffrey Shandler, eds. *Entertaining America: Jews, Movies, and Broadcasting*. Princeton, N.J.: Princeton University Press, 2003.

Holtz, Abraham. "Religion and the Arts in the Theology of Abraham Joshua Heschel." *Conservative Judaism* 28, no. 1 (1973): 27–39.

Howe, Irving. "Philip Roth Reconsidered." *Commentary* 54, no. 6 (1972): 69–77.

Ibn Paquda, R. Bachya ben Joseph. *Duties of the Heart*. Vol. I, trans. Daniel Haberman. Jerusalem and New York: Feldheim, 1996.

Jacobson, Matthew Frye. *Roots Too: White Ethnic Revival in Post-Civil Rights America.* Cambridge, Mass.: Harvard University Press, 2006.

———. *Whiteness of a Different Color: European Immigrants and the Alchemy of Race.* Cambridge, Mass.: Harvard University Press, 1998.

James, William. *The Varieties of Religious Experience.* New York: Modern Library, 1902.

Jay, Martin. *Downcast Eyes: The Denigration of Vision in Twentieth-Century French Thought.* Berkeley: University of California Press, 1993.

Jeffrey, Kirk. "The Family as Utopian Retreat from the City: The Nineteenth-Century Contribution." *Soundings* 55, no. 1 (1972): 21–41.

Joselit, Jenna Weissman. "Bezalel Comes to Town: American Jews and Art." *Jewish Studies Quarterly* 2 (2004): 354–65.

———. "The Jewish Home Beautiful." In *The American Jewish Experience,* 2nd ed., ed. Jonathan Sarna. New York: Holmes & Meier, 1997, 236–42.

———. "Mirror, Mirror on the Wall: Clothing, Identity, and the Modern Jewish Experience." In *Divergent Jewish Cultures: Israel and America,* ed. Deborah Dash Moore and S. Ilan Troen. New Haven, Conn.: Yale University Press, 2001, 107–122.

———. "'A Set Table': Jewish Domestic Culture in the New World, 1880–1950." In *Getting Comfortable in New York: The American Jewish Home, 1880–1950,* ed. Susan Braunstein and Jenna Weissman Joselit. New York: Jewish Museum, 1990, 21–76.

———. *The Wonders of America: Reinventing Jewish Culture, 1880–1950.* New York: Henry Holt and Co., 1994.

Kaplan, Cara. "On Modernism and Race." *Modernism/Modernity* 4, no. 1 (1997): 157–69.

Kaplan, Edward. *Holiness in Words: Abraham Joshua Heschel's Poetics of Piety.* Albany: State University of New York Press, 1996.

———. *Spiritual Radical: Abraham Joshua Heschel in America, 1940–1972.* New Haven, Conn.: Yale University Press, 2007.

Kaplan, Lawrence. "Models of the Ideal Religious Man in Rabbi Soloveitchik's Thought" (Hebrew). *Jerusalem Studies in Jewish Thought* 4, nos. 3–4 (1984–85): 337–39.

———. "Rabbi Joseph B. Soloveitchik's Philosophy of Halakhah." *The Jewish Law Annual* (1988): 139–97.

Kaplan, Mordecai. *Art and Ethics* (Hebrew). Jerusalem: Rubin Mass, 1954.

———. *The Future of the American Jew.* New York: Reconstructionist Press, 1967.

———. *Judaism as a Civilization: Toward a Reconstruction of American-Jewish Life.* New York: Macmillan, 1934.

———. *Questions Jews Ask.* New York: Reconstructionist Press, 1956.

Kasimow, Harold, and Byron Sherwin, eds. *No Religion Is an Island: Abraham Joshua Heschel and Interreligious Dialogue.* Maryknoll, N.Y.: Orbis Books, 1991.

Kauvar, Elaine. "Courier for the Past: Cynthia Ozick and Photography." *Studies in American Jewish Literature* 6 (1987): 129–46.

———. *Cynthia Ozick's Fiction: Tradition and Invention.* Bloomington: Indiana University Press, 1993.

——. "The Dread of Moloch: Idolatry as Metaphor in Cynthia Ozick's Fiction." *Studies in American Jewish Literature* 6 (1987): 111–28.

Kavka, Martin. *Jewish Messianism and the History of Philosophy.* Cambridge: Cambridge University Press, 2004.

Kazin, Alfred. "Review of Bernard Malamud, *The Assistant.*" *Commentary* 24, no. 1 (1957): 89–92.

Kimelman, Reuven. "Rabbis Joseph B. Soloveitchik and Abraham Joshua Heschel on Jewish–Christian Relations." *Modern Judaism* 24, no. 3 (2004): 251–71.

Kirshenblatt-Gimblett, Barbara. *Destination Culture: Tourism, Museums, and Heritage.* Berkeley: University of California Press, 1998.

——. "The Future of Folklore Studies in America: The Urban Frontier." *Folklore Forum* 16, no. 2 (1983): 175–234.

——. "Imagining Europe: The Popular Arts of American Jewish Ethnography." In *Divergent Jewish Cultures: Israel & America,* ed. Deborah Dash Moore and S. Ilan Troen. New Haven, Conn.: Yale University Press, 2001, 155–91.

——. "Kitchen Judaism." In *Getting Comfortable in New York: The American Jewish Home, 1880–1950,* ed. Susan Braunstein and Jenna Weissman Joselit. New York: Jewish Museum, 1990, 77–105.

——. "Theorizing Heritage." *Ethnomusicology: Journal of the Society for Ethnomusicology* 39, no. 3 (1995): 367–80.

Klapper, Melissa. *Jewish Girls Coming of Age in America, 1860–1920.* New York: New York University Press, 2005.

Knopp, Josephine. "The Ways of Mentshlekhayt: A Study of Morality in Some Fiction of Bernard Malamud and Philip Roth." *Tradition* 13, no. 3 (1973): 67–84.

Kramer, Michael, and Hana Wirth-Nesher, eds. *The Cambridge Companion to Jewish American Literature.* Cambridge: Cambridge University Press, 2003.

Lacan, Jacques. *The Four Fundamental Concepts of Psychoanalysis.* New York: W.W. Norton & Co., 1981.

Latour, Bruno. *We Have Never Been Modern.* Cambridge, Mass.: Harvard University Press, 1993.

Le Bon, Gustave. *The Crowd: A Study of the Popular Mind.* Mineola, N.Y.: Dover, 2002.

Levenson, Jon. *Creation and the Persistence of Evil: The Jewish Drama of Divine Omnipotence.* San Francisco: Harper & Row, 1988.

Ley, Sandra. *Fashion for Everyone: The Story of Ready-to-Wear 1870's–1970's.* New York: Charles Scribner's Sons, 1975.

Lhamon, W. T., Jr. *Raising Cain: Blackface Performance from Jim Crow to Hip Hop.* Cambridge, Mass.: Harvard University Press, 1998.

Lichtenstein, Aharon. "R. Joseph Soloveitchik." In *Great Jewish Thinkers of the Twentieth Century,* ed. Simon Noveck. Washington, D.C.: B'nai B'rith Books, 1985, 281–98.

Lichtenstein, Morris. *Peace of Mind: Jewish Science Essays.* New York: Jewish Science Publishing, 1927.

Liebman, Joshua Loth. *Peace of Mind: Insights on Human Nature that Can Change Your Life.* New York: Carol Publishing Group, 1994.

——. *Psychiatry and Religion.* Boston: Beacon Press, 1948.

Lippmann, Walter. *Public Opinion.* New York: Free Press Paperbacks, 1922.

Lott, Eric. *Love & Theft: Blackface Minstrelsy and the American Working Class.* New York: Oxford University Press, 1993.

Lowenthal, David. *The Past Is a Foreign Country.* Cambridge: Cambridge University Press, 1985.

Lowin, Joseph. *Cynthia Ozick.* Boston: Twayne Publishers, 1988.

Lynch, Kevin. *Good City Form.* Cambridge, Mass.: MIT Press, 1981.

Lyons, Bonnie. "The Female Characters in Bernard Malamud's Stories." *Studies in American Jewish Literature* 17 (1998): 129–36.

Malamud, Bernard. *Idiots First.* New York: Dell Publishing Co., 1966.

———. *The Magic Barrel.* New York: Pocket Books, 1972.

———. *Pictures of Fidelman.* New York: Farrar, Straus and Giroux, 1969.

———. *Rembrandt's Hat.* New York: Farrar, Straus and Giroux, 1973.

Manganaro, Marc. *Culture, 1922: The Emergence of a Concept.* Princeton, N.J.: Princeton University Press, 2002.

Mann, Herbert. "The Malamudian World: Method and Meaning." *Studies in American Jewish Literature* 4, no. 1 (1978): 2–12.

Margalit, Avishai. *The Ethics of Memory.* Cambridge, Mass.: Harvard University Press, 2002.

Marini, Stephen. *Sacred Song in America: Religion, Music, and Public Culture.* Urbana: University of Illinois Press, 2003.

Matthews, F. H. "The Americanization of Sigmund Freud: Adaptations of Psychoanalysis before 1917." *Journal of American Studies* 1 (1967): 39–62.

McDannell, Colleen. *The Christian Home in Victorian America, 1840–1900.* Bloomington: Indiana University Press, 1986.

———. *Material Christianity: Religion and Popular Culture in America.* New Haven, Conn.: Yale University Press, 1995.

Melnick, Jeffrey. *A Right to Sing the Blues: African Americans, Jews, and American Popular Song.* Cambridge, Mass.: Harvard University Press, 1999.

Mesher, David. "Malamud's Jewish Metaphors." *Judaism* 26, no. 101 (1977): 18–26.

Meyer, Donald. *The Positive Thinkers: A Study of the American Quest for Health, Wealth and Personal Power from Mary Baker Eddy to Norman Vincent Peale.* New York: Doubleday, 1965.

Michaels, Walter Benn. *Our America: Nativism, Modernism, and Pluralism.* Durham, N.C.: Duke University Press, 1995.

Mitchell, W. J. T. *Iconology: Image, Text, Ideology.* Chicago: University of Chicago Press, 1986.

———. *Picture Theory.* Chicago: University of Chicago Press, 1994.

———. *What Do Pictures Want? The Lives and Loves of Images.* Chicago: University of Chicago Press, 2005.

Moore, Deborah Dash. "Judaism as a Gendered Civilization: The Legacy of Mordecai Kaplan's Magnum Opus." *Jewish Social Studies* 12, no. 2 (2006): 172–86.

Moore, Donald. *The Human and the Holy: The Spirituality of Abraham Joshua Heschel.* New York: Fordham University Press, 1980.

Moore, MacDonald, and Deborah Dash Moore. "Observant Jews and the Photographic Arena of Looks." In *You Should See Yourself: Jewish Identity in Postmodern American Culture,* ed. Vincent Brook. New Brunswick, N.J.: Rutgers University Press, 2006, 176–204.

Morgan, David. *Protestants and Pictures: Religion, Visual Culture, and the Age of American Mass Production.* New York: Oxford University Press, 1999.

——. *The Sacred Gaze: Religious Visual Culture in Theory and Practice.* Berkeley: University of California Press, 2005.

——. *Visual Piety: A History and Theory of Popular Religious Images.* Berkeley: University of California Press, 1998.

Morgan, David, and Sally Promey, eds. *The Visual Culture of American Religions.* Berkeley: University of California Press, 2001.

Nadler, Allan. "Soloveitchik's Halakhic Man: Not a 'Mithnagged'." *Modern Judaism* 13, no. 2 (1993): 119–47.

New, Elisa. "Cynthia Ozick's Timing." *Prooftexts* 9, no. 3 (1989): 288–94.

North, Michael. *Reading 1922: A Return to the Scene of the Modern.* New York: Oxford University Press, 1999.

Ohana, Yolanda. "An Interview with Bernard Malamud: A Remembrance." *Studies in American Jewish Literature* 14 (1995): 64–71.

Okonkwo, Christopher. "Of Repression, Assertion, and the Speakerly Dress: Anzia Yezierska's *Salome of the Tenements*." *MELUS* 25, no. 1 (2000): 129–45.

Orsi, Robert. "Everyday Miracles: The Study of Lived Religion." In *Lived Religion in America,* ed. David Hall. Princeton, N.J.: Princeton University Press, 1997, 3–21.

——. "The Religious Boundaries of an In-between People: Street *Feste* and the Problem of the Dark-Skinned Other in Italian Harlem, 1920–1990." *American Quarterly* 44, no. 3 (1992): 313–47.

Orsi, Robert, ed. *Gods of the City: Religion and the American Urban Landscape.* Bloomington: Indiana University Press, 1999.

Ozick, Cynthia. "America: Toward Yavneh." *Judaism* 19, no. 3 (1970): 264–82.

——. "A Bintel Brief for Jacob Glatstein." *Jewish Heritage* 14, no. 1 (1972): 58–60.

——. "Envy; Or, Yiddish in America: A Novella." *Commentary* 48, no. 5 (1969): 33–53.

——. "Four Questions of the Rabbis." *Reconstructionist* 38, no. 1 (1972): 20–23.

——. "Judaism & Harold Bloom." *Commentary* 67, no. 1 (1979): 43–51.

——. *The Pagan Rabbi and Other Stories.* Syracuse, N.Y.: Syracuse University Press, 1971.

——. "Response to Alan Mintz's 'Is Our Schizophrenia Historically Important?'" *Response* 6, no. 3 (1972): 87–93.

——. "The Riddle of the Ordinary." *Moment* 1, no. 2 (1975): 55–59.

——. *The Shawl.* New York: Vintage Books, 1980.

Parish, Timothy. "Creation's Covenant: The Art of Cynthia Ozick." *Texas Studies in Literature and Language* 43, no. 4 (2001): 440–64.

——. "Women in the Fiction of Bernard Malamud: Springboards for Male Self-Transformation?" *Studies in American Jewish Literature* 16 (1997): 103–14.

Peale, Norman Vincent. *The Power of Positive Thinking: A Practical Guide to Mastering the Problems of Everyday Living.* Philadelphia: Running Press, 1952.

Pianko, Noam. "Reconstructing Judaism, Reconstructing America: The Sources and Functions of Mordecai Kaplan's 'Civilization'." *Jewish Social Studies* 12, no. 2 (2006): 39–55.

Pickford, Mary. *Why Not Try God?* New York: H.C. Kinsey & Co., 1934.

Pinsker, Sanford. "Cityscape as Moral Fable: The Place of Jewish History and American Social Realism in Bernard Malamud's Imagination." *Studies in American Jewish Literature* 14 (1995): 28–38.

Podnieks, Elizabeth. *Daily Modernism: The Literary Diaries of Virginia Woolf, Antonia White, Elizabeth Smart, and Anaïs Nin.* Montreal: McGill-Queen's University Press, 2000.

Prell, Riv-Ellen. *Fighting to Become Americans: Assimilation and the Trouble between Jewish Women and Jewish Men.* Boston: Beacon Press, 1999.

Radway, Janice. *A Feeling for Books: The Book-of-the-Month Club, Literary Taste, and Middle-Class Desire.* Chapel Hill: University of North Carolina Press, 1997.

Raphaelson, Sampson. "The Day of Atonement." In *The Jazz Singer*, ed. Robert Carringer. Madison: University of Wisconsin Press, 1979, 147–67.

Ravitzky, Aviezer. "Rabbi J. B. Soloveitchik on Human Knowledge: Between Maimonidean and Neo-Kantian Philosophy." *Modern Judaism* 6, no. 2 (1986): 157–88.

Reese, Kay, and Mimi Leipzig. Interview with Arnold Eagle. *American Society of Media Photographers.* 1990. http://web.archive.org/web/20060923050059/www.asmp.org/60th/interview_arnold_eagle.php (accessed July, 2009).

Rieff, Philip. *The Triumph of the Therapeutic: Uses of Faith after Freud.* Chicago: University of Chicago Press, 1966.

Rogin, Michael. *Blackface, White Noise: Jewish Immigrants in the Hollywood Melting Pot.* Berkeley: University of California Press, 1996.

Rosenberg, Joel. "Jewish Experience on Film—An American Overview." *American Jewish Year Book* 96 (1996): 3–50.

———. "What You Ain't Heard Yet: The Languages of *The Jazz Singer*." *Prooftexts* 22 (2002): 11–54.

Roth, Philip. "Eli, the Fanatic." *Commentary* 27, no. 4 (1959): 292–309.

———. *Goodbye, Columbus.* New York: Vintage Books, 1959.

———. *Patrimony.* New York: Simon and Schuster, 1991.

———. *Reading Myself and Others.* New York: Vintage Books, 2001.

———. Reply to "Letters from Readers." *Commentary* 37, no. 4 (1964): 16–19.

———. "Writing about Jews." *Commentary* 36, no. 6 (1963): 446–52.

Rubin, Joan Shelley. *The Making of Middle-Brow Culture.* Chapel Hill: University of North Carolina Press, 1992.

Rubin, Steven. "Malamud and the Theme of Love and Sex." *Studies in American Jewish Literature* 4, no. 1 (1978): 19–23.

Rybczynski, Witold. *City Life: Urban Expectations in a New World.* New York: Scribner, 1995.

Schmidt, Leigh Eric. *Consumer Rites: The Buying and Selling of American Holidays.* Princeton, N.J.: Princeton University Press, 1995.

———. *Hearing Things: Religion, Illusion, and the American Enlightenment.* Cambridge, Mass.: Harvard University Press, 2000.

Schneider, Louis, and Stanford Dornbusch. *Popular Religion: Inspirational Books in America.* Chicago: University of Chicago Press, 1958.

Schnur, Susan. "From Prehistoric Cave Art to Your Cookie Pan: Tracing the Hamantasch Herstory." *Lilith* 23, no. 1 (Spring 1998): 22–24.

Schorsch, Ismar. "The Myth of Sephardic Supremacy." *Leo Baeck Institute Year Book* 34 (1989): 47–66.

Scult, Mel. *Judaism Faces the Twentieth Century: A Biography of Mordecai M. Kaplan.* Detroit, Mich.: Wayne State University Press, 1993.

Scult, Mel, ed. *Communings of the Spirit: The Journals of Mordecai M. Kaplan 1913–1934*, vol. 1. Detroit, Mich.: Wayne State University Press and the Reconstructionist Press, 2001.

Shandler, Jeffrey. *Adventures in Yiddishland: Postvernacular Language and Culture.* Berkeley: University of California Press, 2006.

———. "Heschel and Yiddish: A Struggle with Signification." *Journal of Jewish Thought and Philosophy* 2 (1993): 245–99.

———. *Jews, God, and Videotape: Religion and Media in America.* New York: New York University Press, 2009.

Sheen, Fulton. *Peace of Soul.* New York: McGraw-Hill Book Co., 1949.

Singer, David, and Moshe Sokol. "Joseph Soloveitchik: Lonely Man of Faith." *Modern Judaism* 2, no. 3 (1982): 227–72.

Sklare, Marshall. *Conservative Judaism: An American Religious Movement.* New York: Schocken Books, 1955.

Slobin, Mark. *Fiddler on the Move: Exploring the Klezmer World.* Oxford: Oxford University Press, 2000.

Soloveitchik, Joseph. "Confrontation." *Tradition* 6, no. 2 (1964): 5–29.

———. *Halakhic Man*, trans. Lawrence Kaplan. Philadelphia: The Jewish Publication Society, 1983.

———. *The Halakhic Mind: An Essay on Jewish Tradition and Modern Thought.* New York: Seth Press, 1986.

———. *Ish ha-Halakha—Galui ve-Nistar.* Jerusalem: World Zionist Organization, 1979.

———. "Kol Dodi Dofek: It is the Voice of My Beloved That Knocketh." In *Theological and Halakhic Reflections on the Holocaust*, ed. Bernhard H. Rosenberg and Fred Heuman. Hoboken, N.J.: Ktav Publishing House, 1992, 51–117.

———. *The Lonely Man of Faith.* New York: Doubleday, 1965.

———. "U-Vikashtem mi-Sham." In *Ish ha-Halakha—Galui ve-Nistar.* Jerusalem: World Zionist Organization, 1979.

Sontag, Susan. *On Photography.* New York: Farrar, Straus and Giroux, 1973.

Spengemann, William, and L. R. Lundquist. "Autobiography and the American Myth." *American Quarterly* 17, no. 3 (1965): 501–19.

Spengler, Oswald. *The Decline of the West.* New York: Oxford University Press, 1991.

Stern, Josef. *Metaphor in Context.* Cambridge, Mass.: MIT Press, 2000.

Stone, Amy. "Struggling? Juggling? Trying to Integrate Our Multiple Roles." *Lilith* 19 (Spring 1988): 6–7.

Stott, William. *Documentary Expression and Thirties America.* New York: Oxford University Press, 1973.

Stubbs, Katherine. "Reading Material: Contextualizing Clothing in the Work of Anzia Yezierska." *MELUS* 23, no. 2 (1998): 157–72.

Sturken, Marita, and Lisa Cartwright. *Practices of Looking: An Introduction to Visual Culture.* Oxford: Oxford University Press, 2001.

Susman, Warren. *Culture as History: The Transformation of American Society in the Twentieth Century.* Washington, D.C.: Smithsonian Institution Press, 2003.

———. "The Thirties." In *The Development of an American Culture,* ed. Stanley Coben and Lorman Ratner. New York: St. Martin's Press, 1983, 215–60.

Taves, Ann. *Fits, Trances and Visions.* Princeton, N.J.: Princeton University Press, 1999.

Trine, Ralph Waldo. *In Tune with the Infinite.* New York: Dodge Publishing Co., 1910.

Trotter, Wilfred. *Instincts of the Herd in Peace and War.* New York: Cosmo Classics, 2005.

Tye, Larry. *The Father of Spin: Edward L. Bernays and the Birth of Public Relations.* New York: Henry Holt and Co., 1998.

Umansky, Ellen. *From Christian Science to Jewish Science: Spiritual Healing and American Jews.* New York: Oxford University Press, 2005.

———. "Jewish Women in the Twentieth-Century U.S." In *Jewish Women in Historical Perspective,* ed. Judith Baskin. Detroit, Mich.: Wayne State University Press, 1991, 265–88.

van de Wetering, Maxine. "The Popular Concept of 'Home' in Nineteenth-Century America." *Journal of American Studies* 18, no. 1 (1984): 5–28.

Weber, Donald. *Haunted in the New World: Jewish American Culture from Cahan to the Goldbergs.* Bloomington: Indiana University Press, 2005.

Weidman Schneider, Susan. "From the Editor." *Lilith* 28, no. 1 (Spring 2003): 2.

———. "From the Editors." *Lilith* 1, no. 1 (Fall 1976): 3.

———. "Lilith Looks Back." *Lilith* 19, no. 3 (Fall 1994): 14–16.

Weiner, Deborah Heiligman. "Cynthia Ozick, Pagan vs. Jew (1966–1976)." In *Studies in American Jewish Literature: Number 3,* ed. Daniel Walden. Albany: State University of New York Press, 1983, 179–93.

Weiss, Richard. *The American Myth of Success: From Horatio Alger to Norman Vincent Peale.* Urbana: University of Illinois Press, 1969.

Wenger, Beth. *New York Jews and the Great Depression.* New Haven, Conn.: Yale University Press, 1996.

Whitfield, Stephen. *Voices of Jacob, Hands of Esau: Jews in American Life and Thought.* Hamden, Conn.: Archon Books, 1984.

Wirth-Nesher, Hana. "The Languages of Memory: Cynthia Ozick's *The Shawl.*" In *Multilingual America,* ed. Werner Sollors. New York: New York University Press, 1998, 313–26.

———. "Resisting Allegory, or Reading 'Eli, the Fanatic' in Tel Aviv." *Prooftexts* 21, no. 1 (2001): 103–12.

Wisse, Ruth. "American Jewish Writing, Act II." *Commentary* 61, no. 6 (1976): 40–45, reprinted as Ruth Wisse, "Ozick as American Jewish Writer," in *Cynthia Ozick,* ed. Harold Bloom. New York: Chelsea House Publishers, 1986, 35–45.

———. *The Modern Jewish Canon: A Journey through Language and Culture.* New York: Free Press, 2000.

Yerushalmi, Yosef Haymin. *Freud's Moses: Judaism Terminable and Interminable.* New Haven, Conn.: Yale University Press, 1991.

Yezierska, Anzia. *Bread Givers.* Garden City, N.Y.: Doubleday, 1925.

———. *How I Found America: Collected Stories of Anzia Yezierska*. New York: Persia Books, 1991.

———. *Hungry Hearts*. Boston: Houghton Mifflin, 1920.

———. *Red Ribbon on a White Horse*. New York: Scribner, 1950.

———. *Salome of the Tenements*. New York: Grosset and Dunlap, 1923.

Zaborowska, Magdalena. *How We Found America: Reading Gender through East European Immigrant Narratives*. Chapel Hill: University of North Carolina Press, 1995.

Zipperstein, Steven. *Imagining Russian Jewry: Memory, History, Identity*. Seattle: University of Washington Press, 1999.

Zuckoff, Aviva Cantor. "The Lilith Question." *Lilith* 1, no. 1 (Fall 1976): 5–10, 38.

INDEX

Italicized page numbers indicate illustrations.

Abie's Irish Rose (film), 252
adoption, 238
aesthetic movement, 42, 164
aesthetics, and things, 157–164
African Americans, 40, 112
Akiva (Rabbi), 149
Alter, Robert, 213
America, 15, 47, 271; city fascination of, 112; Eastern European Jews coming to, 111–112; Fromm on, 106; for immigrants, 2; Jewish narratives and, 182–183; Jews claim in, 88; Jews visualizing Jews in, 226; Orthodox Jews in, 139; Rome associated with, 169; spiritual roots abandoned by Jews in, 160; triumph of, 92–93. *See also* Jewish America
"America" (Diamond, N.), 263–264, 265
"America: Toward Yavneh" (Ozick), 200
American civilization: building, 40; Freud and, 72
American Jewish literature, 180–224
American journal, 45–49
The American Magazine, 59
American Society of Media Photographers, 249
anti-Semitism, 291n141
anxiety, 23, 47–48
Aperture publication, 246, 252

architecture, 161
archive, of self, 35–36
archive fever, 15, 38, 39, 47
Archive Fever (Derrida), 36
art: civilization and, 42–43; emotions in, 29–30; expansion of, 29; as functional equivalent to religion, 31; Kaplan, M., on, 28–33; modern, 30–31; photography and, 245; revealing self, 40; unifying principle of, 30–31. *See also* museums; photography
Art and Ethics (Kaplan, M.), 29
Art as Experience (Dewey), 42
The Art of Loving (Fromm), 91, 96, 100, 101
Asad, Talal, 227
Ashkenazi tradition, 299n57; beauty in, 158, 160; books of, 154–157, *159*; spirituality of, 160
At Home Only With God (Eagle), 247, 249–250
Augustine, 80
authenticity, 17
authority, 69–70, 106
autobiographical writing, 17
Avot, 115

Bank of the United States, 44
Barbie, 266–268, *267, 269, 277*

Barthes, Roland, 245
Beard, Charles, 40; *The Rise of American Civilization*, 40
Beard, Mary, 40; *The Rise of American Civilization*, 40
beauty, 136, 157; eternity and, 157; experience of aesthetic, 161; in Jewish books, 158; spiritual, in Judaism, 158–160; of things, 177
Bederman, Gail, 40
Bellow, Saul, 181, 225–226, 252
belonging, 17
Benjamin, Walter, 22
Berlin, Irving, 257; "Blue Skies," 257, 265
Bernays, Doris, 287n13
Bernays, Edward, 5, 6, 10, 21, 54, 57, 94, 103, 105–106, 273, 274, 287nn13,25; consumption inversion of, 58; *Crystallizing Public Opinion*, 57, 59, 61, 62, 64, 65, 66, 68, 69, 70, 71; Freud relationship with, 59–60; hair net business, 63, 69; on herd mentality, 6, 56, 58, 60, 61, 63–66, 68–71; on identity, 107; on judgments imprisoning self, 65; Lucky Strike cigarettes, 70; material past of, 108; on past, 55; on personal histories destroying self, 56; *Propaganda*, 59, 64, 66, 68, 69, 70, 71; on propaganda, 60; psychology and herd, 57–71; public basic appeals, 68; public relations counsel, 58–67, 69, 105, 287n13; on self enslavement, 62–63; skeptics of, 58; Torches of Freedom campaign, 70
Biale, David, 270
black history, 83–84
blackness, 191, 197–198, 276
blankness, 35–36, 272
Bloom, Harold, 200
"Blue Skies" (Berlin), 257, 265
books: beauty in Jewish, 158; with emotional power, 159; as sacred things, 153–156
Boston, 128, 129
boundary construction, 124, 135–137
Braiterman, Zachary, 29, 136

Bread Givers (Yezierska), 183
Bronx Lourdes, 8
brotherly love, 101–102
Brown, Bill, 49–50

Call It Sleep (Roth, H.), 212
Calvin, 80
catharsis, 72
Cathedral of Commerce, 161–162
cathedrals, great, 161–162, 165
Cather, Willa, 28; *Death Comes for the Archbishop*, 28
Catholics, 112–113, 135; halakhic man related to, 114–115
Century Theatre, 28
Chagall, Marc, 212
Christianity, 87–89, 135; Feuerbach criticism of, 99; halakhic man related to, 114–115; Sheen on, 92
cities: conceptual models of, 127–128; congregation functioning like, 137; defenses to seductive lures in, 135
cityscape, 139–140; as urban holy, 109–110; urban holy created from, 115–116
civil rights, 143–144
civilization: aesthetic performance of self, 41; as counter-cultural move, 40; Kaplan, M., on art and, 42–43
Civilization in the United States, 40
Clark University, 53
clothing. *See* dress
Cohen, Richard, 247
Cohen, Steven, 236
The Cohens and the Kellys (film), 252
"Coming to America" (Diamond, N.). *See* "America" (Diamond, N.)
Commentary (Roth, P.), 190, 201
confession, 84, 85, 291n140
"Confrontation" (Soloveitchik), 111
connectivity, 75
Connelly, Mark, 83; *Green Pastures*, 83, 91
Conservative Judaism, in America, 174
consumption, 6, 34, 38, 106, 223, 275–276; anxiety of, 47–48; Bernay's inversion of, 58; indecency and

gaudiness of, 165. *See also* material consumerism
conventional symbol, 152
cosmic city, 127–128, 132
counterhistory, 292n159
coveting things, 173–174, 179, 275–276
creation story, 145
"A Creative Partnership" (Liebman), 76
The Crowd: A Study of the Popular Mind (Le Bon), 60
crowds: Le Bon on, 60–61; Trotter on, 61
Crystallizing Public Opinion (Bernays, E.), 57, 59, 61, 62, 64, 65, 66, 68, 69, 70, 71; Freud on, 60
cult of domesticity, 161
cultural amnesia, 160
cultural studies, 281n7
cultural tensions, 16
culture, 40–41

Dale, Mary, 257, 259
dauerhafte Erinnerungsspur (permanent memory trace), 39
Dauerspuren (permanent traces), 39
Day of Atonement, 120, 161
The Day of Atonement (Raphaelson), 254–257
death: fear of, 36; material waste and, 37–38
Death Comes for the Archbishop (Cather), 28
democratic societies, 158
dependence, 96–99
Derrida, Jacques, 15, 36, 37, 38, 41–42; *Archive Fever,* 36; on archiving self, 49; trace, 36; on writing instruments, 39
destiny, 137
devotion, 69
Dewey, John, 42, 183; *Art as Experience,* 42
Diamond, Eitan, 139
Diamond, Neil, 254, 262–264, 265, 269, 313n111; "America," 263–264, 265
diaries: autobiographical writing related to, 17; as emotional confidantes, 20–21. *See also* journal writing

Diner, Hasia, 247
divine, 152; energy, 75, 151; icons and, 165; presence, 149
Dorff, Elliot, 120–123, 127
Dornbusch, Stanford, 74
Douglas, Ann, 52
Douglass, Frederick, 40; *The Reason Why the Colored American Is Not in the World's Columbian Exposition,* 40
dress: as symbol, 191–192; Yezierska and Roth on, 183–199
Dukakis, Michael, 263
Durkheim, 4
Duties of the Heart (ibn Paquda), 25

Eagle, Arnold, 10, 226–227, 243–252, 269, 278; Aperture publication, 246, 252; *At Home Only With God,* 247, 249–250; Orthodox Jews in New York City collection, 226–227
The Earth Is the Lord's (Heschel), 8, 142, 143, 144, 145, 150, 151, 153, 156, 160, 167, 170, 171, 173, 174, 177
Ecclesiastes, 25, 123
Eckhart, Meister, 99
Eisen, Arnold, 144, 167, 236
The Eisenstein Reconstructionist Archives of the Reconstructionist Rabbinal College, 18, 51, 281n11
"Eli, the Fanatic" (Roth, P.), 9, 180, 190, 191–192, 265
Elijah, Meir b., 134
emotions: in art, 29; art and, 31; in Jewish art, 30; that create archive, 36
"Envy; or, Yiddish in America" (Ozick), 9, 182, 201, 202, 225
erotic love, 101–102, 103
Escape from Freedom (Fromm), 94, 274
eternity, 38, 157
existence, 136–137
existential togetherness, 133–134
Exodus, 99, 146, 149, 177

faith, man of, 129–130
fashion, 160. *See also* dress
fate, 136–137
father–son relationship, 260–261

Feuerbach, 99
Fighting to Become American (Prell), 46–49; ghetto girl stereotyping, 48–49; Jewish American Princess, 48, 49; Young Jewish Woman in Search of Marriage, 48, 49
film, 252–266
"The First Seven Years" (Malamud), 215
folksmensh, 212
food, 241, *242*
forgetfulness: false worship and, 165; of life, 39–40; reversing, 167
Forman, Diana, 266
Forum, 59
Fosdick, Harry Emerson, 72
Foucault, Michel, 280n12
Fox, Emmet, 75; *Power through Constructive Thinking,* 75
Fox, William, 253
Freedman, Jonathan, 3, 11, 12, 270–271, 279n3; *Klezmer America,* 3, 11
freedom, 57, 94; Fromm on, 93–103; love and, 102–103
Freeman, Annis, 101
Freud, Sigmund, 6, 15, 21, 36, 37, 38–39, 54, 56, 64, 68, 71–72, 79, 195, 291n145; America influenced by, 59; Americans' rejections of, 72; Bernays, E., relationship with, 59–60; on childhood experiences, 81; *dauerhafte Erinnerungsspur* (permanent memory trace), 39; *Dauerspuren* (permanent traces), 39; God of, 76; guarded pessimism of, 53; on identity, 107; map of human psyche, 76; *Moses and Monotheism,* 36; mystic writing pad (*der Wunderblock*), 39; *Note on the Mystic Writing Pad,* 38; permanent memory trace (*dauerhafte Erinnerungsspur*), 39; permanent traces (*Dauerspuren*), 39; *der Wunderblock* (mystic writing pad), 39. *See also* neo-Freudians
Freud's Moses (Yerushalmi), 36
Friedman, Lester, 253
Fromm, Erich, 2, 5, 6–7, 10, 11, 54, 55, 57, 91, 273, 274; on America, 106;
The Art of Loving, 91, 96, 100, 101; *Escape from Freedom,* 94, 274; on freedom, 93–103; on God, 96, 97, 99, 100; *The Heart of Man,* 100; human freedom and, 93–103; on identity, 107; idolatry of, 98–99, 104; incestuous ties, 97–98; Judaism of, 104–105; liberated self of, 106; male/female roles, 91; *Man for Himself,* 96; material past of, 108; new bondage of, 94; on past, 55; on personal histories destroying self, 56; *Psychoanalysis and Religion,* 95–98; *The Sane Society,* 100; on self, 96–98; "Sex and Character," 91; on story of Isaac, 101; *You Shall Be as Gods,* 94, 103
Fuller, Robert, 94
Funk, Rainer, 101
Furman, Bessie, 240; *Magen David,* 240
"The Future of Folklore Studies in America: The Urban Frontier" (Kirshenblatt-Gimblett), 110–111

Gabler, Neal, 253
Gandhi, 21
Gaon of Vilna, 114, 134
gaze, 280n12
gazing, 227
Gemeinschaft, 44
gender biases, 91
gender constructions, 11, 90
gender images, 61
Genesis, 101, 110, 122, 124, 129, 137, 145, 275
Gilbert, Cass, 162
Gilroy, Paul, 285n120
Glatstein, Jacob, 201
Glatzer, Nahum, 177
God, 75, 99, 122, 140, 275; Adam and, 130, 133, 134; borders and limits created by, 136–137; in city, 115; footprints of, 132; fortune of meeting, 126; Fromm on, 96, 97, 99, 100; in Genesis, 110; Giles finding, 113; ground between space and, 164; halakhic man compared to,

118–119; halakhic man mimicking, 124; holiness as secret of, 166–167; Judaism on, 92; Kaplan, M., disavowing, 16–17; Levenson on, 122; Liebman on, 79, 82; material things restricting, 152; negative theology about, 163; peace of mind and, 80; reverence for, 127; Shimeon condemned by, 170; Soloveitchik meeting, 140; things concealing, 151; things in image of, 148–149; truth revealed by, 76; urban holy and, 110, 116–117, 127. *See also* divine; *Shekhinah* (God's presence)

God in Search of Man (Heschel), 141

golden calf, 146–147, 168

goldeneh medinah (golden land), 112

Goldwyn, Sam, 186

Good Housekeeping, 59

Goodbye, Columbus (Roth, P.), 190

Graham, Billy, 290n124, 292n141

Great Depression, 34, 44

Green Pastures (Connelly), 83; Negro symbolism, 83, 91

Greenberg, Betty, 176

grief, 73

Grinker, Roy, 72

Habertal, Moshe, 165, 166

hair net business, 63, 69

halakhah, act of, 3, 110, 125–126

Halakhic Man (Soloveitchik), 3, 7, 110–111, 114–119, 124, 127–133, 139–140, 274–275; Adam related to, 129–133; cosmic boundaries of, 127–128; God mimicked by, 124, 140; normative framework of perception of, 119; transformations of, 118

The Halakhic Mind (Soloveitchik), 124

Hale, Nathan, 59, 71–72

hamantaschen (Jewish cookie), 241, *242*

Handler, Ruth, 266

Harris, Alice Kessler, 183

Hartman, David, 119, 120, 121, 130, 131

Harvard Medical School, 72

Hasidic movement, on art, 29

Hayyim of Volozhin, 114

healthy-mindedness, 289n97

The Heart of Man (Fromm), 100

Hebrew Union College, 143

Heinze, Andrew, 16, 49, 56, 80, 82, 90, 128–129; adapting to abundance, 34; on material consumerism of Jews, 45–46, 47; on Passover rituals, 46, 47; on Sheen, 88; on Sukkot, 43–44

Herberg, Will, 261; *Protestant, Catholic, Jew*, 261

herd mentality: Bernays, E., 6, 56, 58, 60, 61, 63–66, 68–71; freedom from, 65–67; individual decoupled from, 70; as irrational inheritance, 65. *See also* crowds; social forces

heritage, 227–228; American Jewish identity and, production, 225–269; authenticity of, 269; cultural production and, 228–229, 231–232; in film, 252–266; food and, 241, *242*; after Holocaust, 252; in *The Jazz Singer* films, 252–266; Kirshenblatt-Gimblett on, 243, *244*; *Lilith* production, 243; masculine, 250–251; museums, 238, *239*, 240; photography and, 10, 245–246, 249, 252; turning back on one's, 304n39; visualizing, 228–243

Hertzberg, Arthur, 246–247, 249, 251; *A Jew in America*, 247

Herzl, Theodor, 212

Heschel, Abraham Joshua, 2, 3, 8–11, 44, 136, 183, 208, 275–276; on aesthetics, 157–164; on America, 160; attachment to spatial things, 168; desire of return of, 160; discourse on things, 144–145; discriminatory racial practices battled by, 171; divergent accounts of things, 152–153; *The Earth Is the Lord's*, 8, 142, 143, 144, 145, 150, 151, 153, 156, 160, 167, 170, 171, 173, 174, 177; on feminine, 151; on Genesis, 145; *God in Search of Man*, 141; on holiness, 145–146; on

Maimonides, 163; *Man Is Not Alone,* 141, 150; material presence and *The Sabbath,* 141–179, 180; mystical vision of, 143–144; obsession with things, 142; paganism, 150, 152; real symbol, 152; on reason, 150; *The Sabbath,* 8, 10, 141–179, *178;* Sabbath preparation of, 176; Shimeon admired by, 172; spatial things, 172; spiritual-intellectual conception, 149; symbols, 152; things in time, 173–179; *Torah min-Hashamayim,* 141, 149

"Hester Street Cinderella" (Yezierska), 183

high-brow, 159

Hitler, 99

holiness, 145–146, 153, 159, 162; aesthetics and, 157–158; imitations of, 164; of Sabbath, 141, 147; things and, 146–148, 164, 165; urban roads to, 110

Holocaust, 115, 136, 141, 252

Holy Bible, 104

Holzhandler, Dora, 238

home manuals, 174–176

homo religiosus, 116–117, 119, 120, 123, 126, 127, 135

human flourishing, 54

Hungry Hearts (Yezierska), 183, 185–186

Huxley, Julian, 24

icons, 165

identity: films' impact on, 254; Freud on, 107; Fromm on, 107; of Kaplan, M., 25; narrative uncovering human, 223; personal, 31–32; things, idolatry, and, 165–173; things and personal, 179

Idiots First (Malamud), 9, 213, 215

idleness, 19

idolatry, 57, 97–98, 172, 200; betrayal and, 166; four conceptions of, 165; of Fromm, 98–99, 104; identity, things and, 165–173; material form of, 167; self transformed by, 168

images, 227–269

"Imagining Jews" (Roth, P.), 225

immigrant consumption, 45–47

immigrant literature, 16, 285n120

immigration, 14–15, 112

immortality: plea of Kaplan, M., 50; writing and, 35

In Tune with the Infinite (Trine), 75

incestuous ties, 97–98

independence, 99. *See also* dependence

individuals, true longings of, 69

inheritance, 5, 6, 105; material identity and, 107; renouncing, 57

inherited past, 55

inner life, 123–125; Jewish law and, 126; material things and forgetting, 160

inner maturity, 76

inner peace, 291n140

installment plans, 46–47

Instincts of the Herd (Trotter), 61

intellect, herd mentality and, 61

intermarriage, 312n76, 313n106

Isaac, 101, 103

Ishmael, 103

Ishmael (Rabbi), 149

Israel, 136

"It is the Voice of My Beloved that Knocketh" ("Kol Dodi Dofek") (Soloveitchik), 111. *See also* "Kol Dodi Dofek"

Jacobson, Matthew, 247, 258, 262

James, William, 289n97

The Jazz Singer (film), 3, 10, 11, 226, 228, 252–266, 269, 277

Jesus Christ, 88

Jew(s): constraining narrative of material life, 223–224; consumerism of, 45–47; as cultural pioneers, 30; emulating, in America, 40; labeling, 270–271; standard of living improvements of, 46–47; stereotyping of, 46–47; visual heritage of, 238, 240; visualizing themselves in America, 226. *See also* Sukkot

A Jew in America (Hertzberg), 247

Jewish America, 71–93